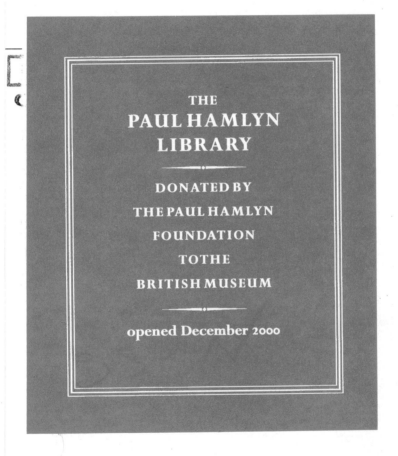
ANF

MARK ANTONY

HIS LIFE AND TIMES

MARK ANTONY

HIS LIFE AND TIMES

Alan Roberts

The Malvern Publishing Company Limited

Published by:
The Malvern Publishing Company Ltd,
32 Old Street,
Upton-upon-Severn
Worcestershire WR8 0HU

ISBN: 0-947993-12-6

Typeset by Printit-Now Ltd
Lloyds Bank Chambers
Upton-upon-Severn
Worcestershire WR8 4HU

Set in Times 12 point

Printed and bound in Great Britain by
Biddles Ltd, Guildford and King's Lynn

To Caritas

Coin portrait of Antony 33 BC

Acknowledgements

My formal acknowledgements are few: to Sir Ronald Syme for his indispensable *Roman Revolution*, to Professor Michael Grant for his invaluable *Cleopatra* and his many other works on Roman history, to the late Sir William Tarn and the late M.P. Charlesworth for their relevant chapters in the *Cambridge Ancient History,* and to the editors and authors of the *Oxford Classical Dictionary,* without whose works this book would be very considerably the poorer, and to my wife without whose support and encouragement it would never have been written.

Contents

PART 1

THE YOUNG ANTONY

PART 2

CONSUL AND TRIUMVIR

PART 3

THE UNEASY ALLIANCE

PART 4

OVERLORD OF THE EAST

PART 5

THE ACTIUM CAMPAIGN

PART 6

REQUIEM IN EGYPT

LIST OF MAPS

Appendix

PART I

The Young Antony

CHAPTER I

Rome

To know Mark Antony one must first understand something of the past and present of the society into which he was born on the 14th January, probably in the year we call 83BC, but to the Romans of the day the 671st of their era, which they reckoned from the founding of Rome. Apparent to us but mercifully hidden from them were the cataclysmic events of their own immediate future, the five turbulent decades which spanned Antony's life and were to see the violent death throes of the Republic and the no less bloody birth pangs of the Empire. For them, whether citizen, freedman or slave, Roman, Italian or foreigner, the social orders and the political institutions of the city state must have seemed immutable, hallowed by time itself.

For all of them alike, the nobles in their fine houses, the bankers and the merchants, the artisans and the shopkeepers, the urban proletariat in the teeming tenement blocks and the unemployed on the streets, the history of Rome stretched reassuringly back, almost to the beginning of time. Then the ancient heroes and the children of the gods had walked the earth, and in that remote antiquity Romulus had founded the city which now was mistress of the world.

And indeed Rome was even older than such legends. Traces of neolithic habitation have been found, and the archaeological evidence suggests that there may have been permanent bronze age settlement on the site from around the middle of the second millennium BC. Perhaps as early as the tenth century a pastoral people of Indo-European origin, speaking an early form of Latin, moved down from the Apennines and began to cultivate the fertile volcanic soil of the plain of Latium; eventually they spread north as far as the Tiber. There, on the flat top of the Palatine hill commanding the lowest practicable crossing of the river, they built a village of mud and wattle huts. The first settlement was followed by others on the nearby hills, first the Quirinal, then the Esquiline, the Capitoline and the Caelian, and gradually these grew together to form the readily defensible centre of a settled agricultural community.

The Tiber marked the boundary of these Latin speaking peoples, and soon Rome came under the influence of the more advanced civilisation of Etruria across the river to the north. During much of the sixth century Etruscan kings ruled in Rome, turning the rural hill town into a small city on the model of their own city states. But the power of Etruria waned after her expansion to the south had been checked by defeats at the hands of the Greek cities. According to Rome's later historians the last of the Tarquin kings was expelled in 510 by Lucius Junius Brutus, who became one of the first consuls of the infant Republic. Certainly by the first half of the fifth century Rome had won her independence from Etruria and was ruled by her own leading families. During this century, in alliance with the other peoples of Latium, she withstood a series of armed incursions from the hill tribes of the Apennines and strengthened her own position by defeating the neighbouring Etruscan city of Veii, only twelve miles away on a tributary of the Tiber.

The brief, factual, necessarily dry account which follows must suffice to cover the next three centuries of rapidly expanding Roman military power and political influence until Antony's grandfather, the first Marcus Antonius, appears in the recorded annals of the Republic as consul in 99, and so steps into history.

In 387 an invading army of Celts sacked Rome, though later legend has it that Marcus Manlius, supposedly warned by the cackling of the sacred geese, managed to save the Capitol, the spiritual and religious centre of the city. Soon afterwards the first stone walls were built round the seven hills, enclosing an area of some 400 hectares. At the beginning of the second half of the fourth century Roman intervention against the Samnites, at the request of the Greek cities of Campania, led to a bitterly contested war with the other Latin states, and eventual victory gave Rome effective control of Latium through a number of separate imposed alliances. When the last of the Samnite wars ended in the first decade of the third century Rome had extended her influence over much of southern Italy by means of further alliances and the establishment of military colonies in sensitive frontier areas. With the help of these new allies she was able to resist an invasion by Phyrrus of Epirus and finally to eject him from Italy.

Thus in the short span of three or four generations the power of Rome had spread rapidly down the length of peninsular Italy, reaching the straits of Messina by the middle of the third century. Inevitably her interests came into conflict over Sicily with those of Carthage, the leading maritime power and trading nation in the central and western Mediterranean. Victory in the first Punic war removed the Carthaginian threat to southern Italy and Sicily passed to Rome becoming her first overseas province; within a few years she ousted Carthage from Corsica and Sardinia and the two islands were made a single Roman province in 227. With the loyal support of most of her Italian allies Rome stubbornly contained Hannibal's long invasion of

Italy during the second Punic War and survived a number of disastrous defeats at his hands; finally Scipio Africanus defeated him and broke the military power of Carthage on African soil at Zama. Exhausted by the struggle, her manpower depleted and her agricultural economy in ruins, Rome nevertheless emerged for the first time as a Mediterranean power in her own right.

At the request of Rhodes, Pergamum and some of the Greek cities, Rome intervened in Greece in 200 to defeat Philip V of Macedon. A few years later an attempt to invade Greece by Antiochus III, ruler of the Seleucid empire, was foiled by Roman arms and he was eventually expelled from Asia Minor. Thus Rome was drawn into the eastern Mediterranean, and with the eclipse of Macedon and the Seleucids only Egypt out of the Hellenistic successor states to Alexander's empire remained independent under the Ptolemies.

The northern part of mainland Greece came under direct Roman rule in 146 as the province of Macedonia, and in the same year the cities of Carthage and Corinth were sacked and destroyed by Roman armies; Carthage's heartland was annexed as the province of Africa. The kingdom of Pergamum was bequeathed to Rome in 133 under the will of its last king and became the province of Asia. Further to the east Cilicia was declared a Roman provincial command in an attempt to deal with the pirates who had set up bases on the mountainous coast from which they preyed on the trade routes of the eastern Mediterranean.

In the west, after the defeat of Hannibal, the new Carthaginian colonies on the southern coast of Spain passed to Rome and became the provinces of Nearer and Further Spain. To secure the northern frontier of Italy the plain of the Po was annexed and colonised during the second century, though it did not become the province of Cisalpine Gaul until the 70's; to protect the land route to Spain Rome moved into southern Gaul, and by 120 the valley of the lower Rhone from the Cevennes to the Alps was under Roman control as the province of Transalpine Gaul. Across the Adriatic maritime Illyricum was administered from Rome.

This wholesale conquest of lands bordering the northern Mediterranean from Spain to Asia Minor was the direct result of Rome being drawn into the vacuum caused by her elimination of Carthage, Macedonia and the Seleucid empire as Mediterranean powers. It was made possible by the disciplined power of the Roman armies and the magnificent roads they built, like the Via Aemilia through northern Italy and the Via Domitia to Spain. But it was not undertaken as a deliberate policy of territorial aggrandisement; the Senate embarked on it haphazardly, often reluctantly, in the belief that they had to do so in order to protect Roman interests and prevent any coalition being formed against them.

The whole system of defensive treaties with allies to secure the boundaries of Roman influence, well proven in the conquest of peninsular Italy, when applied to the wider sphere of the Mediterranean meant that through these allies Rome's political interests were continually being drawn outwards beyond the existing frontiers, to be followed inevitably by her armies. The pressures were economic as well as political: the growing commercial interests of the equites, the knights of the equestrian order which once had found the Roman cavalry and now ranked next below the senatorial class, demanded protection and peace in which to ply their trade, preferably through annexation with its promise of further lands to exploit.

But the political institutions of the city state had evolved too slowly from their tribal origins to meet so rapid an expansion. This inability to adapt, coupled with the ruling oligarchy's determination to retain political power in its own hands though forced to concede an ever greater measure of financial and commercial control to the equites, made the slow death of the Republic inevitable.

In the early days of Rome after the expulsion of the kings, sovereign power had lain, at least in theory, in the Comitia, or Assembly of the Roman people, summoned by the magistrates to meet in a body and voting by tribes, or family clans. But throughout the middle life of the Republic the Senate, though technically an advisory council of nobles, in effect wielded the real power, proposing legislation to the Assembly, ensuring it was passed by means of their control of the property weighted voting system, and then ratifying it. Membership of the Senate was limited to 300, and the senators, though indirectly elected, were in practice drawn almost exclusively from a small group of noble families, which, whether originally patrician or plebeian, by the fourth century had come to form a closely knit hereditary ruling oligarchy. Executive power lay in the hands of two consuls holding office for one year and elected from the ranks of the Senate by a military Assembly over which the senators themselves had complete control.

In a latter day sense there were no political parties. Instead, particularly over the last hundred years of the Republic, there was a constantly changing succession of alliances as the leading senatorial families strove to maintain and improve their positions of power and privilege. During the later years these groupings tended to move into a loose sort of alignment. On the one hand the consulars, the senior senators who had held office as consul and thus permanently enobled their families, formed the inner circle of the oligarchy and controlled

6

the Senate: they were the self-styled boni, the good men or Optimates, conservatives bent on maintaining the political and economic status quo. Their opponents, anyone who wanted to change the existing order of things for whatever reason, were the so-called Populares, though they were led by members of the same ruling families, often young and embittered enemies of the consulars; sometimes for their own ends, sometimes in the interest of social reform, they would secure themselves election as tribunes of the people, and then circumvent the Senate by putting their proposals on issues such as land reform or the extension of citizenship direct to the Assembly.

Dominion over the newly conquered territories brought great wealth to Rome through exploitation of the provinces in the form of taxes and cheap imports of manufactured goods and raw materials and in tribute paid by the client states, formally designated as friends and allies of the Roman people. The senators were debarred by law from engaging in trade or commerce and much of this new wealth accumulated in the hands of the equites: they provided the negotiatores who were bankers, moneylenders and traders, and the publicani who acted as public works contractors and bought the rights of provincial tax collection at auction. Some of them came from the leading families in the Italian cities where their influence was beginning to rival that of the hereditary landed aristocracy with its vast estates carved out of the lands Rome had won in the Italian wars. Italy was little more than a convenient geographical term for the peninsula, and political power remained firmly in the hands of the ruling oligarchy in Rome. Though associated status and then full Roman citizenship were gradually extended to the other Latins, there was no form of representative democracy and to vote in the Assembly any male citizen had to attend in person.

As the rule of Rome expanded and the orbit of her trade widened the influx of slaves of non-Italian origin, which had begun after the second Punic war, changed the whole rural economy. Based on cheap slave labour the great estates were planted with vast vineyards, olive groves and orchards, and operated more as ranches carrying livestock for meat and wool and less as producers of cereals, thus increasing the need to import corn, which in the second century came mainly from Sicily and Sardinia as tax paid in kind. After the booty and spoils from the victories in Macedonia reached Rome direct taxes were no longer levied on Roman citizens in Italy; in a series of attempts to win the votes of the urban proletariat the price of corn was more and more heavily subsidised, until in the last years of the Republic Clodius Pulcher as tribune made it a free issue. As a result many of the tenant farmers and small freeholders, who for centuries had made the

7

agricultural economy self-sufficient as well as providing the backbone of the legions, were ruined and dispossessed. Their farms went to the big estates, and many of them drifted to Rome; there they swelled the ranks of the unemployed and the urban mob, attaching themselves as clients to the great families or the leaders of the Populares, to vote in the Assembly, and on occasion to fight in the streets, as their patrons and paymasters ordered.

Festivals and games, free corn and lavish gladiatorial shows became the accepted way to buy votes in the Assembly and support on the streets. Once the citizen legions raised by the consuls to serve for one year had been Rome's sure shield in defence; now there was a dearth of recruits with the required property qualifications, and the army was fast becoming a professional instrument for the annexation of territory and the acquisition of wealth, with the soldiers demanding a share of the booty and the provision of land on discharge as their right.

In an attempt at reform the young noble, Tiberius Gracchus, tribune in 133, put proposals to the Assembly designed to give effect to an existing law limiting the amount of public land any individual might hold. In a speech about the plight of the urban poor and the rural dispossessed he referred to the fact that they provided most of the manpower for the legions, saying of them: 'They fight and die to give others wealth and luxury, they are called the masters of the world but they have no foot of land to call their own.' Alarmed at this threat to the size of their own estates as well as to the Senate's authority his conservative opponents struck him down on the steps of the Capitol itself. This was the first murder for purely political reasons in the long history of the Republic, a grim foretaste of what was to come as the Optimates continued to refuse to make any concessions and the Populares adopted ever more violent means to achieve their ends.

Ten years later Tiberius's younger brother, Gaius, was elected as tribune of the people, entrusted with safeguarding their rights. During his two years as tribune he put forward a number of measures for social reform, including Tiberius's agrarian proposals, controls for the price of corn, more political influence for the equites and extension of Roman citizenship to all Latins as of right, with associated status for other Italians. In retaliation the Senate passed a decree, later known as the ultimate decree, charging the consuls to see to it that the Republic came to no harm, and in effect outlawing Gaius; he was killed and 3,000 of his supporters were executed without trial.

During the last decade of the second century Gaius Marius was one of the first of the very few 'new men' from outside the senatorial families to rise to office as consul. Helped in his early career by the powerful Metelli he married Julia, the sister of Caesar's father and a member of the patrician Julian family; but it was his espousal of the Populares' cause and his military ability, demonstrated first against Jugurtha in Numidia and then in defending the Alpine frontier against migrant Germanic tribes threatening to erupt into the plain of the Po, which secured him the consulate in five successive years from 104 to 100. As well as being an able general Marius was an excellent administrator and a military innovator and he completely reorganised the army, improving the design of its weapons, replacing the maniple as the tactical unit with the more flexible cohort and giving the legions the standards which became known as eagles. He also speeded up the process of turning the annually conscripted citizen militia into a voluntarily enlisted professional army owing allegiance to its generals rather than to the Senate. By now recruits were found largely from the rural areas with two thirds coming from the Italian allies. In Rome skilled trades and crafts were mainly in the hands of freedmen and slaves from the East, and already the majority of the free inhabitants were of non-Italian or servile origin; to them, as Scipio Aemilianus put it, Italy was but a stepmother.

In the Social war, so called because Rome fought to resist the demand of her Italian allies, or socii, for extension of Roman citizenship to them, Marius served under Gnaeus Pompeius Strabo in the north, while Cornelius Sulla, nicknamed Felix, commanded in the south. Pompeius and Sulla managed to win most of the battles, but the allies achieved their aim and to end the war Rome was forced to concede citizenship to all mainland Italians south of the Po.

Sulla's election as consul for 88 gave him Asia as his proconsular province and command against Mithridates VI of Pontus, who had overrun much of Asia Minor including the province of Asia and had then established himself in Greece. Marius tried to oust Sulla, but he was forced to flee from Italy when Sulla marched on Rome and took the city, the first Roman general to do so by force of arms, and another ominous precedent for the future.

But with Sulla away in the east Marius returned to Italy, raised an army, and acting in concert with Lucius Cornelius Cinna, who had been deposed as consul in 87, he sacked Ostia and took Rome; the Senate was obliged to appoint him and Cinna as consuls for 86. Marius died seventeen days later but not before he had hunted down and killed many of his enemies among them Antony's grandfather.

Though originally plebeian as opposed to patrician, the Antonii, who affected to trace their descent back to Anton a son of Hercules, were by now one of the noble senatorial families of Rome. Antony's grandfather, also Marcus, was the leading orator of his day, when the ability to speak cogently and persuasively, particularly in the Senate and the law courts, was of first importance for a Roman noble in his public career. As a youth Cicero heard him speak and so admired his style that he later cited it as an example in his 'De Oratore'. As praetor, one of the magistrates who at this time governed the provinces, Antonius was given command in 102 against the pirates in Cilicia. Inscriptions indicate that he hauled his fleet across the isthmus of Corinth to avoid a winter passage round the Peloponnese and he was successful enough in this campaign to be voted a Triumph in 100. He was elected consul for 99, and in 97 he held office as one of the two censors who supervised much of the administration of the city ranging from public morals to the registration of citizens on the electoral lists, and who had the right to strike off members from the rolls of the Senate for misconduct. Though later the powers of the censors were greatly curtailed, at this time the office marked the apex of a career in the public service in pursuit of Fama, Gloria, Auctoritas and Dignitas. During his censorship he began the process of enrolling non-Roman Italians living in the city as Roman citizens.

Antonius had family connections in Arpinum and at first he supported Marius who came from that district. But later they quarrelled, perhaps over the rights of the Italian allies, for Antonius was prosecuted but acquitted for inciting them to revolt. When Marius seized power in 87 he took his revenge on those of his enemies who had once been his friends and supporters. Among them were the brothers Lucius and Gaius Julius Caesar, Publius Licinius Crassus and his sons, and Antonius; the Caesar brothers were arrested in the street and summarily executed; Crassus committed suicide and one of his sons was killed, but another, Marcus, escaped to Spain.

Antonius fled to the country where friends arranged for him to hide on a farm. Appian describes how the farmer, embarrassed at the thought of offering rough country wine to a noble consular such as Antonius, sent a slave to fetch a flask of better wine from the local inn; there, in response to a casual enquiry, he let slip whom the wine was for. The innkeeper reported this to Marius's agents who despatched a detachment of soldiers under a military tribune, Publius Annius, with orders to kill Antonius. Annius sent his men into the farmhouse; then surprised at how long they were taking he went in himself. Upstairs he found Antonius trying to divert the soldiers from their task with an involved dialectical dissertation; this he cut short with a stroke of his sword. He sent Antonius's head to Marius as the customary proof of orders executed and notice of head money expected; Marius is said to have put it facing him across his dining table to gloat over it. Not long afterwards Antonius's son, also Marcus, married Julia, daughter of the Lucius Julius Caesar who had been killed on Marius's orders; their first-born was Mark Antony.

Though outlawed by Cinna and denied supplies and reinforcements from Italy, Sulla succeeded in driving Mithridates out of Greece, and in 85 at Dardanus he forced him to sue for peace and surrender all the territory he had conquered in Asia Minor. He fined the independent kingdoms and the Hellenistic cities which had supported Mithridates a total of 20,000 talents and obliged them to pay tribute. Thus for the first time Rome's interests in the East came face to face with Parthia's.

When news of Cinna's death reached Sulla he set out for Italy; there he was joined by Gnaeus Pompeius, still in his twenties, who had raised a private army of three legions from his father's veterans on the family estates in Picenum. With the help of Pompey, Quintus Metellus Pius, and Marcus Crassus who had returned from Spain, Sulla defeated Marius and the consular armies in the ensuing civil war. At the final battle at the Colline Gate Crassus won the day, and Sulla entered Rome as the victor. He had himself made dictator, an emergency office limited to six months under the constitution of the Republic and not used since the Second Punic war; the appointment of a dictator automatically suspended all the other magistrates except the tribunes.

Sulla at once set about eliminating his own enemies and all those who had supported Marius. But this time, for the sake of efficiency and economy of effort and to give a semblance of the State's authority to the process of murder without trial, he instituted proscriptions. This sinister innovation, again pointing the way of things to come, meant that simply by publishing their names on a list Roman citizens were outlawed and made liable to summary execution; their property was forfeited to the State and their sons and their children's sons were debarred from holding public office. The hunting down of the proscribed, the sound of marching soldiers echoing through the empty streets at night and the rattle of sword hilts on the doors of private houses in the small hours, formed the background to a reign of terror which was long to be remembered. At least forty senators and 1,600 equites died in Sulla's proscriptions; Orosius puts the total killed at 9,000.

Having disposed of his enemies by death or flight and thus acquired their property Sulla took further steps to consolidate his position as dictator and his control of the Senate. He replaced more than one hundred senators who had died or been proscribed in the civil war and he doubled the membership of the Senate to 600, promoting his own men, many from the equites. To govern the provinces, now ten in all, he increased the number of praetors to eight and their financial officers, the quaestors, to twenty, making the latter members of the

11

Senate. He laid down a scale of minimum ages for all magistrates and passed measures designed to enable the Senate to control provincial governors.

Another precedent was Sulla's arbitrary confiscation of land from the districts which had resisted him and its use for resettling his veterans. Towards the middle of the second century the Senate had ceased allotting public land to discharged soldiers, largely because of the difficulty in finding enough of it; Sulla now revived and extended the practice. He had brought five legions back from the East, but he gave land grants to veterans from all the twenty three legions he had deployed in the civil war. This set a pattern for future demands from discharged soldiers, most of them peasants to whom land of their own was even more important than money; soon they came to look to their generals as the providers of both land and money, thus extending their loyalties in a client patron relationship after their discharge.

Then in 79, to the surprise and relief of Rome, Sulla resigned his office as dictator. This was a precedent of a different kind, and one not to be repeated for nearly four hundred years when in ill health Diocletian would abdicate and retire to his palace near Salonae. Why Sulla did so is not clear: perhaps, as the story went, an old prophecy had convinced him that he had not long to live, but more probably he knew that he was seriously ill.

The measures which he took to restore to the Senate the executive powers which he himself had curtailed were swept away within a decade. He had demonstrated only too clearly how to use the army to abrogate the Senate's authority, though Marcus Aemilius Lepidus was defeated when he tried to emulate him in 77 by marching on Rome with the army of Gaul. In the proscriptions Sulla had eliminated all those most able and willing to defend the political institutions of the Republic, and in so doing he had given impetus to the decline of the senatorial oligarchy. It was too late to reverse or even to stay the process for the economics and politics of real power were moving the Republic inexorably towards its end. Already the man whom only assassins' daggers would force to surrender his office as dictator was in his early twenties, the man who was to remark that Sulla did not understand the ABC of power or he would never have let it slip from his hands.

Sulla died a year later, his epitaph, which he was said to have composed himself, that he had not been outdone in good by his friends or in evil by his enemies. For the next decade a three cornered struggle went on between the Optimates stubbornly defending their birthright, the Populares demanding reform in ever more forthright terms, and the growing commercial and financial interests of the equites seeking political power and control of the courts. The last of Sulla's constitutional reforms was repealed during the consulate of Pompey and Crassus in 70, the year which has been said to mark the beginning of the final stage in the slow but violent death of the Republic.

During the civil war which brought Sulla to power the brash young Pompey proved the ablest of his generals and was perhaps mockingly nicknamed Magnus. Sulla forced him to divorce his wife, Antistia, in order to marry his own wife's daughter, Aemilia, who, though pregnant, was obliged to divorce her husband; she died soon after in childbirth. Remarking that men paid more heed to the rising than the setting sun Pompey insisted on triumphing for the victories he had won in Sicily and Africa, and Sulla grudgingly gave way to his young son-in-law. In 77 Pompey trapped Lepidus's legate, Marcus Iunius Brutus, in Mutina and executed him after a promise of safe conduct. Then from 76 to 72 with proconsular powers voted him by the Senate he fought a series of bitter campaigns in Spain against Quintus Sertorius, who in 83 had been sent as praetor to govern the two Spanish provinces. Driven out by pro-Sullan forces in 81, Sertorius had returned at the invitation of the Lusitanians in the west of the peninsula and had succeeded in recovering much of Roman Spain. Moderate, able, and popular with the Spaniards, he carried on a long and successful guerrilla war against the Roman armies sent to dislodge him; it was only when he was murdered by his own Roman officers in 71 that Pompey was able to finish the war.

In 73 Spartacus, a Thracian gladiator, led a slave revolt in southern Italy; he defeated several consular armies and at one point reached Cisalpine Gaul. Crassus finally cornered him in Lucania, but Pompey returned from Spain in time to cut off the survivors in Etruria and to receive more acclaim for Spartacus's defeat than Crassus felt he deserved.

As one of Sulla's principal backers Crassus had appropriated much of the property of the proscribed. During the 70's he used his financial talents to increase his already considerable wealth which he put to work to further his own political advancement. It was in this decade that Marcus Tullius Cicero and Gaius Julius Caesar began their public careers. Cicero was born into a well-to-do equestrian family near Arpinum in 106, in the same year as Pompey. In 81 and 80 he began to make a name for himself in the law courts of Rome, and he then spent two years at universities in Greece and Rhodes. His first appointment in the public service came when as a 'new man' he was elected as quaestor for 75, an office which carried with it membership of the Senate, and sent to Sicily. Back in Rome he set the seal on his growing reputation as an advocate when in 70 he prosecuted Gaius Verres, recently returned from governing Sicily where his extortion and corruption had become a public scandal even by the current standards of provincial administration.

In contrast to Cicero, Caesar was a member of one of Rome's ancient patrician families, the Julii. In 84, when he was sixteen or seventeen, he married Cinna's daughter, Cornelia, and a year or so later he fled from Italy rather than obey Sulla's order to divorce her. After military service in Asia Minor, where he won the civic crown for gallantry in saving the life of a soldier, he studied at the university of Rhodes and then served on the staff in a campaign against the pirates of Cilicia. During Pompey's consulate he helped him to restore the powers of the tribunes of the people which Sulla had curtailed. He showed legal and rhetorical skills and won public acclaim as prosecutor in two corruption trials. In 68 he gave the funeral oration for his aunt Julia, Marius's widow; Cornelia died in that year, and despite his Marian connections he married Sulla's granddaughter, Pompeia. As aedile in 65 he publicly honoured Marius's memory, and he spent borrowed money with abandon to provide lavish gladiatorial shows for the popular entertainment.

At times Caesar showed a degree of self-confident arrogance which was rare even in a young Roman noble, and in his dealings with the pirates who kidnapped him in Asia Minor he revealed a strange blend of ruthlessness and cynical humour. Telling them that the twenty talents they asked was too low a ransom for him, he sent to Miletus for fifty. Though he remained their prisoner until the money arrived, he managed to dominate his captors and warned them that he would come back with Roman troops to punish them. They would have done better to have heeded him for he returned to capture, imprison, and crucify them all, though in token of the friendly way in which they had treated him he saw to it that they died a quick death. But, such incidents apart, he had given no indication of anything unusual in his make-up, no hint of the political ambition and the military talent which lay within him.

In spite of his marriage to Julia, which had allied the noble but impoverished Antonii with the patrician but equally impoverished Julii, Antony's father made no great mark in the life of Rome. He was remembered as an honest kindly man, feckless and easy-going, and, as such men often are, generous to a fault; it fell to Julia to look after the straitened family finances as well as managing the household. Plutarch describes how when one of his friends came to borrow money, Antonius, with none to give him, sent a slave to fetch some water knowing that it would be brought in a silver bowl; he gave the bowl to his friend, telling him to make what use of it he could. Later when Julia missed it, and thinking it stolen started to question the slaves, he confessed and asked her to forgive him.

Like his father before him, Antonius as praetor in 74 was given a special imperium to deal with the pirates who had again become a serious threat to trade and shipping over the length and breadth of the Mediterranean and were even interfering with the vital corn supply to Rome. After inconclusive naval engagements off the Spanish and Ligurian coasts the pirates defeated him off Crete and he was obliged to make a humiliating treaty with them; in Rome he was given the ironical cognomen, or nickname, Creticus.

Antonius died in 72, leaving Julia with their three sons, the eleven year old Antony and his younger brothers Gaius and Lucius, and a mortgaged villa at Misenum. A year later she married Publius Cornelius Lentulus, and it was in his house that the three Antonius brothers grew up. Lentulus had been involved in a financial scandal as quaestor in 81, but he was elected praetor in the same year as Antony's father, and then consul in 71. In the following year the censors took the exemplary, and in the case of a consular, as Lentulus now was, the unusual step of striking him off the rolls of the Senate for misconduct; Antony's uncle, Gaius Antonius, was struck off at the same time.

As a youth in the 60's Antony became a close friend of Gaius Scribonius Curio, and later of Clodius, both of them wild and dissolute young aristocrats some years older than him. With Curio as his drinking and gambling companion Antony ran up large debts, amounting, according to Plutarch, to 250 talents. The talent, originally a Greek term describing the load of gold or silver a man could carry, is difficult to translate into later monetary terms, but it was an enormous debt for the penniless young Antony and Curio used his father's name to guarantee it. The elder Curio had been a supporter of Sulla, and like Crassus he had grown rich on the proceeds of the proscriptions; as soon as he heard that his son was using his name to underwrite his friend's debts he forbade Antony his house.

When Curio deserted the Populares and joined his father in backing the Optimates Antony turned to Clodius. A patrician by birth Clodius adopted an individual and wholly unscrupulous approach to politics, manipulating the urban mob to advance his own interests. In 63 he acted as prosecutor in the trial of Catiline; Cicero decided at the last moment that it would not be to his political advantage to accept the defence. Lucius Sergius Catilina had been praetor in 68, and for the next two years he had governed Spain as propraetor; on his return to Rome he was accused of having abused his powers and put on trial.

As chairman of the court Caesar took a neutral attitude, and with the connivance of Clodius, and some judicious bribery by Crassus, Catiline was acquitted. But the delay in bringing him to trial had debarred him from standing in the consular elections for 65 and 64. In the election for 63 he was backed by both Crassus and Caesar, and he made an electoral pact with Antony's uncle, Gaius Antonius, who was another candidate; but the Optimates united to oppose him, thus opening the way for Cicero as a compromise candidate. Cicero was elected with Antonius as his colleague and so became the first 'new man' to gain office as consul for several decades.

Early in 63, playing on his patrician ancestry and his known sympathy for the Populares through his Marian connections, Caesar bribed his way with Crassus's help to election to the office of Pontifex Maximus, head of the board which controlled all State religious affairs and vacant on the death of Metellus Pius.

After Crassus had withdrawn his financial backing, Catiline, ambitious but now frustrated and disillusioned, began to gather round him the disaffected from every class, all those who had a grievance against the system and the establishment. Encouraged by these new supporters and further embittered by another defeat in the consular elections for 62, he began to organise a widely based conspiracy against the State. As consul Cicero was kept well informed by his spies, but as a 'new man' he felt that he had to have irrefutable written evidence before he moved against aristocrats such as Catiline and his influential friends. After Cicero had denounced him in the Senate Catiline left Rome to head a group of rebellious Sullan veterans in Etruria; Cicero then obtained the evidence he needed by means of a dubious but effective strategem in which he used delegates to Rome from the Allbroges in Gaul, whom the conspirators had approached, as unwitting agents provocateurs. He immediately arrested five of the ringleaders, among them Antony's stepfather, Lentulus, who was urban praetor.

When the Senate debated what was to be done with the conspirators most of the speakers argued that they deserved to die, though Caesar advocated imprisonment; the younger Cato proposed their death, his motion was carried, and on Cicero's orders the five were immediately executed without trial. During the debate a letter was handed to Caesar and Cato at once accused him of treasonable correspondence with the conspirators; Caesar silently passed the letter to Cato who was dismayed to see it was a love note from his step-sister, Servilia, who was Caesar's mistress. For his part in unmasking Catiline's plot Cicero had been acclaimed as the saviour of the Republic, but the summary executions brought a revulsion of feeling in the Senate. He tried to justify his action on the grounds that although, as his critics maintained, any immediate threat to the State had been removed by the arrest of the ringleaders, they had nevertheless been outlawed and so deprived of any right to trial by the ultimate decree, 'senatus consultum ultimum', which the Senate had passed a month before, charging him as consul to take all necessary steps to safeguard the Republic. But some doubted the validity of this argument in law and others distrusted Cicero's smooth tongue and disliked him as a 'new man'. Many felt that the danger to the State had not been grave enough to warrant the execution of their own peers without trial and feared that Cicero had established a precedent which could rebound on their own heads.

It was alleged that Cicero at first refused to hand over Lentulus's body to Julia for burial. Whatever the truth of this Antony doubtless took his mother's part, and Cicero's hatred of him may date from this time. As Cicero's colleague Gaius Antonius found himself obliged to take the field against Cataline, though a timely attack of gout prevented him from being present at the final battle in January 62 when Cataline was defeated and killed by Gaius's legate, Marcus Petreius. However self-interested Cataline's motives for championing their cause may have been, his tomb became a place of pilgrimage for the outcast and the oppressed over many years to come.

After their defeat of Antonius the Cilician pirates had prospered. In the absence of a standing Roman fleet and with no other maritime power to hold them in check they gradually extended their operations, and by the early 60's their well-handled squadrons were ranging virtually unchecked over the whole Mediterranean. At times they brought the sea borne trade of Italy to a standstill, and it was the disastrous effect of their attacks on shipping, in particular the soaring price of corn, which led to persistent demands for action against them. This pressure enabled Aulus Gabinius, tribune in 67, to get measures agreed by the Assembly for raising large naval and military forces despite a storm of protest in the Senate, where only Caesar supported the proposals; an 'imperium infinitum' was approved, giving one man unprecedented powers of command for three years over the whole Mediterranean and inland to a distance of fifty miles from the coasts.

When this Lex Gabinia was passed Pompey, who had taken no proconsular province to govern, was the natural choice for supreme command. The news of his appointment was enough to bring a sharp fall in the corn price. His detailed and carefully co-ordinated plan was brilliantly executed and in forty days his legates swept the western Mediterranean clear of pirates, the discomfited survivors making the best of their way home to what they hoped was the safe haven of their fortified bases. But Pompey defeated them off the Cilician coast and then landed and took their main fortress of Coracesium by assault; encouraged by the clemency he showed to the prisoners the rest of the inland strongholds surrendered. He put his army into winter quarters and attempted to find a more lasting solution to the problem of the pirates by resettling them in various towns and communities in southern Asia Minor and Achaea.

At the time there was another Roman army in Asia Minor, commanded by Lucius Licinius Lucullus, which had been engaged since 73 in a long and difficult war against the indomitable Mithridates VI. Nicomedes III, the last king of Bithynia, had bequeathed his kingdom to Rome and on his death in 75 or 74 it became the province of Bithynia. But Mithridates was not prepared to accept direct Roman control of the Bosporus and he quickly overran the new province, slaughtering every Roman who fell into his hands. Lucullus, despatched by the Senate to restore Roman rule, was an able and resourceful general and at first all went well: he drove Mithridates out of Bithynia, occupied his kingdom of Pontus, and then crossed the Euphrates to defeat his son-in-law, Tigranes, the king of Armenia.

But Lucullus, an aristocrat by birth, was an honest and upright man and a strict disciplinarian. At one point his troops, irked by his refusal to allow them to loot and seeing no end to the war, refused to obey his orders. His measures to protect the local inhabitants and limit the exploitation of the Roman controlled areas of Asia Minor alienated the powerful tax companies and other commercial interests in Rome, and they retaliated by interfering with his supplies and reinforcements from Italy.

After regrouping in the mountains of Armenia, Tigranes and Mithridates launched a counter-offensive in which Tigranes overran Cappodocia and Mithridates recovered much of Pontus. Faced with a shortage of supplies and further mutinies, one at least instigated by his brother-in-law, Clodius, there was little Lucullus could do; the Roman governors of Bithynia and Cilicia refused to move to his assistance beyond the borders of their own provinces and the war reached a stalemate in the difficult terrain of the central Anatolian plateau.

The Senate appointed Pompey, in winter quarters with his army in southern Asia Minor, to replace Lucullus and take command against Mithridates. They renewed his Mediterranean-wide imperium as high admiral of the Roman fleet and also made him governor of both Bithynia and Pontus, thus bringing all the Roman forces in Asia Minor under his command. His first move was to reach an agreement with Phraates, king of Parthia, which isolated Mithridates from Tigranes and effectively recognised the Euphrates as the common boundary between the Roman and Parthian spheres of interest. After a short campaign in eastern Pontus during the summer of 66, Pompey cornered Mithridates in the valley of the upper Lycus and defeated him in a night battle; Mithridates managed to escape and fled to Colchis on the eastern coast of the Black Sea. Pompey then crossed the Euphrates into Armenia where Tigranes surrendered his capital, Artaxata.

Early in 65 Pompey marched north, but Mithridates was already beyond the Caucasus engaged in raising the tribes round the Sea of Azov against his own son, Machares, who ruled the Bosporan Crimea as his viceroy. After driving his son to suicide Mithridates established himself in the province, which stretched west from the Crimea along the coastal plain of the Black Sea. Pompey had to content himself with defeating the Iberians in the southern foothills of the Caucasus; then, leaving his fleet to watch Mithridates, he marched east towards the Caspian. In another brief campaign he defeated the Albanians, whose tribal territory ran down from the Caucasus to the plain of the Cyrus and the Caspian; he then moved south to winter quarters west of the Euphrates in Armenia Minor.

During 65 Pompey's legates, Lucius Afranius and Gabinius, had crossed the Euphrates and seized the border province of Gordyene, which was in dispute between Parthia and Armenia. Phraates sent envoys to remonstrate with Pompey and to remind him that they had agreed the Euphrates as a common boundary, but Pompey brushed his protest aside with the arrogant retort that the frontier which he chose would be a just one. Thus an opportunity to negotiate with Parthia from a position of strength and to agree a lasting frontier on a natural river boundary was lost to Rome. It was not to occur again, and Pompey's abrogation of his agreement with Phraates sowed the seeds of enduring Parthian distrust of Roman good faith and was to cost Rome dearly in blood, material and prestige.

Early in 64 Pompey ordered Gabinius and Afranius to take over Syria, once the heartland of the Seleucid empire, but presently in a state of anarchy as the local princes fought among themselves. Gabinius occupied Damascus where he was joined by Pompey's quaestor, Marcus Aemilius Scaurus, and Afranius forced the Syrian Gates to open the coast road to Antioch and the lower Orontes valley. After a brief visit to Amisus to organise the defences of Pontus against any counter-attack by Mithridates Pompey joined Afranius in Antioch and spent the winter making Syria into a new Roman province.

Again in 63 he gave his legates an independent role, directing Gabinius and Scaurus south into Judaea. Here Hyrcanus and his younger brother, Aristobulus, of the ruling Hasmonaean dynasty were disputing the throne, with Hyrcanus helped by Aretas, king of

Arabian Nabataea, besieging Aristobulus in Jerusalem. Gabinius and Scaurus took Aristobulus's part, perhaps because they considered him more likely to pay the bribes which both he and Hyrcanus offered for Roman backing.

But Pompey summoned the brothers to Damascus and decided that Hyrcanus would prove more compliant as Rome's client ruler of Judaea. He arrested Aristobulus and ordered Marcus Pupius Piso to reinstate Hyrcanus in Jerusalem. The priests and the Jewish officers refused to surrender the Temple and Piso had to bring up artillery, battering rams and other siege equipment, and even then it took him two months to reduce the inner citadel of the Temple. Sulla's son, Faustus, led the final assault, but the frustrated Roman troops got out of hand, butchering thousands of Jews and cutting down the priests as they officiated at the Temple altars.

Pompey insisted on viewing the sanctuary of the Temple; he did nothing but indulge his curiosity, no doubt marvelling at the absence of the image of any god. But his very presence infuriated the Jews who felt that his eyes had defiled their holy of holies. Pompey confirmed Hyrcanus as High Priest and Ethnarch with the Idumaean Antipater as his chief minister, but he drastically reduced the territory of Judaea, removing all non-Jewish areas acquired under the Hasmonaeans. Ten towns east of the Jordan known as the Decapolis came under indirect Roman rule from Syria, as did the Greek and Phoenician cities on the coast, thus depriving Judaea of her only outlet to the sea. Samaria was also detached from Judaea, and, with the plain of Esdraelon, formed a corridor of Roman administered territory between Judaea proper and the recently Judaised province of Galilee.

Aretas of Nabataea had thought his desert kingdom safely beyond the reach of Rome, but after his intervention in Judaea, albeit on the side of the Roman-backed Hyrcanus, he felt it prudent to send an embassy offering to submit to Pompey. To make sure that this was something more than a politic but empty gesture on Aretas's part Pompey crossed the Jordan and marched into Nabataea. He was nearing the capital, Petra, when couriers caught up with him bringing news that Mithridates at last was dead, killed by his son Pharnaces who was now seeking to make his peace with Rome. After a brief celebration Pompey turned in his tracks and set off on the long march back to Asia Minor, leaving Scaurus to continue the advance on Petra.

Envoys were awaiting him at Amisus with presents as tokens of Pharnaces's submission and the decaying body of Mithridates as evidence of his father's death. Thus, with the help of Pharnaces, Pompey had brought the third war which Rome had fought against Mithridates to a successful end, and his task in the East was complete.

Although he had turned down the proffered settlement with Parthia, he had detached her client states west of the Euphrates and reoriented them to look to Rome as overlord. In doing so he set up the framework of Roman rule for centuries to come over the whole of Asia Minor and the Levant, from the Pontic shore of the Black Sea eastward to the Caucasus and the Euphrates and south to the deserts of Arabia and the Red Sea.

He had made himself the most powerful man in the Roman world, and the shadow of his power was long enough to reach to Rome and there keep men guessing as to how he would use it when he returned. His campaigns in the East had provided him with the wealth to back his military and political power and had given him a reputation for invincibility and a semi-divine authority. He was truly Pompey the Great, and he had confounded those who had slightingly nicknamed him Magnus in his youth.

In his absence the struggle for political advantage in Rome had gone on unabated, with Caesar strengthening his position in spite of growing opposition from Cicero and Crassus finding political power harder to acquire than wealth. In 63 Caesar followed up his election as Pontifex Maximus by winning office as praetor for 62. In December of that year Clodius was involved in a scandal at the ancient festival of Bona Dea, the goddess worshipped only by women with sacred rites deriving from remote antiquity and a strictly enforced taboo that no male, man or animal, might defile the ceremonies by their presence. It was as urban praetor for the year that the ceremonies were held in Caesar's house under the auspices of his mother, Aurelia. It was alleged that the beardless and youthful looking Clodius managed to get into the house dressed as a woman, perhaps with the connivance of a female slave. But a servant whom he met in a passage saw through his disguise and rushed to report the male intruder to Aurelia who was said to have identified Clodius. It was the kind of bizarre practical joke which might well have appealed to him for its own sake, but when the story spread rapidly through Rome the next morning it was widely assumed that his purpose had been to further an affair with Caesar's wife, Pompeia.

When Clodius was arraigned on charges of sacrilege he maintained that he had been ninety miles away from Rome that night. As prosecutor Cicero did his utmost to break this alibi, but to his considerable chagrin Aurelia either could not, or would not, name the intruder as Clodius. Caesar offered no evidence, and helped it was said by bribes from Crassus Clodius was acquitted. One result was that in Clodius Cicero made himself an implacable enemy; another was Caesar's divorce of Pompeia with the remark that his wife, as the wife of the Pontifex Maximus, must be above suspicion.

Later in the same month Pompey landed in Italy, and Rome paused, looking to Brundisium and wondering what he would do, for it seemed that all Sulla had won through civil war was his for the taking. Thanks to him the pirates no longer preyed on the seaways of the Mediterranean and imported corn was cheap and plentiful in Rome. Mithridates, that wily old enemy of Rome, was dead and part of his kingdom of Pontus added to the province of Bithynia. Pompey had carved a new Roman province out of Syria and made Judaea a client state. He had established Rome's authority from the Hellespont to the Euphrates and from the Caucasus to the frontiers of Egypt. Wherever he had led his army Roman arms had triumphed, and now those battle hardened legions, heavy with loot, hungry for land, loyal to the last man, stood behind their general on Italian soil. It was small wonder that Rome caught her breath.

But Pompey had no wish for absolute power, no mind to impose his will on Rome. For his soldiers he wanted the land he had promised them, and for himself a Triumph and some small show of gratitude and respect for all he had achieved in the name of Rome. When the reception he expected did not materialise he hesitated, as if at a loss: the only positive step he took was to send word to Rome to divorce his wife, Mucia, apparently on suspicion of adultery with Caesar. He began to demobilise his legions, asking the Senate only for land for his soldiers and leave to hold his Triumph. He then set out for Rome, travelling as a private citizen and escorted only by a few friends.

In spite of, or perhaps because of Pompey's divorce of Mucia, Caesar took the lead in the Senate in proposing honours for him. But the Optimates distrusted Pompey, and their leader, Cato, brother-in-law of Lucullus whom Pompey had replaced in Asia Minor, opposed many of Caesar's proposals. With the support of the powerful Metelli angered by Pompey's divorce of their kinswoman, Cato succeeded in blocking motions to ratify Pompey's settlement of the East and provide land for his veterans. Thus the Optimates frustrated and antagonised Pompey, but they could not deny him his Triumph which he held on the 28th and 29th September 61, the latter his forty fifth birthday. He had triumphed after his campaigns in Africa and Spain, and in Plutarch's eyes this third Triumph meant that he had led all the three continents captive to Rome. It was more lavish and spectacular than anything the city had ever seen before. Banners and floats proclaimed victories over fourteen countries and the capture of 900 cities and 800 ships; they announced the raising of the public revenue from fifty to eighty-five million denarii and the enormous capital sum of 20,000 talents which he had paid into the Treasury. The prisoners from the conquered lands walked in the procession led by the captive princes, among them Aristobulus and his sons; at the end of the Triumph, contrary to the Roman practice of killing the leading prisoners as a symbolic sacrifice to the gods of Rome, their lives were spared on Pompey's orders.

Soon afterwards Caesar borrowed heavily from Crassus to disentangle himself from his creditors and left quietly to take up his appointment as propraetor in Further Spain. Here at the age of forty he was to command an army in battle for the first time, revealing talents as a general which his contemporaries, and perhaps even he himself, had not suspected he possessed. During 60 he returned to hold a Triumph to mark his first victories in Spain and to stand for election as consul for 59. But Cato insisted that the letter of the law be observed, whereby Caesar was not allowed to enter the city before his Triumph, knowing full well that he had to do so to be accepted in time as a candidate for the coming consular election. Caesar chose to forgo his Triumph, and he was elected as consul with the Optimates' candidate, Marcus Calpurnius Bibulus, as his colleague. In a further ill-considered attempt to thwart him the Senate decided that after their term of office the consuls of 59 should only be given supervisory duties over State forests and other public lands instead of the customary proconsular provinces to govern, thus sacrificing Bibulus's legitimate expectations in spiting Caesar.

So, as if driven by some death wish, Cato and the Optimates made it certain that Caesar would never come to terms with the old oligarchy. Not content with alienating him and rebuffing Pompey they also antagonised Crassus by making a number of abortive attempts to interfere with his complex financial enterprises. As a result Pompey and Caesar, the two most powerful men in Rome, were driven into a tacit mutual understanding to protect their own interests. To cement this accord with a personal and binding tie Pompey married Julia, Caesar's daughter and only child; unlike some marriages arranged for political ends it was to bring them both great happiness. Deluded by an exaggerated notion of his own capacity as a statesman Cicero cherished the idea that with the help of a soldier such as Pompey, or possibly Caesar, he could bring about a new concord between the senatorial and equestrian orders. But he was unwilling to commit his legal and rhetorical skills to further Pompey and Caesar's interests, and Caesar decided that other means would have to be found to silence him. Crassus's business ventures had prospered: he had acquired much property at a fraction of its true value by making the owners offers for their houses when they were threatened by one of the numerous fires which swept Rome, while his own private fire brigade waited nearby in a side street to put them out. But his political intrigues had been less successful and he had failed to persuade the Senate to annex Egypt. Now he readily agreed to support Caesar and Pompey and out of this understanding the first Triumvirate developed.

If the consulate of Pompey and Crassus in 70 began the final stage of the decay of the Republic, that of Caesar and the ineffective Bibulus in 59 marked the point from which there could be no recovery. This was largely due to Cato's stubborn refusal to compromise his Republican principles and the intransigence of his two principal supporters, the Metelli cousins, both Quintus Caecilius but distinguished by the nicknames Celer and Creticus. Caesar made effective use of every conceivable political stratagem to outwit the Optimates, and with the added threat of Pompey's veterans he reduced the Senate to impotence and forced through bills to ratify Pompey's settlement of the East and provide land for his soldiers. In May Publius Vatinius, acting in Caesar's interest as tribune, got the Senate's previous arrangements set aside and Cisalpine Gaul and Illyricum were allotted to Caesar as proconsular provinces for a term of five years which ran to the last day of February 54; Pompey's tenure of Spain was similarly extended. A month later, on Pompey's initiative, the province of Transalpine Gaul, vacant on the death of Metellus Celer, was also given to Caesar.

With Caesar's backing Clodius renounced his patrician status so that he was eligible to stand for office as tribune of the people; he was elected for 58, when the consuls were Pompey's legate, Gabinius, and Lucius Calpurnius Piso, whose daughter Calpurnia, Caesar had married the year before. When Cicero declined an appointment on Caesar's staff in Gaul, Clodius, with Caesar's support and Pompey's tacit approval, arraigned him on the charge that he had acted illegally in executing the Catiline conspirators without trial. After a fruitless appeal to Pompey Cicero evaded trial by fleeing from Rome, and in his absence Clodius had no difficulty in securing a formal sentence of exile against him. By now Clodius was the acknowledged leader of the more extreme radicals and controlled what amounted to a private army on the streets of Rome, using it in his own interest as much as those of Caesar and Crassus, or against Pompey's.

Some years earlier, in an attempt to win back popular support for the Optimates, Cato had got the corn subsidy increased so that more than 300,000, perhaps a third of the adult population, received a monthly issue of five modii of corn at half the market price. Clodius now retaliated by making it free; to finance this he proposed the annexation of Cyprus which was ruled by Ptolemy, brother of

Ptolemy XII of Egypt. But unlike his brother, Ptolemy of Cyprus had not insured his throne by paying Caesar and Pompey to secure him formal recognition as friend and ally of the Roman people. With Caesar's approval, Clodius used the pretext of collusion with the pirates to oust Ptolemy, who committed suicide. He then got Cato appointed as governor; this was an astute move, for it was difficult for Cato to refuse and it deprived the Optimates in Rome of their only effective leader.

Later in 58 Clodius over-reached himself in opposing Pompey, who reacted by employing another tribune, Titus Annius Milo, to recruit gangs to combat Clodius and break his hold on the urban mob and streets of Rome. Pompey was mainly responsible for securing Cicero's triumphant return from exile in September 57, despite Clodius's every effort to prevent it. Cicero at once began to try and undermine Pompey's understanding with Caesar and Crassus. It was on his initiative in the Senate that Pompey was given wide powers to resolve a sudden corn shortage, possibly engineered by speculators, which arose that autumn. Pompey sailed himself to Sardinia, Sicily and Africa during the dangerous closed winter season to buy corn and charter vessels to transport it to Rome; it was now that he coined the phrase, beloved of sailors, 'Navigare necesse est, vivere non est necesse'.

Earlier Antony had been a close friend of Clodius and his wife, Fulvia, and one of their principal associates. But, according to Plutarch, he grew tired of Clodius's constant intrigues and alarmed at the mounting opposition his activities as tribune were arousing. Whether or not this was the only reason, Antony, now twenty-five, left Rome, probably during the latter half of 58, to study at the universities of Athens and Rhodes.

CHAPTER II

Syria, Judaea and Egypt

After his consulate in 58 Gabinius received Syria as his proconsular province, partly through Clodius's good offices. His colleague, Piso, now Caesar's father-in-law, was allotted Macedonia. On his way to Syria Gabinius met Antony in Greece and invited him to serve on his staff; at first Antony declined, but he accepted when Gabinius offered him command of the cavalry in Syria and they travelled on together to Antioch. There Gabinius was met with the news that civil war had again broken out in Judaea, which after Pompey's reorganisation was little more than a Jewish ethnarchy under the Roman governor of Syria.

After walking in Pompey's Triumph Aristobulus had been imprisoned in Rome. But one of his sons, Alexander, had raised an army in Judaea against his uncle, Hyrcanus, who as High Priest and Ethnarch had remained loyal to Pompey's legate, Scaurus, the previous governor of Syria. His army numbered some 1,500 cavalry and 10,000 infantry and with it Alexander had already won control of much of Judaea. He had fortified Alexandreum in southern Samaria, Hyrcanium, and Machaerus in the hills east of where the Jordan flows into the Dead Sea; in Jerusalem he had begun to rebuild the sections of the walls which Pompey had demolished six years before, when he took the city.

Gabinius marched with part of the army of Syria down the coast road through Byblos, Sidon, Tyre and Acre and then inland across the plain of Esdraelon. He sent Antony ahead in command of a mixed force of cavalry and auxiliary light infantry with orders to locate Alexander's army and maintain contact with it until the main body of the Roman army arrived. Antony came up with the Jewish army, and while he waited for Gabinius he was joined by Antipater with forces loyal to Hyrcanus.

As soon as he was faced by the whole Roman army Alexander withdrew, but Gabinius succeeded in bringing him to battle near Jerusalem. According to Josephus, Alexander lost 3,000 dead and 3,000 prisoners before he managed to extricate the remnants of his army and retreat into Samaria. He refused the terms which Gabinius offered, and after getting the worst of another battle he withdrew into the mountain fortress of Alexandreum commanding the road to

Jericho; in his account of this second battle Josephus mentions Antony's personal courage and ability as a leader. Gabinius left a force to cover Alexandreum and marched off with the rest of the army to re-establish Roman control over Judaea. On his return he tightened the siege and Alexander asked for terms, offering to surrender Hyrcanium and Machaerus as well. But these two fortresses were handed over to Gabinius on the instructions of Alexander's mother who feared for the lives of her husband, Aristobulus, and their other children, still held prisoners in Rome.

Eventually Alexander was forced to surrender, and Gabinius ordered the fortifications of Alexandreum to be demolished. He confirmed Hyrcanus as High Priest, though not as Ethnarch, and he allowed Antipater to remain as chief minister. He divided Judaea into five autonomous districts, each to be ruled by local leaders whom he selected. He then returned with the army to Syria. His campaign in Judaea had been a model of its kind: with a small force he had won a swift, decisive and economical victory, and he had then reimposed indirect Roman rule through local clients who owed their positions to Roman arms.

But Aristobulus and another son, Antigonus, escaped from prison in Rome, and it was not long before they made their way back to Judaea where they raised another army and refortified Alexandreum. This time Gabinius remained in Syria, sending an army south under Servilius, Antony and Sisenna to deal with this new revolt. When they reached Samaria Aristobulus abandoned Alexandreum, withdrew across the Jordan and fell back with his army of 8,000 towards Machaerus. But before he could reach the dubious safety of its partly destroyed walls the Romans caught up with him and forced him to give battle. At first Aristobulus managed to hold his hastily prepared positions, but at the second Roman assault his line broke. The Jews lost 5,000 dead before Aristobulus managed to escape to Machaerus with 1,000 men, but Antony, following up rapidly, arrived before they could start to rebuild the walls.

Aristobulus held out for two days, but then with Antony leading the final assault the Romans took the town. Aristobulus was captured but Antony spared his life and that of his son, Antigonus, sending them both back to Gabinius who returned them as prisoners to Rome. There Aristobulus was put back into prison, but Antigonus and Aristobulus's other children were freed as a result of the agreement Gabinius had made with their mother over the surrender of Hyrcanium and Machaerus, and which he now persuaded the Senate to honour.

From Josephus's account of these two minor Judaean campaigns of 57/56 it is clear that Antony, now twenty seven, made a name for himself as a cavalry commander of resource and initiative and an officer who was to be found leading his men from the front wherever the fighting was heaviest. In less than two years he had come a long way from the university student in Greece learning the finer points of the Asiatic style of rhetoric, which Plutarch describes as having much in common with his way of life, being boastful, insolent, and full of empty bravado and misguided aspirations.

These Judaean campaigns demonstrated the importance of the new province of Syria as the keystone of Roman power in the East and the forward base from which the Levant could be controlled and the Parthian frontier guarded. They also served to concentrate Rome's attention on Egypt, now the only independent country bordering the eastern Mediterranean.

Ever since Rome's power and influence had extended eastward in the second century there had been a growing temptation to meddle in the internal affairs of Egypt. After the death of Alexander Egypt had been ruled by the dynasty established by his general, Ptolemy. At one time the dominions of the Ptolemies had included Cyrenaica, Cyprus and Cilicia, as well as the province known as Coele, or hollow, Syria, which stretched in a wide arc from the Mediterranean coast between Sidon and the mouth of the Orontes through northern Judaea to Damascus and the area east and south-east of the anti-Lebanon. But the power of the Ptolemaic empire declined, partly as the result of constant and bitter feuds within the ruling house, and Coele Syria passed to the Seleucids, from whom Judaea won independence under Jannaeus and his Hasmonaean successors. By the beginning of the first century, though still a sovereign state, Egypt had become dependent on the whim and the goodwill of whoever ruled in Rome.

From 110 Ptolemy IX and his brother, Ptolemy X, were spasmodically engaged in civil war over two decades for the throne of Egypt and control of her remaining overseas possessions. After being deposed by a military revolt Ptolemy X borrowed heavily from Roman bankers to finance a series of attempts to re-establish himself. When he died in a naval battle in 88 the Senate, despite the demands of his Roman creditors, made no move either to depose Ptolemy IX or to annex Egypt. But on Ptolemy IX's death in 81 Sulla did intervene to appoint the last legitimate heir as Ptolemy XI. He was assassinated by the Alexandrians in the same year and succeeded by Ptolemy XII, nicknamed Auletes, or Fluteplayer, the bastard son of Ptolemy IX and father of the Cleopatra, who as Cleopatra VII was destined to be the last of the Ptolemies to rule Egypt. The will in which Egypt, like Pergamum and Bithynia, was supposed to have been bequeathed to Rome, if in fact it ever existed, was made either by Ptolemy X in an

28

effort to buy Roman backing or possibly by Ptolemy XI at Sulla's dictation.

Cyrenaica was bequeathed to Rome by Ptolemy Apion on his death in 96, but the Optimate majority in the Senate, reluctant to extend their commitment to administer overseas territories, did not make it a province until 74, and then only to prevent the pirates using it as a base. In an effort to forestall any move to annex Egypt Ptolemy XII, or Auletes as he is commonly known, adopted a conciliatory pro-Roman policy. In 63 he sent a large cavalry force to assist Pompey at Jerusalem, and perhaps also to demonstrate that he had no designs on Judaea which once had been part of the Ptolemaic province of Coele Syria. But this only alienated the Egyptians, in particular the cosmopolitan Alexandrians who feared and despised the Romans, regarding them as little better than armed and disciplined savages.

Over the years Auletes's hold on the throne of Egypt became less secure, and in 59 Caesar and Pompey, acting in concert, agreed to underwrite him as king of Egypt and obtain for him formal acknowledgement from the Senate as friend and ally of the Roman people; their price was the huge sum of 6,000 talents. Egypt was still a wealthy country; among her exports were precious stones, flax for making linen, and glass. The Nile valley produced a surplus of corn and was the only source of the marsh plant papyrus used throughout the Mediterranean world as paper. Egypt also controlled the river and seaborne trade routes from Africa and the East, which carried the bulk of the luxury goods such as silks from China, ivory from Ethiopia, pearls, spices, tortoiseshell and gemstones from India, perfumes and incense from southern Arabia and the Horn of Africa, all of which were much in demand in Rome.

But the gross annual product of Egypt was perhaps no more than 10,000 talents, and despite the comprehensive and efficient taxation system which covered every aspect of Egyptian life and the income from the lucrative and tightly controlled State monopolies such as export of grain, 6,000 talents was more than Auletes could hope to raise in a short time. But Caesar and Pompey had to be paid promptly so he borrowed from a consortium of Roman bankers headed by Gaius Rabirius Postumus. The heavy taxes which he proposed to levy in order to repay this loan with its high interest charges increased anti-Roman feeling and made him even more unpopular. His inability to prevent the annexation of Cyprus and his failure even to protest at the deposing of his own brother as ruler so inflamed the Egyptians that he was forced to flee the country.

Cleopatra's eldest sister, or perhaps half-sister, also called Cleopatra, became ruler of Egypt in her father's place as Cleopatra VI, but she was soon succeeded by her next sister, Berenice. In Rhodes Auletes appealed to Cato, who was on his way to take up his post as governor of Cyprus, but he was boorishly rebuffed. He then travelled on to Rome to enlist the help of Pompey, who received him well and lodged him in some style in his own villa outside the city.

In Rome there was speculative trading in the promissory notes which Auletes had given to Rabirius and the bankers. After some unedifying debates the Senate, swayed by the majority who had no financial interest in Auletes' restoration, decided not to help him. They came to this decision despite the fact that Berenice had married Archelaus of Pontus without their leave, after Gabinius had vetoed the Alexandrians' first choice of a consort who was living in Syria. Though he sympathised with Auletes Pompey had already been paid and he was not prepared to oppose the Senate over the Egyptian succession.

In Parthia Phraates was deposed and murdered by two of his sons, Orodes and Mithridates, acting together. But their accord was short-lived: Orodes won the throne, and Mithridates fled to Gabinius who welcomed a pretext to intervene in Parthia. He was already across the Euphrates when news reached him that Auletes had arrived in Syria, apparently with Pompey's backing in his attempt to recover Egypt. Gabinius returned at once to Syria and Auletes appealed to him for military assistance. In this he had Pompey's support and probably the approval of Crassus and also of Caesar, now far away campaigning in Gaul. But Gabinius must have been well aware of the Senate's attitude to such a venture. As a governor of a province he was expressly forbidden to wage war outside that province without the Senate's leave, which in the case of Egypt was unlikely to be forthcoming. He had to weigh the possible consequences of flouting the Senate's authority against the likely financial rewards and the degree of protection he could expect from Pompey.

Gabinius called a council of war. Then, as indeed it is now, an attack on Egypt mounted from Syria and Judaea was a difficult and complex operation. Gabinius had no fleet and not enough transports to make a seaborne invasion feasible. The problem was one of logistics, of how to move and supply an army in adequate strength for its task, overland from Judaea to Egypt; the principal hazard was not the Egyptian army but the Sinai desert which in the past had defeated generals and their armies and in the future was to tax the skill, resource and tenacity of many more.

As governor of Syria the political gamble was Gabinius's, but the military problems were plain enough to his staff and at the council of war the majority opposed the operation. Antony, his appetite for action whetted by the Judaean campaigns, was one of the few who spoke in favour. But it was probably Pompey's covert support coupled with the dazzling promise of the riches of Egypt, rather than Antony's enthusiasm, which helped Gabinius to overcome his military reservations and his fear of the Senate's reaction.

The price Gabinius asked, and Auletes perforce agreed, was 10,000 talents, 4,000 more than Auletes had already paid to Pompey and Caesar but still owed to Rabirius and the Roman bankers. To have any hope of raising it Auletes plainly had to be reinstated on the throne of Egypt. If this was successfully accomplished the rewards would be immense, even though Pompey, and perhaps Caesar and Crassus as well, would have to be paid their share. If it failed Gabinius knew well enough that he could expect neither payment from Auletes nor the triumvirs' protection from prosecution.

In the autumn of 56 Gabinius again marched south from Syria, this time at the head of a formidable army consisting of seven Roman legions, a contingent of auxiliary light infantry, and a cavalry force commanded by Antony and composed mainly of regiments of Gallic or Galatian origin.

Beyond Gaza Gabinius took the classic invasion route along the desert coast road. Antony commanded the advanced guard and in person led the final assault which took the key frontier city of Pelusium at the north-eastern mouth of the Nile delta and opened the way into Egypt for the army. After the fall of the city Antony restrained Auletes from a wholesale slaughter of the Egyptian prisoners, an act which the Egyptians long remembered as they did the honourable burial he gave Berenice's husband, Archelaus, who had once entertained him in Pontus. According to Plutarch the personal courage and the qualities of leadership which Antony displayed during this brief campaign won him a name as a brilliant soldier and were recognised with honours and decorations.

Gabinius duly restored Auletes to the throne of Egypt; Berenice was strangled on her father's orders and Cleopatra became heir apparent. It was probably now that Antony met the fourteen year old Cleopatra for the first time, though there is some evidence that Auletes may have taken her with him when he fled from Egypt; if he did, Antony would have met her in Syria at the start of the campaign.

Gabinius had to leave Egypt in early 55 with the field army to put down yet another revolt against Hyrcanus in Judaea led by Alexander; Antony accompanied him with the cavalry. Gabinius left behind several thousand soldiers, mainly time-expired Gauls and Germans, and most of them took service with Auletes as mercenaries, becoming known as Gabinians. This was a prudent precaution designed to keep

31

Auletes on the throne and insure repayment of his debt to Gabinius without leaving Roman legions in Egypt.

But Auletes also had to repay Rabirius and the bankers. In April 55 Rabirius arrived in Egypt to try and collect his debt, and to this end he contrived to get himself appointed as financial adviser to Auletes. Over the next eighteen months he accumulated all the money and goods he could lay his hands on to set against his loan and shipped them back to Italy. When towards the end of 54 he returned to Rome his enemies indicted him on charges of corruption. He was defended by Cicero, who put forward a bizarre plea of poverty and secured his acquittal on technical grounds. Despairing of ever being able to recover what Auletes still owed him Rabirius made over the balance of the debt to Caesar, perhaps in token of the part Caesar had played in persuading Cicero to undertake his defence.

Gabinius, who returned to Rome before Rabirius, was arraigned on charges of bribery and of making war outside his province. At least in public Cicero was by now reduced to acting as little more than an unwilling spokesman for the triumvirs, and, in spite of the violent attacks he had made on Gabinius, pressure from Pompey forced him to overcome his scruples and accept the defence; however Gabinius was convicted on one count of abusing his power and sentenced to exile.

In 56 Caesar returned briefly from Gaul to meet Crassus at Ravenna, and from there they travelled on to confer with Pompey at Luca. Attended by two hundred senators the three leaders renewed the triumvirate, this time on a more formal basis; they agreed that Caesar's tenure of Gaul would be extended for a further five years and Pompey and Crassus would be the consuls for 55, with Crassus taking Syria as his proconsular province in 54 and Pompey Spain, both for a five year period to match Caesar's in Gaul. It seems probable that this second five year term, which in Caesar's case apparently applied to his three provinces of Illyricum and the two Gauls, ran from November 55 and thus began before his original tenure of Cisalpine Gaul and Illyricum expired at the end of February 54. If this was so it would have ensured that all three triumvirs' appointments took effect from the same date, since it appears that the five year terms voted to Pompey for Spain and Crassus for Syria both ran from the Ides of November 55.

The Senate had little option but to endorse the triumvirs' arrangements and to give them power to appoint their own legates, found colonies and make war and peace in their own provinces, all without reference to Rome. Caesar returned to Gaul with his standing enhanced and command of the army and control of the wealth of the province assured to him for the next five years. As consuls Pompey and Crassus began to work together effectively. Their election prevented one of the other candidates, Lucius Domitius Ahenobarbus, from carrying out his pre-election promise to deprive Caesar of Transalpine Gaul. Cato had returned from Cyprus to stand as praetor but Pompey blocked his election.

During 55 the stone amphitheatre which Pompey had built on the Campus Martius was dedicated with opening games including a staged elephant hunt and the slaughter of five hundred lions. A porticoed building forming part of the theatre complex was designed to accommodate meetings of the Senate. With the completion of this theatre and his defeat of the pirates and reorganisation of the corn supply it could be truly said of Pompey that he had given the Roman people bread and circuses.

At the end of 55 with Ahenobarbus and Clodius's brother, Appius Claudius Pulcher, as the new consuls and Cato this time securing election as urban praetor, Pompey decided to remain in Italy and send legates to rule the Spanish provinces on his behalf. But in mid-November 55 Crassus, now in his late fifties, set off for his province of Syria with the avowed intention of launching an unprovoked attack on Parthia and winning himself a military reputation to match those of his two colleagues.

After plundering Judaea and robbing the Temple in Jerusalem of its treasure Crassus crossed the Euphrates and attacked Parthia. In 53 his army was defeated at Carrhae and he and his son Publius were killed. Some survivors under his quaestor, Gaius Cassius Longinus, managed to reach safety in Syria, but the main field army was overwhelmed and destroyed. The news of this defeat for Roman arms at the hands of the Parthians, underlined as it was by the loss of seven legionary eagle standards, shocked Rome; it was seen as a disaster unparalleled since Cannae in the second Punic war and like Cannae it was to be mourned by generations of Romans as yet unborn.

CHAPTER III

Caesar's Lieutenant

Antony left Syria in the summer of 54 and returned to Italy travelling overland through Asia Minor and Greece. He had been away for four years, but instead of going to Rome he made his way north, deliberately avoiding the city. Evidently he had already been in touch with Caesar for he continued straight on over the Alpine passes to join the army in Gaul.

Caesar had left his deputy, Titus Labienus, in command in northern Gaul, while he was away on his second expedition to Britain. Reports of the spectacular victories he had won in conquering all Gaul from the Rhine to the Atlantic and the Channel had resounded across the Roman world. In the East Antony had developed a taste for action beyond putting down revolts of the turbulent Jews; he was now twenty nine, and it was natural for him to want to serve under Caesar the great proconsul of Gaul and his own kinsman on his mother's side.

Caesar had embarked on his first Gallic campaign in 58 to prevent a mass westward migration by the Helvetii from the area of Geneva which threatened his province of Transalpine Gaul, already known to the Romans simply as The Province from which the name Provence derives. But he had quickly made up his mind to reduce all Gaul and to establish a frontier on the Rhine to contain the German tribes whom he had defeated in 58 and thrown back across the river. This wholesale annexation of Gaul, accomplished in the campaigning seasons of 57 and 56, was undertaken as much for his own greater military glory and political and financial aggrandizement as for any valid strategic reasons.

The disunited Gallic tribes could not resist the ruthless efficiency of Caesar's comparatively small army, never more than eight legions strong during his first years in Gaul. Its high morale and disciplined fighting power sprang in part from the devotion he inspired in his centurions and soldiers. The professional competence of his largely unknown staff officers allowed full play to his own rare military talent and in their consistent achievement of the apparently impossible they made his victories possible. Among his senior officers, the legionary legates were Gaius Fabius, Cicero's brother Quintus, Gaius Trebonius, Decimus Brutus who had commanded the fleet Caesar had built to defeat the Veneti off the southern coast of Brittany, and Crassus's younger son Publius, whose handling of the reserve had won the day against Ariovistus and who subsequently had conquered Normandy and Aquitania. Caesar picked all his subordinates with an instinct which seldom erred, at least as far as their military ability was concerned.

He must have considered that for the moment Antony would be more use to him in the field in Gaul than on the streets and at the hustings in Rome. The image of the dissolute young noble, abetting Clodius in manipulating the urban mob, had been overlaid by the repute Antony had won as a cavalry commander in Judaea and Egypt.

It was in the late summer of 54 that Caesar returned for the second time from Britain. After an unopposed landing on the coast of Kent, followed by a storm which wrecked part of his huge fleet, he had forced the crossing of the Great Stour and defeated the confederate army of the tribes of the south-east under the command of Cassivellaunus, whose own kingdom lay north of the Thames. The local levies melted away before the Roman advance, and after fording the Thames, Caesar marched north on Cassivellaunus's capital. By now some of the southern tribes were assisting him, and Cassivellaunus accepted his terms, giving him hostages and agreeing to pay an annual tribute.

On his return to Gaul Caesar received the news that Julia, his daughter and only child and Pompey's young and much loved wife, had died in childbirth. Her untimely death broke the one personal link between Caesar and Pompey, and in Rome the implicit threat to peace was widely recognised. Large crowds mourned her death and insisted on giving her a public funeral on the Campus Martius. She was to prove the only issue of Caesar's four marriages, and with the probable exception of Cleopatra's son Caesarion, the only child he is known to have fathered in a lifetime of extra-marital liaisons with a succession of mistresses.

Though the tribes of northern Gaul had been subdued they were far from pacified and a poor harvest that autumn added to their unrest. To hold down the newly won territories Caesar dispersed his legions in winter quarters across northern Gaul, but even so there were a series of sporadic, ill co-ordinated revolts, in one of which a legion and a half were lost and their two legates killed. For this Caesar took savage reprisals and exacted a barbarous revenge on the tribal leaders. He remained in Gaul himself, abandoning his usual practice of spending the winter months in the Cisalpina where he was better placed to influence events in Rome. During that winter he raised two more legions, bringing his strength to ten including one he had borrowed from Pompey.

His expeditions across the northern ocean to Britain and his feat of bridging the Rhine in ten days and crossing it to terrorize the German tribes may have fired the imagination of the more chauvinistic in Rome, but they served no real strategic purpose. Cato censured him for his unprovoked aggression and his merciless repression of the Gallic and Geman tribes, and Pompey sneered that the ocean between Gaul and Britain was no more than a stretch of mudflats. But it was the military power Caesar had won for himself and the good use his agents were making of his new found wealth to further his political interests which made the Optimates increasingly apprehensive as to what he would do when his provincial commands expired in the winter of 50/49; the triumphant army of Gaul, so conveniently placed, if Caesar so decided, to deny Pompey's legions the land route to Italy or even to make a sudden move on Rome, posed a constant, if veiled, threat.

As a result the Optimates turned to Pompey, but as the lesser, nearer and more predictable of two evils rather than as their natural leader; for he had never been one of their own number and they distrusted his popularity with the common people and his working arrangement with Caesar. For his part Pompey had neither forgotten nor forgiven the rebuff which the Senate had given him when he returned from the East in 62. And though perhaps he too felt a vague disquiet as to Caesar's intentions he was not the man to go back on the agreement he had made at Luca without good and evident cause.

When Domitius Ahenobarbus took office as consul in January 54 there was little he could do to make good his pledge to remove Caesar from command in Gaul. His colleague, Appius Claudius Pulcher, though himself no partisan of Caesar's, was Clodius's brother and family ties were strong; Clodius had changed his spelling of the family name to the more plebeian form when he renounced his patrician status to stand as tribune of the people.

Domitius Ahenobarbus and Claudius Pulcher were both implicated in a corruption scandal during the consular elections for 53. As a result these elections were not finally held until July 53 when Domitius Calvinus and Valerius Messalla Rufus were elected for the remaining months of the year. That there were no elected consuls for the first six months of 53 is a measure of the political malaise in Rome, with Milo, now in the pay of the Optimates, fighting on the streets against Clodius, who was using his private army mainly in Caesar's interest. Meanwhile Pompey punctiliously observed the law which precluded him as a proconsul from entering the city to restore law and order. In the autumn of 53 Caesar returned to the Cisalpina, and with ample funds at their disposal from the rape of Gaul his agents intensified their campaign of political bribery on his behalf in Rome. It was probably in 53, perhaps after the news of Carrhae reached him, that Caesar proposed a new marriage alliance to Pompey. He suggested that he should marry Pompey's daughter, Pompeia, and that Pompey should marry his great niece, Octavia. Both women were already married, as was Caesar himself, but for such high dynastic purposes divorce could readily be imposed should he and Pompey be so minded.

But for one reason or another Pompey did not agree, and he closed the door on Caesar's proposal by marrying Cornelia, daughter of Quintus Caecilius Metellus Pius, usually known as Metellus Scipio, who happened to be one of the consular candidates for 52. Cornelia had just been widowed by the death at Carrhae of her husband, Crassus's younger son Publius, who had left Gaul to go to the East with his father. Pompey's reasons for declining Caesar's proposal and marrying Cornelia can only be conjectured. The Metelli were one of the most powerful of the patrician families, and it is possible that he sought to repair the rift with them caused by his divorce of Mucia and through them to align himself more closely with the Optimates. But it seems at least as likely that a man such as Pompey might well have been reluctant to call on his happily married only daughter to divorce her husband, Faustus Cornelius Sulla, in order to marry Caesar; another factor may have been the antagonism that this would certainly have aroused among Sulla's relations, friends and clients.

Caesar's proposal would also have meant Octavia divorcing her husband, Gaius Claudius Marcellus, and the consequent alienation of another influential family. And of course it is possible that Pompey may simply have preferred the vivacious, talented and highly intelligent Cornelia to the beautiful and virtuous Octavia. Whatever his reasons, his decision was to have far-reaching consequences, again bringing him love, loyalty and happiness in marriage, but at the same time strengthening his ties with the Optimates and so contributing to the final break with Caesar.

Antony returned to Rome for some months in the autumn of 53 or the spring of 52 to stand for office as quaestor. He was now thirty one and it was six years since he had last been in Rome. With Caesar's backing he was elected, thus becoming a member of the Senate; he then went back to Gaul to take up his new appointment on Caesar's staff.

It was perhaps on this visit to Rome that Antony married his first cousin, Antonia, daughter of his uncle, Gaius Antonius; a daughter, also named Antonia, was born of this marriage some time before 49.

Cicero's taunts in the Philippics about an earlier marriage to Fadia, the daughter of a freedman, were probably a sarcastic reference to a liaison Antony had with her; there is no other evidence that he married her.

It may have been now that Antony's habit of affecting the uniform of the Gallic cavalry began to be remarked upon in Rome. Plutarch describes him as wearing a low-belted tunic, with a heavy curved sword at the hip and a cavalry cloak overall. This would hardly have caused comment when he commanded Gabinius's cavalry in Syria or served on Caesar's staff in Gaul. But such dress must have stood out among the conservative togas in the streets and public places of Rome and may well tell something of Antony himself, a certain extrovert flamboyance, a wish to be seen to be different. Plutarch also refers to the tradition that the Antonii were descended from Anton and mentions that Antony liked to foster physical comparison with the conventional portrayal of Hercules in statues and pictures, believing that his own aquiline features and his powerful body, bigger, stronger and taller than most men's, gave credibility to the legend. Plutarch describes his appearance as noble and dignified, with a wide forehead, a prominent straight nose and full beard giving him a virile swashbuckling air. This coupled with a brash and impatient arrogance and a quality of personal magnetism made Antony a man whom soldiers would follow and women would love, whom many of his peers would fear and hate but no man or woman would ignore.

A number of surviving statues and busts have been tentatively identified as being of Antony, but in every case the attribution is doubtful and none are authenticated by inscriptions. His coin portraits date from 44 onwards and with the exception of the earliest, bearded and veiled in mourning for Caesar, all are clean-shaven. They show a strong head and thick neck set on powerful shoulders, but the immediate and lasting visual impact which makes most of them instantly recognisable is the unusual and highly individual profile with its straight almost continuous vertical line formed by forehead, nose and chin, looking as if it had been cut from one straight edge.

The portrayal of the heads of living men on Roman coins only began with Caesar and then only in the last years of his life. These coin portraits from the first issues of Caesar, Antony, and others in the Imperatorial period, which followed the Republican and preceded the Imperial, and indeed right through the first three centuries of the Empire, were reasonably accurate likenesses. For those who ruled in Rome coins were the only certain means of communication with the great mass of the peoples they ruled and the only way of making the features of the ruler familiar in every corner of the Roman world;

accuracy was considered of more importance than any stylised flattery. The reverses were used for messages which the emperors wished to circulate, often employing graphic imagery and religious symbolism to advertise their achievements and emphasise the benefits of their rule, sometimes degenerating into no more than propaganda slogans based on pious hopes and wishful thinking.

Plutarch's description and the coin portraits can be taken as the only reliable guides to Antony's physical appearance. Evidence from coin hoards proves that at the time Plutarch wrote, around the turn of the first century AD, Antony's legionary denarii were still in circulation. It seems likely that at least some of his portrait coins, perhaps those on which his head was coupled with Octavian's or Octavia's were also still in use, and if they were, Plutarch would have been familiar with them.

Plutarch also had primary sources to draw upon, most of them now lost, and his detailed description of Antony's appearance is probably reasonably accurate. The picture he paints fits well enough with Antony's character as he and others describe it: an impatience with the forms and conventions of Roman life, a liking for the low company of actors, artists and musicians, the habit of drinking in public and eating with his soldiers, these were qualities which may have endeared him to the legions and the common people but were hardly calculated to impress the establishment, which, as always, deeply distrusted the common touch in one of their own number. A generous nature, open, outgoing and lacking any real capacity for intrigue, and an uninhibited and catholic taste for women which they reciprocated in full measure only served to add jealousy to the distaste of the conservatives. Military talent and proven qualities of leadership turned distrust and jealousy into fear and hatred, and in Cicero's Philippics provoked a master of language to a sustained level of abuse unmatched for two millennia.

But much of this lay in the future, and it is hindsight that enables us to identify the threads of that past present, which woven together into one particular pattern makes our history out of their future. It is clearly a mistake, though a common one in historical analysis, to look on this history as inevitable, as the only possible outcome for that past which was their present, perhaps because our own present rests upon it. In the hands of the same actors the same threads could have been woven into many different patterns to form many different futures, any one of which might have been our history and thus have changed our present beyond our imagining. On reflection this must be self-evident to all but the fatalist, though perhaps unpalatable and therefore not at once apparent.

In the winter of 53/52 the immediate future seemed particularly uncertain and fraught with danger. In Rome there was widespread rioting as the bitter gang warfare between Clodius and Milo reached new heights of violence. The Optimates and Caesar's agents were busily trying to outbid one another in bribing the electors and corrupting the current holders of office. As a result the consuls and other magistrates, with no police or troops to call on, were unable to maintain law and order on the streets. Charge and counter charge in the law courts again forced the postponement of the consular elections, and, as in 53, the year began with no elected consuls to take office.

As well as battling against Milo on the streets Clodius pursued his own private vendetta against Cicero, who continued to take little part in public life. When he did attend the Senate he made a bitter and intemperate attack on Caesar's father-in-law, Piso, taunting him with having Gallic blood because his wife's family came from Placentia, despite the fact that, like Cicero himself, her father, Calventius, was of Latin provincial origin, and there had been hardly a Gaul south of the Po for more than a hundred years. He was met by an equally vicious but masterly piece of written invective, attributed to the pen of Gaius Sallustius, better known as Sallust the historian. In 52 Cicero was nominated by the Senate to govern Cilicia for one year, and he left Rome somewhat reluctantly in 51 to take up this appointment.

Clodius was a candidate for the office of praetor in 52, but these elections also had to be postponed because of the civil disorders in Rome, and they still had not been held when on 18th January 52 he was killed in a street battle against Milo. Enraged at their leader's death the Populares mob stormed the Curia Hostilia, set it on fire and used the blazing building as a funeral pyre for Clodius's body. Milo was put on trial, and despite Cicero's efforts in his defence he was found guilty and exiled.

Clodius's death had two far reaching consequences. The senators, already alarmed at the breakdown of law and order, had their minds concentrated by the destruction of their own Senate building. As a result they appointed Pompey as sole consul and extended his Spanish imperium to run for a new five year period from 52. Carrying with it, as it did, control of the army of Spain, this upset the delicate balance of power with Caesar, whose tenure of the two Gallic provinces and Illyricum was due to end during the winter of 50/49. It is not clear whether the initiative for extending Pompey's command of Spain came from the Senate, possibly in order to persuade him to accept office as consul for the third time, or whether Pompey himself specifically asked for it; but whichever was the case the implications must have been obvious, both to Pompey and the Senate.

As sole consul Pompey acted promptly and effectively. His emergency legislation and his local recruiting of troops, both undertaken with Caesar's knowledge and approval, were designed to restore the rule of law in the city and were not aimed either at Caesar or the Populares. Nevertheless the Senate's extension of Pompey's imperium together with the growing support for him from the Optimates undoubtedly increased Caesar's concern as to his own position when he relinquished command in Gaul. As the law stood he could not hold office again as consul until 48, and he was well enough aware that his enemies would seize the opportunity to attack him in the law courts after he had given up command in Gaul and before he was protected by election as consul. Though the more moderate of the Optimates recognised his dilemma they feared that he might react by attempting a military coup, and consequently they were determined that he should not stand in the consular elections for 48 with the army of Gaul still under his command; this too made them turn to Pompey.

Pompey also recognised the dilemma; he tried to resolve it by proposing legislation designed to safeguard Caesar during the crucial early months of 49, after he handed over in Gaul and before he was protected as consul designate elect, but this came to nothing. It has been suggested that with the two surviving triumvirs still acting in uneasy concert it would have been simple to have waived the ten year rule in Caesar's favour. But this would not have met the objections of the Optimates, for Caesar would then have stood for election while absent from Rome and still the legally appointed proconsul of Gaul; it might also have stretched Pompey's trust in his colleague too far.

It has also been suggested that Pompey acted with such studied rectitude in not entering the city to restore law and order until he was appointed consul that he must have had some devious motive. Both such views underestimate the continuing strength of the old Republican forms and the necessity for both the triumvirs at least to give the appearance of acting within the framework of the law and the constitution.

Later in 52 Pompey managed to extricate his new father-in-law, Metellus Scipio, from a web of corruption charges and have him appointed as his colleague in the consulate for the remaining months of the year. Gradually as his ties with the Optimates strengthened and their support for him grew Pompey's attitude to Caesar became less conciliatory. He began to listen to flatterers' tales which his officers brought back from visits to Gaul telling him that if he appealed to Caesar's troops they would defect. When others expressed alarm at the power of Caesar's army Pompey declared: 'I have only to stamp my foot anywhere in Italy and armies will rise up out of the ground.'

Caesar held that the other consequence of Clodius's murder was to lead the tribal chieftains in Gaul to believe that he was too involved with internal politics in Rome to return to his army, and thus was one of the main causes of the last and greatest Gallic revolt in 52. For the first time a leader of talent and ability emerged in Vercengetorix of the Averni, and soon all central and north-west Gaul had joined in the revolt, though Aquitania and the Belgic tribes of the north-west held back.

But Caesar acted with speed and decision; from Narbo he crossed the snow-bound Cevennes in midwinter to rejoin Labienus. In a short campaign, after a frustrating defeat at Gergovia, he finally trapped Vercingetorix at Alesia, where Antony and Trebonius commanded legions, and forced him to surrender. During the autumn the army in the north put down a tardy uprising, and in the Dordogne Caesar made a savage and cruel example of the last desperate defenders of Uxellodunum by cutting off the hands of the prisoners so that they should not bear arms again.

That winter Antony commanded fifteen cohorts holding down the Bellovaci in their tribal territory between the Somme, the lower Seine and the Aisne. When Commius of the neighbouring Atrebates finally submitted Antony agreed to his condition that he should not be required to come face to face with any Roman; but the following year Commius decided that he preferred freedom to Roman rule, however remote, and he escaped to Britain.

For the first time Caesar showed some moderation in his treatment of Gaul; he did not interfere with the organisation of the tribes and he allowed their leaders to collect the taxes. This time there were to be no more revolts and the Gallic war at last was over. In eight years Caesar had matched, if not surpassed, Pompey's conquests in the East; to set against Asia Minor and the Levant he had added the western half of Europe to the Mediterranean provinces and made Rome a continental power. In the process the Celtic civilization of Gaul had been ruthlessly destroyed at an incalculable cost in human suffering and the seeds of another great civilization had been sown.

Caesar's victories had stemmed from a latent military talent coupled with decisive speed of thought and action, the whole controlled by a clear analytical mind and powered by a ruthless will; they had been made possible by the devoted efforts of his small staff and by his own gift of rapport with his soldiers who gave him their unswerving loyalty and an affection, sometimes grudging and cynical, but based on an uncomplicated belief in his luck and in his star.

In Rome Curio, who had taken Clodius's place as leader of the

Populares, was elected as tribune for 50, and in this year he married Clodius's widow, Fulvia. With all the wealth of Gaul at his disposal Caesar obtained Curio's services for a large cash bribe, and with another considerable sum, said to be 1,500 talents, he bought Lucius Aemilius Paullus one of the consuls for 50. However the other consul, Gaius Marcellus, unwilling to forgive Caesar's offer of his young wife Octavia in marriage to Pompey, remained an uncompromising enemy. Since constitutionally Caesar could not be relieved of his command in Gaul until a successor was appointed one of Curio's first moves as tribune in Caesar's interest was to veto all discussion on who should replace him.

Curio served Caesar well, but his term of office would expire in December 50 and the early months of 49 were likely to be critical. With the Senate controlled by the Optimates and his enemies waiting the opportunity to arraign him in the courts only a tribune of the people could give Caesar effective political protection. To replace Curio he needed a committed supporter on whose loyalty he could rely, whose political judgement he could trust and whose character and moral courage would be equal to outfacing a hostile Senate. In the summer of 50 he sent Antony to stand for election as tribune for 49.

When Antony arrived in Rome he found that an unexpected vacancy had occurred in the college of augurs, whose function was to interpret the signs, often from animal sacrifices, and determine whether or not they were auspicious for some particular course of action. Antony decided to stand for election as augur as well as tribune; he was elected to both offices, and he then returned to Gaul.

For a time in May of 50 Pompey lay seriously ill on his estate near Neapolis. The widespread and spontaneous expressions of relief which greeted his recovery may have made him overestimate the popular support he could count on in a trial of strength with Caesar. Though in the summer of 50 there was no sign of an open break between the two men, the pressure of events was driving both of them into positions which left little room for manoeuvre or compromise.

When Bibulus, now governor of Syria, asked for reinforcements to meet an anticipated Parthian invasion the Senate called on Pompey and Caesar to provide one legion each. Pompey volunteered the one which he had lent to Caesar some years before and Caesar nominated the Ist Legion from southern Gaul and the XVth from the Cisalpina; before they left he gave every soldier a cash bonus. He replaced the XVth, his only legion south of the Alps, with the XIIIth from Transalpine Gaul. Neither he nor Pompey made any other movement of troops during the autumn of 50 and by mid-November Caesar's eight remaining legions were dispersed in winter quarters in Gaul.

In Rome a dangerous impasse developed with Pompey and the Senate combining to insist that Caesar should hand over Transalpine Gaul by the Ides of November. Curio was active on Caesar's behalf, stirring up the people against the Senate, vetoing all discussion of Caesar's successor and any proposal that he alone should relinquish his provincial command, and putting forward the not unreasonable counter proposal that both he and Pompey should do so at the same time. By now Antony was again in Rome waiting to take over from Curio as tribune on 8th December.

But in November Marcellus persuaded the Senate to pass a motion that Caesar alone should give up his command at the end of the year. A few days later Curio's amendment requiring both Caesar and Pompey to hand over their commands was also passed, this time by the overwhelming majority of 370 to 22. These wholly contradictory results, in what were to be almost the last free votes on an important issue by the Senate of the Republic, paradoxically perhaps do indicate that they were democratically decided. They also show a compelling desire for compromise and peace, if these could be bought by appeasing Caesar. But pursuing his personal feud against Caesar Marcellus was determined to force the issue while he was still consul. On the 2nd December, acting without the Senate's authority though in concert with the consuls elect, his own first cousin Gaius Claudius Marcellus and Lucius Cornelius Lentulus Crus, he formally offered Pompey a sword and charged him to defend the State. From his headquarters at Ravenna, just inside the southern boundary of Cisalpine Gaul, Caesar had already sent Aulus Hirtius to Rome to try to reach a compromise through Pompey's father-in-law, Metellus Scipio. When the news of Marcellus's move reached Caesar he at once ordered couriers to ride for Gaul with orders for the VIIIth and XIIth Legions to march south at once.

Hirtius reached Rome on 6th December, but judging that there was no longer any room for negotiation he did not approach Scipio. On the 9th December, his first day in office as tribune, Antony denounced Marcellus in the Senate and then went on to make a violent attack on Pompey and the Optimates, but this only hardened their resolve. Curio had left to join Caesar, but when he reached Ravenna Caesar sent him back to Rome with a letter to the Senate offering to give up his command on the sole condition that Pompey should do the same. That in early winter, late autumn by the season, Curio took only three days to ride the 250 miles to Rome by way of Fanum and the Via Flaminia over the Apennine passes suggests that this offer of Caesar's was more than an empty gesture.

But on 1st January 49 Antony had difficulty in persuading the

Senate even to listen to Caesar's letter. When he insisted on reading it himself the new consuls, Marcellus and Lentulus Crus, blocked all debate. Antony then summoned the Assembly to hear Caesar's proposals. In the Senate a motion calling on Caesar to lay down his command or be declared a public enemy was passed by a large majority, but Antony and another Caesarian tribune, Quintus Cassius Longinus, immediately vetoed it.

More clearly than the rest of the Optimates Cicero foresaw the likely effect of civil war on the institutions of the Republic which he had so consistently defended; he initiated private talks and attempted to mediate on the basis of Caesar retaining Illyricum only, but nothing came of this.

On 7th January the Senate passed the ultimate decree, declaring a public emergency and charging the consuls to take all steps to safeguard the State. The Senate thus tacitly endorsed Marcellus's approach to Pompey and in effect outlawed Caesar though without naming him. Before the decree was passed Antony and Cassius hurriedly left Rome to avoid arrest as Caesar's supporters; Curio and Cicero's young friend and correspondent, the aedile, Marcus Caelius Rufus, fled with them. Whether they really had to disguise themselves as slaves to escape from the city is uncertain, but when they reached Ravenna on 10th January this is how Caesar put it to his single legion: elected tribunes of the Roman people, one of them a member of the college of augurs, forced to flee from Rome disguised as slaves and in fear of their lives at the hands of the Optimates.

At about this time Lucius Julius Caesar, Antony's first cousin and a kinsman of Caesar's, and a praetor, Lucius Roscius, left Rome with a personal message for Caesar from Pompey suggesting a compromise. Some of Pompey's closest friends were privy to this move, but it seems that it was not debated in the Senate for Cicero knew nothing of it. In reply Caesar proposed that they should both disband their forces in Italy, that Pompey should leave for his province and that free elections should then be held. He also suggested that he and Pompey should meet, and he intimated that he would be prepared to retain one legion only, together with either the Cisalpina or Illyricum; he sent his father-in-law, Piso, and Roscius to take this reply back to Pompey.

But clearly Caesar felt that with the Senate's passing of the ultimate decree the time for negotiation and compromise had gone. To wait any further on events might well prove fatal; if he was to survive he had to act at once.

On the night of 11th January he slipped away from a dinner party at his headquarters to the XIIIth Legion's camp and gave the order to march south through the night down the coast road from Ravenna;

Antony and Curio rode with him. At the Rubicon, the small river running into the Adriatic which marked the southern boundary of the province of Cisalpine Gaul, he halted and conferred with his legate, Gaius Asinius Pollio; but to enter Italy at the head of an army was an act of armed rebellion and the decision could be Caesar's alone. After a brief pause he said:- 'Let the die be cast', and ordered the XIIIth to cross the Rubicon and continue the march at full speed; before dawn on the 12th his cavalry were in Ariminum.

As reports of Caesar's move fanned out ahead they were embellished by every kind of rumour. Alarm quickly turned into widespread panic, and everywhere people abandoned their homes and fled in all directions. A rumour that Caesar had taken the Via Flaminia and was heading for Rome brought panic to the city.

With no reliable intelligence as to Caesar's movements or intentions Pompey hesitated. Apart from some newly raised levies the only troops he could call on, though perhaps hardly rely on, were the Ist and XVth Legions, still in Campania waiting transports for Syria. Marcus Favonius, one of the praetors and no respecter of persons, suggested that he should try stamping his foot on the ground. The consuls and the Senate offered him a variety of conflicting and constantly changing advice, but the overall responsibility was his and he failed to act with authority or decision.

For a time he did nothing to abate or control the mounting turmoil in Rome. Then he suddenly declared that he was abandoning the city as it was in a state of anarchy and ordered the Senate, the magistrates, and all citizens loyal to the Republic to follow him south. Though from a purely military point of view he needed time to concentrate a field army, such a precipitate evacuation was unworthy of him and a recipe for political disaster. Most of the senators and magistrates obeyed his order, but in their terror-stricken concern for their own lives and property they forgot the Treasury. Rome was left to the Populares, who prepared to welcome Caesar, and to the great mass of the city's inhabitants who had nothing to fear from him.

Caesar took Pisaurum and Fanum where the two northern ends of the Via Flaminia joined the Via Aemilia on the Adriatic coast. He sent Antony south with five cohorts across the Apennines to seize Arretium on the Via Cassia and Curio with four cohorts down the Via Flaminia towards Iguvium. He continued his own march down the Adriatic coast road, shrugging off the unwelcome though not wholly unexpected news that Labienus, his legate and deputy in Gaul, had declared for Pompey; however the army in Gaul had remained loyal and the reinforcements he had sent for were already on the march. Events were moving almost as fast as messengers and Pompey was at

46

Capua when Piso and Roscius finally caught up with him to deliver Caesar's reply. By now Pompey knew that the time for compromise had gone, and perhaps he already realised that he was going to be forced to abandon Italy; but he replied that he would go to Spain if Caesar returned to Gaul, though he refused to suspend his recruiting.

That Ancona, ninety miles from Ravenna, fell to Caesar on 14th January gives some measure of the speed of his march and the lack of any effective resistance. Indeed his advance gained momentum as the towns in his path opened their gates and their demoralised garrisons went over to him. But as Attius Varus, the Pompeian commander in Auximum, was trying to persuade his troops to retire rather than surrender, Pompey's personal legate, Vibullius Rufus, arrived and managed to hold together thirteen cohorts and withdraw them to Corfinium on the lateral Via Valeria east of Rome.

Domitius Ahenobarbus was in command at Corfinium, once the capital of the Italic League in the Social War, and here he was determined to stand and fight. Ahenobarbus, the nickname Brazenbeard had originally been given to one of his ancestors, was an old enemy of Caesar's and now his designated successor in Gaul. He lacked military talent but not courage, and as an aristocrat and uncompromising Republican he did not consider himself in any sense Pompey's subordinate. He ignored orders from Pompey, now at Luceria, to withdraw south and join the main body of the army which the consuls were bringing down the Via Appia towards Brundisium. Unmoved by a further appeal from Pompey he dug in and prepared to defend the town with his thirty cohorts.

As Caesar halted and deployed before Corfinium the reinforcements from Gaul caught up with him, first the XIIth Legion and then the VIIIth with twenty two cohorts of new levies. The soldiers of the legions were volunteers, but these recruits may not have been, for in emergencies such as civil war recourse was had to conscription. When Antony with his five cohorts captured Sulmo on the Via Minucia, the only practicable road south from Corfinium, Ahenobarbus's line of retreat was cut and Caesar was able to tighten his investment; after seven days the garrison forced their leaders to surrender without a fight. In contrast to his punitive reprisals in Gaul Caesar had decided on a calculated policy of clemency to his Roman enemies, and he pardoned Ahenobarbus and accepted the soldiers into his army.

From Corfinium Caesar sent a small detachment to secure the Treasury in Rome and pressed on himself by forced marches down the Adriatic coast. Four days after Corfinium fell Pompey reached Brundisium where he fortified the city and entrenched positions covering the harbour. His army now consisted of the two legions earmarked for Syria, the XVth now apparently renumbered the IIIrd, and some thirty cohorts of new levies. Caesar sent ahead a captured Pompeian officer, Numerius Magius, with peace proposals, but Pompey rejected Caesar's suggestion that they should meet to discuss terms. On 4th March he embarked the main body of his army on transports which he had collected at Brundisium and ordered the two consuls to sail with the convoy for Dyrrachium; he stayed in Brundisium himself with a garrison of twenty cohorts.

On 9th March Caesar arrived before the city, having covered the 290 miles from Corfinium in seventeen days; he now had six legions, three veteran, and three newly formed from recruits and defecting Pompeians. He at once took up positions to cover the harbour and prevent Pompey from escaping; to this end he started work on a mole to seal off the inner harbour basin. He again attempted to open negotiations through Numerius Magius in the belief that if he could only meet Pompey he would be able to detach him from the Optimates, and that this was perhaps the last opportunity to do so. But Pompey replied that he could not meet Caesar or discuss terms in the absence of the consuls.

Then on 15th or 16th March Pompey's transports returned. He had evidently been waiting for them for he immediately put into operation a carefully prepared deception plan. Under its cover and displaying something of his old expertise in amphibious operations he disengaged his army before Caesar realised what was happening, embarked it on 17th March with minimal losses and successfully cleared Brundisium harbour for the eighty mile passage to Dyrrachium.

Thus having outmanoeuvred Pompey throughout the campaign Caesar was himself outwitted at the last. Faced with the sails of Pompey's transports disappearing below the horizon there was little he could do, for he had neither the fleet nor the transports to carry his pursuit across the Adriatic. Indeed Pompey's 500 warships gave him undisputed naval command, not only of the Adriatic, but of the central Mediterranean and the sea routes to Italy.

Foiled by Pompey's evacuation and his own lack of a fleet Caesar entered Brundisium through its hastily opened gates. In no more than nine weeks and without a single battle the whole Italian peninsula had fallen to him like some overripe fruit; he had yet to digest it.

CHAPTER IV

Master of Horse

After a brief stay in Brundisium Caesar set out for Rome, sending the two tribunes, Antony and Cassius, on ahead to summon the rump of the Senate to meet on 1st April. On his way up the Via Appia Caesar met Cicero on 27th March at Formiae on the Gulf of Gaeta, but he failed to persuade him to return to Rome for the meeting of the Senate.

Unlike the majority of the senators who had obeyed Pompey's call to follow him across the Adriatic, Cicero had remained at his villa at Formiae where he had spent much of his time since returning from Cilicia in November 50. It is evident from the letters he wrote to Atticus, the wealthy banker who was his kinsman and his correspondent in Rome, that he stayed in Italy principally because he could not make up his mind what to do. They show distrust of Caesar, whom he regarded as a dangerous revolutionary, and a carping, querulous criticism of Pompey whose reasons for abandoning Italy he could not understand. They also reveal a degree of self-deception and attempted self-justification, which made it difficult for him to reconcile his own high moral standards and his genuine concern for the Republic with his subconscious search for where his own best interest lay.

Marcus Aemilius Lepidus, son of the consul of 78 and one of the praetors for 49, had no such scruples, for he always acted in his own self-interest and he had a talent for perceiving where it lay. He too had evaded Pompey's call, skulking in a villa near Cicero's during the Italian campaign; as soon as it was clear that Caesar would win he had hurried back to Rome and taken his side. Marcus Junius Brutus, on the other hand, put what he felt were Rome's best interests before his private feelings when he joined Pompey. That such a man as Brutus, well known for his filial piety, should stifle his natural hatred of his father's murderer for the good of Rome was to his contemporaries a measure of his high principles: he was to give them further proof.

Preserved with Cicero's correspondence are letters from Caesar and his agents, Gaius Oppius and Lucius Cornelius Balbus, which taken together suggest that Caesar genuinely sought a reconciliation with Pompey, though no doubt on his own terms and possibly only as a means of detaching him from the Optimates. These letters show that Oppius and Balbus, often subtle and devious on Caesar's behalf, considered Cicero susceptible to the most unsubtle flattery; they also reveal an attempt to subvert Lentulus Crus, one of the consuls.

When Caesar reached Rome at the end of March, it was the first time he had entered the city for nine years. At a sparsely attended meeting of the Senate on 1st April the debt which he owed the inhabitants of the Cisalpina for the support they had given him was repaid promptly, and in good measure, when a bill put forward by Roscius was passed extending full citizenship to the whole of Cisalpine Gaul. At the same meeting the cowed senators formally authorised Caesar to use the State reserves in the Treasury; in spite of a veto by the tribune, Metellus, and his courageous if misguided attempt to deny him access to the Treasury, Caesar removed huge quantities of gold and silver in bullion and coin.

In an attempt to secure the vital corn supply against Pompey's command of the sea Caesar sent Curio to Sicily with two legions formed from surrendered Pompeians; another legate with one legion was sent to Sardinia, where the Pompeian garrison anticipated his arrival by declaring for Caesar. By the end of May Curio had driven Cato out of Sicily and Caesar ordered him to cross to Africa and take over the province.

In Gaul Caesar replaced Labienus, who had joined Pompey in Italy and accompanied him to Greece, with Crassus's elder son, Marcus, who previously had served him well as quaestor in the province. Antony's brother, Gaius, was sent to Illyricum to counter any move Pompey might make up the eastern coast of the Adriatic and to cover the vulnerable land approaches to Italy from the north-east. Caesar had ordered the building of some two hundred warships to protect the eastern coast of Italy and challenge Pompey's command of the Adriatic, and he now appointed Cicero's son-in-law, Publius Cornelius Dolabella, to command this new fleet.

After barely two weeks in Rome Caesar left for the Spanish provinces, the only Pompeian stronghold which he could reach by land. He left Antony as his deputy and Master of Horse in Italy, in command of the army and in overall control of administration, with Lepidus as urban praetor responsible for Rome itself. In selecting his lieutenants Caesar showed shrewdness and insight and during the civil war Labienus was the only one of importance who defected to Pompey. Loyalty and popularity with the army were probably Caesar's main considerations in Antony's appointment and political expediency in Lepidus's; with most of the consulars and senators in Pompey's camp Lepidus was the only prominent member of the old senatorial oligarchy among his supporters. As such he could allay some of the fears of the Optimates who had remained in Rome, and as elected praetor lend an air of respectability to Caesar's new administration. Though his loyalty was primarily to himself Lepidus had committed himself in espousing Caesar's cause and he seemed hardly the man to attempt a coup on his own account, let alone Pompey's.

Antony had proved himself in independent commands, and, like Lepidus as praetor, he held elected office as tribune and augur, though neither he nor Lepidus had much political experience. Nor, according to Plutarch, had Antony the inclination or the patience to follow the normal processes of law and administration. But as well as using Livy's and Pollio's contemporary histories, both now lost, Plutarch drew heavily on Cicero's letters and speeches; these have survived, and they show an uncompromising hatred for Antony, which makes it as difficult today to form any objective judgement from them as it must once have been for Plutarch. The few letters of Antony's which have survived because Cicero quoted them against him tend to throw a different light on his political acumen and his administrative capacity.

After refusing Caesar's plea to return to Rome at the end of March Cicero received a formal summons from Pompey to attend a meeting of his counter-Senate at Thessalonica in May. He was in two minds whether to go, and it seems that he may have disclosed his indecision to Curio, who had called to see him at Cumae on his way to Sicily. He told Curio that he wanted to leave Italy, either for Malta or Greece, and Curio apparently reported this both to Caesar and Antony.

Caesar who was nearing Massalia on his march to Spain, and Caelius accompanying him on his staff, both wrote to Cicero on 16th April from Intimillium urging him to stay neutral and remain in Italy. On 24th April Antony, who it seems was due at Misenum on 3rd May, wrote to Cicero from Rome:-

'Antonius, Tribune, Propraetor, Greeting to Cicero, Imperator.

Had I not been very attached to you, much more so than you think, I would not have been alarmed by a rumour which is being spread about you, particularly as I thought it false. But because I do esteem you so highly I cannot hide the fact that such a rumour, however groundless, caused me great concern. I cannot believe that you are about to go abroad when you prize Dolabella and that paragon among women, Tullia, so greatly, and you yourself are valued so highly by us, to whom by Hercules your honour and standing are almost dearer than they are to yourself. Yet it is not the part of a friend to be unmoved by gossip, even from

51

men of ill repute, and I have been the more particular, because I felt strongly that this was incumbent on me as a result of our disagreement, which derived more from jealousy on my part than from any injury you have done me. For I want to convince you that no one except Caesar is dearer to me than you are, and that at the same time Caesar ranks Cicero high among his friends. Therefore, my dear Cicero, I beg you not to commit yourself to the good faith of a man who has only benefited you by righting a wrong he had already done you, and not to fly from a man who, even if he no longer loved you and that could not happen, would still desire your safety and your highest standing. I have deliberately sent you my dearest friend, Calpurnius, so that you may know my great concern for your life and your honour.'

This letter has survived because Cicero forwarded a copy of it with a copy of Caesar's when he wrote to Atticus on 2nd May, referring to it as 'odiosus'. By any normal standards Antony's letter can be described as friendly and courteous, more so indeed than Caesar's, and if it contained a warning this was suitably veiled. Cicero's comment perhaps stems from his own indecision, his frustration at the turn events had taken and his inability to influence them, and his irritation that a man whom he detested should be in a position of authority as Caesar's deputy.

On 3rd May Cicero wrote to Atticus twice. In his first letter he said that he had made up his mind to go to Malta; with it he enclosed a copy of Caelius's letter, complaining of his advice to stay in Italy. He had evidently answered Antony's letter, for his second letter to Atticus included extracts from Antony's reply. Cicero protested that he had repeatedly told Antony he had no plans against Caesar, that if he had he would be with Pompey, and that he was conscious of Dolabella's position as his son-in-law. He went on to say that he wanted to leave the country because he did not like having to be escorted by lictors wherever he went in Italy; he criticised Antony for having his actress mistress Cytheris and his other friends carried with him in litters. He quotes from Antony's second letter to instance what he calls its peremptory and hectoring tone:-

'Your decision is perfectly correct,' Antony had written. 'He who wishes to be neutral remains in this country, for he who leaves is seen to take one side or the other. But it is not for me to decide who may go and who may not. Caesar has charged me to see that no one leaves Italy. So it matters little whether I agree with your plan since I am not empowered to relax this ruling. In my opinion you should send to Caesar and put your request to him. I have no doubt that you will be successful, especially as you promise to bear our friendship in mind.'

These two letters of Antony's give a glimpse of him which is at some variance with the picture Cicero paints of Caesar's arrogant, coarse and licentious deputy riding roughshod over the people of Italy, too impatient and drink befuddled for the niceties of law and diplomacy. While their style can match neither Cicero's own genius for the polished use of language, nor Caesar's lucid and economical prose, they are nevertheless written in the Latin of an educated man and in this respect compare favourably with Pompey's letters. The first is courteously phrased, and if the second is more abrupt it seems likely that Antony wanted to make it clear that he meant exactly what he wrote.

Cicero waited for another month in his seaside villas, first at Cumae then at Formiae, unable to decide how to escape from Italy or where to go. Antony left Misenum on 10th May for Capua without having seen him; instead he sent a message saying he was ashamed not to have visited him, but felt that Cicero bore him a grudge. On 18th May Cicero's daughter, Tullia, who was with him at Cumae, gave birth two months prematurely to a son for Dolabella.

The letters Cicero wrote to Atticus during May not only show his indecision, but also something of the confusion and despair he felt at the eclipse of the Republic's institutions in which he so wholeheartedly believed and around which he had built his career in public life. In them he complains that Antony summoned fourteen local leaders to come early one morning to his villa at Misenum, but then discovered that they were from Cumae and Neapolis and told them to go away and come back the next day as he wanted to clear his bowels and take a bath. Cicero quotes this as an example of Antony's boorish and arrogant behaviour, but adds that Cumae and Neapolis had offended Caesar; it seems possible that Antony's treatment of their leading citizens was a deliberate slight, intended to show Caesar's displeasure.

At the beginning of June Cicero finally took ship for Greece; over optimistic reports that Caesar was in difficulties at Massalia perhaps helped him to make up his mind at last. Caesar had indeed been checked at Massalia where the city was held against him by Domitius Ahenobarbus, whom he had pardoned at Corfinium; with no fleet he was forced to wait while warships were built to complete the investment from the seaward side.

But carpenters could be found in the ranks of the legions, and under the direction of local shipwrights twelve warships were completed in two months. In June Caesar continued on his march to Spain with a small force of cavalry, leaving Gaius Trebonius with three legions to besiege Massalia and Decimus Brutus in command of the newly built blockading squadron. Soon afterwards Decimus defeated a relieving Pompeian squadron under Quintus Nasidius and sealed off the seaward approaches, enabling Trebonius to tighten the siege.

Caesar had ordered Gaius Fabius, one of his most able and experienced legates, to bring six legions and 6,000 cavalry from Gaul for the war in Spain. Fabius forced the Pyrenean passes and established himself north of Ilerda facing the Pompeians on the Segre, a tributary of the Ebro. Pompey's legate, Lucius Afranius, had three legions in Nearer Spain and he had been joined by his colleague, Marcus Petreius, with two legions from Further Spain; they had also raised some eighty cohorts of Spanish auxiliaries and 5,000 cavalry. In Lusitania, the most western part of Further Spain, there were two more Pompeian legions under Marcus Terentius Varro, better known as Varro the writer and historian, and perhaps the greatest scholar Rome ever produced.

Caesar joined Fabius and the army on 22nd June, still mid-April by the season which was some two and a half months behind the calendar. After an inconclusive encounter battle Caesar found himself trapped between two rivers by rising flood water, but he managed to extricate his army by building coracle-type boats and using them to improvise pontoon bridges. Exaggerated reports of their successes from Afranius and Petreius encouraged Varro to set off on the long march to join them; they also prompted some of the senators who were still wavering in Rome to leave to join Pompey in Greece.

But Caesar outmanoeuvred Afranius and Petreius; first he cut them off from their base in Ilerda, then from their local water supply, and on 27th August 49 they were forced to surrender. Caesar rode on with a single cavalry regiment across the Ebro into Further Spain, and resistance crumbled before him; at Corduba Varro and his two legions asked for terms. Caesar made Quintus Cassius governor of Further Spain, leaving him with four legions, among them the IInd, XXIst, and XXXth, in charge of both provinces; on his way back to Italy Massalia surrendered to him, but this time Domitius Ahenobarbus escaped by sea.

Elsewhere during the summer of 49 things had not gone so well for Caesar. In the Adriatic Dolabella, commanding the new Caesarian fleet, was defeated by the Pompeian admirals, Marcus Octavius and Lucius Scribonius Libo. After losing forty ships in a battle at sea he beached the rest of his fleet and fell back on land towards Gaius Antonius who occupied an island, probably Curicta, to cover his withdrawal. The Pompeians blockaded the island while two Caesarian legions on the mainland watched helplessly from across the strait. Some of Antonius's men escaped on rafts, but he was eventually forced to surrender with fifteen cohorts. Antonius himself was held prisoner and his soldiers were drafted into the Pompeian army.

After expelling Cato from Sicily Curio carried out Caesar's orders and invaded the province of Africa, held for Pompey by Varus who had taken over command after escaping from Corfinium. Probably because of shortage of transports Curio embarked only two legions, and these were largely composed of Pompeians who had surrendered at Corfinium. He dispersed a squadron of Pompeian transports off the African coast, captured some of them and then landed unopposed near Cape Bon.

After establishing a base at Castra Cornelia Curio forced Lucius Caesar to abandon Clupea and then advanced on Utica which was held by Varus; he had the better of a battle outside the city and Varus withdrew inside the walls. Curio foiled an attempt to subvert the loyalty of his two ex-Pompeian legions, and though he had no siege artillery he invested Utica closely while he waited for his other two legions to arrive from Sicily.

Juba, the client king of Numidia, who bore a personal grudge against both Curio and Caesar, set out to relieve Varus in Utica. Without waiting for his reinforcements to arrive Curio moved to intercept Juba and prevent him from joining forces with Varus. At the first encounter his infantry threw back the Numidian cavalry, but perhaps made over-confident by this success and still without cavalry or auxiliaries he followed up a feigned retreat by Juba's general, Saburra, and was drawn into a carefully sprung trap in the Bagrades valley. His two legions fought desperately but in the end they were overwhelmed and destroyed. Disdaining flight or surrender Curio died sword in hand with his soldiers; so for the second time Fulvia was widowed.

At Castra Cornelia Pollio did his best to rally the garrison, but after many were lost in a panic-stricken attempt at evacuation by sea the rest surrendered, only to be massacred on Juba's orders; Pollio succeeded in escaping. Thus thanks to Juba Africa remained in the hands of the Pompeians, and their fleets continued to dominate the Sicilian strait and the seaways of the central Mediterranean.

On his return from Massalia Caesar was faced with a mutiny in the

IXth Legion at Placentia. He dealt with it by threatening decimation, an ancient Roman military disciplinary process whereby every tenth man was executed; he contented himself with executing twelve of the ringleaders, ostensibly chosen by lot, and noting the names of the others.

Soon afterwards he entered Rome for the second time that year. His first concern was to arrange some measure of constitutional authority for himself, since with the two consuls absent with Pompey in Greece he could not be elected in the normal way as consul designate for 48. This problem was neatly solved by Lepidus, who, as praetor, nominated Caesar as dictator, thus allowing him to call consular elections at which he was elected with Publius Servilius as his colleague.

As dictator Caesar was also empowered to allot the consular provinces, and before resigning the office he did so. Lepidus, who was married to the daughter of Caesar's mistress, Servilia, was rewarded with Nearer Spain, Aulus Albinus received Sicily, Sextus Peducaeus Sardinia and Decimus Brutus Transalpine Gaul. Caesar's choice was restricted by a dearth of consulars among his supporters; only twenty six were alive in 48 and of these twelve were with Pompey; from the remaining fourteen Caesar reinstated Gaius Antonius, Gabinius and Messala, all of whom had been debarred from public office, but of the others only Domitius Calvinus was an active supporter and a competent general.

The other problem which faced Caesar was economic, and thus less susceptible to a quick and easy solution by stroke of sword or pen. The civil war had exacerbated the financial chaos and social unrest caused by the severe and archaic laws on debts and debtors. Interest rates had risen sharply, there was a critical shortage of corn, and throughout Italy there were few citizens who, in one way or another, did not owe money to the bankers, merchants and moneylenders. The leaders of the Populares advocated the popular but simplistic solution of cancelling all debts by decree. The merchants and the bankers were appalled by such a threat to their livelihood and its effect on trade and business. Caesar drew his support from both equites and Populares, and it was important that both should continue to back him. He was forced into a compromise: the holding of cash to more than 60,000 sesterces was forbidden, as was the hoarding of grain and other food supplies: outstanding interest on debts was remitted, and creditors were obliged to accept land or goods if debtors offered them in repayment of cash loans. Though these concessions did not solve the problem, they kept the Populares on Caesar's side and allayed the worst fears of the middle classes.

But the most pressing need, economic as well as political, was to deal with Pompey, first to forestall any move he might make to recover Italy, and then to reopen the flow of corn from Egypt and tax revenues and tribute from the East. This was more to Caesar's liking, and after spending only eleven days in Rome he set out for Brundisium, where he had ordered the army to concentrate, together with every warship and transport his staff could muster.

Pompey had called on his legates in the eastern provinces and the client kings to provide contingents for the army he was assembling in Thessalonica. Inevitably this took some considerable time, but he appears to have acted without any sense of urgency, almost as if he felt that time was on his side. And perhaps he had good reason to believe that it was, for his admirals had defeated the Caesarians in the Adriatic and now controlled that sea and most of its eastern seaboard, and despite the loss of Spain, Sicily and Sardinia, Varus's successful defence of Africa meant that he still had naval command of the central as well as the eastern Mediterranean.

Bibulus commanded the whole Pompeian fleet which included squadrons from Egypt under command of Pompey's son Gnaeus, from Syria under Gaius Cassius, Rhodes under Gaius Marcellus, Achaea under Octavius, and a composite squadron from Asia Minor; in the Adriatic there were one or more squadrons of native Liburnians. Bibulus was based on Corcyra with two squadrons, each of some fifty ships, and the self-imposed task of covering the straits at the entrance to the Adriatic and denying Caesar the crossing from Italy. Pompey himself seemed confident that Caesar had neither the means in the shape of transports, nor the will, to attempt an opposed passage in winter.

By the end of 49 Caesar had concentrated twelve legions and a large force of cavalry at Brundisium. The legions were under strength, but nine of them were experienced and battle hardened formations from the army of Gaul; of these, three had fought at Massalia and the other six in the recent Spanish campaign; the remaining three were newly raised. But despite their every effort his staff had only managed to find enough transports to carry 15,000 infantry and 500 cavalry.

On 4th January 48, still late autumn by the season, Caesar embarked seven legions and one cavalry regiment, all that he could cram on to the available transports. His security must have been good and the Pompeians' intelligence poor, for no word reached Bibulus ashore on Corcyra. The convoy slipped across the Adriatic undetected and Caesar landed unopposed on an open beach near Palaeste. Bibulus put to sea as soon as he heard that Caesar had sailed, but he was too late and all he could do was to capture thirty of the transports returning empty to Italy; in his fury and frustration at failing to intercept Caesar he burned them at sea with their crews still on board. Soon after landing Caesar sent Vibullius Rufus, whom he had captured, with peace proposals to Pompey, but nothing came of them.

When reports of Caesar's landing reached Pompey in Thessalonica he started to move his army on the long march westward up the Via Egnatia. Caesar secured his bridgehead and then seized the nearby port of Oricum. Back at Brundisium Antony was in command, charged with ferrying the rest of the army across as quickly as possible. But Libo appeared off Brundisium with his Liburnians, seized the island of Santa Andrea commanding the entrance to the harbour and destroyed more of the precious transports. He reported to Pompey that he had sealed off Brundisium and could deny Caesar reinforcements; he did not exaggerate. But there was no fresh water on the island, and this Antony tried to exploit by mounting standing patrols to prevent Libo's men from landing on the mainland to refill their water casks.

After capturing Oricum, which had been the base for one of the Pompeian squadrons, Caesar marched north on Apollonia and the city quickly declared for him as did a number of others to the south in Epirus. But Pompey forestalled him by reaching Dyrrachium first and so securing his base port at the western end of the Via Egnatia. Caesar tried to return to Brundisium in a small boat to speed up the despatch of the rest of the army, but he was foiled by a sudden storm and had to content himself with sending a series of urgent messages to Antony.

But Libo still commanded the seaward approaches to Brundisium. In an attempt to dislodge him Antony had sixty ship's boats fitted with protective wicker screens, manned them with picked crews and concealed them on the mainland opposite the island. He then ordered two newly built warships to put out from the inner harbour and manoeuvre as if they were on sea trials. Libo tried to cut them off and pursued them as they withdrew; when Antony judged that the Liburnians had been drawn far enough away from the island he launched the sixty boats, and they succeeded in capturing one of the enemy ships though the others escaped.

Across the Adriatic Pompey and Caesar faced each other with their armies encamped on either bank of the Apsus, which ran into the sea north of Apollonia. Caesar was outnumbered and he sent another peremptory message to Antony and his lieutenant, Fufius Calenus, urging them to sail as soon as they got anything approaching a favourable enough wind to lay a course for Apollonia, even if it meant that they might be unable to join him from their landing point.

Despatches for Caesar from Rome reached Antony at Brundisium. Caelius, now a praetor, had proposed the deferment of all debts for six years free of any accumulating iterest. As consul Servilius opposed this, and he was supported by Gaius Trebonius, the urban praetor, but after a long dispute Caelius persisted in refusing to amend or withdraw his proposals. Finally the Senate passed the ultimate decree against him, but he escaped from Rome and joined Milo, who had broken his exile to return to southern Italy and stir up a revolt. Eventually Milo was killed by the troops he was trying to subvert and Caelius was captured and executed.

At Brundisium Antony's tactics at last bore fruit and shortage of fresh water forced Libo to abandon the island and lift the blockade. Antony and Calenus at once embarked the rest of the army and in response to Caesar's orders sailed on a south-west wind, when to hold a course for Oricum they needed a wind from north of west, or at the worst due west.

They cleared Brundisium in the late afternoon, and under cover of the long winter night they crossed the straits undetected by the Pompeians. But in the morning the wind backed south and freshened, making it impossible to set a course for Oricum or even Apollonia; they were driven north up the coast, past the mouth of the Apsus in full view of both armies and on towards Pompey's base at Dyrrachium. Pompey alerted his admirals and as Antony's transports swept past the Rhodian squadron put out from Dyrrachium in their oared warships to give chase. Then to Antony's dismay the wind dropped, and the Rhodians had almost closed with the slowest of his ships when it suddenly freshened again, still from the south, and the convoy was able to draw away.

But every mile they sailed north up the enemy held coast was a mile further from a junction with Caesar. In desperation Antony gave the signal to put into the small harbour of Nympheaeum, some thirty miles north of Dyrrachium, though it offered no protection from southerly and south-easterly winds and Lissus garrisoned by the Pompeians was only three miles away. But with 'incredibili fortuna' as Caesar himself put it, the wind veered south-west with the setting sun and strengthened giving Antony's transports shelter in Nympheaeum and putting the Rhodians on a lee shore where they lost all sixteen of their bigger warships.

During the night two of Antony's stragglers anchored off Lissus. One was carrying recruits who surrendered after a promise of quarter, but Otacilius Crassus, commander of the Lissus garrison, had them all executed. The veterans managed to get ashore from the other ship and eventually fought their way through the enemy lines to join Caesar.

The next day Crassus abandoned Lissus, and the town declared for Caesar and opened its gates to Antony.

Antony moved his transports round from Nympheaeum to Lissus where he disembarked his four legions and 800 cavalry and auxiliaries, and sent a courier to Caesar to tell him that they were all safely ashore. He ordered most of the transports to return empty to Brundisium, but he kept thirty at Lissus so that if Pompey invaded Italy Caesar could at least follow him with a small force.

As soon as Antony's convoy had sailed past them Caesar and Pompey both moved out from their camps on the Apsus, Caesar to cover Antony's approach march and Pompey to intercept and destroy him before he and Caesar could join forces. Pompey marched rapidly north and set up an ambush on Antony's expected line of march, but, forewarned, Antony halted before he reached it. The next day Caesar arrived and to avoid being trapped between the two Caesarian armies Pompey withdrew south of Dyrrachium to Asparagium on the river Genusus.

Antony joined Caesar who at once followed Pompey and offered battle; when this was refused Caesar made a sudden move on Dyrrachium. As soon as Pompey realised the threat he hurried to protect his main base, but when he debouched on the coastal plain south-east of Dyrrachium he found Caesar already in position between him and the city.

Pompey seized the high ground at Petra, some two miles to the south of Caesar's camp, and secured his seaward communications by occupying a strip of coast running five miles south from Petra and extending about a mile inland. Caesar tried to cut this strip with a thrust towards the sea, but Pompey held and repulsed this attack. Caesar then set about the formidable task of investing his still numerically superior enemy from the landward side by throwing up some fifteen miles of continuous ditch and wall, which he strengthened at intervals with forts.

Though penned in with his back to the sea Pompey was not too concerned: his supplies were sufficient for the moment and when he needed more he could ferry them in by sea from Dyrrachium: his fleet controlled the Adriatic and could deny Caesar supplies and reinforcements from Italy: his position at Petra would give Afranius the chance to join him with the remnants of the defeated army from Spain, the so-called Afranian cohorts.

Pompey had nine legions to set against Caesar's under-strength eleven. He had brought with him the two Gallic legions together with three more raised by the consuls in southern Italy. To these five he had added four more: one largely made up of re-enlisted veterans from

Macedonia and Crete, two which Lentulus had raised as consul in the province of Asia, and one formed by amalgamating the two depleted Cilician legions and consequently named Gemini. He had used the soldiers from Gaius Antonius's fifteen surrendered cohorts as reinforcements, bringing the average strength of his nine legions to over 4,000.

Unlike Pompey it was not Caesar's normal practice to make up the strength of his veteran legions with new drafts, and his eleven legions were at little more than half strength giving him less legionary infantry than Pompey; but the nine legions from the army of Gaul were far superior in quality to Pompey's.

Pompey's main advantage, numerically at least, lay in his cavalry and auxiliaries made up of small contingents drawn from every part of the Roman East. The cavalry, 7,000 strong according to Caesar, were commanded by the various client princes or their generals, and only the Galatians with their Celtic expertise in horsemanship could compare with Caesar's three elite regiments of Gallic horse. The auxiliaries included archers from Crete, Sparta and Pontus, mounted archers from Syria and two cohorts of slingers, perhaps 4,000 men in all; Caesar had only a few hundred slingers whom Antony had brought with him.

But Pompey was content to wait until Metellus Scipio arrived with the two veteran legions from Syria and gave him a decisive numerical advantage. Already Caesar was almost certainly running short of supplies, and Pompey must have felt that with his command of the Adriatic time was on his side.

Exploiting his naval superiority Gnaeus Pompeius made a surprise attack with his Egyptian squadron on Caesar's base port of Oricum. He seized the entrance to the outer harbour and managed to remove the block ship closing the inner basin, only to find that the channel was neither wide nor deep enough to take his ships; nothing daunted he hauled four of them overland into the inner basin, defeated the Caesarians and took Oricum. Leaving a garrison there he sailed on up the coast to Lissus, and though he failed to take the town he succeeded in burning Antony's thirty transports.

At Petra the two armies were facing one another, each dug in behind a complex system of trenches and field works. Caesar tried to break the deadlock with a general assault on Pompey's lines, mounting co-ordinated attacks at six different points, but they were all repulsed. Pompey then began to run short of fodder for his large cavalry force; though his supply route by sea was open, the amount he needed proved beyond the capacity of his transports to carry and land across an open beach, so he tried to transfer the bulk of his cavalry to

Dyrrachium by sea, but Caesar blocked this move.

With the spring grass only just beginning to shoot, Caesar too was short of fodder as well as food. This need for forage and food was probably one reason why he split his army and sent three separate forces east to raise support in Greece and harass Scipio's approach march: Domitius Calvinus with the XIth and XIIth Legions to Macedonia, Gnaeus Calvisius Sabinus with five cohorts to Aetolia, and Lucius Cassius Longinus with the XXVIIth Legion to Thessaly.

Foiled in his attempt to transfer his cavalry Pompey tried to break out from the Petra perimeter; he concentrated four legions but Publius Cornelius Sulla held their two pronged attack. Then with the help of deserters Pompey identified a weak point in the southern sector between Caesar's quaestor, Cornelius Marcellinus, and Antony with the IXth Legion. This time he used six legions in a phased attack on a narrow front. The full brunt of their assault fell on the IXth Legion, and though Antony managed to contain the initial penetration he had to signal for reinforcement. Caesar moved up thirty three cohorts, but their counter-attack broke down in the maze of trenches, ditches and field works. At the critical moment, before they could consolidate and reorganise, Pompey threw in his reserve and flung the Caesarians back in disorder, though Antony managed to stop the rout. Perhaps not realising the extent of the victory he had won, Pompey failed to follow up and exploit it; Caesar's comment that Pompey was no general showed his relief.

Caesar's close investment of the Petra perimeter was broken by this defeat at Pompey's hands, and he pulled back to regroup in his old lines at Asparagium. Pompey followed cautiously, but when Caesar abandoned his camp and withdrew east down the Via Egnatia he again failed to make effective use of his cavalry to harass Caesar's retreat.

Afranius, who by now had joined Pompey with several cohorts of survivors from Spain, urged him to seize the opportunity to invade Italy. But Pompey was afraid that if he did so Caesar's army in Gaul would intervene. He was also unwilling to leave Scipio to almost certain defeat and cut himself off from the East by abandoning Greece. So, setting aside Afranius's advice, he too marched down the Via Egnatia for the junction he had arranged with Scipio at Larissa.

In Macedonia Domitius Calvinus got the best of an inconclusive battle with Scipio, who then moved against Cassius in Thessaly; failing to take him by surprise Scipio turned back again on Domitius. After further marches and countermarches Domitius joined Caesar and Cassius at Aeginem while Scipio seized Larissa and waited there for Pompey.

When Gomphi and Metropolis in Thessaly failed to open their gates to Caesar he handed them over to his soldiers to loot and pillage. As well as giving a boost to the morale of the legions and a warning to the rest of Thessaly the sack of the two cities also probably provided urgently needed food and grain, for though it was late July by the calendar it was still only early summer by the season and the harvest was not yet ripe. The evidence suggests that with the army once again concentrated and insufficient cavalry to cover wide-ranging foraging parties Caesar was seriously short of essential supplies.

Early in August he set up his camp near Pharsalus, which lay twenty five miles south of Larissa where the main road to central Greece reached the foothills on the southern edge of the plain of Thessaly. He does not mention Pharsalus himself, but four of the ancient sources say that the battle was fought near old Pharsalus which has never been identified on the ground but was certainly in the upper basin of the Epineus, a tributary of the Peneus.

A day or so later Pompey moved from Larissa to Pharsalus where he entrenched his camp on rising ground facing Caesar. On successive days Caesar drew up his army in order of battle, but Pompey made no move to accept the challenge and Caesar was not prepared to risk an uphill assault on his fortified camp. Caesar then decided to break camp and march off, probably because he was running short of supplies, but possibly to force Pompey to accept battle in order to protect his communications with Larissa.

On the night of the 8th of August Caesar issued orders for the army to march the next morning. But as the legions were forming up to move off in column of route Pompey flew his battle ensign and his army began to move out and take up their line of battle; Caesar at once gave the order to form his own line.

In infantry Pompey had some numerical advantage, according to Caesar deploying 110 cohorts against his own eighty. But the quality still lay with Caesar's veterans in spite of the defeat they had suffered at Petra, a defeat which they were anxious to avenge and a victory which Pompey may have been over confident that he could repeat. In his cavalry, which Plutarch described as the flower of Italy, and in his auxiliaries Pompey held an overwhelming numerical advantage.

Caesar has it that it was the senators in Pompey's camp, eager to finish the war and return to their accustomed life in Rome, who made him decide on battle at this last hour. This may have been so, for Plutarch describes how some of them were arranging the next year's magistracies between themselves and how Lentulus Spinther, Domitius Ahenobarbus and Scipio were quarrelling over who should succeed Caesar as Pontifex Maximus; but in war, at least, Pompey had never shown himself the man to be influenced by such pressures.

Except for the garrison of fifteen cohorts at Dyrrachium Pompey had concentrated his whole available strength, and he knew that Caesar could call on Calenus's fifteen cohorts which were still in Achaea. He may have wanted to fight before his numerical advantage slipped away and his soldiers forgot how they had put Caesar's legions to flight at Petra. When he realised, probably through intelligence on the night of the 8th, that he had delayed long enough in the hope of enticing Caesar into a frontal attack and instead there was a risk of his slipping away, he decided on battle the next day. It is possible that he did fear a threat to his communications, but this was not the main reason which made him decide to fight at Pharsalus.

Pompey left seven cohorts to guard his camp, and with his army drawn up in front of it he still had a strong position on rising ground with Caesar slightly below him. The open plain stretching away into the distance was ideal ground for cavalry and Labienus had convinced him that his cavalry could win the day. He took command of his more open left flank himself with the two Gallic legions directly under his eye and Labienus with the main body of the cavalry on their left. Scipio commanded the centre with the Syrian legions, and on the right, partly protected by the ground and the river Epineus, Afranius had the Gemini legion and the Spanish cohorts. Caesar took his own right with the Xth Legion facing Pompey, Domitius Calvinus the centre, and Antony the left with the VIIIth and IXth Legions which had suffered heavy casualties at Petra.

Pompey's plan, devised by Labienus, was to hold Caesar's line with his infantry and to use his cavalry to brush aside the small force of enemy cavalry and encircle the Caesarian infantry from flank and rear. At the last moment Caesar apparently divined Pompey's intention: he withdrew one cohort from the third line of each legion and formed them into a flank guard, telling them only to attack on his orders and then to thrust with their javelins instead of throwing them, predicting that the gilded youth of Pompey's cavalry would not be able to stand steel in their faces.

The battle began with Caesar's line advancing slowly uphill to close with Pompey's infantry who stood their ground. On the open flank Pompey's massed cavalry forced back Caesar's cavalry. Supported by covering fire from slingers and archers Labienus then wheeled to begin his encircling movement. But as he did so the eight cohorts of Caesar's flank guard, who had stepped their long throwing javelins in the ground to present a defensive line of sharp iron stakes, went over to the attack on his signal. Taken in the flank and surprised by this unexpected assault the Pompeian cavalry recoiled and then fled in disorder. Pompey's left flank was now open and his slingers and archers unprotected as Caesar threw in his third line. When Labienus failed to rally the cavalry Pompey must have realised that the result of the battle was virtually settled for he left the field and made his way back to his camp.

The Pompeian infantry fought on desperately, but Caesar gradually rolled up their line from the open flank and then the two Gallic legions broke and fled; the legions and independent cohorts of the centre and right managed to withdraw in good order. As Caesar's troops broke into his camp Pompey removed his general's insignia and rode for Larissa with a small escort. Antony took command of the Gallic cavalry, setting up a controlled and relentless pursuit which allowed the fleeing enemy no chance to stand and regroup. With four legions Caesar cut off the main body of the Pompeian infantry and the next morning they asked for terms; in all nearly 25,000 surrendered and of these 20,000 were absorbed into Caesar's army.

The dead on the plain of Pharsalus numbered 15,000, the vast majority from Pompey's army. Less than half of them were Roman, but of these a disproportionate number were young nobles from the ancient families of Rome who had chosen to fight to the end rather than surrender or flee. Among the leaders Ahenobarus died though his son escaped, as did Labienus who before the battle had been foremost in swearing to conquer or die. Caesar's comment when he surveyed the battlefield, 'They would have it so', provided a terse epitaph for the Pompeian dead.

The victory at Pharsalus was complete and decisive, but it came only just in time. Pompey's admiral, Decimus Laelius, had again sealed off Brundisium by seizing the island commanding the harbour entrance, and, though Caesar's legate, Publius Varinius, tried the same tactics to dislodge him as Antony had used, Laelius had arranged for fresh water supplies to be ferried from Dyrrachium and Corcyra. The Pompeian admiral, Gaius Cassius, brother of Caesar's general, attacked the naval base at Messina with the Syrian squadron, using fireships to destroy the Caesarian fleet; from here he sailed on to Vibo. But when Labienus brought the news of Pharsalus to Dyrrachium Laelius called off the blockade of Brundisium and Cassius withdrew from Vibo.

In the spring of 48 Caesar had sent two legions to reinforce Illyricum where Quintus Cornificius was hard pressed by Marcus Octavius. Gabinius was now despatched with more troops, but the Pompeians' naval hold on the Adriatic forced him to take the overland route and he did not reach Illyricum until the autumn; eventually he was besieged in Salonae where he died. As soon as Laelius withdrew from Brundisium Vatinius embarked what troops he could muster and sailed for Illyricum where he defeated Octavius off the island of Tauris.

After escaping from Pharsalus to Larissa Pompey rode for Amphiopolis where he took ship for Mytilene. Here he picked up Cornelia and his younger son, Sextus, and they sailed on for the eastern Mediterranean. But when news of the outcome of the battle reached Rhodes and Antioch both cities declared for Caesar and closed their harbours to Pompey and his followers. After a brief stop in Cilicia he sailed for Egypt, sending envoys ahead of him to Alexandria.

When Pompey left Greece it is not clear why he did not make for the province of Africa, still firmly held for him by Varus; the rest of his supporters were to find refuge there and it would seem to have been the better choice. But it is probably wrong to assume that when he sailed from Amphipolis he had already decided to go to Egypt; it was only when Asia Minor, Syria and the Levant all declared for Caesar that he headed for Egypt.

At the start of the war Gnaeus Pompeius had visited Alexandria to enforce his father's demands for assistance; Egypt had provided a squadron of warships and 500 Gabinians and had sent supplies and war materials to Dyrrachium. Auletes had died in 51; in his will he left the throne jointly to Cleopatra, then eighteen, and her twelve year old brother Ptolemy. He also appointed the Senate as executor, and Lepidus was sent to Egypt to supervise the carrying out of the terms of the will. Cleopatra married her brother, as was the custom in the royal house of Egypt, and they became joint rulers as Cleopatra VII and Ptolemy XIII. When Bibulus, as governor of Syria, recalled the Gabinians to defend the province from a threatened Parthian invasion they not only refused to go, but they murdered Bibulus's two sons whom he had sent to order them to return. Cleopatra insisted on the murderers being handed over to Bibulus, and this enraged the Alexandrians who saw it as an act of appeasement to the Romans. It also alienated the council of ministers, headed by the Egyptian eunuch, Pothinus, the Greek rhetorician, Theodotus, and their Greek/Egyptian general Achillas, who wanted to continue to rule Egypt themselves.

Early in 48 the council deposed Cleopatra and ruled in the name of Ptolemy who was now fourteen. But Cleopatra managed to raise considerable support, probably in Upper Egypt and perhaps from Nabataea, and by the autumn of 48 she and her brother were at war for the succession with their armies facing each other north of Pelusium.

When Pompey's envoys reached Alexandria Theodotus and

Pothinus decided that it would be prudent to kill him if he tried to seek refuge in Egypt, and they sent secret instructions to Achillas to this effect; as Theodotus put it:- 'Dead men don't bite'. When Pompey's ship arrived off Mons Casius, north of Pelusium, on 28th September Achillas went out to welcome him, supposedly with friendly greetings from Ptolemy; he took with him two Gabinian officers, one of whom, Septimius, had served as a centurion under Pompey in the pirate war. Achillas persuaded him to come ashore with them while Cornelia and Sextus waited on their anchored ship. As Pompey stepped from the boat Septimius stabbed him in the back and the others finished him off with their swords. Thus on the day before his fifty eighth birthday the great Pompey died, treacherously struck down on a foreign shore while his wife and son watched helplessly from their ship. Achillas sent his head to Theodotus in Alexandria.

On the day after the battle at Pharsalus Caesar rode for Larissa, but when he got there that evening Pompey was already gone. Two days later he set out for the East, taking the Via Egnatia for the Hellespont. With him he took the VIth Legion, now reduced to half strength, and a regiment of cavalry, and he sent orders to Calenus in Achaea for the XXVIIth Legion to join him in Asia Minor. Probably after he had established that Pompey had sailed for Egypt he gave Domitius Calvinus three legions, among them the ex-Pompeian XXVIth and XXXVIIth, and the task of taking over Syria. As Master of Horse Antony was to take the rest of the army back to Italy and again act as his deputy there, in command of the army and in control of civil administration.

At the Hellespont Caesar took over part of a Pompeian squadron of warships and requisitioned some transports. He then crossed over to the province of Asia, reaching Ephesus in time to save the treasures of the Temple of Artemis from looting Pompeians. He earned the gratitude of the inhabitants by removing the right to collect taxes from the venal hands of the publicani, and instead allowing the local municipal councils to levy them; so corrupt were the tax farmers, that although the same amount of money accrued to the provincial revenues, the burden on individual taxpayers was cut by a third.

As soon as it was clear that Pompey had made for Egypt Caesar followed him, sailing from Asia Minor with the VIth and XXXVIIth Legions; they were both so under strength that his total infantry numbered only 3,200. He reached Alexandria on 1st or 2nd October and there was met by Theodotus bearing Pompey's head as if it were some propitiatory offering. With an outward show of grief, which though probably genuine perhaps also concealed an inward sense of relief, Caesar gave orders that it should be buried, choosing whether

67

by accident or design, a mausoleum dedicated to Nemesis.

He landed wearing the full dress of a Roman general, and preceded by lictors bearing fasces, the symbol of his Roman imperium, he marched through the city at the head of his troops. This provoked the Alexandrians, who saw it as an affront to Egypt's sovereignty and a threat to her independence, to protest and riot.

Caesar deployed his troops along the southern side of the Great Harbour in the Bruchium quarter and installed himself in the adjoining royal palace. He summoned Pothinus, and turned his mind to extracting the money he needed to pay his armies and prosecute the war against the Pompeians in Africa. Despite the profligacy of Auletes Egypt was still the richest country in the Mediterranean, and Caesar claimed that he was owed the debt he had taken over from Rabirius, who in his turn had lent the money to Auletes so that he could pay Caesar and Pompey for reinstating him; it was a neat Roman argument and difficult for the Egyptians to refute. Pothinus tried to demonstrate Egypt's poverty, and because of Pompey's death Caesar agreed to halve his demands, but they still amounted to far more than Pothinus could readily find from the Egyptian treasury.

As the representative magistrate of the Roman people, Egypt's friends and allies, Caesar announced his intention of arbitrating in the dispute over the succession and ordered Pothinus to bring Ptolemy to the palace. When Cleopatra heard this she was afraid that Caesar would decide in favour of her brother, whose army under Pothinus's orders already controlled Alexandria, so that he could continue on his way against the Pompeians in the province of Africa before sailings out of Alexandria were stopped for the winter by the etesian winds.

Leaving her army north of Pelusium the twenty one year old Cleopatra made her way secretly to Alexandria and there had herself smuggled into Caesar's presence. He was captivated by her wit and spirit, and soon she was established as his mistress in the palace where her brother and rival for the throne was held under virtual house arrest.

Though the rioting which followed Caesar's first march through the city subsided the Alexandrians still resented the presence of Roman troops and Caesar's arbitrary assumption of power. He tried to placate them by offering to return Cyprus to Egyptian rule; he designated Cleopatra's younger sister, Arsinoe, and their eleven year old youngest brother, also Ptolemy, as joint rulers, but continued to hold both of them in the palace.

Pothinus stirred up the mob who killed one of Caesar's envoys and maltreated another; he secretly ordered Achillas to bring back his army of 20,000 infantry and 2,000 cavalry from Pelusium and drive the

Romans out of Alexandria. Caesar was dangerously outnumbered, but before he was too closely besieged he managed to get messengers out with urgent calls for help to Domitius Calvinus and the pro-Roman client prince, Mithridates of Pergamum. Domitius was attempting to restore Roman rule in the eastern province of Syria, bordering the Euphrates, when Caesar's message reached him. He detached the XXXVIIth Legion and ordered the Rhodian admiral Euphranor, to embark it and escort it to Alexandria; he may also have sent a second legion overland on the long march to Egypt.

Caesar was soon closely invested from the landward side by Achillas and held only the Palace quarter on the eastern side of the Great Harbour and part of the Bruchium quarter on its southern side. He was cut off from the open sea by part of the Egyptian fleet lying in the Great Harbour between the inner basin, where the Roman ships were berthed, and the polygonal three storied lighthouse, faced in white marble and surmounted by a statue of Zeus Soter, which towered 100 metres above the entrance at the eastern end of Pharos island. Caesar had Pothinus executed when he discovered that he had ordered Achillas to Alexandria. Arsinoe escaped from the place with her tutor, Ganymede, and she had Achillas killed and appointed Ganymede to command the army in his place.

In a surprise attack Caesar burned seventy two of the Egyptian ships at their berths and destroyed thirty more on the harbour slips. He then seized the Pharos lighthouse, thus reopening the harbour entrance. Showing more resource and resolution than Achillas, Ganymede tightened the landward investment and contaminated the Romans' water supplies by pumping sea water into the underground cisterns; Caesar managed to obtain drinking water by sinking wells.

Euphranor arrived off Alexandria with the Rhodian squadron escorting the transports carrying the XXXVIIth Legion; despite an attempt by the Egyptian fleet from the western or Eunostos harbour, the harbour of Happy Return, to intercept them, they disembarked the legion safely, effectively doubling the strength of Caesar's army. But Ganymede won control of the western end of Pharos island and reinforced the Egyptian fleet in the Eunostos harbour. Supported by the Rhodian squadron Caesar counter-attacked and secured the whole of Pharos island. Euphranor was then able to force the seaward entrance to the Eunostos harbour, and though he was killed in the battle the Rhodians bottled up the Egyptian fleet in the inner Kibitos basin.

Caesar now held Pharos island and both ends of the Heptastadion, the causeway, seven stades long as its name indicates, which ran south from the middle of Pharos island to the Alexandrian shore and separated the Great Harbour from the Eunostos harbour; half-way along it two channels, normally spanned by bridges, allowed ships to pass from one harbour to the other. Caesar then captured the whole length of the Heptastadion, but the Egyptians counter-attacked and cut him off on the centre section; in order to escape he and his soldiers had to swim for their lives. With the Heptastadion again in Egyptian hands their fleet was able to retake the Eunostos harbour.

For reasons which are not clear Caesar released Ptolemy who promptly took his place at the head of the Egyptian army; the author of the contemporary Alexandrian War, probably Caesar's lieutenant, Hirtius, says that this occurred before Pelusium fell to Mithridates's relieving army, and he is to be preferred to Dio who postdates it. In response to Caesar's call Mithridates had raised an army in Asia Minor and marched south; he was reinforced by infantry raised by Antipater in Judaea and cavalry sent by Malchus from Nabataea. After taking Pelusium early in 47 he marched up the eastern Pelusiac branch of the Nile to avoid the intricate network of waterways in the lower delta, and then crossed the river and turned down the western Canopic branch towards Alexandria.

After feinting a move by sea to meet Mithridates Caesar marched west round the end of the Mareotic Lake and joined him on the west bank of the Canopic branch. Though Ptolemy and the Egyptian army failed to prevent this junction they succeeded in placing themselves in a strong position between Caesar and Alexandria; but they were overwhelmed in the battle which followed on 27th March, and Ptolemy himself was drowned trying to escape by swimming the river.

With the Alexandrian War at an end Caesar confirmed Cleopatra as sole ruler and kept his promise to return Cyprus to Egypt, though Arsinoe, the younger sister whom Cleopatra hated, was imprisoned for her part in the war. Some of the secondary sources, though none of the primary, have it that Caesar stayed with Cleopatra for some months, accompanying her on a royal progress through Upper Egypt and a holiday trip up the Nile. Such stories are no more than a pleasing fiction. By the end of March at the latest reports reached Caesar that during the winter Pharnaces had defeated Domitius and overrun much of Asia Minor. It can be shown that Caesar left Egypt probably by mid-April, certainly by the first week in May: the battle of Zela was fought on 2nd August 47, and considerations of time and space applied to Caesar's movements by sea or land make it certain that he did not dally in Egypt.

Before he left Caesar probably knew that Cleopatra was carrying his child. To support her as ruler and to protect Egypt against any incursions by the Pompeians he left behind the XXVIIth and XXXVIIth Legions, and possibly also the XXXVIIIth which may have been sent overland by Domitius and could have arrived with Mithridates. Caesar apparently had with him no one of rank in whose loyalty he could place sufficient trust to warrant leaving him as legate in Egypt: instead he appointed a certain Rufinus, said to have been the son of a freedman, to command the Roman army of Egypt.

Caesar again took the redoubtable VIth Legion with him, now little more than a thousand strong. It was still the winter season of prevailing etesian winds and he almost certainly marched overland from Alexandria to Ptolemais Ace. In Judaea he rewarded Hyrcanus and Antipater for their assistance to Mithridates, confirming Hyrcanus as High Priest and Antipater as Chief Minister; he returned Jaffa to Judaea, thus restoring her vital outlet to the Mediterranean, and he authorised the reconstruction of the walls of Jerusalem. He exempted the Jews from paying tribute to Rome, and from providing winter quarters for Roman troops; this included supplying food, a costly and much resented imposition which the Cypriots had been happy to pay 200 talents to be excused when Cicero was governor of Cilicia. Thus Caesar handsomely repaid his debts to the Jews, both in Judaea and in the other Jewish communities in the Roman world, notably Alexandria, and this they long remembered.

He left his kinsman, Sextus Julius Caesar, in Antioch as governor of Syria and sailed from Seleuceia for Tarsus on the river Cydnus. Here the good offices of Marcus Junius Brutus, son of Caesar's lifelong friend and mistress, Servilia, and himself pardoned after Pharsalus, secured pardon for Gaius Cassius, brother of Caesar's general, Lucius Cassius. The story that Gaius planned to assassinate Caesar at Tarsus, but waited for him on the wrong bank of the Cydnus was probably concocted afterwards.

Pharnaces had taken advantage of Roman preoccupation with the civil war to emerge from his Crimean kingdom in an attempt to recover Pontus. First he attacked Ariobarzanes of Cappadocia and then Deiotarus in Lesser Armenia, two client princes who had supported Pompey but had been quick to transfer their allegiance to Caesar. Domitius marched against him with four legions, two of Galatians found by Deiotarus, one from Pontus, and his own XXXVIth; but Pharnaces defeated him at Nicopolis and then overran Pontus where he took a bloody revenge on every Roman he found.

From Tarsus Caesar marched north to meet Domitius; between them they had four legions, Caesar's VIth, Domitius's XXXVIth, one Pontic and one Galatian, and some auxiliaries. With Caesar in command this proved enough; on 2nd August 47 at Zela in southern

Pontus, where twenty five years before Pharnaces's father, Mithridates, had destroyed another Roman army, Caesar inflicted a crushing and decisive defeat on an over-confident Pharnaces who played into his hands by launching an uphill frontal attack on the entrenched legions.

This victory promoted the laconic epigram in Caesar's letter to a friend in Rome: 'Veni, vidi, vici', which later was carried on a placard at his Triumph and was to be remembered and quoted over the centuries to come.

Pharnaces escaped to the Crimea only to be murdered by rebels; Caesar then rewarded Mithridates with the Bosporan kingdom, but he was defeated and killed while attempting to take it over. Deiotarus was confirmed as ruler of Galatia, but its eastern province was ceded to Ariobarzanes. The depleted and battle scarred VIth Legion was sent back to Italy to rest and refit. Domitius stayed in Asia Minor to supervise the reorganisation of the client kingdoms. Caesar left at the beginning of September, arriving at Brundisium on the 24th, more than a year after the battle of Pharsalus.

The news of Pharsalus had reached Rome quickly, though it was not until the late autumn of 48 that Antony returned to Italy with the main body of the army. No consular elections for 47 had been held, but the instructions Antony brought with him put an end to speculation about Caesar's intentions: he was to be reappointed as dictator for 47, with Antony as his Master of Horse.

As Caesar's deputy the supreme authority again was Antony's and the manner in which he exercised it was perhaps predictable: without personal ambition and in loyalty to Caesar, but with uninhibited licence and ill concealed contempt for the niceties of the law and the conventions of Roman life. Plutarch's account of Antony's stewardship during the year after Pharsalus, when Caesar was absent from Italy, derives in part from Cicero's letters and his later speeches. Doubtless there was some substance in Cicero's accusations against Antony, but he certainly embellished and exaggerated these stories out of malice towards him and resentment and frustration at being confined at Brundisium on his orders. Though he had left Italy Cicero had taken no part in the war and after Pharsalus he had refused to take over command from Cato at Dyrrachium; instead he had returned to try and make his peace with Caesar, but Antony was adamant in refusing to allow him to leave Brundisium.

Plutarch describes Antony's journeys through Italy on affairs of state as being like some parody of a royal progress: his golden drinking cups ceremoniously carried before him instead of the lictors' fasces, his mistress, the actress Cytheris, accompanying him in an open litter, his extravagant banquets in tented pavilions set up for the occasion on sylvan river banks, his low-born entourage, and his forcible billeting of courtesans and sambuca players on respectable citizens.

Much of Antony's behaviour would have passed uncriticised, if not unnoticed, in the person of Caesar's deputy, had not Antony himself delighted in flaunting his contempt for the conventions, his impatience with the tedious processes of law, and his own preference for the company of actors, dancers and musicians. For the conservatives these insults were made even less palatable, because, in Caesar's deputy, they were obliged to swallow them.

Much of the unrest and civil disorder during the twenty months Caesar was away from Italy stemmed from the intractable problems of debts and debtors and the interim measures he had taken to relieve them; for the merchant bankers and the creditors these had gone altogether too far, but for the great mass of citizens and freedmen, overburdened as they were with debts, they had not gone nearly far enough.

Courting popularity as a tribune Dolabella proposed the simplistic solution of cancelling all debts, and when his motion was opposed by his fellow tribune, Trebellius, he appealed to Antony to support him. But, with the ultimate responsibility for law and order, Antony saw only too clearly that the result of such a measure would be economic anarchy and widespread disorder, and he prepared to thwart Dolabella's proposal. Apparently he also had some reason to suspect Dolabella of having seduced his wife, Antonia, and he formally divorced her by turning her out of his house.

Dolabella had no difficulty in finding followers ready and eager to back his proposals to cancel debts and he occupied the Forum with a large crowd of them. Antony warned him that he would use force if necessary to clear the Forum, but Dolabella's response was to move in more of his supporters from the urban mob. With the backing of the Senate and the magistrates, including the other tribunes, Antony brought up troops and ordered the mob to disperse. But incited by an inflammatory speech from Dolabella they resisted the troops and refused to move; nearly a thousand died before the Forum was cleared. There was a lack of balance in Dolabella's make-up, as later he was to show only too clearly, but on this occasion he may have defied Antony mainly because of their personal quarrel over Antonia and Antony may have over-reacted for the same reason.

Civil disturbances continued in Rome, some instigated by Dolabella, and in an attempt to restore order the Senate passed a number of emergency decrees. And despite Antony's popularity with the army and his standing as Caesar's lieutenant at Pharsalus there was growing unrest among the legions, now idle in their home stations, because they had not yet been given the land grants and gratuities which Caesar had promised them when the civil war ended.

The property of the defeated Pompeians was put up for auction, even though many of their wives and families were still living in Italy. Much of this forfeited property was sold at a fraction of its real value because no one dared to run up the bidding against the Caesarians. In this way Antony acquired Pompey's house, known as the House of Ships from the trophies in the shape of bronze beaks and trident rams from captured ships which decorated its front.

CHAPTER V

Caesar: Dictator and Triumphator

On his return to Italy Caesar was perhaps relieved to find his quarrelling lieutenants still loyal to him and the widespread civil disaffection directed against the general economic malaise caused by the war, and not aimed at him in person. He did no more than remonstrate with Antony and Dolabella over the blood which had been shed in the Forum and the emergency decrees which the Senate had seen fit to pass, and insist that those who had bought the property of the dead or outlawed Pompeians should at least pay what they had bid.

But before he left for his next campaign in Africa he appointed Lepidus as Master of the Horse in place of Antony, and he was careful to take Dolabella with him. Calenus and Vatinius were rewarded with the consulate for the rest of the year, and though he was still dictator Caesar was himself elected consul for 46 with Lepidus as his colleague. But he had neither the time, nor perhaps the inclination, to make any real effort to solve the pressing economic problems of Italy resulting directly from the war and aggravated by the laws on debts. He did little more than buy time by putting a moratorium on interest on all debts incurred during the war, and by remitting for a period of one year all rents up to an annual figure of five hundred denarii in Rome and one hundred and twenty five denarii in the rest of Italy; this differential, presumably designed to provide roughly equal treatment, indicates the disparity between property values in Rome and those in the rest of the country. Caesar's mind was on the Pompeians who had rallied and concentrated their forces across the Sicilian strait in the province of Africa, and he may well have hoped that victory in Africa would bring with it a ready-made solution for the economic ills of Italy.

After defeating Curio Varus had continued to hold the province for Pompey with the help of Juba of Numidia. After Pharsalus all the surviving Pompeian leaders, except Pompey himself, had made their several ways to Africa. Scipio, Afranius and Petreius were there, as was Labienus with the Gallic and Germanic cavalry he had brought from Buthrotum in Epirus. Cato had crossed to Cyrenaica with the fifteen cohorts which had garrisoned Dyrrachium, and finally he too arrived in Utica after a long and arduous march up the coast road.

Pompey's two sons, Gnaeus and Sextus, had also reached Africa, though after a dispute with the other leaders Gnaeus had sailed on to the Balearics.

The Pompeians had mustered a formidable army of ten legions and 15,000 cavalry in Africa and a fleet of some fifty warships. They could also count on Juba to provide the four legions which he had trained on Roman lines, as well as a considerable force of slingers, archers and cavalry, and some war elephants. From Rome all Caesar could do was to have Juba declared an enemy of the Roman people and his hereditary rivals, the Mauretanian princes Bogud and Bocchus, formally adopted as friends and allies of Rome.

Caesar's preparations for the African campaign were disrupted by a mutiny among the veteran legions, who refused to serve overseas again until their promised bounties had been paid. When he sent a commission, headed by Sallust, to offer them one thousand denarii a head as an interim payment their response was to kill one praetor and to stone Sallust and make him flee for his life. In an attempt to force Caesar's hand elements of the Xth Legion marched on Rome and he went out to meet them himself. He disconcerted them by offering them their discharge and addressing them as if they were already civilians; he told them that they would not qualify for the generous gratuities which he had promised at the end of the civil war and which he would give to every soldier when he held his Triumph. The mutiny collapsed, and Caesar did no more than take the names of the ringleaders; but both at Thapsus and at Munda the Xth Legion was to find itself in the forefront of the battle.

On 25th December 47 Caesar embarked six legions, seven independent cohorts and 2,000 cavalry at Libylaeum in western Sicily. Again the limiting factor seems to have been shortage of transports, though there may have been continuing disaffection among the veterans, for among the six legions were the Gallic Alaudae, or Larks, now numbered the Vth, the XXVIth, and the newly raised XXVth, XXVIIIth and XXIXth.

After a storm had scattered the convoy Caesar landed near Hadrumetum with one legion and two squadrons of cavalry. Hadrumetum itself was firmly held by Gaius Considius Longus, and harassed by the Pompeian cavalry Caesar marched seven miles south to Leptis which opened its gates thus providing him with a much needed port. Leaving six cohorts there as a garrison, he moved the rest of his small force on 3rd January to Ruspina between Leptis and Hadrumetum. Here he entrenched his camp and set about training his recruits while he waited for the rest of the legions from the convoy to join him.

The Pompeians had strong garrisons in the more important towns, where they had concentrated most of the available food supplies in depots. Cato commanded their main base at Utica, and Scipio was encamped nearby with the field army of eight legions and a large force of cavalry; during the first weeks of the campaign he made no attempt to seek out Caesar and destroy his scattered army. This failure to take the offensive when Caesar was at his weakest and most vulnerable was a blunder on Scipio's part, perhaps deriving from his reluctance to face Caesar in battle when it seemed that victory could be won by using delaying tactics to wear him down.

Caesar sent Rabirius Postumus back to Sicily to expedite the despatch of some of the veteran legions on a second convoy. His immediate problem was shortage of food for his soldiers and fodder for what cavalry he had. He was forced to mount a series of foraging expeditions and so expose his infantry in open country without enough cavalry to provide an adequate screen. Labienus showed skill and determination in using his own cavalry to intercept and harass these foraging parties; on one occasion, when he co-ordinated an attack with Petreius's infantry, Caesar only managed to extricate his force after his soldiers had fought back to back to beat off simultaneous attacks on their front and rear.

Scipio then moved south with the main Pompeian army; Juba advanced to join him from Numidia, but a threat to his rear from Bocchus's Roman general, Sittius, forced him to withdraw, though he left some cavalry and elephants with Scipio. Caesar remained on the defensive at Ruspina until the second convoy reached Leptis with the XIIIth and XIVth Legions, a regiment of cavalry and some thousand archers and slingers. Then, towards the end of January, he left Ruspina for a position inland from Leptis where supplies were easier to obtain. Scipio countered by entrenching his army on rising ground covering Uzita; he was joined by Juba, who had left his general, Saburra, to watch Bocchus and Sittius. It was now midwinter, and with the Pompeians holding nearly all the food supplies in the towns and Labienus continuing to harass foraging parties, Caesar found it increasingly difficult to feed his army, now, with the arrival of the IXth and Xth, ten legions strong. He tried to force a battle, but Scipio, confident that shortage of supplies would force Caesar to disperse his army, was determined to fight only in entrenched positions on ground of his own choosing.

Towards the middle of March, still January by the season, Caesar marched south in an attempt to bring on a decisive battle by threatening Zeta and Thysdrus, both held by Pompeian garrisons. But in a complicated sequence of march and counter march Scipio and

Labienus covered his every move, and after three months of inconclusive manoeuvring it seemed that their strategy of wearing him down and denying him supplies was succeeding.

Caesar evidently decided that he could only break this impasse by forcing the Pompeians to fight in defence of one of their main bases. He chose Thapsus on its coastal promontory east of Leptis; the city and its port were cut off from the hinterland by a large salt lake and could only be reached along two narrow isthmuses between the lake and the sea, one running west and the other south.

After a surprise approach march under cover of darkness Caesar arrived before the walls of Thapsus early on the morning of 5th April, having left detachments to hold the southern isthmus behind him. Although it meant dividing his army Scipio decided to seize the opportunity to trap Caesar between the sea and the lake. He left Juba and Afranius to seal off the southern isthmus, and on the night of the 5th he marched round the landward side of the lake with the rest of his army. By dawn on the 6th he was at the narrowest part of the western isthmus and here he halted and dug in; Caesar moved west from the city and faced him a mile away. Scipio had succeeded in trapping him but in doing so he had himself been manoeuvred into a position in which he had no choice but to fight; for his part Caesar had gambled in forcing the decisive battle he had sought so long. Now it was in the hands of their soldiers.

It was said afterwards that Caesar had an attack of the fainting sickness as his army formed up on the morning of 6th April 46. Certainly he did not exercise his usual tight control, for before the left of his line was ready the Xth Legion on the right advanced without orders. There was little he and his staff could do but attempt to co-ordinate the rest of the line and leave the outcome to his soldiers; they were not to fail him.

The Vth Legion had been specially trained to meet a frontal assault by war elephants; now they channelled them into gaps which they opened in their own ranks and then turned them back on to the Pompeian infantry. Attacked by the Xth Legion and charged by their own elephants Scipio's left broke. His centre and right had already given ground, and now they too broke and fled. Caesar pursued them past the walls of Thapsus to the southern isthmus, but his force there could not hold the flood of defeated Pompeians. Juba and Afranius abandoned their positions and joined the remnants of Scipio's beaten army to the south-west of the lake.

Completely out of their officers' control Caesar's legions took a bloody revenge for all the frustrations of the long winter campaign, slaughtering the Pompeians who were trying to surrender. Afranius was captured and executed. Scipio tried to escape by sea, but he was intercepted by Sittius and only evaded capture by taking his own life. Juba and Petreius got away from the battle, but died by each other's hands in a suicide pact at Zama. Of the other leaders only Sextus, Labienus and Varus escaped from Africa to the Balearics, and from there joined Gnaeus in Spain. Within the week Caesar's cavalry were at Utica, and in despair Cato took his own life.

All Roman Africa was now in Caesar's hands, and he carved out a new province, Nova Africa, from the eastern part of Numidia. Sallust was appointed to govern both African provinces, his immediate tasks to get supplies of oil and corn flowing again to Rome and to extract the heavy reparations in cash and kind imposed on the towns and cities which had supported the Pompeians. Caesar insisted that the two African provinces could, and in future would, supply Rome with an annual quota of 200,000 Attic bushels of grain and three million pounds of olive oil. On 13th June he sailed from Utica, and after delays caused by bad weather and a brief visit to Sardinia he arrived back in Rome on 23rd July.

Gnaeus Pompeius had established himself without much difficulty in Further Spain, largely because of the unpopularity of Caesar's governor, Quintus Cassius. Since Caesar had first appointed him in the autumn of 49 there had been growing unrest in the two provinces caused by his corruption and extortion, which surpassed even his own notorious record as Pompey's quaestor in Further Spain in 52. When in accordance with Caesar's instructions Cassius had prepared to invade Africa in 48 some of his troops mutinied and joined the Roman provincials and Spanish tribes in open rebellion.

Cassius had called on Lepidus and Bogud of Mauretania for assistance. Lepidus had recently taken over Nearer Spain, and together he and Cassius restored the provincial administration in most of Further Spain, though they failed to stamp out the revolt in the extreme west of the province. When Gnaeus arrived in the autumn of 47, followed by his brother Sextus, Labienus and Varus in the spring of 46, they were welcomed by the rebels, Roman and Spanish alike, and soon won control of much of Further Spain. Caesar recalled Cassius and sent Trebonius to replace him; when Cassius sailed for Rome he so overloaded his ship with bullion and treasure extorted from the Spaniards that it foundered at sea and he was drowned. Lepidus meanwhile had returned to Rome to triumph.

With Pompey dead and his followers defeated on every front, Caesar decided that the time had come to celebrate the official end of the civil war. The Pompeians who had escaped to Spain could be treated as rebels and dealt with by Trebonius, supported by an army under command of Quintus Fabius Maximus and Caesar's own kinsman, Quintus Pedius. His Triumphs would celebrate his victories and mark the end of the war; they would also give the people of Rome a public holiday and a spectacle to impress them with his power and authority.

To this end an unprecedented period of forty days was given over to the most lavish public celebrations Rome had ever seen. As well as four separate formal Triumphs to acclaim Caesar's victories in Gaul, Egypt, Asia Minor and Africa, this protracted holiday festival included gladiatorial games, public banquets, athletic contests and wild beast hunts. Prisoners and criminals were used in a series of staged battles fought to the death between infantry, cavalry and specially imported elephants, and part of the Campus Martius was excavated and flooded for a naval battle. Dedication ceremonies were held for Caesar's newly completed Julian Forum and his Temple to Venus Genetrix the patron goddess of the Julian family; in her honour, and incongruously in memory of Caesar's daughter and Pompey's wife the gentle and much loved Julia, four hundred lions and a herd of giraffes specially shipped by Sallust from Africa were slaughtered to make a public show.

During the last ten days of September 46, high summer by the season, the four Triumphs were watched by huge crowds from temporary stands fitted with luxurious silken awnings provided by Caesar to protect them from the sun and impress them with his munificence. He gave every spectator measures of oil and corn, and one hundred denarii in cash, perhaps the equivalent of a year's wages for the poorer classes; afterwards, seated at 22,000 tables, they were served with the best Falernian wine at a huge open air public banquet in the Forum.

To accord with the long standing custom that victories over fellow Romans were never publicly commemorated Caesar's four Triumphs officially celebrated the defeat of foreign enemies in Gaul, Egypt, Pontus and Africa. There was a distinctive motif for each Triumph, with the processional floats and ornaments embellished with four different materials, citrus wood, acanthus, tortoiseshell and ivory.

The Gallic Triumph was the first and most splendid of the four, but near its start the axle of Caesar's own triumphal chariot broke and the superstitious Romans were not slow to note that it happened as he passed the Temple of Fortune. Vercingetorix walked in the procession loaded with chains to mark the conquest of Gaul, and a gilded statue of Ocean, also in chains, symbolised the reaching out of Roman power across the northern seas to Britain. The climax of the Triumph came when in the fading evening light the procession wound its way up to the Capitol lit by flaring torches carried on the backs of elephants; Caesar climbed the steps to the Temple of Jupiter Optimus Maximus on his knees, some said to expiate the ill omens threatened by the breaking of his chariot axle. There he placed his triumphal laurel wreath on the altar of the god, while the gallant Vercingetorix after six years in prison was led away to be publicly strangled.

One float in the Pontic Triumph carried a placard reading 'Veni, Vidi, Vici' to proclaim the victory at Zela, and the crowds laughed and jeered at a picture of Pharnaces fleeing from the battle. They laughed too at effigies of Achillas and Pothinus in the Egyptian procession and marvelled at a model of the Pharos lighthouse. But all was not applause for Caesar: the sight of Cleopatra's younger sister, Arsinoe, shackled in golden chains moved the cruel but sentimental Romans to voice their protest. And in the African Triumph, though the prisoners were led by Juba, the four year old son of the dead king, large pictures showing how Cato, Scipio and Petreius had met their deaths spoiled the non-Roman effect and were received in silence; doubtless they also disturbed the peace of mind of the watching senators who only a month before had been obliged to renew Caesar's term of office as dictator for the unprecedented period of ten years.

As was their custom the legions sung their marching songs, rude and lewd, cynical and sentimental, as such soldier's songs always are; some with bawdy references to Caesar's sexual prowess and his supposed youthful liaison with the king of Bithynia showed scant respect for their general. But instead of his usual amused and indulgent tolerance for his soldiers Caesar displayed impatience and irritation.

Drawing on the State Treasury, which he now controlled, and his own private funds swollen by his victories, Caesar gave every soldier 5,000 denarii; this was three times more than Pompey had given his veterans sixteen years before, and a generous enough bounty when related to their pay, which after Caesar himself had doubled it was now 225 denarii a year. But as always in any army there was a group of soldiers who complained loudly that if the Triumphs had not been staged on so lavish a scale their bounties could have been larger. When this came to Caesar's ears it so enraged him that he ordered the arrest of the most outspoken, and if Dio is to be believed three of them were executed as a sacrifice to Mars.

Already absolute power had begun to erode the normal human restraints of prudence and self-interest and open the door to despotism. Like Alexander before him and others yet to come Caesar planned and ordered a grandiose programme of public building which included a bigger and better theatre, a new complex to house all the law courts called the Basilica Julia, and a huge hall with a portico a mile in circumference designed to hold the entire Assembly of the Roman people.

But the Pompeians put a temporary halt to some of his plans. As happened in Caesar's absence in many of the campaigns of the civil war, his lieutenants had proved no match for the Pompeian generals in Spain. Gnaeus, Sextus and Labienus had raised thirteen legions, largely of Spanish origin, 6,000 cavalry and a similar number of auxiliaries. Trebonius, Quintus Fabius and Pedius had failed to make any headway against them, and once more Caesar had to take the field himself.

In November 46 he set out for the fourth time for Spain. Travelling in the unsprung carriage of the time he covered fifty to sixty miles a day, in itself a feat of endurance for a man in his middle fifties. Seventeen days after leaving Rome he was at Saguntum on the Gulf of Valencia, and less than two weeks later he joined the army which he had ordered to concentrate near Corduba, deep in Pompeian held Further Spain. The army consisted of eight legions and 8,000 cavalry; of the legions, four at least, the IIIrd, Vth, VIth and Xth, were experienced veteran formations.

In its initial stage the campaign developed in much the same way as the middle phase of the war in Africa; the Pompeians had permanent garrisons in the towns where they had collected all available supplies from the surrounding countryside, and Gnaeus with the field army used delaying tactics and refused battle, apparently in the hope that shortage of supplies would weaken Caesar and force him to disperse his army.

But Caesar captured first one town and then another, until on 17th March 45 by the new Julian calendar he outmanoeuvred Gnaeus and forced him to give battle at Munda. Bogud, the client prince of Mauretania, handled Caesar's cavalry with skill, keeping them firmly under control after they had repulsed Labienus's cavalry in the opening stages of the battle, which developed into a long and bitterly contested struggle between the legions. In the end Caesar's veterans won the day, partly because the embattled Pompeian infantry mistook a move by Labienus to counter Bogud's cavalry as the first stage of disengagement prior to withdrawal.

The Pompeians lost 30,000 men, among them Labienus and Varus, and all thirteen legionary eagles. Gnaeus fled to the Pompeian naval base at Carteia, but there he was wounded and then betrayed and killed; his head was displayed at Hispalis so that all Further Spain could see that Pompey's eldest son and heir was dead. When Corduba fell a few days later amidst confusion and further slaughter Sextus managed to make good his escape. Though he did pardon Quintus Ligarius for the second time, Caesar no longer applied his calculated policy of clemency; as he saw it the civil war was already over and won, and in Spain he had put down an armed rebellion led by renegade Romans. As in Africa he exacted punitive fines from the towns which had supported the Pompeians, but he rewarded Balbus's home city of Gades.

The reorganisation of Spain took several months, and it was not until September 45 that he left to return to Italy. Many of the senators and most of the Caesarian leaders travelled to the frontier to meet him; among them was Antony, perhaps prompted by Fulvia, widow of Clodius and Curio, whom he had married, probably during the previous year. Fulvia was a woman of forthright character, with political ambitions which she sought to realise through a husband in a position of authority; according to Plutarch she had already cured Antony of his more extravagant excesses.

Antony, apparently dropped for the past two years, was seen to be restored to favour, and even recognised as Caesar's deputy, when he was accorded the place of honour beside him in the leading carriage, in what soon became a triumphal progress back to Rome. Decimus Brutus rode in the following carriage with Caesar's great-nephew, the eighteen year old Gaius Octavius who had served on the staff, though recurrent illness had prevented him from taking an active part in the campaign. Trebonius also returned from Spain with Caesar; later he was to maintain that on the journey he attempted to sound out the extent of Antony's loyalty to Caesar, and, though he had not responded, neither had he reported his approach.

Plutarch tells a story, which he describes as typical of Antony, of how when they were nearing Rome a rumour spread in the capital that Caesar was dead; disguising himself as a courier Antony rode ahead carrying a letter in his own hand to Fulvia; muffled and cloaked he was admitted unrecognised to his own house and taken to Fulvia, who, alarmed for her husband's life, demanded to know if he was safe; Antony then threw off his cloak and took her in his arms. Though Plutarch cites this as an instance of Antony's love of practical jokes, it could also point to a human need for reassurance.

For the ten months that Caesar had been in Spain the normal business of state had been carried on by Lepidus as Master of Horse and consul, with the aid of eight prefects who ranked as praetors. But Lepidus was little more than a figurehead, and the Senate was reluctant to pass any new laws or take any policy decisions without first discovering Caesar's views and obtaining his approval. It took at least two months to get a reply from Spain, and the inevitable delay in the conduct of public affairs only emphasised Caesar's autocracy, which was made even less palatable by his practice of sending his instructions in private code to Oppius and Balbus who then made his wishes known to the Senate. The measures which Caesar himself had initiated before he left for Spain, particularly social reforms and correction of abuses, went ahead in his absence.

During the civil war he had implemented policies which he had previously decided upon such as the enfranchisement of Cisalpine Gaul, but otherwise his legislation was confined to emergency measures designed to keep Italy quiet while he prosecuted the war. After Thapsus he turned his attention to the future, and the result was a comprehensive programme of administrative and legislative reform and a vast scheme of public works. Among the latter engineering studies were undertaken to improve the port of Ostia and to drain the Fucine Lake and the Pontine marshes: the first two projects were to be completed by his Imperial successors, but the last would wait two millennia to be realised by another dictator and a more advanced technology. A new highway was to be driven across the Apennines to the Adriatic, and a temple to Mars was planned on the site of the artificial lake on the Campus Martius; Varro, now pardoned and restored to academic life, was given the task of assembling the first public library in Rome.

Alterations were made to the criminal law in respect of offences against the State and to provide more effective control over the provincial governors. Legislation was passed in an attempt, largely abortive as such attempts always are, to regulate public morals and restrict private extravagance. To replace some of the human losses in the civil war and to turn the birth rate upwards fathers of large families were rewarded. And the daunting task of codifying the whole body of Roman civil law was begun; it was to be completed nearly six hundred years later under Justinian.

One much needed reform was that of the calendar, by now nearly three months out of phase with the seasons. On the advice of the mathematician and astronomer, Sosigenes, whom Caesar had met in Alexandria, the year 708/46 was lengthened to four hundred and forty five days so that the solar and calendar years coincided on 1st January 45, and a modified version of the Egyptian calendar was then adopted. Sosigenes's calculations were made with such accuracy that the Julian calendar has only required a single fine adjustment under the auspices of Pope Gregory, one of Caesar's successors in the office of Pontifex Maximus.

On his return from Spain in September 45 Caesar spent a few days at his country villa at Lavicum; while he was there he made a new will, which he deposited, as was customary, in the safe keeping of the Vestal Virgins. Though it was known that he had done so his friends considered it a private matter, for to make such a will was no more than a prudent act on the part of a wealthy nobleman who was the head of the Julian family. There was some speculation as to whom he had named to replace Pompey, who as his son-in-law had been the principal heir to his personal fortune which in size now rivalled that of the State Treasury itself.

Occasionally Caesar discussed the possibility of an early death, but at no time according to one of his closest friends, Gaius Matius, did he refer to whom might take his place or how the political vacuum would be filled on his death. The severe headaches and intermittent fainting fits which he suffered from in Gaul seem to have grown more frequent in his last campaigns in Africa and Spain. During these attacks of the fainting sickness, as it was called, he would fall unconscious to the ground and froth at the mouth; if, as has been suggested, he was an epileptic this had no effect on his mental and physical abilities.

Indeed when he arrived in Rome from Lavicum to hold his Spanish Triumph he began an astonishing period of sustained mental activity. It seemed that the six months he had allowed himself before setting out for Parthia were all too short to accomplish all that he wanted to do, all that he knew had to be done, all that he knew that he alone could do. In Spain he had made no secret of the fact that his mind and purpose were set on a final grand campaign in the East; to avenge Carrhae and recover Crassus's lost eagles would settle Rome's account with Parthia, resolve the question of the eastern frontier and set the final seal on his own military reputation. There was also a threat to Macedonia from Dacia which he planned to deal with as a prelude, and a rebellion to be put down in Syria in which Sextus Caesar had been killed by Quintus Caecilius Bassus.

Caesar's main reason for mounting this major expedition against Parthia such a short time after the end of the civil war may simply have been the feeling that, at fifty five, if he was to undertake it, then the sooner he did so the better. During the past fifteen years war and conquest had become a way of life for him which gave full play to his genius and to his talent for finding a triumphant solution through battle. His own careful and detailed arrangements covering the provinces over the next two years, and the time his staff needed to plan and make the preliminary preparations for the campaign, make it certain that the decision to attack Parthia in the summer of 44 must have been taken by September 45 at the latest; it was a calculated one, not made as has been suggested out of sudden disenchantment with the intractable economic problems of Italy and the political intrigues in Rome.

When the news of Munda reached Rome on 20th April a ceremonial thanksgiving procession had been held in which a statue of the absent Caesar had been carried alongside that of the goddess of Victory, making no clear distinction in the estimation of some between the living Caesar and one of the immortal gods. For the Triumph which he staged on his return he took Liberty as the central theme, but this time he made no attempt to conceal that it was the defeat of the sons of Pompey and their Roman officers which was being publicly celebrated; in Caesar's eyes they were no more than rebels, and liberty itself perhaps synonymous with their downfall.

To Cicero, and to what remained of the old senatorial oligarchy, liberty meant the restoration of executive power to the Senate and the elected magistrates of Rome. Cicero had allowed himself to hope that this is what Caesar would do at the end of the civil war, perhaps remaining himself as protector of the State. At the time this was not so insubstantial an expectation as it might later appear, for after Pharsalus the hopes of most of Italy had been pinned on a speedy end to the civil war. With Caesar continuing to use the old Republican forms, the opposition was split into those who stood uncompromisingly with Cato and those who reluctantly accepted Caesar's dictatorship as a necessary prerequisite for ending the war. These hopes faded after Cato's suicide and the eclipse of the Pompeians, but by then the remaining Republicans were already compromised, and they could only hope and pray that Caesar, like Sulla before him, would decide to restore the Republic.

Another source of irritation, voiced in private by Cicero, was the presence in Rome of Cleopatra with her brother Ptolemy XIV and her infant son Caesarion, and Caesar's relations with this foreign queen. She had come to Rome during the winter of 46/45, ostensibly to negotiate a formal treaty with Rome, but also to use her hold over Caesar to ensure that he made no plans to annex Egypt. She may well have hoped that Caesar would publicly accept Caesarion as his son; Cicero certainly assumed that he was the father. But Caesar made no such public acknowledgement, though he lodged Cleopatra openly in his villa at Trastavere across the Tiber and set up a gilded statue of her beside the cult image in the new temple to Venus. During 46 Cicero divorced Terentia and married his rich ward Publilia.

It was perhaps only in the autumn of 45 that the great families who had ruled Rome for so long came to realise that Caesar had no intention of restoring the Republic or resigning his office as dictator. At last it became clear to them that he was merely using the framework of Republican government to consolidate his own autocratic powers, while his patronage and gifts of office were widening the base of his support and weakening his opponents; on the last day of 45 his appointment of Caninius Rebilus as consul for less than a day provided a focus for their grievances and gave rise to bitter and ribald comment.

Wherever they turned the evidence was there before their eyes: statues raised to Caesar, a temple dedicated to his clemency, a cult set up in his honour with his principal lieutenant, Antony, as its priest, all this against a backcloth of public buildings rising on his orders. In every aspect of their daily life they felt the effect of his decrees: they saw the tribunes again bereft of power, the other magistrates his clients and the Sentate his obedient tool.

During 46 and 45 Caesar increased the membership of the Senate to nine hundred, largely by appointing new members from among his friends and supporters, including some from Roman Gaul, all men whom he thought he could rely upon in the Senate and who would help to keep rural Italy and the provinces loyal to him. In Sicily, and in southern Gaul and southern Spain, he speeded up the granting of citizenship to the leading families, thus binding them to him as clients; though Italy was still little more than a name for the peninsula, this extension of Roman citizenship accelerated the process of national identification under the military and political hegemony of Rome. The Gallic Alaudae, now the Vth Legion, were rewarded with a block grant of citizenship, which was also extended to all foreign doctors and teachers in Rome.

To administer the new provinces Caesar increased the number of praetors to sixteen and quaestors to forty; most of the men he appointed owed, and knew they owed, their advancement solely to him. In this reorganisation of the Senate and the magistrates Caesar either overlooked, or deliberately ignored, the discontent it caused amongst the cowed and silenced rump of the old oligarchy. Though they had already lost effective power, until now they had retained the outward trappings of that power and the privileges which went with it. Caesar's wholesale appointment of new senators and other magistrates from obscure provincial families threatened the very structure of Roman political life as they had always known it. It was this threat, and the erosion of their own privilieged status, which made the old guard of the traditional ruling families close its ranks, and it was one of the factors which led to the opposition to Caesar coalescing into a conspiracy against his life.

Caesar's supporters, among them many who had compromised their political principles out of self-interest, could point to Pompey's statues re-erected on Caesar's orders and to the undoubted benefits brought by many of his measures like the reform of the calendar; another such was the halving of the recipients of the corn dole to 150,000, and the forcible resettlement of the hard core of the urban proletariat who had no wish to work in new colonies in Spain and across the Adriatic in Illyricum.

But Caesar's hand indeed lay heavily on Rome for at long last the absolute power, which perhaps at first he had not sought, was his, and he had no mind to let it go. To many of the old aristocracy he was a tyrant, even a despot who threatened liberty and constitutional freedom, though in reality it was only their own power and privilege which were at risk. Herein lay their fundamental weakness and Caesar's strength, for to the great mass of the common people of Rome and Italy he was their benefactor, with an aura of divinity, whose autocracy they found preferable to the rule of the old oligarchy.

Caesar was determined to use his power to carry through all the projects which his brilliant intellect conceived. His clear mind fastened quickly on the essentials of what had to be done and what he wanted to do, and showed him the way to accomplish both. He behaved like a man without enough time, almost as if he saw his own time running out, though this may have arisen from the schedule he had set himself for the Parthian expedition.

In his haste he began to show more openly his contempt for the old Republican forms and his impatience with inferior minds which could not see with his vision. His personal charm and his tact and courtesy which had served him so well began to wear thin, perhaps because he no longer felt the need to exercise them. In his determination to let nothing stand in his way it was but a small step from autocracy to tyranny. But unlike other despots his self-confidence and his contempt for his enemies made him ignore their resentment and discount the possibility that such men might be capable of translating their opposition into action against his person. This belief in himself, in his star and in his destiny, made him something of a fatalist and at the same time convinced him of his own inviolability. In spite of the concern expressed by his friends and supporters he dispensed with his personal bodyguard. Instead he called on the members of the Senate to take a personal oath of loyalty to him, and this he planned to extend to all Roman citizens.

The preparations for the Parthian campaign went ahead for all to see, as much in the appointments of provincial governors for the next two years as in the disposition of the legions, most of which were outside Italy. After holding the consulate as Caesar's colleague for 44 Antony was to take over Macedonia as proconsul; Dolabella was to govern Syria when Bassus had been expelled, though Caesar allowed Antony, as augur, to veto his proposal that Dolabella should become Antony's colleague as consul when he left for the East. When someone suggested to Caesar that Antony and Dolabella might be plotting against him he remarked 'It's not these well fed long-haired fellows I fear, but the lean and hungry ones.'.

Under a plebiscite proposed by Antony's brother, Lucius, as tribune, Caesar was constitutionally empowered to nominate the consuls for the following two years. He selected Hirtius and Gaius Vibius Pansa for 43, and Decimus Brutus and Lucius Munatius Plancus for 42; in the meantime Decimus would govern the Cisalpina and Plancus the remainder of Gaul. At some point in 44 Lepidus would hand over to Domitius Calvinus as Master of Horse and take over command in southern Gaul and Nearer Spain. Pollio would govern Further Spain, Titus Sextius would take over from Sallust in Africa, and Vatinius would continue operations against the tribes in Illyricum during 44; in the East Trebonius would govern Asia from mid 44, and Lucius Tillius Cimber Bithynia.

These comprehensive forward arrangements ensured that while Caesar undertook the Parthian expedition lieutenants whom he trusted would hold the whole ring of Roman provinces from Africa, through Spain and Gaul, across the Adriatic to Macedonia, and beyond the Hellespont to Asia Minor and Syria. He allotted a total of sixteen legions to these legates and retained another sixteen and 10,000 cavalry and archers for his field army. With the three legions supporting Cleopatra in Egypt this made a total of thirty five legions; during the winter of 45/44 their pay and maintenance and the provision of a war chest for Parthia proved a heavy drain on the Roman Treasury.

It was Caesar's practice to raise new legions rather than bring the old ones up to strength with drafts of recruits, though he had reinforced the VIth for the Munda campaign. Between 47 and 45 nine veteran legions, the VIth to the XIVth, were disbanded and their soldiers resettled with gratuities and lands grants. The XIth and XIIth which did not take part in the African campaign were given land in Italy, as were the VIIth and VIIIth for whom colonies were founded in Campania. Several new colonies were set up in Africa, and after Munda two legions were given generous land grants in southern Gaul, the Xth at Narbo and the VIth near Arelate. New veteran colonies were also established at Corinth, at Sinope on the northern coast of Asia Minor, and in Spain and Illyricum. All these would help to keep Italy and the provinces loyal to their patron.

It was in the late autumn or early winter of 45 when Gaius Cassius found himself only designated as rural praetor for 44, and so passed over for provincial governorship or command in the field army despite his previous experience in Parthia as Crassus's quaestor, that the conspiracy against Caesar began to take shape. His pride slighted and his ambition thwarted Cassius began to sound out others, who for one reason or another were opposed to Caesar.

He found many ready to listen, some aggrieved like him because Caesar's favours had passed them by, and others like Decimus Brutus among the trusted lieutenants who owed their advancement to Caesar. The evidence of Caesar's cults and statues and his exercise of patronage was there before their eyes, and it was easy to read into them regal or even divine aspirations. This in itself was bad enough, but a dictator absent in the East meant a repetition of the period after Pharsalus with indirect rule through men such as Antony and Lepidus, and Balbus and Oppius again conveying to the Senate what they alleged were Caesar's instructions, as they had during the Munda campaign. And who could tell how long this might last, or indeed whether Caesar intended to return to Rome at all, for there were rumours that he had designs to move the capital to a rebuilt Ilium or found a new dynasty with Cleopatra in Alexandria. There is no evidence at all that Caesar had any such plans, but these stories played insidiously on abiding Roman fears of the East. It was but a short step to suggest that the only certain way to restrain Caesar and restore the Republic was to strike him down before he left for Parthia.

Thus Cassius set himself a target in time. His thoughts turned to his brother-in-law, Marcus Brutus, as the man who could head the conspiracy and give it respectability. After pardoning Brutus at Pharsalus Caesar had appointed him to Cisalpine Gaul in 46 and he had proved an able and honest governor. This enhanced his reputation as a man of principle, serious minded and independent in outlook; his piety and concern for the ancient traditions of his family were well known, and he had given ample proof of his disinterested devotion to Rome and the ideals of the Republic when he had joined Pompey.

Brutus had recently divorced his wife, and during 45 he married Cato's daughter, Porcia, widow of Bibulus who had died worn out by his efforts to close the Adriatic to Caesar in 48. Thus his loyalties were divided, for his mother, Servilia, as well as being Cato's sister, was Caesar's old friend and one-time mistress; at least until the late summer of 45 he remained loyal to Caesar. But Cassius was not slow to remind him of the history of his family in the service of the Republic, and in particular to point to the Junius Brutus who had expelled the last of the seven kings and was revered as one of the founders of the Republic. The statue of that Brutus now stood on the

Capitol with those of the seven kings and recently Caesar's had been placed beside them; the inference was obvious even without the graffiti which began to appear calling on Brutus, and which may have been a factor in winning him over and so giving the conspirators both a figurehead and a leader. Soon there were sixty of them; the names of twenty are known, no less than nine of whom Caesar had pardoned after they had fought for Pompey; of the others seven were committed Caesarians, among them Trebonius, Tillius Cimber and Decimus Brutus.

From January 44 events themselves and Caesar's own acts served to emphasise the fears of the conspirators and to endorse their purpose and harden their resolve. Two of the tribunes made a show of removing diadems placed on Caesar's statues either by his supporters or his enemies. Then they arrested spectators who raised the cry of Rex as Caesar passed; though he replied 'I am not Rex, but Caesar', he saw to it that the two tribunes were removed from office and struck off the Senate's rolls for their pains. Coins were struck and came into circulation early in 44 bearing Caesar's head; this was a radical departure from the time-honoured Republican custom of never depicting the heads of living men on coins and could readily be represented as evidence of regal ambitions.

On 14th February the Senate changed Caesar's ten year tenure of office as dictator to appointment for life by making him 'Dictator Perpetuo'; further honours were lavished on him, among them the title of 'Father of the Country', the renaming of the month Quintilis July, and the grant of a tribune's personal inviolability. All these were engraved on silver tablets, and the whole Senate led by Antony as consul carried them in solemn procession to lay them in the temple on the Capitol. As they passed through the Forum Caesar was sitting there at work on the plans for his Julian Basilica, and when the senators approached to show him the tablets he did not rise but received them seated. This was widely interpreted, not only as evidence of his contempt for the Senate which many shared, but also as a deliberate slight on the people of Rome; the fact that no less than six of the ancient sources mention this incident, some of them excusing Caesar's discourtesy in various ways, is evidence of the effect it had.

During the fertility rites at the ancient festival of the Lupercalia in February Antony offered Caesar a ritual crown in mime, and perhaps in jest, though Cassius and Casca went down on their knees to press him to accept. It is possible that Caesar had prearranged this with Antony to demonstrate his refusal in public and put an end to growing rumours that he wished to be king. If this was so Cassius and Casca may well have intervened to provoke Caesar into accepting, though it does not explain why Lepidus openly wept.

Someone discovered an obscure extract in the Roman version of the Sibylline Books which was interpreted as prophesying that Parthia would only be defeated if Rome was led by a king. Again the motives for circulating this story are not clear, but it forced Caesar, concerned for the morale of his superstitious soldiers, to compromise by saying that he would only be a king in the East. There is little real evidence that Caesar wished to become king in Rome, and none at all that he sought to set up a hereditary monarchy.

Equally nothing in the primary sources indicates that he believed himself especially favoured of the gods, let alone one of their immortal company. In the East the dividing line between human and divine was blurred in the persons of the rulers and some of the Roman proconsuls, but as yet this was not so in Rome. In 46 someone, whether friend or enemy, had scratched 'Divus Est' on the base of one of Caesar's statues and he had ordered it to be removed; a graffiti reading 'To the Unconquered God' now appeared on his statue in the Quirinus temple of the deified Romulus. Caesar certainly believed in his star and his destiny, but it was his contemporaries and his murderers who formally deified him immediately after his death, thus setting the pattern of divinity for those who came after him.

But whether he was called god, king or perpetual dictator mattered little to the conspirators. They were determined to strike before he left for the East and another period of rule by proxy began, before he had time to dismantle what remained of the framework of Republican government. Cicero himself still knew nothing of the plot for the conspirators were well aware that they could not trust his tongue.

The fears of the sixty men, united in their purpose through fear of each other, fear of betrayal, and even fear of the consequences of calling off their enterprise, gave the conspiracy a momentum of its own as the days moved on to the last practicable moment, the morning of the Ides of March, when Caesar would attend the Senate before leaving for Parthia two days later. Despite their constant fear of discovery they could not steel themselves to advance their plans before this last possible hour, and so completely did the conspiracy absorb them that they could not force their minds beyond the deed itself to what would follow when the tyrant was slain.

On that morning of 15th March 44, in spite of all alarms and prophecies, Caesar was escorted to Pompey's theatre where the Senate awaited him. At the door Trebonius, and perhaps Decimus Brutus, detained Antony in conversation, for even at these odds the conspirators feared his courage and his physical strength.

After Caesar had impatiently rejected his plea on behalf of his exiled brother Cimber pulled at his toga, and as he did so Casca struck the first blow with his dagger, closely followed by Cassius. Unarmed, Caesar tried to defend himself from the encircling daggers with his stylus. Then, realising that there was no escape, he covered his face with his toga, shutting out the contorted faces of the conspirators as they pressed round him, each trying to strike the blow which each had sworn to strike; he fell dying at the base of Pompey's statue.

PART 2

Consul and Triumvir

CHAPTER VI

Consul in Rome

Of all the senators who were not privy to the plot only two, Lucius Marcius Censorinus and Gaius Calvisius Sabinus, moved to Caesar's aid. As the conspirators milled around him the rest of the senators stared amazed, frozen in their disbelief. Then as they saw him fall and realised that what they saw was actually happening their instinctive reaction was to get out of the building as fast as they could. In the confusion it was hard to tell who all the conspirators were, let alone who else they planned to kill; fear turned to panic as the senators jostled and fought to get through the doors and away to safety.

Brutus had planned to ask the Senate to give its formal approval to the slaying of the tyrant and the annullment of all his acts and then to dispose of the body by throwing it without ceremony into the Tiber, as was the practice for common criminals. But the panicking senators, appalled at what they had witnessed and spurred on by the fear of a sudden dagger thrust in their own backs, were in no mood to stop and listen to Brutus or anyone else. Decimus's gladiators, stationed outside the theatre to protect the Senate from any spontaneous retaliation by the urban mob, would have been better deployed to hold the doors and keep the senators inside.

Antony was still outside with Trebonius. As soon as he realised what had happened he hurried off through back streets to his home, discarding his consular insignia as he went. He ordered his household staff to barricade the doors and windows and prepare for an attack.

Waving their bloodied daggers the conspirators ran through the Forum, calling on Cicero's name and shouting that they had struck for Liberty, and so on up to the Capitol. On the way they were joined by others, who, as Appian aptly comments, 'had not shared the deed, but wanted the glory, and were to find, not glory, but death with the guilty'. Prominent among them were Dolabella and others like him who owed their advancement to Caesar.

The sight of the terror-stricken senators running wildly through the streets brought alarm and consternation to all who saw them, and in their turn they hurried to put up the shutters on their shops and bolt the doors of their houses behind them. As the news of Caesar's assassination spread rapidly through the city, embroidered by every kind of rumour, the streets emptied and a hush fell on Rome.

Lepidus happened to be in the Forum as the senators came running from Pompey's Theatre on the Campus Martius, and he made his way as quickly as he could to the island in the Tiber where his single legion, the only troops in Rome, was encamped; from there he sent a message to Antony placing himself and his soldiers at the consul's disposal.

In the empty stillness of the Curia Caesar's body lay where it had fallen at the foot of Pompey's statue. After a time three of his household slaves stole quietly in, laid the body in a litter with one arm hanging down over the side and carried it awkwardly, as three men must a litter, along the streets he had walked that morning, busy then with noisy crowds but now deserted, and so back to his house and the waiting Calpurnia.

For a time silence lay like a threat on the stilled heart of Rome. But there were no further alarms, no tramp of marching soldiers, no more men running through the streets, and people ventured out in ones and twos and gathered in small groups on the street corners. Then they began to drift towards the centre of the city, anxious to find out what had happened and what was going to happen, and soon a crowd had assembled in the Forum.

Dolabella addressed them: he began by announcing that he had assumed the office of consul which he claimed was to have been his when Caesar left for Parthia; then he went on to make a violent attack on the dead Caesar. They heard him out, though without much enthusiasm, and then a section of the crowd, whose support had perhaps been bought by the conspirators, began to call for Brutus and Cassius to come down and speak to them.

On the Capitol the self-styled liberators had no coherent plan. Brutus had failed to hold the Senate and obtain its sanction for the killing of Caesar and the annullment of all his acts and measures; other than this they had not planned beyond the deed itself. Caesar had loomed so large over Rome, and the hazard of their enterprise had appeared so great, that it had seemed to them if only they could kill him the Republic would be of itself restored and everything would fall back in its old accustomed place. Even their rush through the Fr to the Capitol had been unpremeditated, perhaps the result of a subconscious wish to seek the approval of Jupiter himself in place of endorsement by their peers in the Senate.

In response to the crowd some of the senators went up to the Capitol and escorted Brutus and Cassius down to the Forum. When Brutus mounted the rostra the crowd listened quietly as in the language of an intellectual and the accent of a Roman aristocrat he expounded his abstract theme of liberation and the restoration of the

Republic. Among the leaders of the conspiracy he was perhaps the only one whose conscious motives were altruistic, based as they were on what he believed to be the ideal of liberty under the Republic, but which in effect was no more than liberty and privilege for the hereditary ruling class. What he said, and his manner of saying it, struck no chord and brought him no rapport with the crowd. The terms he used were unfamiliar, and what he was trying to say meant nothing at all to those who heard him; for what was this cry of Liberty, when to them Caesar had been not a tyrant but their leader and all they felt was a dull anger and an uncomprehending sense of personal loss. In respect for Brutus they heard him out in silence; for his part he failed to sense their mood or their feelings.

When Lucius Cornelius Cinna took Brutus's place on the rostra and at once launched into a bitter attack on Caesar and all his works this was something the crowd could better understand, and they soon made it clear that they did not like what they heard. At first they were merely restive, but soon they began to heckle him, and finally they became so incensed and threatening that all the conspirators cravenly withdrew back to the safety of the Capitol.

They had not planned a coup, in fact they had no plan at all, but with this retreat their second opportunity to control events was gone. Cicero at least saw this clearly enough and overcoming the slight to his self-esteem caused by their failure to make him a party to their plot he went up to the Capitol. There he urged them to call an immediate emergency meeting of the Senate and at it to announce that they would take the lead in restoring the Republic. But, in spite of his pleading, fear of Antony and Lepidus's troops lost them this third chance to assert their authority. It was to be their last, for discounting Cicero's advice they sent envoys to Antony asking him to help them prevent disorder in the city, thus confessing their lack of purpose and surrendering the initiative to him as consul.

Expecting an assault at any moment on his barricaded house, Antony had thought his escape from the assassins' daggers due to some lucky chance and no more than a temporary respite; he had good reason, for Cicero soon made it clear that had he been consulted Antony would have died with Caesar, whatever Brutus might have said. This had been advocated by Cassius and some of the conspirators with a more practical turn of mind, but Brutus had insisted that only Caesar should die. He had done so not because of his personal friendship with Antony, for he was a man always prepared to sacrifice a friend for a principle which he held dear; indeed it was this trait in Brutus which to his contemporaries spelt true nobility of spirit. Rather he had argued that to kill Antony or any of

99

Caesar's supporters would invalidate their claim to be tyrannicides; since Caesar was the tyrant, to kill him, and him alone, would achieve their end.

When Antony received Lepidus's message and then the envoys from Caesar's murderers he acted quickly. He told Lepidus to move his legion to the Campus Martius, where it could be seen and from whence it could be rapidly deployed in the centre of Rome. He ordered the city magistrates to have the streets patrolled, and he sent instructions to Balbus, Caesar's agent and the city prefect, and to Hirtius, another Caesarian and one of the consuls designate for 43.

Though the city was quiet that night, it was an uneasy quiet. Friends and relatives of the conspirators hurried from house to house trying to raise support among the other senators, many of whom, though sympathetic, were reluctant to commit themselves. Decimus returned to his house escorted by his gladiators, but the rest of the conspirators spent the night on the Capitol. As the realisation of how few they were and how little support they commanded spread through the city the fears of the people lessened and their anger at Caesar's murder grew.

On the morning of the 16th Lepidus seized the Temple of Ops, which housed part of the State Treasury, and moved detachments of his legion into the Forum prior to an assault on the Capitol. But Antony, with the ultimate responsibility now his as surviving consul, feared that the use of troops to storm the Capitol and kill Caesar's murderers, among them many of the leading men in Rome, would antagonise the uncommitted senators and precipitate further violence with the risk of civil war; with Hirtius's backing he restrained Lepidus.

Instead he summoned the Senate to meet on the following day at the Temple of Tellus on the Esquiline, conveniently close to his own house in the Carinae which once had been Pompey's. Meanwhile he conferred with Calpurnia, and no doubt with her father, Piso. During the day the conspirators remained immured on the Capitol, afraid either to venture down into the Forum or go back to their houses. As the shops reopened and normal life began to return to the streets the leaders of the urban mob started to swing opinion against Caesar's murderers; those who secretly sympathised with them kept their own counsel and the safety of their homes.

Antony was in a difficult position as consul and a potentially dangerous one as the principal Caesarian. He could count on Lepidus and his legion and on the backing of Caesar's veterans, many of whom were in Rome, and probably also on the street gangs, always provided that he could control Dolabella. But he knew that many of the Optimates, among them most of the more experienced and influential senators, sympathised with the conspirators. Of the rest of the citizens of Rome, the middle classes and the great mass of the common people, he could not be certain, and in any dispute with the Senate and the Optimates their support might prove vital.

So Antony bided his time. He handled the meeting of the Senate on 17th March with tact, moderation and considerable skill. In spite of their own personal differences he recognised Dolabella as his consular colleague. He ensured a full hearing for every senator who wished to speak, allowing them to express the whole gamut of views, ranging from special honours for the tyrannicides and liberators and annullment of all Caesar's acts, proposed by the staunch Republican, Tiberius Nero, to forthright and unequivocal condemnation of the assassins who had murdered Caesar. He adroitly turned aside the motion to annul all Caesar's acts, pointing out that to do so would not only cause administrative chaos but would also deprive most of the senators of their present offices and their future appointments.

This reminder of their own interests coupled with the unseen but real threat of Lepidus's troops, discreetly concealed not far away, made many of the less extreme think again. After Cicero and Lucius Munatius Plancus had advocated moderation a decree was passed offering the conspirators an amnesty but at the same time confirming all Caesar's acts and measures. This practical Roman compromise, based as it was on pragmatism and self-interest, was inconsequently followed by a unanimous vote that the dead Caesar should in future be worshipped as a god. Then from all sides of a relieved Senate came a vote of thanks to Antony, congratulating him, in the words of the formal motion, on the prudent and statesmanlike manner in which he had resolved a most difficult, dangerous and confused situation. Outside the waiting crowd cheered him, when, as was the custom for the consul, he announced the decisions the Senate had taken.

He had found himself suddenly thrust to the centre of affairs for the first time and in a crisis of the gravest kind, and the senators were clearly surprised and impressed by the way he had handled the meeting. To them and to his own supporters, and perhaps to himself, this was a new and unsuspected Antony. Some of them, recalling his reputation and his open careless nature, made the mistake of thinking him incapable of dissembling his feelings and intentions and assumed that he meant precisely what he said, when in fact he was feeling his way, trying to reassure the confused Senate and consolidate his own authority as consul and at the same time widen the base of his support beyond that of Caesar's veterans and committed followers.

After the meeting he sent a message to the conspirators telling them that they had nothing to fear and inviting them to come down from the

Capitol. But they distrusted him, and they feared that Lepidus, although his soldiers had already rescued Cinna from an angry mob, might use his legion in a bid to put himself in Caesar's place. A letter Decimus wrote from his house, probably on the morning of the 17th, to Brutus and Cassius on the Capitol reveals his concern at the conspirators' disarray. In the end, to show their good faith, Antony and Lepidus had to send their sons, the infant Marcus Antonius, later to be nicknamed Anyllus by the Alexandrians, and the young Marcus Lepidus, up to the Capitol as hostages before the conspirators dared to come down. A public reconciliation was staged in the Forum, and that evening Cassius dined with Antony and Brutus with his brother-in-law, Lepidus.

The Senate met again the next morning, this time with the conspirators present. First there was another spontaneous and unanimous vote of thanks to Antony for averting civil war; then they passed a motion commending Brutus, Cassius and the other tyrannicides and liberators. After this they turned to more practical matters, confirming Caesar's provisional arrangements for the provinces, Asia to Trebonius, Bithynia to Cimber and Cisalpine Gaul to Decimus; according to Plutarch, they also gave Crete to Brutus and Africa to Cassius. There were two legions in the Cisalpina, and Caesar's legate, Sextius, held Africa Nova with three, and though Antony did not openly demur he must have viewed this allotment of provinces to the conspirators with misgiving, if only as a potential threat to himself at the end of his year as consul. The allotment of the consular provinces, Macedonia to Antony and Syria to Dolabella, again followed Caesar's plans and was endorsed by the Senate some two weeks later; there were six legions in each province and this redressed the military balance.

Next on the agenda was Caesar's will and the arrangements for his funeral. There was wide support for Cassius when he argued that the reading of the will and the funeral itself should be held in private. Cassius was a realist and he knew well enough, as Atticus was to comment to Cicero, that if Caesar were given a public funeral their cause could well be lost. But Antony, and Piso as Caesar's father-in-law, were adamant that the will should be read in public and Caesar accorded the State funeral customary for a consul who died in office. Cassius continued to object, but to his dismay Brutus gave way and agreed to both being held in public.

While Caesar was alive his will in the safe keeping of the Vestal Virgins was sacrosanct, but it seems likely that both Piso and Antony knew the contents before the formal reading in Antony's house, and perhaps even before the debate in the Senate. On the sole evidence of remarks by Cicero in the 2nd and 3rd Philippics, where he made use of any and every means to vilify Antony, it has been widely supposed that as Caesar's deputy Antony had expected to be named as his principal heir. This is to mistake both the context of the time and the nature of the will itself, which was a private testament properly drawn in the traditional manner and such as any wealthy Roman noble might make. It was not a political document covering the succession, for Caesar never looked on himself as the founder of a hereditary dynasty. The confusion arose at the time, and arises now, partly because, as dictator, Caesar was so powerful that no will of his could in effect be wholly private, and partly because of the significance which Octavian succeeded in attaching to his adoption into Caesar's branch of the Julian family. It is in no sense to belittle Cicero's literary genius or the debt Western civilization owes him to recognise that, in the Senate and elsewhere, he did not scruple to use his rhetorical talent to pervert the truth in discrediting his enemies, justifying his own failures and hiding his political inadequacy.

In his will Caesar named his sister's grandson, Gaius Octavius, son of his niece Atia, as heir to three quarters of his estate, unless in the meantime Calpurnia had borne him a son, and he expressed the wish, not unusual in the circumstances, that as his heir Octavius should be adopted into his own branch of the Julian family and take the name of Caesar. The remaining quarter of his estate he left jointly to his nephew, Quintus Pedius, and another great-nephew, Lucius Pinarius Scarpus; Antony and Decimus were named as secondary or alternate heirs, an appointment which carried some of the duties of executors and with a number of others, including some of his murderers, they were made trustees and guardians of any infant male heir. From his will it is evident Caesar had still hoped that Calpurnia might bear him a son; it was some of the detailed provisions designed to cover this event which Octavian took out of their intended context to substantiate his claim to be Caesar's son as well as heir to his name.

Caesar left his gardens by the Tiber to the people of Rome and three hundred sesterces to every citizen. As this news spread through the city grief at his death and anger with his murderers mounted. Thus it was in an already highly charged emotional atmosphere that the funeral procession entered the Forum for the oration, before proceeding to the Campus Martius where a cremation pyre had been built beside the tomb of his daughter, Julia.

Caesar's principal heir, and other than Pedius his nearest male relative, the eighteen year old Gaius Octavius was on the other side of the Adriatic at Apollonia, where he was continuing his studies and military training while waiting to accompany Caesar on the Parthian campaign, and it fell to Antony to deliver the funeral speech from the new rostra which Caesar had built. In front of it Caesar's supporters had set up a gilded shrine modelled on his Temple to Venus, the patron goddess of the Julian family; in it they had placed an ivory couch on which they had laid his torn and bloodstained toga. The cortege halted in front of the rostra and the bier was set down beside this shrine.

Though the four main secondary sources differ in their accounts, all agree that Antony made the funeral oration; Cicero, the only primary source, bears this out in two passing references. Antony apparently instructed heralds to recite the customary preliminaries, the account of Caesar's life, his victorious campaigns, the battles he had won, the lands he had conquered, the booty he had brought back to swell the Roman Treasury and the honours a grateful Senate had given him. He may have used the heralds to heighten the effect, or perhaps to avoid appearing too partisan himself after the amnesty and his reconciliation with the conspirators. But whatever the reason, he had planned the ceremony with skill and care, and now he made sure that it was dominated by the dead Caesar.

As a prelude to the funeral speech itself the heralds recited the personal oath of loyalty which all the senators, among them most of his murderers, had sworn to Caesar. This repetition of the form and words of the oath could so easily have been omitted that its inclusion can only have been a calculated act on Antony's part, and perhaps indicated his feelings, if not his purpose.

All the while the tattered toga lay in silent reproach on the couch before the rostra, and by the time Antony began to speak the crowd was filled with compassion for Caesar and anger with his assassins; there can be little doubt that he sensed their mood. According to Plutarch, on whose biography of Antony Shakespeare based his famous funeral speech, he struck a note of pity for Caesar and indignation at his fate. This is borne out by Cicero's sarcastic tirade in the 2nd Philippic, written in October 44: 'You treacherously officiated at the funeral of the tyrant, if funeral it can be called; yours was that handsome eulogy; yours the pity, yours the incitement; you, I repeat you, lit the fires . . .' However he makes no mention of this in a letter written in April 44 containing a brief reference to the funeral.

Whether carried away by his own words and the frenzy of the crowd, or perhaps with deliberate intent, when Antony came to the end of his speech he held up Caesar's torn and bloody toga and cried out that the conspirators were no more than murderers and common criminals. As the crowd shouted for the blood of the assassins, unseen hands, probably those of the professional mourners, raised high for all to see a wax image of Caesar on which every one of his twenty three stab wounds had been faithfully reproduced; someone in the crowd called out a line from Pacuvius, 'Pardoned I these men that they should murder me?'. This was a familiar as well as an apt quotation and the anonymous voice may have quoted it spontaneously, but the production of the wax image can only have been prearranged.

A brief debate as to where the cremation should take place was cut short by someone setting fire to the bier where it rested before the rostra, on the spot where later the Temple to the Divine Julius would be built. The crowd piled benches and market stalls on the improvised pyre, the mourners threw on their triumphal robes, the veterans their weapons, the women their jewellery, and the Jews of Rome, specially favoured by Caesar, added their wailing laments.

Some of the crowd snatched up flaming brands and ran to fire the homes of the assassins while others went to search them out in person, but they had hidden themselves too well. The only casualty was Gaius Helvius Cinna, the poet, who had come as a personal friend to honour Caesar; the mob mistook him for Cinna the praetor, one of the assassins, and tore him limb from limb in the street. One house belonging to Lucius Bellienus, a Pompeian senator, was burned to the ground, and it was with some difficulty that Antony and the city magistrates managed to prevent a general conflagration in which the whole of Rome would have burned as Caesar's pyre.

Antony's conduct of the funeral strengthened his hand as consul, and by the following morning he was in undisputed control of Rome. The conspirators remained divided among themselves, united only in their fear of a repetition of the mob violence which the day before had erupted against them and their property. By now Antony knew that he had the backing of the majority of the people of Rome as well as that of the veterans and the Caesarians. He could rely on the army in Italy, and he tried to ensure Lepidus's continued support by securing him the coveted office of Pontifex Maximus made vacant by Caesar's death, using a legal device to do so which Cicero at once declared unconstitutional.

In the Senate where he was weakest and his authority rested only on his office as consul and his ability to carry the members with him and so control the proceedings, Antony continued to handle affairs with skill and with unexpected tact and moderation. He was punctilious in consulting the inner circle of consulars on every aspect of all the business which he put before the Senate. His proposal to abolish the office of dictator was acclaimed with enthusiasm and passed unanimously, though it is not clear whether in fact it did remove provision for such office from the constitution or merely made it illegal for anyone to arrogate it to himself as Caesar had done. Whichever the case, it was an astute move on Antony's part for it cost him nothing and served to widen his support among the moderate senators.

Without demur Calpurnia had handed over all the State papers to Antony as Caesar's deputy, together with the greater part of the money in the house at the time of his death, amounting, according to Plutarch, to 4,000 talents; it was probably impracticable, if not impossible, to separate his private funds from the public monies, for Caesar had made no such distinction. The Senate had already endorsed all his acts and measures, and with the State papers in his hands and the co-operation of Caesar's secretary, Faberius, Antony had the initiative and he used it to good effect. He could lend Caesar's authority to every proposal and when the papers required amendment to meet a change in circumstances or to suit his own purpose this could readily be arranged, though during the first few weeks he did so sparingly enough to avoid challenge.

Since his return from Cilicia Cicero had taken little active part in politics, but it is surprising that in the period following Caesar's death he did not once attend the Senate after 17th March, despite his later claim that he never deserted his post at this time of danger. With opinion hardening against Caesar's murderers and isolating them from public affairs the Optimates were without a leader. Brutus had gravely miscalculated in assuming that the death of the tyrant would of itself allow his killers to participate in the return to Republican government. They had succeeded in turning the clock back five years in that power no longer lay in the hands of one man, but the conditions which had made the rise of one man to absolute power inevitable remained unchanged; the old oligarchy had once more shown itself incapable of ruling Rome, let alone of amending the constitution of a city state to enable it to rule an empire. Had it not been for the army there might have been one more chance of making the old system work, given a change of heart and purpose on the part of the Optimates. But here again Brutus and Cassius had miscalculated, here the clock could not be turned back; the process begun by Marius and perfected by Caesar, whereby the legions gave their loyalty to their generals and not to the Senate or the Republic, could not be reversed.

It was clear, both to the moderates in the Senate and to Rome's powerful commercial interests, that with Caesar's death control of the new provinces and the client states could only too easily be lost. That there was no widespread revolt is a tribute both to the Caesarian governors, who held down vast territories with minimal forces and no civil administrative service, and to the real benefits of Roman law and order. But Gaul remained far from pacified, in Syria the Pompeian, Caecilius Bassus, besieged in Apamea by Staius Murcus and Marcius Crispus, was making overtures to Parthia, and in Spain Sextus Pompeius had raised six legions against the Caesarian legates. It was essential that Rome should present a united front to her subject territories; to the majority in Rome the consensus policy which Antony was pursuing seemed the best way to achieve this end.

As for the liberators, feeling ran so strongly against them that they were all but prisoners in their own houses for fear of the urban mob and Caesar's veterans, and this in spite of the fact that Brutus and Cassius held office as praetors. Early in April Trebonius left the city and set off on the long journey to take up his appointment as governor of Asia, and at about the same time Decimus slipped quietly away to his province of Cisalpine Gaul. Cleopatra also left Rome shortly after Caesar's death and returned to Egypt with Caesarion and her young brother and co-ruler, Ptolemy.

Brutus and Cassius decided that it would be prudent to absent themselves in the hope that the outcry against them would die down. In the normal course of events Brutus, as urban praetor, was not allowed to leave the city for more than ten days at a time; in an interview with Antony he asked leave to be absent for longer than this and Antony was no doubt happy to be relieved of his presence in Rome. Between the 9th and 13th of April Brutus and Cassius both left for Antium where they waited in the hope of better news from Rome. Brutus still planned to preside at the July games in honour of Apollo, which it was his responsibility to finance and supervise as urban praetor; threats by Caesar's veterans against his life if he tried to return were to some extent offset by reports reaching Antium that the Senate was taking action against the ringleaders of the mob which had attacked the houses of the conspirators.

These reports may have stemmed from Antony's steps to maintain law and order. While the leaders of the conspiracy were still in Rome he had turned a blind eye to the more extravagant excesses of the mob, which at least served to check any move by the conspirators to rectify their failure to kill him, a mistake some of them made clear they regretted. But when the four principals all left Rome during the first two weeks of April, apparently as the result of a joint decision, Antony took action against the ringleaders of the mob. He arrested some of them and executed a certain Amatius, a Greek horse-doctor who had passed himself off as a descendant of Marius and thus a kinsman of Caesar's and had started a cult to honour him, setting up an altar and a column on the spot in the Forum where he had been cremated. In the Senate Antony acted with caution, presenting each proposal as implementing Caesar's plans and continuing to consult the consulars on every detail; even the absent Cicero gave his grudging approval.

Except for Spain and Syria the Roman world outside Italy remained quiet. It took a week for the news of Caesar's death to reach the German tribes beyond the Rhine, and a week later it was known in Rome that they had sent envoys to Aurelius, the commander on the Rhine, pledging their obedience to his instructions. But it was still too early to expect reports from Asia Minor on how the client rulers were reacting; Publius Servilius Isauricus, who had governed Asia for Caesar since 46, was himself due to return to Rome during the summer. In mid-April Lepidus left to take over his provinces of Nearer Spain and Narbonese Gaul, the latter so named from the capital Narbo and now including all southern Gaul from the Pyrenees to the Alps and often simply referred to as the Province. He carried instructions from Antony to open negotiations with Sextus when opportunity offered; in another attempt to ensure his loyalty Antony had betrothed his daughter, Antonia, to Lepidus's son, Marcus. Pollio already held Further Spain, and during the summer Plancus, who with Decimus was consul designate for 42, took over as his province the rest of Gaul, the part which Caesar had conquered and was known as Gallia Comata, long-haired Gaul, or merely Transalpine Gaul to distinguish it from Lepidus's province of Narbonese or Old Gaul.

It seems unlikely that at this time Lepidus contemplated a bid for supreme power on his own account, as some alleged; though he was a man whose conceit far outran his ability his attempt at such a coup would come later. And there is no evidence that Antony had any such aspirations, although from all that is known of Fulvia she had ambition enough for two. As the leading Caesarian general Antony could rely on the army, and as consul he had shown statesmanlike qualities and unsuspected political skill which had put him comfortably in control of Rome. But he lacked Caesar's belief in himself and his destiny, and above all his certainty of purpose, his conviction that only he had the will and the ability to accomplish what only he could see must be done.

With Caesar's death many of his veterans who were in Rome awaiting resettlement had feared, not without reason, that the Senate would try to find some excuse to cancel their land grants. Now that the political situation had almost returned to normal Antony determined to reap the credit for allaying these fears and at the same time consolidate his support in the army by officiating at the founding ceremony for a new veteran colony in Campania. Probably during the third week in April he left Rome for Casilinum where he presided at the foundation of the new colony, which he named Julia Antonia.

Denarii struck in Rome during the summer or autumn of 44 bear Antony's head on the obverse, bearded and veiled in mourning for Caesar. This was only the second regular issue of Roman coins to bear the head of a living man; coins bearing Pompey's head were struck after his death by his son. It was a calculated act of policy on Antony's part, but other than to emphasise his loyalty to Caesar widely and in a lasting manner his motives are obscure. He had shown skill and judgement in using his consular authority and the force of his own personality to hold the balance between the Optimates and the Caesarians; so far he had made no move to avenge Caesar, nor since his speech at the funeral had he attacked the conspirators openly.

But the factor which he and everyone else had failed to take into account was how the eighteen year old Octavius would react to his unexpected inheritance. The first news of the assassination came to him in a letter from his mother, Atia, written in haste on the same day; she told him the bare facts of Caesar's death with no hint of the contents of the will, of which she probably knew nothing, advised caution and urged him to come back to Italy as soon as he could.

Octavius discussed what he should do with his friends and brother officers, Marcus Agrippa and Salvidienus Rufus. The leading citizens of Apollonia pledged their support, and the commander of the garrison offered his troops to escort him back to Italy and there avenge Caesar. But he decided to return quietly as a private citizen so that he could better judge the prevailing mood. He took the first available ship, and avoiding Brundisium he landed at the small port of Lupia. From there he travelled to Brundisium and thence to Neapolis where he arrived on 18th April. Three days later he was at Puteoli with his mother and stepfather, Lucius Marcius Philippus, who were staying at their villa next to Cicero's. His journey had given him an idea of the support he could expect: the soldiers and the veterans had acclaimed him as Caesar's heir, but the cities and towns had been less enthusiastic.

Both Atia, and Philippus who had been consul in 56, advised him not to accept the adoption. Three parts of the estate were his, they argued, but Caesar could not have foreseen the circumstances of his own death and so there was no obligation for Octavius to take his name; they warned him that if he did so he could not inherit Caesar's position but would take upon himself the moral duty to avenge his death and thus enter into a blood feud with sixty of the leading families in Rome; perhaps the cautious but experienced Philippus added that even if he did take Caesar's name there was no established precedent for the adoption of a son in a will, and this might prove of doubtful validity in law.

As well as meeting Cicero at Puteoli Octavius was visited by Balbus and the two consuls designate for 43, Hirtius and Pansa; probably they all wanted a chance to reassess this eighteen year old who had been so suddenly thrust into the centre of the political arena, while Balbus may also have been concerned about the fate of the war chest for Parthia, part of which was at Brundisium and part already in Asia.

Thus far Octavius had behaved with circumspection, but now he revealed something of what lay within him; putting aside the advice of Philippus and Atia he decided to accept the adoption and take the name of Caesar with all it implied for good or ill, declaring that it would be wrong to do otherwise if Caesar had thought him fit to bear his name.

So a few days later when he set off up the Via Appia for Rome, though the adoption still had to be legally ratified, by the custom of the time he was Gaius Julius Caesar Octavianus; he had taken the name of Caesar and from now on this is what his contemporaries called him. Except for what Caesar himself had endowed it with, magic or odium, it was no more than the name of a branch of the patrician Julian family, but from the outset Octavius divined what it could mean for him. The cognomen, Octavianus, indicated that he had been adopted from the family of Octavius and this was something that he had no wish to stress. It is only to avoid confusion with Caesar that history has called him Octavian until later he became Augustus.

When he arrived in Rome towards the end of April or the beginning of May, Antony was still in Campania, and Octavian persuaded Lucius Antonius, as tribune, to call a meeting of the people; at it he announced that he proposed to accept the adoption and to put the necessary legal process in hand. On 12th May at the postponed spring games in honour of Mars he attempted to have the golden throne, awarded to Caesar by the Senate, and the golden diadem with which Antony had tried to crown him at the Lupercalia, set up in Caesar's honour in the place he would have occupied, but two of the tribunes refused to allow it.

It may have been reports of Octavian's activities in Rome and the manner in which the veterans and the more extreme Caesarians had welcomed him, that alarmed Antony in Campania, though it seems more likely that rumours had reached him of a plot against his person by some of the conspirators: abetted by Cicero many of them continued to make no secret of their regret that they had allowed him to survive Caesar. Whichever it was, when Antony returned to Rome towards the end of May he brought with him a personal bodyguard several thousand strong recruited by his lieutenant, Publius Ventidius, from the veterans in Campania.

Octavian made a courtesy call on Antony as consul and leading Caesarian; he reminded him that he was principal heir to Caesar's private fortune, which he alleged was in Antony's hands and which he now required to pay Caesar's legacy to the citizens of Rome. This was their first meeting since they had travelled back together in Caesar's train after Munda. As well, no doubt, as maintaining that it was the public monies which as consul he had removed from Caesar's house, and this with Calpurnia's leave, Antony warned Octavian of the burden he would take upon himself with Caesar's name. But this was no more than his parents had said, and it was Antony's refusal to take him seriously which offended Octavian, who felt that as Caesar's heir he had been rebuffed by Caesar's principal lieutenant.

It was a grave mistake on Antony's part and it was to have far-reaching and incalculable consequences. But it was understandable enough, and perhaps inevitable, when the burly and impulsive Antony, a big man in every sense and in his late thirties at the height of his physical powers, Caesar's general who had proved himself at Pharsalus and presently the consul in unchallenged command of Rome, found himself faced with this seemingly callow and frail youth whom sickness had denied an active part at Munda, but who now, with a disconcerting stare from unsmiling eyes, was stating his intention of carrying out his filial duty to his new and newly divine father and insisting on his rights as heir to Caesar's name and fortune.

This meeting set the tone for a relationship in which neither was ever really to trust the other. It seems doubtful whether there could have been trust and confidence between two men so different in character and temperament: the young Octavian, cool and calculating beyond his years, ruthless and devious in his means, but unswerving in his purpose and single-minded in his goal, and the flamboyant and extrovert Antony, by nature an easy-going hedonist with a talent for action and a charisma all his own, which moved some to idolise him and others to fear him, a man whom fate had raised to power and political necessity had made a pragmatist and an opportunist.

One result of Octavian's insistence on discharging his obligations as Caesar's heir to the citizens of Rome and the veterans was to make Antony harden his attitude to the conspirators in order to prevent his own standing from being undermined. In his conduct of public affairs he abandoned his previous policy of conciliation and moderation, and he made little attempt to disguise the use he was making of Caesar's papers to consolidate his own support by such means as the sale of tax exemptions and grants of land and citizenship.

Cicero's accusations in the Philippics castigating Antony's every move are exaggerated to a degree which makes it difficult to sift distortion from invention, and impossible to arrive at the truth. As well as vilifying Antony they were also designed to throw the blame on him for every measure of Caesar's with which Cicero disagreed. Having voted for the ratification of all Caesar's acts Cicero found himself obliged to justify them as good and necessary while rejoicing in the death of their author; a convenient way of concealing the paradox of his own stance and continuing to attack Antony was to represent the ones he did not like as Antony's forgeries.

Among those in doubt are some of the provisions for extra land for the veterans, the extension of citizenship to Sicily, the cession of Armenia Minor to Deiotarus and the inclusion of ex-centurions with property qualifications on the rolls for jury service. But further land had to be found for the veterans and State funds were used for its purchase, Caesar had already granted the Sicilians Latin rights, the pro-Roman Deiotarus, one of the key client princes in Asia Minor, had annexed Armenia Minor and there was little Antony or the Senate could do but recognise the fact, and widening the qualifications for jury service continued Caesar's own policy. It had never been agreed in the Senate that new legislation could only be introduced if it could be shown to have been included in Caesar's acts or papers; Antony merely found it simpler to enact new measures if he could attach the seal of Caesar's approval to them and thus include them in the Senate's bloc endorsement of all his acts.

There is no real evidence that Antony exceeded the normal and accepted bounds of consular patronage, but Cicero accused him of emptying the State Treasury and embezzling the vast sum of 700 million sesterces from the Temple of Ops. According to Cicero's own testimony precisely the same sum was available a few months later to compensate Sextus for the confiscation and sale of the Pompeius family property, though this may have been found from the Temple of Saturn. To Cicero, and to Octavian who charged him with misappropriating Caesar's private fortune, Antony replied that both had been used on the normal business of State.

By the last week in May it was generally known that Antony had decided to remove Decimus from Cisalpine Gaul, apparently on the grounds that he could not be allowed to remain so close to Rome with an army under his command, and that the presence there as governor of one of Caesar's murderers was an affront to the soldiers and in their eyes damaging to Antony's standing. Decimus had taken over the two regular legions of the province and was known to be recruiting more. But Antony may have had other reasons: Cicero was believed to be negotiating with both Decimus and Octavian and he could conceivably attempt to reconcile Caesar's heir with Caesar's murderer, an alliance, which however unholy and unlikely it might seem, could only be aimed at Antony and would produce a potential threat too near to Rome for comfort.

Antony called a meeting of the Senate for 1st June at which he planned to deprive Decimus of the Cisalpina. Rumours that he intended to quell the expected opposition and browbeat the Senate into agreement with the threat of troops were enough to stop most of the senators from attending. But he was determined to have his way; without waiting for one of the statutory seventeen days he summoned the Assembly to meet the next day. With the help of his brother Lucius as people's tribune and official patron of the thirty five tribes, a title he had received for services to Caesar, he had little difficulty in persuading the Assembly to cancel Decimus's appointment. Instead they allotted the Cisalpina to Antony together with Transalpine Gaul, both for a term of six years; Dolabella's tenure of Syria was similarly extended. In return Antony gave up Macedonia, but it was agreed that he should keep the army of the province consisting of six of Caesar's best legions which had been earmarked for the Parthian campaign. This was a remarkable change of policy on Antony's part, and provided Decimus could be made to surrender the Cisalpina it would immensely strengthen his hand at the end of the year.

On 5th June, with Antony's agreement and possibly at his prompting, the Senate appointed Brutus and Cassius as commissioners to supervise the corn supply from the provinces, thus giving them an excuse as praetors to absent themselves from Italy and a hint to do so; their allotment of provinces for 43, Crete to Brutus and Cyrenaica instead of Africa to Cassius, was not confirmed but held over to a later date. Brutus was still hoping to preside at the games in honour of Apollo in early July, and both he and Cassius took this move by Antony and the Senate as a deliberate insult. Brutus's mother, Servilia, called a family conference at Antium to discuss what was to be done; Cicero arrived while this was going on, and his letter to Atticus describing the meeting gives some idea of the total disarray to which the conspirators had been reduced; it also provides an insight into his own fear and hatred of Antony when he refers bitterly to their failure to kill him with Caesar, careful though he is not to mention him by name.

Throughout June Antony was still in effective control as consul, though his move against Decimus cost him the backing of some moderates in the Senate, and Octavian continued to erode his standing among the veterans and more extreme Caesarians with a judicious blend of cash, promises and inflammatory speeches; his constant theme was adulation of the dead Caesar and the need to avenge his death, coupled with emphasis on his own filial but disinterested obligations as heir, all indirectly but pointedly contrasted with Antony's conduct.

In the end Brutus decided not to return for the Apollinaris Games from the 7th to the 13th of July, and as praetor Gaius Antonius presided in his place. The newly constituted games to commemorate Caesar's victories were staged during the last ten days of July, the month, formerly Quintilis, which had been renamed in his honour. Gaius Matius and Rabirius Postumus were among those who financed them on Octavian's behalf and helped him to pay Caesar's legacy to every citizen. The spectators applauded when he again tried to have Caesar's golden throne and diadem set up in the place of honour and noisily voiced their disapproval when this was again vetoed, this time by Antony in person.

During the games a comet appeared in the northern sky on seven successive evenings, providing a sure sign for the superstitious Romans that Caesar was indeed with the immortals, and that the gods themselves favoured the heir who bore his name and had given the games in his memory. And it seems that Octavian himself may have taken it as a private and personal endorsement of his purpose; at the least it was a propitious omen and he took care to impress it on the public memory by placing a flaming star on the foreheads of Caesar's statues. Antony tried to counter this, and at the same time emphasise his own loyalty, by raising a statue to Caesar on the new rostra, inscribing it simply but enigmatically, 'Patri optime merito'.

He was evidently alarmed by the hostility of the spectators at the games and the mounting support for Octavian, particularly among the veterans and the Caesarians. As a result he changed his tactics again; at a public meeting during the games he took a much more moderate line and in the Senate he reverted to a policy of conciliation. With his agreement, and after representations from Servilia, Brutus and Cassius's appointments as corn commissioners were cancelled and perhaps on his initiative the Senate confirmed them as governors of Crete and Cyrenaica respectively. These were minor provinces usually governed by the same man, but at least these new posts were not an affront to their dignity and standing.

In Spain Lepidus was negotiating with Sextus, who was insisting on compensation for the expropriated family property and public office commensurate with his standing as Pompey's son, as well as the freedom to return to Rome which Antony had offered; eventually his demands were agreed. In mid-July, after another lengthy period of indecision and heart searching, Cicero made up his mind to leave for Greece with the intention of returning the following year when Antony would no longer be consul. But the ship which he took from Syracuse was forced to shelter from the weather in Leucopetra, and when news reached him there of Antony's seeming change of heart he decided to return to Rome.

On 1st August Piso attacked Antony in the Senate, but he got no support in criticising his handling of affairs since Caesar's death. Piso, an experienced consular, had consistently used his influence on the side of moderation and peace, and it is not clear why he chose this moment when Antony was again taking a conciliatory line in the Senate to attack him. It is also not clear why during the last days of July, or possibly on 1st August, Antony decided to issue a formal consular edict against Brutus and Cassius accusing them of having deserted their posts as praetors, when previously he had at least acquiesced in their provincial appointments. Octavian's activities may have made him take a firmer stand against Caesar's murderers, but there may also have been rumours that Brutus and Cassius did not intend to go to their allotted provinces but to Greece and Syria instead.

Two joint letters from Brutus and Cassius to Antony have survived with Cicero's correspondence. In the first, written towards the end of May at Lanuvium and courteously expressed, they seek to clarify their position if they return to Rome and ask for assurances as to their safety. The second, dated 4th August and in reply to Antony's consular edict, is phrased in altogether different language and warns Antony to remember not how long Caesar lived, but how short a time he held supreme power.

At Velia on 17th August Cicero, on his way back to Rome, met Brutus who was travelling south to collect some ships before leaving Italy; he sailed a few days later, but Cassius seems to have waited for some weeks before he also left Italy, though Plutarch says they left together and parted in Athens. Cicero arrived in Rome in time for the meeting of the Senate which Antony had called for 1st September, but he did not attend. His reason for not doing so may simply have been, as he said himself, that he was tired by the journey; he may also have wanted to consult his friends and take the political pulse of Rome. But Antony took offence at his absence and threatened him with the statutory penalties if he did not attend; then, as a rebuke to Cicero, he foolishly decided not to attend himself on the following day, pleading illness as an excuse.

Cicero however did attend, and on this, his first appearance in the Senate since 17th March, he took the opportunity to attack the absent Antony. His speech which came to be known as the 1st Philippic was comparatively moderate, certainly in relation to what was to come, and on this occasion he avoided personal abuse and concentrated on

Antony's actions as consul. Although he was supported by Servilius, now returned to Rome, and by some other members, this immediate and open opposition to Antony perhaps indicates that he was already looking outside the Senate to Octavian; among the consulars only Philippus and Marcellus gave Octavian their reluctant and generally ineffective backing in the Senate, as they were bound by family ties to do. Antony had already seen his authority as consul undermined by Octavian's arrival in Rome and his suborning of the Caesarians. With Cicero adding his rhetorical gifts to attacks in the Senate by Piso and Servilius on his arbitrary conduct as consul, and Octavian's complaints that he was far too accommodating with Caesar's murderers, Antony now found himself in some danger of isolation.

As a result he became increasingly concerned about what would happen when he relinquished executive power at the end of the year, soon after his brothers, Gaius and Lucius, gave up their offices as praetor and tribune. With Octavian controlling the extreme Caesarians in Rome, and some of the conspirators commanding armies in the provinces, Antony had to be able to defend himself when January came. Soon after the Assembly had allotted him Gaul he had ordered four of the Macedonian legions to Italy, and they were due to reach Brundisium at the beginning of October; with them and the two regular legions in the Cisalpina he would be able to counter any military move against him and watch events in Italy from Cisalpine Gaul.

To Antony, the attacks on him in the Senate were not only a threat to his authority, but also an affront to his dignity and an insult to his person; it was not in his character to ignore them, rather to hit back in the same vein. On 19th September the Senate met in the Temple of Concord, but Cicero did not attend, excusing himself on the grounds that he feared for his life at the hands of Antony's bodyguard; Piso and Servilius also absented themselves.

Antony made a violent speech denouncing Cicero; he began by accusing him of deliberately fermenting trouble between Caesar and Pompey and working to widen the breach between them which had led to the civil war; this was not only true, but commonly known to be true. He then charged him with having engineered the death of Clodius and with complicity in Caesar's murder; in the former Fulvia's hand can perhaps be detected. In reply to Cicero's attack on his recruiting of a bodyguard Antony retorted that Cicero had employed armed slaves to protect himself during his consulate; from here he went on to accuse him of executing his stepfather, Lentulus, without trial and then refusing to hand over his body for burial.

Though Cicero did not hear the speech it did not prevent him from describing Antony's delivery of it as the spewing out of words, a comment in a letter to Cassius which perhaps came from the heart, for though himself a master of personal abuse Cicero was always constrained by his feelings for the niceties of language to phrase his most vicious attacks in impeccable and mellifluous Latin. He retired to one of his eight villas to write his reply; in it he put all his malice into a diatribe against Antony, curiously interspersed with lengthy periods of self-justification and self-congratulation; he accused him of every form of vice and crime and of being the cause of the State's every ill. It has been hailed as a masterpiece of invective; it is perhaps a masterly exercise in misrepresentation, for in his frustration Cicero abandoned all regard for the truth and made a number of charges against Antony which were demonstrably false, among them cowardice and implication in Caesar's murder, which he paradoxically described as a glorious deed. For a masterpiece it is inordinately long and verbose; if Cicero had ever delivered it to the Senate it would have taken him some two hours, but he was afraid to do so and until December he circulated it as a pamphlet among his close and trusted friends.

Some of the officers of the army, Caesarians at heart rather than committed supporters of either Antony or Octavian, were becoming more and more alarmed at the rift between the two leaders, in their eyes Caesar's deputy and Caesar's heir. Towards the end of September they persuaded them both to take part in a formal reconciliation staged in public in the temple of Jupiter on the Capitol. But neither trusted the other: Octavian felt that Antony had compromised with Caesar's murderers and slighted him when as Caesar's heir he had turned naturally to him for help; for his part Antony still could not bring himself to take Octavian altogether seriously, though he realised that, ably abetted behind the scenes by Caesar's agents, Octavian was using Caesar's name to erode his authority as consul and usurp his leadership of the Caesarians.

At a public meeting on 2nd October Tiberius Cannutius, a tribune and a client of Servilius's, cross questioned Antony, insinuating that he had no real intention of punishing Caesar's murderers; Antony responded angrily with a forthright condemnation of the conspirators, the first time he had attacked them in public since the funeral, and then went on to accuse Cicero of organising and directing them.

A few days later Antony claimed to have uncovered a plot to assassinate him and said that interrogation of some members of his own bodyguard who were implicated had revealed that Octavian's agents were behind it. This Octavian vehemently denied, calling at Antony's house to protest his innocence; Antony persisted in his allegation that Octavian's agents had subverted his bodyguard in an attempt to kill him. The truth of the matter is lost, if indeed it were ever known except to the principals. In a contemporary letter Cicero suggests that it was an invention of Antony's to win himself sympathy; he comments that many believed it to be true, but admits that he did not himself know the truth of it.

Antony was clearly alarmed, both about his present safety and what might happen at the end of the year, for accompanied by Fulvia he left Rome on 9th October to meet the Macedonian legions at Brundisium. There is no evidence that he intended to use these four legions for any purpose other than to form the core of his proconsular army in Gaul. Cicero however at once put it about that he was planning a coup in Rome, and many believed him.

Octavian certainly saw, or pretended to see, this move of Antony's as a direct threat; perhaps he sensed an opportunity as well, for he sent agents to Brundisium with large sums of money to undermine the legions' loyalty to Antony. A few days later he set off himself for a tour of the Caesarian veterans' colonies in Campania accompanied by five trusted friends, among them Agrippa and Gaius Maecenas, a wealthy Etruscan nobleman from Arretium. Their object was to recruit what could be no more than a private army, for, though he now bore the name of Caesar, Octavian was a private citizen and to raise such an army was a revolutionary act amounting to treason.

They took with them several wagons loaded with coin, and Octavian's cash offer of more than two years pay in the form of a bounty of 500 denarii together with the promise of 5,000 denarii if his enterprise, ostensibly to avenge Caesar, succeeded, was enough to make many of the younger veterans lay down their ploughs and take up their swords; they were in their late twenties and early thirties, mainly from Caesar's VIIth and VIIIth Legions, and soon Octavian had a force of trained soldiers, according to the various ancient sources 3,000 to 10,000 strong.

In spite of his allegations about Antony's embezzlement of public money Octavian evidently had very considerable funds at his own disposal. Despite his later denials he had probably himself misappropriated the bulk of Caesar's war chest for Parthia, and he was certainly being financed by Balbus, Maecenas, Oppius and other wealthy Caesarians.

His agents did their work well at Brundisium for when Antony arrived he was met with noisy complaints from the soldiers about their bounties, which they contrasted unfavourably with Octavian's payments in Campania, and with pointed questions asking why Caesar's murderers had not been punished. They derided his offer of one hundred denarii to compensate them for their transfer to Italy and

118

refused to listen to his explanations as to why Caesar's death had not yet been avenged. Angered by their mutinous attitude Antony ordered the arrest and execution of the ringleaders, which was watched, according to her enemies, by a gloating Fulvia. This summary action was within the letter of Roman military law and for the moment discipline was restored, but Antony did not have sufficient funds readily available to match or outbid Octavian's agents, who continued their attempts to subvert the three legions which had arrived from Macedonia. To allow them to remain idle any longer in their camps near Brundisium was to play into Octavian's hands and Antony decided not to wait for the fourth legion; he ordered the other three to march north up the Adriatic coastal road for Ariminum in the Cisalpina, evidence in itself that he did not intend to use them against Rome. He set off himself for Rome, probably after receiving reports of Octavian's recruiting in Campania, taking with him the Vth Legion, the Gallic Larks, which he had re-embodied and on whose loyalty he could rely.

News of Antony's march put Octavian in a quandary. Strategically placed in Campania he could either interpose his army to block Antony's return to Rome and at the same time appeal to the three Macedonian legions to defect, or he could march on Rome himself and forestall Antony by getting there first. This was the crucial choice which faced him as a revolutionary leader who by taking up arms had committed himself; there could be no going back, and to do nothing was to invite defeat and retribution at Antony's hands.

If the Macedonian legions remained loyal to Antony, their legal commander as well as the elected consul, Octavian would be outnumbered; politically he had no rallying cry other than to avenge Caesar. In this dilemma he turned to Cicero, sending him a succession of envoys and bombarding him with letters seeking advice. What he really needed was the political backing of an elder statesman who could sway the Senate in his favour and give what was now revealed as a revolutionary movement some semblance of respectability, if not constitutional authority. Not one of Octavian's letters to Cicero has survived later editing, and indeed it would have been surprising if they had, for as Oppius indicated to Cicero, Octavian was prepared to compromise with Caesar's murderers for the sake of Cicero's support. At this stage, as his private letters show, Cicero discounted Octavian's chances of success and refused to commit himself beyond advising him, somewhat cryptically, to go to Rome where his strength lay. And, though perhaps not in the way Cicero intended, this is what Octavian decided to do; to march on Rome at the head of his private army and get there before Antony. It was a bold decision, though in the classic dilemma facing a revolutionary leader who has declared himself there could have been no other choice, for once back in Rome Antony would undoubtedly pass the ultimate decree to outlaw him.

Octavian reached Rome during the second week in November; he encamped the main body of his army outside the city and sent in a detachment to seize and occupy the Forum. Alarmed by rumours of Cassius's intentions Dolabella had left some weeks before to secure his province of Syria, and there was no consul to resist Octavian; but with Antony approaching by forced marches none of the senators were prepared to commit themselves. Instead, on November 9th Octavian addressed a public meeting which Cannutius, as tribune, called at his bidding: he claimed that he had acted only to protect Rome and forestall Antony, who he said was marching on the city with the Macedonian legions to usurp power on his own account. He went on to praise Caesar to whom he said all power had justly been bequeathed and then to pledge his unconquerable determination to win for himself the honours and the standing his adoptive father had enjoyed, stretching out his hand to Caesar's statue on the rostra to emphasise the binding nature of his solemn oath. Cicero's comment was, 'So much for salvation with a saviour such as that'; he added that the test would come the following month when Casca, one of Caesar's murderers, was due to take office as tribune.

But the crowd did not react with much enthusiasm to Octavian's sudden attack on Antony, whom many of them respected as a popular Caesarian leader and the consul who had averted civil war. When they realised what he planned Octavian's own troops showed even less enthusiasm for an armed confrontation with Antony and their erstwhile comrades in Caesar's legions. They complained that they had been deceived: Octavian had told them that they were to defend their colonies against Caesar's murderers and avenge his death, and now they found Caesar's deputy and their own general at Pharsalus cast as the enemy. Even the magic of Caesar's name could no longer conceal the fact that Octavian's enterprise was revolutionary, and they would not accept Antony as their enemy; with embarrassed excuses and Octavian's money still in their purses they made their way back to their farms in Campania. Octavian had gambled and lost; his army had melted away, and with Antony nearing Rome he had no choice but to escape with his remaining supporters to Arretium, where through Maecenas and his own family connections he could find sanctuary and perhaps raise another army.

A few days later Antony arrived in Rome; he must have received the news of the failure of Octavian's bid and the desertion of his army with relief and satisfaction. At last the issue was clear: Octavian had raised an army without a vestige of legal authority and was in open rebellion against the State; what was more he had committed himself, and he had failed. Antony called a meeting of the Senate for 24th November to pass the ultimate decree against him and ordered the senators to attend on pain of being themselves arraigned on charges of treason.

But on the morning of the 24th news came that the Martial Legion, one of the three on the march up the east coast, had declared for Octavian and had turned west to join him. This was completely unexpected, for Antony thought he had overcome the crisis of discipline at Brundisium; if the other two legions followed the Martial's example it spelt disaster.

Octavian's agents had done their work perhaps better than they knew, and the executions at Brundisium were bearing their bitter fruit. In contrast to Caesar's treatment of the Xth Legion when they mutinied before the African campaign Antony had acted precipitately and in anger. If, as Cicero says, Fulvia had hardened Antony's resolve at Brundisium, her determination had served him ill, and if, as he also alleges, she witnessed the executions and openly expressed her satisfaction this must have increased the rancour and the bitterness. But whatever part she played it was in loyalty to Antony, and he too had acted in character: as Plutarch notes his impulsive nature made him hasty in anger and over-generous in rewards, though he adds that he usually erred on the side of leniency and generosity.

Thus the 24th November proved a dramatic turning-point, both for Antony and for Octavian. At one moment Antony was firmly in control with four legions to reinforce his authority as consul, and Octavian was a failed revolutionary whom the Senate would declare a public enemy that evening; the next moment the turn about was complete. Such was the power of the army and the importance of its loyalty to whoever aspired to rule in Rome.

However a crisis brought out the best in Antony. He acted at once to cancel the meeting of the Senate and then rode himself for Alba Fucens, on the Via Valeria some sixty miles from Rome, to meet the Martial Legion. But they closed the gates of the town, jeered at him from the walls and refused to listen. Unable to move them and unwilling to waste further time in fruitless parley he set off with a small escort to ride back through the night to Rome. Before he left he tried to insure against further defections by ordering a cash bounty of 500 denarii to be paid to the other three Macedonian legions.

By the morning of the 28th he was in Rome; he called a meeting of the Senate for late the same evening with the intention of declaring Octavian a public enemy, the unprecedented hour a measure of his urgency. With Dolabella on his way to Syria Antony must have accepted that when the Senate passed the ultimate decree against Octavian, he as consul would have to take the field against him, and thus leave Rome undefended and open to him and his agents.

But as the meeting opened news came that the IVth Legion had also defected. The implications were grave enough to make Antony decide to leave at once for Cisalpine Gaul despite the fact that his term of office still had more than a month to run; it was of overriding importance to secure the Gallic provinces, and in particular the Cisalpina, as his firm base.

The motion to declare Octavian a public enemy was not put to the Senate and the rest of that evening's business was quickly despatched. Macedonia was allotted to Gaius Antonius, and for the other provinces which were reallocated the lot fell consistently in favour of Antony's supporters; among them Sabinus, who had tried to defend Caesar, received Africa, and Lepidus, whose support in Provence could prove vital, was rewarded with a special commendation which Antony knew would gratify his passion for formal honours.

CHAPTER VII

Mutina

After the meeting of the Senate finished late that evening, Antony put on his general's uniform, and cloaked and accoutred for war he rode for Tibur where his troops were encamped. The next morning he reviewed the Vth Legion and perhaps one other legion, which may by now have been formed from veterans recruited by Decidius Saxa; the whole parade took an oath of loyalty to his person. Later the same day, according to both Appian and Dio, most of the senators and many of the leading citizens travelled out from Rome to Antony's camp at Tibur and pledged him their backing, of their own free will swearing the same oath of allegiance to him as his soldiers had done.

This spontaneous and voluntary demonstration of support after he had left the city must have heartened Antony. It also indicates widespread distrust of Octavian's intentions and fear of his revolutionary band of disaffected veterans and financial opportunists waiting on the sidelines in Etruria and the threat they posed to life and property in Rome; and it puts into perspective Cicero's spurious portrayal in the subsequent Philippics of the circumstances in which Antony left Rome.

Before he set off on the long march north up the Via Flaminia to meet the two remaining Macedonian legions at Ariminum Antony sent a courier to Decimus with a formal summons to hand over the Cisalpina.

Decimus had the two regular legions of the province together with two or three others which he had recently raised; these he had managed to provide with some battle experience in a short campaign against the Alpine tribes, as a result of which he wrote to Cicero asking for a Triumph. Saxa continued to recruit for Antony in Campania; in Etruria Octavian had raised his strength to two legions of veterans and one of recruits, and he now set out for Alba Fucens to join the IVth and Martial Legions.

The provinces beyond the Alps were held by three Caesarian legates: Plancus had recently taken over Transalpine Gaul with three legions; Lepidus, who also governed Nearer Spain, was strategically placed with four legions in Provence commanding the coastal route to Italy and Spain; Pollio with two legions held Further Spain, more than a months march from northern Italy and forty days by courier from

Rome. No one could be certain how they would react. Pollio, a friend and old comrade of Antony's, the most competent general of the three and a historian in his own right, a man of independent mind and spirit who deplored the ravages of civil war, was likely to put what he saw as the best interests of Rome before his own or Antony's. And if Lepidus and Plancus could be relied upon for nothing else they were certain to temporise and procrastinate in order to emerge on the winning side.

Cicero was in constant touch by letter with Decimus and Plancus, exhorting them to stand firm for the Republic. Decimus was also in contact with Plancus, while Antony apparently remained in touch with Lepidus, and possibly with Plancus as well. The sailing season was closed for the winter, and there was as yet no firm news in Rome from Brutus or Cassius though there were many rumours. With Antony on the march to Ariminum it was Decimus who first had to decide what to do, whether to fight or submit. He was a realist, and after Caesar's death his aim had been to establish himself as governor of Cisalpine Gaul with an army under his command. Since leaving Rome in April he had kept in touch with Brutus and Cassius, urging them in his letters to provide themselves with armies.

Decimus had been one of Caesar's most trusted and able lieutenants and he knew that the Caesarians would exact revenge for his treachery; the fast approaching Antony threatened such retribution. Though now that Antony had left Rome the news reaching the Cisalpina must have seemed more encouraging: Cicero had ventured back to the city after prudently keeping out of the way at Arpinum and was busily engaged in his self-imposed role as the saviour of the Republic, with Octavian as the instrument which destiny had chosen for him. Decimus might discount Cicero's political acumen and distrust Octavian as Caesar's heir; but from his letters Cicero appeared to be convinced that he could manipulate Octavian, who it was true had raised no objection to Casca holding office as tribune. Decimus had not seen Octavian since they had ridden back together after Munda, and as Cicero so plausibly maintained it was conceivable that he was not implacably hostile to the liberators and Antony was in fact the only enemy; certainly it was Antony and not Octavian who was now marching on the Cisalpina. Decimus had little real choice: he refused to hand over the province, declaring that the decision was not a difficult one and he had had no need of Cicero's or Pansa's advice in reaching it.

At Ariminum Antony met the two remaining Macedonian legions; to his relief both had remained loyal. So it was at the head of an army of either three or four legions that he marched on across the Rubicon and into Cisalpine Gaul. The cities threw open their gates and he was welcomed in the towns and the countryside. Decimus had been in the north of the province, and when Antony approached he avoided battle and withdrew southwards. He halted at Mutina, not to stand and fight, but to take refuge behind the walls of the city; he prepared for a siege by requisitioning food and property and slaughtering and salting down all the cattle he could find. Antony invested Mutina with a ditch and rampart and set about building artillery and siege engines; by now he controlled the entire province, but he needed the whole of his army to keep Decimus securely bottled up in Mutina and prosecute the siege.

With no consul there was political stalemate in Rome. The consulars gave no lead, either because of age and infirmity or through lack of nerve and will. The new tribunes who took office on 9th December, Casca among them, called a meeting of the Senate for the 20th, supposedly to arrange that the new consuls, Hirtius and Pansa, could be inaugurated in safety on 1st January, but probably to allow the Senate to hear Decimus's despatches. Cicero returned from Arpinum on the 9th; he sensed that at last the chance had come to redeem his past failures, to wipe away the political frustrations of the last ten years, to revenge himself on Antony, and above all to save the Republic to which he had given a lifetime's devoted service.

His plan was to use consular armies under the two consuls elect, both moderate Caesarians and 'new men', acting in concert with Octavian and his private army to defeat Antony and so weaken and divide the Caesarians. Then through the consuls in Rome and the proconsuls in the provinces he as elder statesman would direct the fortunes of the restored Republic until the old senatorial oligarchy was firmly back in control. He had convinced himself that Octavian was 'sound', and he was to aver that he knew the inmost secrets of his heart. And when the fighting was done he could curtail Octavian's powers and restrict his ambition within the confines of the constitution, perhaps himself acting as political mentor to this enigmatic young man who called him 'father'. But first Antony had to be outlawed, defeated, hunted down as a public enemy and destroyed.

Such was Cicero's plan. It could be said to reveal a self-induced fantasy world in that it displays a failure to understand Octavian or assess his purpose, an inflated opinion of his own political capacity and standing with his contemporaries, inability to appreciate the changed role of the army and the power it wielded, and an obsessional hatred of Antony. But with Octavian having been forced to withdraw to Etruria and Antony fleeing Rome to besiege Decimus in Mutina, it was perhaps not so impracticable a design for Cicero, who had built his life round the Republican institutions which had already endured for centuries and in which he believed so passionately. The essential paradox in Cicero lay in his self-knowledge of his own unquestioned genius as a man of letters and his refusal to recognise his inability to translate his skills as writer, philosopher and advocate into the current world of affairs.

He had not proposed to attend the meeting of the Senate on 20th December, but he changed his mind when a despatch arrived from Decimus saying that he had refused to hand over the Cisalpina. He opened the debate with the 3rd Philippic, concentrating all the fury of his oratory in another vicious attack on Antony in which he blended calumny and derision with allegations that he intended to enslave the Roman people. He commended Decimus for his refusal to hand over his province and the defecting legions for the loyalty they had shown to the Senate. For Octavian he had nothing but praise: he referred to him as a young man of semi-divine intelligence and courage who had disinterestedly invested his patrimony to raise an army and by his own initiative had saved Rome from destruction at Antony's hands.

But not even Cicero could disguise the fact that Antony was the elected consul. After the meeting of the Senate when he addressed the crowd in the Forum in the speech known as the 4th Philippic he attempted to explain away this unpalatable fact with the most brazen and involute sophistry: he argued that if Octavian, Decimus, and the IVth and Martial Legions had taken up arms against a Roman consul they would be guilty of the most heinous crime of treason against the State, but since the Senate had commended all of them they could not then be guilty of such a crime, and therefore it must follow that Antony could not be consul and instead was thus proved to be an enemy of the State.

On New Year's Day 43 the new consuls, Hirtius and Pansa, duly took office. They were both of Italian provincial origin, and they owed their position to the ability they had shown in Caesar's service. It may well be that he had nominated them for the consulate in 43, the year in which he had expected to be away in Parthia, for the very reason that lacking noble senatorial connections they would be less likely to intrigue against him in his absence. But what their attitude would be now to Caesar's murderers and how they would react with Antony and Octavian on the brink of conflict was more difficult to predict.

Pansa took the chair at the meeting of the Senate which followed the inauguration ceremony. After he and Hirtius had spoken, perhaps in the interests of peace and moderation he next called on Calenus, his own father-in-law and a friend of Antony's. Calenus proposed that they should send envoys to negotiate with Antony and persuade him to raise the siege of Mutina and acknowledge the authority of the Senate. Though it was Antony, and not Decimus, who was strictly within his constitutional rights, Calenus's motion was pre-emptive, made in anticipation of what Cicero would propose.

Cicero began his speech, the 5th Philippic, by chiding Calenus and deriding his proposal, arguing that it would be madness to send envoys to a man such as Antony, whom even if they had not formally outlawed they had effectively branded as a public enemy when they commended Decimus and Octavian and their armies. Once again, and at some length, he catalogued the crimes which he said Antony had committed as consul and described him as a debauched and frenzied animal bent on devouring the State. He went on to move formal motions, again commending Decimus and this time including Lepidus for his part in reconciling Sextus Pompeius to the Senate; he proposed that a golden equestrian statue of Lepidus should be placed on the rostra or wherever else he chose. The Senate repealed Antony's agrarian law providing land for all Caesar's veterans, but Cicero proposed land grants specifically to reward the IVth and Martial Legions; in the end these were whittled down to cash bounties. Cicero told the Senate that Octavian was marching north to Decimus's relief, calling him the heaven sent young man on whom their hopes of liberty rested; he claimed that he had given Octavian authority to raise an army from Caesar's veterans, and ignoring the fact that this was an act of treason, brushing aside the other constitutional niceties, he went on to invoke what he called a higher legality to cover any action which he considered was designed to protect the State.

He proposed that Octavian's assumption of command should be regularised by giving him imperium as a propraetor, and that, despite the fact that the Senate had no powers to appoint its own members, he should be made a senator and allowed to stand for the consulate ten years before the normal age; as Octavian was only nineteen this meant that he would still have to wait for eleven years.

In reply to reservations voiced by some senators on the grounds of Octavian's expressed hostility to Caesar's murderers, Cicero declared that Octavian was devoted to the Senate and nothing was of more importance to him than its authority; on this Cicero solemnly pledged himself to the Senate and the Roman people. When he gave his word it was in good faith, and herein lay the mistake which was to prove fatal to his cause and to his person: carried away by pride in his own sagacity and hatred for Antony, he had allowed himself to be convinced by his own rhetoric that he could manipulate Octavian as he wished.

Pansa next called on Piso who took Antony's part, rebutting much of what Cicero had said, and in a shrewd thrust at his summary execution of the Catiline conspirators reminding the Senate that it was neither proper nor their custom to condemn consulars unheard. He pointed out that it was Antony who was acting within the law, while Decimus and Octavian certainly were not; then he turned on Cicero accusing him of malice and charging him with acting out of fear and hatred of Antony.

The debate continued all day until Pansa adjourned the meeting in the evening. When the Senate reassembled the next morning Salvius used his tribune's veto to prevent Antony from being declared a public enemy. Cicero's friends abused him for doing so and tried to stir up the crowd in the Forum against him, but when he offered to speak to them they were quick to stop him for fear he might move them in Antony's favour. At the end of the second day Cicero's motions were passed, commending Decimus and Lepidus, giving Octavian imperium as a propraetor, appointing him as a senator with rank of a consular and offering him a golden statue.

It looked as if there would be little that Piso, Sulpicius Rufus, Salvius and Antony's other friends would be able to do on the following day to prevent his being outlawed. That evening Fulvia and Antony's mother, Julia, both dressed in black and taking with them the young Marcus Antonius, called at the homes of the senators to canvass their support and appeal for moderation.

The next morning Cicero pressed for the ultimate decree, but Piso managed to circumvent him, and the Senate then considered Calenus's proposal to send an embassy to Antony. On the fourth day of the debate Salvius vetoed Cicero's motion that no embassy should be sent, and Calenus's proposal was passed. It was agreed after further discussion that the envoys should be Piso, Sulpicius, who had seconded Calenus, and Octavian's father-in-law, Philippus. The allotment of provinces made on 28th November was then cancelled, Decimus's tenure of Cisalpine Gaul was confirmed, and on the insistence of the friends and relatives of the conspirators, who feared that Octavian and Antony might make common cause against them, Antony was offered Macedonia instead of Transalpine Gaul.

According to Appian Cicero redrafted the text of the Senate's despatch to Antony, phrasing it in more peremptory terms. There is no other evidence that he did so, and Appian's statement may derive from Pollio who was no admirer of Cicero as a man or as a politician. Whether amended or not, the letter the envoys took ordered Antony to lift the siege of Mutina forthwith and then hand the province back to Decimus and withdraw south of the Rubicon: there he was to stay, remaining 200 miles from Rome, until he received further instructions from the Senate.

Sulpicius was nearly sixty and a sick man; the winter journey up the Via Cassia and over the Apennine passes proved too much for him and he died within sight of Mutina. Piso and Philippus found the city closely invested and Antony bombarding the walls with his artillery; he was determined to reduce Mutina and eliminate Decimus before Hirtius could march north with the new consular levies and join Octavian near Bononia.

Piso and Philippus delivered the Senate's message, which they realised amounted to an ultimatum. Then the two Caesarian consulars, Caesar's father-in-law and Octavian's stepfather, found themselves listening in embarrassed silence to an angry tirade from Antony; he accused Cicero of manipulating the constitution and he denounced the Senate for sustaining Caesar's murderers and rewarding the IVth and Martial Legions for mutiny; he refused to raise the siege or allow them through his lines to see Decimus. In private he indicated to them that he would be prepared to surrender the Cisalpina if instead he were given Transalpine Gaul with an army of six legions for a period of five years. This he insisted was the minimum which would leave him able to defend himself while Brutus and Cassius were consuls in 41 and then held proconsular provinces in 40.

He reminded Piso and Philippus that he had only agreed to the amnesty of 17th March because of his personal regard for Brutus and his respect for him and Cassius, and for them alone out of all the conspirators; now he feared and distrusted them both. Whether he already knew that Brutus had taken over Macedonia and was investing his brother, Gaius, in Apollonia is uncertain; the news reached Rome at the beginning of February. He insisted that the Senate must abide by the legislation passed during his consulate, and in particular his land grants to the veterans must be honoured.

Part of Antony's official reply to the Senate survives in the 8th Philippic because Cicero quoted extracts in order to refute them item by item. In his letter Antony made the same conditions for surrendering the Cisalpina as he had put to Piso and Philippus: that he should hold Transalpine Gaul with six legions until the end of 39 when Brutus and Cassius would be due to give up their proconuslar provinces; in prudence he could scarcely ask for less. It is significant that he still accepted Brutus and Cassius as the consuls designate for 41, and so apparently had not closed the door on an agreement with them.

According to Appian part of his reply was aimed directly at Cicero:-

The Assembly of the Roman people lawfully appointed

me to the provinces of Gaul and I will prosecute Decimus for not obeying this law; I will punish him for Caesar's death, and him alone as representative of all the murderers, so that the Senate, which now shares the guilt through Cicero's support of Decimus, shall be purged of that blood guilt.

When the two envoys left with his reply Antony sent his quaestor, Lucius Varius, to watch his interests in Rome. Piso and Philippus arrived back during the first week of February, and Pansa called a meeting of the Senate to consider Antony's letter. The Senate rejected his conditions for giving up the Cisalpina, and then despite the efforts of his supporters they passed the ultimate decree calling on the consuls to take all measures to defend the State. But on a motion put by Lucius Julius Caesar, Antony's uncle and a committed Republican, and supported by Calenus and Pansa himself, Antony was not declared a public enemy, though a proposal by Calenus that another embassy should be sent was defeated.

On the following day Cicero took Calenus to task in the 8th Philippic for supporting Antony and attacked his motives. Then he went on to analyse Antony's reply sentence by sentence, calling it bloody, savage, criminal, and abhorrent to gods and men, and its author a dangerous wild beast. In a letter to Cassius he described Antony's terms as intolerable and the envoys' behaviour as disgraceful, despite the fact that by his own testimony he had prayed that they would fail.

Antony intensified his efforts to batter a breach in the walls of Mutina. But Octavian, encamped at Forum Cornelii on the Via Aemilia half-way between Mutina and Ariminum, made no move to relieve Decimus, even when Hirtius advanced further up the Aemilia and drove Antony's cavalry out of Claterna; here he too halted like Octavian to wait on events. Throughout February they were probably both secretly in touch with Antony; certainly Octavian hesitated to ask his soldiers, among them veterans of Caesar's VIIth and VIIIth Legions, to fight old comrades and fellow Caesarians in an attempt to relieve the most detested of Caesar's murderers.

The extent to which either Octavian or Antony could act in concert with the conspirators was restricted by the abiding loyalty of Caesar's soldiers to his memory. He had taken these tough but simple peasants from the poverty and squalor of rural Italy and given them pride in themselves and their legions. Their fortitude, courage and discipline had given him the mastery of the Roman world. To them Caesar had been more than a successful general: he had given them hope of a better life on their own land when their service was done, and they had revered him as their protector against both the Republican oligarchy which for generations had ground them into the soil and the merchants and moneylenders who had bled them white. To avenge his death was a sacred obligation and in fulfilling it they saw no reaon to fight each other. Antony and Octavian had each been obliged to plead expediency and lack of opportunity to excuse their delay in bringing Caesar's murderers to account. They had each discovered to their cost how difficult it was to persuade their soldiers to fight one another, Antony when the two legions had defected, and Octavian when his army had melted away after his first march on Rome rather than fight Antony. As events were to show it was a lesson both men heeded and a reminder that the soldiers were at last beginning to realise their power.

But for a prudent regard for their soldiers' feeling Antony and Octavian would both have been prepared to go further in accommodation with Caesar's murderers. Octavian would use any means to achieve his single-minded end of supreme power; with Caesar's name he had taken on himself the duty to avenge his murder and this he would do when it suited his long term purpose, though whether out of filial duty or merely to enhance his own reputation is hard to determine.

By nature less devious, and lacking Octavian's ambition, Antony would have been prepared to compromise with Brutus out of respect for his motives, and in the knowledge that but for him he would have died with Caesar. As for Cassius and the others who had advocated his death he would subordinate revenge for its own sake or Caesar's to his own best interest. At the moment he had probably only decided that Cicero would pay with his life for the Philippics and Decimus with his for baulking him at Mutina.

Early in February a despatch from Brutus to the consuls reached Rome: he said that he controlled the three provinces of Macedonia, Achaea and Illyricum with an army of six legions and asked the Senate for ratification. When he left Italy he had sailed to Athens; from there he established himself first in Achaea, and then in Macedonia with the help of his kinsman, Quintus Hortensius, the governor. When Gaius Antonius arrived in January to take over the province Hortensius declared for Brutus and invested Antonius and his single legion in Apollonia. Vatinius, proconsul of Illyricum and a loyal Caesarian, moved south against Hortensius but his three legions went over to Brutus. With the whole of Greece under his control Brutus was able to intercept the quaestors of Asia and Syria on their way back to Rome with the annual tax revenues and persuade them to join him. With the

131

opening of the sailing season news came from the East which seemed to confirm rumours current in Rome during the winter that Cassius had obtained troops and supplies from Trebonius in Asia and then sailed for Syria where the Syrian legions were believed to have gone over to him.

In the Senate Calenus attacked Brutus for illegally seizing power outside his own province, but Cicero's motion commending him and endorsing his new command was passed. The next despatch from the East which arrived in Rome in late February or early March shocked the Senate with the news that Dolabella had executed Trebonius. The cause of the dispute, which arose when Dolabella reached Trebonius's province of Asia on his way to Syria, is obscure, but it may have arisen from the aid Trebonius had given Cassius against Syria. After an initial skirmish Dolabella attacked Smyrna and captured Trebonius; according to one account he tortured him before putting him to death and then allowing the soldiers to kick his severed head through the streets.

This time the outraged Senate was unanimous in condemning Dolabella, Calenus himself proposing that he should be outlawed. In the 11th Philippic Cicero took the opportunity to move that Cassius should be given command against Dolabella with a special imperium over the whole of the Roman East; but this was further than the Senate was prepared to go, and Pansa himself reproved Cicero for putting such a motion. After a long debate the two consuls were authorised to appoint deputies against Dolabella, until the war in the Cisalpina was finished and one of them could take the field himself.

The reports from Syria were to prove well founded, though it was almost another two months before confirmation reached Rome that Cassius controlled the whole province. When he got there he had found the two Caesarians, Murcus the governor and Crispus the governor of Bithynia, besieging the Pompeian, Caecilius Bassus, in Apamaea; two years earlier Bassus had led the revolt in which Sextus was killed. Cassius's arrival brought an abrupt end to the siege, with Murcus's three Syrian legions, the three which Crispus had brought from Bithynia, and Bassus's garrison of a single legion all going over to him. Allienus, the Roman legate in Egypt, had marched north in response to Dolabella's call to join him in Syria; now he had no choice but to join Cassius, who without having to fight a single battle found himself in command of twelve legions and in control of the whole of Asia Minor and the Levant. Though Cassius was known in Syria, where he had served as Crassus's quaestor and after Carrhae as proquaestor until 51, the way in which the whole Roman East fell into his hands is a tribute to his reputation and personality.

Antony's friends in Rome, concerned at the rumoured outcome in the East but encouraged by the rebuff to Cicero over Cassius's imperium, renewed their efforts to negotiate a compromise. The Senate agreed to send another embassy consisting of Piso, Calenus, Cicero himself, Lucius Caesar, and Servilius who had been their choice to take command against Dolabella but had managed to excuse himself; this time he again withdrew, as did Cicero who pleaded the physical dangers of the journey and accused Calenus of deceit, and in the end no embassy was sent.

Pansa left Rome on 19th March with four new legions and marched north to join Hirtius and Octavian. Hirtius advanced up the Via Aemila towards Bononia and Antony's cavalry screen withdrew before him. Pansa found his easiest route up the Via Flaminia covered by Ventidius with the three legions he had raised for Antony in Picenum, and he was forced to cross the Apennines by the more westerly Via Cassia. Ventidius had returned to Rome after his earlier recruiting for Antony, but, according to Appian, he left again early in December to avoid Cicero's reprisals against Antony's supporters and his demands on them for money to fund the war against him. Ventidius came from Asculum in Picenum and had been one of Caesar's supply and transport specialists in Gaul; Cicero contemptuously called him a mule driver, but there is no contemporary evidence for the cognomen, Bassus, which is sometimes given him.

During the second half of March despatches from Plancus and Lepidus reached Rome; they both reiterated their loyalty to the Senate, Plancus in his elegant polished style which mirrored Cicero's. But what they wrote was not to Cicero's liking, for they advocated compromise and peace instead of the holy war against Antony on which he was resolved. Though neither mentioned it in their despatches Antony appears to have been in touch with both of them. Lepidus in fact had sent his praetorian cohort to Italy, telling its commander, Marcus Junius Silanus, to join whichever side seemed likely to win. This move, allowing him to disown Silanus if his choice proved wrong, was characteristic of Lepidus; Silanus chose Antony.

On 20th March Cicero wrote to Plancus: under the guise of friendship he warned him of the effect on his career and his prospect of holding the consulate with Decimus in 42 if he did not dissociate himself from Antony. A week later he wrote to Lepidus in similar vein, but in such a patronising tone that a man like Lepidus, so conscious of his dignity and his patrician ancestors, was bound to take offence.

Some time in March Antony published an open letter to Hirtius and Octavian as they pushed tentatively forward beyond Bononia towards

Mutina. Much of it has survived since Hirtius sent a copy to Cicero, who quoted from it extensively in the 13th Philippic to refute what Antony had written. Cicero concluded by joining Servilius in congratulating Lepidus on reconciling Sextus with the Senate, adding a special commendation for Sextus. But the greater part of his speech was given over to pouring scorn, abuse and ridicule on Antony; that Antony's letter was shrewdly aimed at the weak point in Cicero's coalition against him, the alliance between Caesarians and neo-Pompeians, is evident from Cicero's fury as he analysed and tried to demolish it phrase by phrase.

> 'When I heard of Trebonius's death', Antony wrote, 'I rejoiced that the murder of a great man had been avenged, but grieved that an assassin's life seemed dearer to the people of Rome than Caesar's. Hirtius,' he went on, 'has Caesar alone to thank for his present office, and Octavian is no more than a boy who owes all to Caesar's name, yet here they are attempting to succour his murderer, the poisonous Decimus. The consuls and the Senate have tried to justify the outlawing of Dolabella who rightly executed Trebonius, they have allowed Casca to take office as tribune and the twice pardoned Varus to hold Africa, and they have condoned the illegal seizure of power by Brutus and Cassius in Macedonia and Syria. They have deprived Caesar's veterans of their land grants and deceived some of them into enlisting to avenge Caesar when in fact they are consorting with Caesar's murderers. In Hirtius's own camp one of the legionary commanders, Servius Sulpicius Galba, is openly flaunting the very dagger he used to strike Caesar down.
>
> 'They have resurrected Pompey's cause, and they are apeing the Pompeians who in the civil war tried to set up an anti-Senate in Pompey's camp. For their ringmaster they have the discredited Cicero who once boasted that he had deceived Caesar, and soon would serve them in like manner. For my part,' Antony declared, 'I am resolved to avenge Caesar: I will never abandon his cause or allow his veterans to be stripped of their lands; I will tolerate no further insults, I will never be false to my pact with Lepidus or break faith with Plancus.'

This last thrust must have struck a chord of doubt and fear in Cicero despite all his brave words.

> 'So far', Antony went on, 'no blood has been shed between Caesarians, but if it comes to battle, whoever may win, only our enemies and Caesar's will profit. My cause is just and with the help of the gods I will prevail; but if I die my fate will soon be yours, and you will discover how defeated Pompeians behave in victory. Lastly, I can put behind me the injuries done me by my friends if they will put behind them what they have done and join me in avenging Caesar.'

Inside Mutina Decimus was critically short of supplies and war material; his soldiers were near starvation and the civilian population already starving. Hirtius ordered Galba to meet Pansa a hundred miles down the Via Aemilia. But Antony had decided to intercept and destroy Pansa before he could join Hirtius and Octavian. Leaving his brother, Lucius, in charge of the siege, he moved out from Mutina with the IInd and XXXVth Legions, his own and Lepidus's praetorian cohorts and several regiments of Gallic cavalry, an adequate enough force to deal with Pansa's four legions of recruits.

But on 13th April Hirtius sent the Martial Legion and both his own and Octavian's praetorian cohorts to meet Pansa and cover his final approach march. With this escort Pansa moved out from his overnight camp on the morning of the 14th and resumed his march up the Via Aemilia. Expecting to meet only Pansa's four new legions, Antony deployed his cavalry on either side of the road near Forum Gallorum, some ten miles south east of Mutina, and set up an ambush with his infantry behind the village.

As soon as Pansa met Antony's cavalry he deployed eight cohorts of the Martial Legion north of the road with its other two cohorts and Hirtius's praetorians to the south, leaving Octavian's praetorian cohort in the centre astride the embankment which carried the road across the flat marshy land. But before Pansa could bring up his other legions Antony ordered his infantry forward with one legion on each flank and both praetorian cohorts on the road itself.

As soon as the soldiers on either side realised whom they were facing a savage and desperate battle began, for these erstwhile comrades in the army of Macedonia had personal scores to settle: the ringleaders of the mutineers executed at Brundisium had been largely from the Martial Legion which now eagerly seized the chance to avenge them, while to Antony's IInd and XXXVth Legions the soldiers of the Martial Legion were deserters and traitors.

On the north side of the road the eight cohorts of the Martial Legion under Galba and Carfulenus slowly pushed back the XXXVth; but to the south of the road the other two cohorts of the Martial Legion and Hirtius's praetorians could not hold the IInd Legion; on the central embankment Octavian's praetorian cohort stood their ground against a fierce assault, outnumbered though they were by Antony and Lepidus's praetorians; Octavian himself had been left by Pansa to defend their camp.

When the XXXVth had been forced back half a mile Antony launched his cavalry round the flank of the two embattled legions. His timing was perfect: the Gallic horse caught Pansa's legions on the march to join the battle, cut through them and wheeled back to complete their rout. The news that Pansa himself had been severely wounded added to the panic as his soldiers fled back to their camp, where Octavian managed to rally them. Octavian's praetorians died almost to a man on the road, and only the badly mauled Martial Legion remained an effective fighting unit. Though his cavalry failed to capture the enemy camp Antony had won the day.

Appian, possibly again drawing on a lost contemporary source, gives a lurid description of the two legions locked together as they fought grimly and, except for the clash of arms, in terrifying silence, with the veterans of the Martial Legion telling Pansa's frightened recruits to keep out of the way while they settled with Antony. Galba's account of the battle in a letter written to Cicero the following day is of considerable interest as a report written in the field by one of the legionary commanders concerned.

Elated by their victory, but exhausted and in some disarray Antony's infantry formed up in column and set off on the march back to Mutina. At Forum Gallorum, where the battle had started that morning, they suddenly met Hirtius marching to Pansa's aid with the IVth and VIIth Legions. In a fiercely fought encounter battle Hirtius's fresh troops defeated Antony's battle weary infantry and captured the eagles of the IInd and XXXVth. Though they had ridden and fought all day Antony's Gallic cavalry set up a defensive screen and succeeded in preventing Hirtius from exploiting his victory; long into the night they covered the retreat of the survivors and carried stragglers back to their lines at Mutina.

There Decimus was on the point of surrender, and Antony intensified his artillery bombardment. But Hirtius and Octavian closed in, and after Antony refused their offer of battle they moved round to the far side of the city, where because of the ground Antony's fieldworks were further from the walls. With his infantry depleted Antony tried to hold them off with his cavalry, but Hirtius began to harass his lines from the rear.

On 21st April Antony countered by moving out two legions and a piecemeal engagement developed into a full scale battle. Antony called up reinforcements, but before they arrived Hirtius broke into Antony's camp with the IVth Legion. In the confused fighting Hirtius was killed, but Octavian managed to recover his body before Antony counter-attacked with the Vth Legion and drove him out.

Like the first battle of Mutina the second produced no clear cut result. Antony's officers urged him to continue the siege: Decimus was trapped, they argued, Hirtius dead and Pansa unlikely to recover, and, while the losses in infantry had been roughly the same, their own cavalry was virtually intact and vastly superior in number and quality.

But Antony took little time to make up his mind to break off the siege and withdraw to Gaul, there to find himself another army and call on Lepidus and Plancus to join him. He may have calculated that he was no longer strong enough to reduce Mutina with Octavian threatening his rear. But with Hirtius dead and Pansa wounded the consular armies were leaderless, leaving Caesar's heir in arms against Caesar's deputy and in support of the most execrated of Caesar's murderers. It was unlikely that such an alliance would be acceptable to Octavian or his army, and neither he nor Antony could be sure that their soldiers would follow them against old comrades; for the ultimate survival of the Caesarians it made no sense at all. With Brutus and Cassius disposing seventeen legions, and between them controlling Greece, Asia Minor and the East, and with the neo-Pompeian Republicans dominating Rome, every consideration of self-interest and self-preservation demanded that Antony and Octavian should make common cause.

Appian's account of Pansa on his death bed urging Octavian to seek a rapprochement with Antony is perhaps apocryphal: in most of the secondary sources such purported verbatim speeches are no more than dramatised versions of what the writer thought should or might have been said. Whether true or not, Pansa's advice to Octavian was probably superfluous, though the time was not yet ripe either for him or Antony: Octavian required from the Senate a more substantive appointment than that of supernumerary propraetor by Cicero's favour, and Antony had first to secure himself a province and a proconsular army.

Antony must have known what a propaganda triumph Cicero would make of his lifting of the siege of Mutina and withdrawal to Gaul, and he must have been aware of the hazards of such a retreat. But he seems to have been confident that he could rely on Lepidus and Plancus despite their reputation as time-serving opportunists. He had been in contact with both of them, but the news from Mutina could be expected to make them think again. It seems possible, even likely, that while Octavian waited to see what he could extract from the Senate he was already secretly in touch with Antony and with the three Caesarian generals beyond the Alps.

CHAPTER VIII

The Caesarians Unite

Though Pansa's defeat caused consternation and panic among Antony's enemies in Rome this was soon relieved by reports of Hirtius's victory. A week later news of the second battle and the raising of the siege of Mutina brought general relief at this end to civil war in Italy, and on the part of Cicero and his supporters jubilation at Antony's defeat.

Victory celebrations were held on 27th April, and despite the deaths of the two consuls the Senate decreed a festival of thanksgiving to last for an unprecedented fifty days. Decimus was voted a Triumph, given overall command of the consular armies and ordered to pursue Antony and destroy him; now that it seemed safe to do so Antony and his officers were declared public enemies, to be denied fire and water and outlawed. Sextus, prudently waiting on events after Lepidus had reconciled him with Cicero and the Senate, was made High Admiral of the Roman fleet with responsibility for the coasts of Italy; though the absence of a regular navy, other than Sextus's own fleet made this no more than a titular appointment, it indicates the growing strength of the neo-Pompeians in Rome.

With the two consuls dead Cicero was able to get Cassius appointed to command against Dolabella and at last succeeded in having his imperium ratified and extended to embrace the whole Roman East. For Octavian he proposed an ovation, a kind of minor triumph, but this was defeated by the more extreme Republicans, who then made sure that a motion was passed inviting Brutus, now conveniently poised at Dyrrachium with five legions, to cross over to Italy.

The Senate nominated a commission of ten to supervise the payment of the promised bounties to the victorious armies, but omitted to include either Decimus or Octavian among its members. Now that the danger seemed to have been averted it was decided to halve the cash payments and restrict them to the IVth and Martial Legions, the soldiers of the other legions being promised land grants on discharge. Though admittedly the Treasury was depleted by the war, and Brutus and Cassius were appropriating the tax revenues of the East for their own purposes, this attempt to economise at the expense of the army was ill judged. A 1% property tax was passed to raise money in Italy, but the wealthy had little difficulty and less scruples in evading it.

When reports of these moves by the Senate reached Octavian in camp near Bononia they confirmed his suspicion of those who were gaining control in Rome; perhaps he recalled the warning in Antony's letter of what might be expected from renascent Pompeians. Certainly he had no intention of allowing himself to be praised, rewarded and removed in the words of the epigram rightly or wrongly attributed to Cicero who never explicitly denied that he was the author: the double meaning in the use of tollendum, implying removal to a higher plane of existence was not only worthy of him but also summed up his attitude to Octavian accurately enough.

Back in early November Cicero had been wary of Octavian's intentions and dubious of his chances of success; but in trying to bring about Antony's downfall any means would serve his end and Octavian quickly became the heaven sent youth who had saved Rome; he seems to have convinced himself that he could subordinate Octavian to the will of the Senate and against all the mounting evidence he continued to maintain this, both in public, and in private letters.

But Octavian had no mind to be the servant of a Republic dominated by Cicero and neo-Pompeians in league with his father's murderers; with them in control of Rome, Cassius holding the Roman East and Brutus with his army a day's sail away across the Adriatic, he was still precariously placed. He had no wish to see the three Caesarian generals in the west manipulated by Cicero into an alliance with Decimus and he was already in touch with Lepidus and Pollio. Now that Antony was no longer consul Octavian had no quarrel with him and no interest in seeing him destroyed. Events were confirming Antony's predictions, and Octavian knew that the Caesarians had to come together if they were not to be defeated in detail. His own freedom of action was limited by the reluctance of his soldiers to fight against old Caesarian comrades, though he hardly needed this constraint to appreciate that if the Caesarians did not soon join forces their cause could well be lost. Something of his strength of character and the maturity of his political judgement at the age of nineteen is shown by the fact that at this critical juncture he was prepared to wait and bide his time, allowing Antony to unite the Caesarians in the West while he extracted what he wanted from the Senate either by diplomacy or force of arms.

He refused to hand over the consular legions, remarking that anyway no soldiers of his would agree to serve under one of Caesar's murderers, and he declined to negotiate with Decimus or even to meet him. Instead he helped Antony's stragglers, releasing Decius, one of his officers captured at Mutina, and telling him that he was free to rejoin Antony. Before Decius left he asked Octavian what his attitude was to Antony: Octavian replied that he had surely made this clear enough to the discerning and there was no point in saying more to fools.

Decimus wrote to Octavian urging him at least to block Ventidius's march to join Antony; but Octavian ignored him and made no attempt to intercept Ventidius when he set off with the three legions he had recruited for Antony. During the operations round Mutina Ventidius had remained encamped on the Via Flaminia and had made no move to come to Antony's assistance. In both cases the reason may have been that two of Ventidius's three legions, like two of Octavian's, had been raised from veterans of Caesar's old VIIth and VIIIth Legions who were not prepared to fight their old comrades, providing another example of how the abiding loyalty of Caesar's soldiers restricted the Caesarian generals.

Despite the confident tone of his despatches to Rome and his letters to Cicero, Decimus and his army were in no shape to carry out the Senate's instructions to destroy Antony. His soldiers were sick and half starved, his baggage animals long since eaten, and he had no cavalry. He proceeded to waste two more days in going to confer with Pansa, only to find that he had died from his wounds.

In contrast Antony acted with speed and decision. On 22nd April, the day after the second battle, he marched west from Mutina up the Via Aemilia with the Vth Alaudae, two other weary and battle scarred legions, and the survivors of Lepidus's praetorian cohort under Silanus. The column was screened by his Gallic cavalry under command of his brother, Lucius, and Lucius Trebellius. No longer consul, and without Rome's authority to sustain him, everything now depended on Antony and whether he could hold his army together. But it was just such a pass as this which brought out the best in him; generous in victory, disaster was a challenge to be met with a joke on his lips and a sword in his hand. He drew deep on some inner reserves of mental and physical strength to lift his soldiers, discounting their hardships by sharing them, inspiring them with his fatalistic humour and his ability to outmarch and outride them. It was this facet of Antony's character, together with the loyalty and fortitude of his exhausted soldiers, and above all the discipline and professional competence of the Gallic cavalry, which prevented the long and arduous retreat from degenerating into the rout which his enemies so confidently predicted.

Antony marched up the Via Aemilia by Rhegium Lepidii and Parma to Placentia and then west along the Via Postumia to Dertona, recruiting reinforcements as he went, according to Decimus from the gaols he opened and the slaves he freed. Behind him Decimus trailed doggedly along the same road, the gap between them widening with every day's march. At Dertona Antony turned south-west on to the minor road, later the Via Julia Augusta, to Aquae Statiellae and the difficult passes over the coastal mountains where the Apennines meet the Maritime Alps. Here hunger and exhaustion took their toll, and Plutarch describes how Antony and his soldiers were reduced to gnawing bark and roots and eating creatures which no man had tasted before. But he held the army together, and on 3rd May, only two weeks after leaving Mutina, he reached his rendezvous with Ventidius at Vada Sabata on the Ligurian coast some thirty miles west of Genoa.

Here he was joined by some of his stragglers, perhaps Decius among them with news of Octavian's overtures. Here too he would have received despatches from his agents and supporters in Rome telling him that he and his officers had been outlawed, and letters from Fulvia who had been helped by Atticus and had found refuge in Calenus's house. He would have heard of the Senate's slighting of Octavian and his refusal to hand over the consular legions to Decimus, how Cassius now held the East with the Senate's authority and confirmation of reports that his own brother, Gaius, was a prisoner in Brutus's hands.

Decimus was just west of Dertona when he received a report that Antony had halted at Vada Sabata because his soldiers had refused to continue the march west along the coastal road and were insisting on heading north for Pollentia and the Little St. Bernard pass. This may have been part of a deception plan; if so it was a plausible enough story for this was the shortest way home for Antony's Gallic troops. Decimus at any rate believed it and sent detachments to intercept Antony at Pollentia; all they found waiting for them was an ambush mounted by Antony's far ranging cavalry under Trebellius.

Encouraged by the junction with Ventidius the soldiers quickly recovered from their ordeal in the mountains, and Antony, now with six legions, continued the march along the corniche road. Lepidus had stationed Quintus Terentius Culleo to guard the road where it passed through a coastal defile and entered his province; but Culleo went over to Antony, perhaps persuaded to do so by Silanus. Confident now that Lepidus would not oppose him Antony rode on with the advanced guard, leaving Ventidius in command of the main body of the army. Lucius's cavalry screen reached Forum Julii on 12th May, and three days later Antony camped beyond the town on the eastern bank of the Argenteus. The retreat from Mutina had been a notable feat of arms; after the junction with Ventidius it became an advance into Narbonese Gaul; now on the banks of the Argenteus it remained for Antony and Lepidus to come to terms.

When he heard that Antony had entered his province Lepidus had moved his army out from their camp at Avenio on the Rhone; by forced marches he reached the Argenteus three days after Antony and camped facing him across the river. In a letter to Cicero on 22nd May he protested his loyalty to the Senate and added that Antony's soldiers were deserting him. Indeed there was contact across the river for Antony had deliberately made no move to entrench his camp, as was the standard practice for a Roman army in hostile territory, and old comrades in the two armies began to fraternise; others eager for news of family and friends from Italy soon joined in.

While Antony was investing Mutina the Senate had ordered Plancus to bring reinforcements from Transalpine Gaul for the consular armies advancing to Decimus's relief. The high Alpine passes were still blocked by snow, and on 26th April Plancus crossed the upper Rhone into Lepidus's province en route for the Little St. Bernard pass and northern Italy. But fearing that Lepidus might join Antony, he halted when reports reached him that the siege of Mutina had been lifted and Antony was retreating across the Cisalpina.

An exchange of letters followed between Plancus and Lepidus, and then through an envoy, Marcus Juventius Laterensis, Lepidus assured Plancus that he would resist if Antony tried to enter his province and asked Plancus to join him. Plancus agreed and crossed the Isara on 12th May, to be met with a further message from Lepidus saying that he could handle Antony on his own and telling him to wait on the Isara; Plancus also received a private letter from Laterensis, who was back with Lepidus, warning him not to trust either Lepidus or his army.

Plancus stayed for a few days on the Isara in the vain hope that Decimus would catch up with him; then he decided to ignore Lepidus's last message and march south to stiffen his resolve to resist Antony. He garrisoned his bridge across the Isara, leaving it standing for Decimus to use, and on 20th May set off for Forum Volconii, eight days march away, where he believed Lepidus was.

On the Argenteus contact continued across the river between the two armies camped on either bank. Among Lepidus's seven legions the Xth had many soldiers who had served under Antony's command in Caesar's old Xth; they fraternised with erstwhile Caesarian comrades in Ventidius's VIIth, VIIIth and IXth, at first circumspectly and in small groups, but soon they were openly entertaining each other and finally they built a bridge of boats to get back more easily across the river at night to their own camps.

It is difficult to say whether Lepidus acquiesced in these exchanges by design or force of circumstances. Apparently he made no attempt to stop them, but to some extent he was the servant rather than the master of events, and even if he had been so minded it is doubtful whether his troops would have fought Antony's. While it may be that he owed his position as much to his powerful patrician connections as to his own ability, he had still been a loyal lieutenant of Caesar's; now, like the other Caesarian generals, he found himself as a friend of Antony's in a dilemma not of his own making or seeking. Rome was speaking with many voices, and it is hardly surprising that he thought first of his own interest in alliance with his old Caesarian colleagues.

When Laterensis remonstrated with him at the open fraternisation and urged him to put the loyalty of his own troops to the test by calling a halt to it, the Xth Legion took things into their own hands, opening the gates of their camp to Antony one evening and escorting him to Lepidus's tent; there, after Lepidus in his night-shirt had feigned surprise and dismay, he and Antony were reconciled. Laterensis was the only casualty: loyal to the Senate, disgusted by Lepidus breaking his word and reproaching himself for the breach of the agreement he had negotiated for Plancus he fell on his sword. Perhaps to protect his own family in Rome Lepidus wrote to the Senate still protesting his loyalty and pleading that his soldiers had forced his hand.

Plancus was forty miles away when on 30th May news reached him that Antony and Lepidus had joined forces and were marching towards him. He withdrew, recrossing the Isara on 4th June and this time breaking up his bridge behind him; at Cularo he halted to wait for Decimus. As soon as reports of the agreement between Antony and Lepidus reached Sextus in Massalia he sailed for his base in the Balearics.

In Further Spain Pollio had received no instructions from the Senate. Despatches from Rome were sent overland during the winter months and they normally took thirty to forty days to reach the province; they were often held up by bandits in the Pyrenean passes, and now they were being intercepted by Lepidus's agents and further delayed. The news of the battles at Mutina did not reach Pollio until nearly the end of May. By 8th June he knew that Antony and Lepidus had joined forces ten days earlier, for on that day he wrote to Cicero from his headquarters at Corduba. He describes how his proquaestor, Lucius Cornelius Balbus, nephew of Caesar's agent, had absconded to Mauretania with the contents of the provincial treasury; he went on to say that Antony and Lepidus had been trying to tamper with his soldiers' loyalty, mentioning the XXVIIth and XXXth Legions, and adding that so far he had managed to keep his army intact and within his own province.

But by now Octavian was almost certainly in touch with Pollio, insisting that the Caesarians must close their ranks and stand together; Antony was saying much the same. Pollio had been one of Caesar's most able and trusted officers and he was an old comrade and friend of Antony's. From a provincial Italian background himself he disliked Cicero, distrusted the intrigues in Rome and deplored the effect of civil war on Italy. When he left Corduba in mid-June and marched east with his three legions he had made up his mind to join Antony and Lepidus. It has been said that with their thirteen legions astride his lines of communication he had little choice; but he could still have stayed in Further Spain without committing himself. His own inclinations, his soldiers' loyalties, his friendship with Antony and Octavian's letters all prompted his decision as much as the reality of the military arithmetic.

When the news reached Rome that, instead of resisting Antony, Lepidus had joined forces with him, there was consternation, both in the Senate and among the families and supporters of the conspirators who were terrified of the retribution which they feared would surely follow if Octavian now joined Antony and Lepidus. In a last minute attempt to forestall this the Senate appointed Octavian to joint command with Decimus against Antony and Lepidus. But this was a despairing gesture, for Octavian had made it clear enough that he had no intention of co-operating with Decimus, who anyway was by now across the Alps and approaching Cularo. In his official despatches to the Senate and in his private letters to Cicero Decimus continued to blame Octavian for not intercepting Ventidius and to demand that he should hand over the IVth and Martial Legions.

Cicero vented his frustration on Lepidus, and the Senate took what revenge it could when on 30th June he was declared a public enemy on a motion put by his own brother and seconded by Antony's uncle, Lucius Caesar, thus rendering his property forfeit and debarring his sons from public office. But internal jealousies again blocked the appointment of new consuls to replace Hirtius and Pansa, and no practical steps were taken to support Decimus, the Senate confining itself to expressing its fervent hope that Plancus would remain loyal.

In little more than two months the euphoria brought about by the relief of Mutina had faded, and the high hopes of restoring the Republic had been replaced by despondency and despair. The defeated and outlawed Antony had somehow escaped to Provence where Lepidus had proved a man of straw. Instead of crossing with his army to Italy Brutus had left Dyrrachium and was rumoured to be marching away east along the Via Egnatia. Octavian was still in camp near Bononia, but instead of being discarded and isolated the threat of his eight legions grew ever more menacing. Cicero had good reason when he described the Senate as a tool which had broken in his hands, but that it was he himself who had first blunted it was beyond his understanding.

In their search for a scapegoat many of the Republicans blamed Brutus for not bringing his army to Italy. But he can hardly have forgotten how, after Caesar's death, public opinion had forced him and Cassius and the others to leave Rome and eventually Italy, though to judge solely by his private letters to Cicero he had convinced himself that it was Antony's ambition to assume Caesar's kingly power which had driven him from Italy. He feared that his presence in Italy might bring Octavian and Antony together and unite the Caesarians against him, and in the East Dolabella threatened his communications with Cassius. He continued to hold Gaius Antonius prisoner instead of executing him as Cicero urged, and it seems possible that he had not given up hope of an agreement with Antony, who as recently as February had tacitly recognised his claim and Cassius's to the consulate of 41. He also tried to restrain Cicero from venting his spite on Lepidus's children, whose mother was his own half-sister, Junia; his other half-sister was married to Cassius.

From his letters to Cicero during May and June it is evident that Brutus not only found Cicero's obsessional hatred of Antony distasteful but also felt that it was clouding his judgement; he tried to convince him that, with Caesar dead and Antony thwarted in his ambition to succeed him, it was Octavian who posed the real threat to all of them and to the Republic. This Cicero refused to admit, even in private or to himself. When Atticus sent Brutus an extract from a letter Cicero had written to Octavian, pleading for the safety of the men who had killed Caesar, he lost all patience. 'Recall your words' he wrote to Cicero, 'And dare to deny that they are the plea of a serf to his lord', adding 'Better not to be, than by his leave to be'.

This letter to Cicero and his reply to Atticus reveal Brutus's insight into both Cicero's and Octavian's character. 'What good is it to me' he asks Atticus, 'If the price for overthrowing Antony is to put another in his place? If he who righted that wrong supports another who will take a firmer hold and strike a deeper root? How strangely blind is fear: you guard against what you fear from one, yet bring it on yourself from another when you might have escaped it altogether . . . Cicero fears death, exile and poverty too much . . . What use are his fine speeches on his country's liberty, his exquisitely composed treatises on dignity, death, exile and poverty? . . . Let him fawn and serve; for my part nothing will stop me fighting against monarchy and all absolute and unconstitutional powers above the law'. Though it has been suggested that both letters are later interpolations there is no good reason to doubt their authenticity.

From Bononia Octavian continued to correspond secretly with the Caesarian generals in the West, and his agents kept him informed of every move in Rome; there it soon became evident that he wanted the consulate for himself. From an outburst of Cicero's it seems likely that Philippus and Marcellus were canvassing for him, and possible that they may have put forward Servilius as his colleague; his daughter was betrothed to Octavian during 43.

After Mutina Cicero may have aspired to a second term as consul; Appian, Dio and Plutarch all refer to a proposal that he and Octavian should be colleagues, and Brutus even received a report that Cicero had been elected. Cicero still believed that he could manage Octavian, and the idea of directing the fortunes of the Republic as elder statesman and guiding the military ambitions of a younger colleague had long been a dream close to his heart. It was a partnership which Brutus, with a more realistic appraisal of the likely outcome, profoundly distrusted.

The Senate too took a different view, recalling that except in civil war or like emergency no consular had been freely elected to a second term for more than a hundred years; there was nothing in Cicero's record as a politician which inclined the senators to contemplate making an exception for him. With their minds on protocol and precedent they were blind to the emergency facing them and the civil war which threatened, and they still could not agree the appointment of new consuls.

At Bononia Octavian's soldiers were becoming bored and increasingly impatient with the delays in paying them their bounties; Octavian had little difficulty in directing their frustration at the Senate. He emphasised the slights put on him as their general and the effect of excluding him from the commission of ten, telling them that it was ridiculous for the Senate to expect them to undertake another campaign before their bounties for the last one had been paid; at his prompting the army decided to send a delegation of centurions to Rome to demand payment. As a result the Senate sent representatives to discuss the soldiers' grievances; but misjudging their mood and the efficacy of Octavian's intellignce they made the mistake of sending the IVth and Martial Legions a secret offer to pay their bounties in full if they transferred their allegiance to Decimus.

Octavian handled the situation with skill and finesse; hints that if he were consul he would make it his business to see that all his soldiers were paid in full were enough to despatch another party of armed centurions to Rome to insist that he should be made consul. Though obliged to deposit their arms outside the Senate they made it clear that they were prepared to use them to have their way. However after reprimanding them for their threatening behaviour the senators managed to stall them with promises.

But when they returned empty handed, without the consulate for Octavian or bounties for their comrades, there was such an outburst of resentment and anger that Octavian decided to turn it to his advantage: he ordered the whole army of eight legions, together with the cavalry and auxiliaries, to march on Rome. As soon as the main body was on its way he rode on himself at the head of a small body of picked troops.

Once again reports of a general marching on Rome brought confusion and panic to the city. As rumours spread that Octavian aimed higher than the consulate, coupled with prophecies of the revenge he would take on Caesar's murderers, those who knew or felt they were at risk fled to the country with their families and their more portable possessions; others who feared the violence of the mob barricaded themselves in their houses.

The senators were in a ferment of self-recrimination, each trying to blame the other for antagonising Octavian and procrastinating over the bounties. Cicero had gone into hiding, and in their panic the Senate sent envoys to offer Octavian all he had asked and more: leave to stand for the consulate, and immediate payment of 5,000 denarii to each of his soldiers to be supervised by him instead of the commission of ten.

After the envoys had left came the unexpected and apparently providential news that two legions, long awaited from Africa as reinforcements for the consular armies, had at last arrived. This brought a sudden change of heart and a stiffening mood of resistance in the Senate, with shame for the craven manner in which they had given in and talk of defending the ancient liberties of Rome. They sent further envoys to rescind their offer, but their arrival just as the first envoys were delivering the original message added fuel to the soldiers' fury. Secure now in the knowledge that he had Rome at his mercy Octavian continued his march.

He halted with his advanced guard outside the walls and sent messengers into the city to reassure the people and tell them that they had nothing to fear. The two ex-Africa legions promptly declared for him, and the only other troops in Rome, some of Pansa's recruits, quickly followed their example. Then a group of senators went out to Octavian's camp to try and make their peace with him. That evening a rumour spread through Rome that the IVth and Martial Legions had changed sides again and declared for the Senate. Some believed this and tried to put the city into a state of defence and prepare for a siege;

others continued to load their possessions on to ships at Ostia. At this late stage someone thought of the value of Octavian's mother and sister as hostages, but his agents had foreseen and forestalled this by placing them in the care of the Vestal Virgins. In fact the IVth and Martial Legions knew well enough where their best interest lay and the rumour proved false. The next morning all resistance collapsed when Octavian marched into the city and occupied the Campus Martius. Of the senators who had remained in Rome the last to emerge from hiding was Cicero, to be met according to Appian, with Octavian's ironic comment, 'Ah, the last of my friends to greet me'.

Octavian's first act was to seize enough money from the Treasury to pay all his soldiers their bounties in full, though he only gave them half, promising them the other 2,500 denarii as soon as he was consul; they did not have long to wait until he was elected with his kinsman, Quintus Pedius, as his colleague. On the 19th of the month, which would later be renamed August in his honour, he made his formal entrance into Rome as consul; his twentieth birthday was still five weeks away.

Later it was said that at his inauguration ceremony twelve vultures hovered above the ritual sacrifices, emulating the twelve which according to tradition had watched over Romulus as he laid the foundation stone of the city.

As soon as he was formally installed Octavian lost no time in having his adoption as Caesar's son and heir ratified by the Senate. Next he arranged to try Caesar's murderers in their absence. As well as the sixty who were directly implicated others were arraigned and accused of having prior knowledge of the plot, among them the absent Sextus Pompeius. With Octavian presiding the court completed the trial in a single day; only one member of the panel of judges voted for acquittal, thus spoiling an otherwise unanimous verdict of guilty, and this Octavian did not forget.

Leaving Pedius in charge of Rome with instructions to repeal the decrees outlawing Antony and Lepidus, Octavian marched north up the Via Flaminia; with the two African legions and one formed from Pansa's recruits he now had eleven legions. He would be able to counter any attempt by Decimus to recover the province or to withdraw through it and round the head of the Adriatic to join Brutus and Cassius in Illyricum. But Octavian's main object was to come to an agreement with Antony and Lepidus; he wrote offering Antony assistance against Decimus, but Antony replied that he would himself settle Caesar's account with Decimus and his own with Plancus.

In mid-June Decimus joined Plancus at Cularo. Between them the consuls designate for 42 disposed a considerable army: Plancus had four experienced legions and a large force of Gallic cavalry: Decimus had no less than ten legions, but six of those he had recruited on his march across northern Italy, and the morale of the other four had suffered in Mutina and during their ineffectual pursuit of Antony. They were together at Cularo from mid-June to early August, but little is known of what passed between them; in a letter to Cicero written in June Plancus's envoy, Gaius Furnius, referred to the friendly relations between them. But by the end of July, according to a letter Plancus wrote to Cicero on the 28th, Furnius was negotiating on his behalf with Octavian, supposedly to obtain help against Antony and Lepidus; in this letter Plancus reiterates his loyalty to the Senate and the Republic and blames Octavian for not coming to his aid. However there can be little doubt that Furnius brought Plancus back letters from Octavian repeating his refusal to co-operate with Decimus and invoking Caesar's name in urging him to come to terms with the other Caesarian generals; Plancus had been Caesar's lieutenant, and unlike Decimus his freedom of action had not been compromised by involvement in Caesar's murder. When Pollio joined Antony and Lepidus in July he added his voice to their appeals to Plancus. It was perhaps the knowledge that Antony too would have nothing to do with Decimus which helped Plancus to make up his mind to join the other Caesarians. Like Lepidus he was to some extent the victim of circumstances, but he was already adept in concealing his lack of principle and he was beginning to show the talent for survival which was to serve him so well over the next few years. In mid-August he marched south to join Antony and Lepidus, leaving Decimus at Cularo.

Decimus was now isolated west of the Alps with the Caesarians in control of all Gaul and northern Italy; his only hope was to reach Illyricum and join Brutus, and the direct and only practicable way was to recross the Alps and march east for Aquiliea, trusting that he could either evade Octavian or brush him aside. Instead he chose the long, difficult and circuitous route skirting the western and northern foothills of the Alps to the crossing of the upper Rhine, and thence by way of the Tyrol, the Brenner and the passes of the Julian Alps to Illyricum. It was a plan born of despair, and it took no account of the distance and terrain involved, nor of the fact that beyond the Rhine lay unknown barbarian territory and the formidable barrier of the main Alpine massif.

His army soon melted away; the six new legions declared for Octavian, and then the four from Mutina turned about and marched south with the main body of the cavalry to join Antony. Decimus rode on to the Rhine with a regiment of cavalry; after allowing them to return to their homes in Gaul he crossed the river with a small escort and headed east. He tried to pass himself off as a Gaul, but eventually he was captured by a tribal chieftain, and, according to Appian, executed on Antony's orders.

CHAPTER IX

The Triumvirs

Negotiations between Octavian and Antony continued by letter. They were both in a much stronger position than they had been a few months before. Antony was no longer consul, but all the Caesarian legates in the West had joined him with their armies and he held the four western provinces from the Atlantic to the Alps with some twenty three legions. Octavian was no longer the revolutionary leader of a private army but an elected consul of Rome, and when Decimus's six legions joined him on the Via Flaminia they brought his strength to seventeen legions. Between them the two Caesarian leaders controlled all Italy and the West, with Brutus and Cassius holding the other half of the Roman world from the Adriatic to the Euphrates. Logic, self-preservation and the mood of their soldiers made an agreement between Antony and Octavian a matter of political and military necessity for both of them.

In October Antony with Lepidus, Pollio, Plancus and Ventidius marched back along the coast road into Italy at the head of seventeen legions; Antony's lieutenant Varius, disparagingly or perhaps affectionately nicknamed Cotyla, or half pint, was left to hold the western provinces with six legions. Octavian moved slowly up the Via Flaminia and into Cisalpine Gaul to meet the other Caesarians. Lepidus was acceptable to both Antony and Octavian and he acted as intermediary. His vain ineffectual nature, coupled with his inability to inspire loyalty in his soldiers and the ignominious end to his soaring ambition in Sicily seven years later, all tend to obscure the fact that he had been one of Caesar's most trusted lieutenants and had shown considerable administrative capacity as his Master of Horse and deputy in Rome.

It was these qualities, positive as well as negative, though perhaps not these alone, which now prompted Antony and Octavian to make him the third partner in the alliance they were to form. With their past experience of each other they both felt that they needed a third man to hold the balance and one who would not aspire to usurp their own positions; Lepidus was the obvious choice. And if Lepidus could not allay the fears of the old senatorial oligarchy he could at least provide some air of respectability as a patrician from one of the great families of Rome with a long tradition of service to the Republic. Though

Octavian was now consul his followers remained the motley collection of soldiers of fortune, political extremists and financial opportunists, which a revolutionary leader inevitably gathers around him. Of Antony's lieutenants only Plancus was a member of a senatorial family, and though Antony was himself a noble and a consular there were many in Rome who remembered his cavalier behaviour as Caesar's deputy; they distrusted his character and his associates, and they feared the revenge he would wreak on those who had opposed him as consul and fought against him at Mutina.

The meeting took place in October or early in November on a small island in the river Lavinius, which runs down from the northern foothills of the Apennines and passes near Bononia on its way to the Adriatic north of Ravenna. Lepidus stage-managed the arrangements with flair and skill. Antony and Octavian approached from opposite directions, each with five legions, and camped facing one another across the river. Lepidus had bridges built from either bank to the island, where tents were pitched and a dais set up in sight of both armies. The two principals waited at the bridges, each with an escort from his praetorian cohort, while Lepidus made a show of searching the island and then waved his cloak as a signal that it was free of any ambush.

When Antony and Octavian met on the island it was for the first time for more than a year; in full view of the armies they took their seats with Lepidus on the dais, Octavian as consul sitting in the centre. They resolved to take upon themselves the task of restoring the Roman State. To this end they accorded themselves legislative and executive powers for five years, including the right to appoint the consuls, provincial governors, magistrates and other officers of State; this would be ratified and given statutory authority by the Assembly. Thus on an island in the Lavinius the second Triumvirate was set up, its ultimate authority the swords of the watching legions.

Still in sight of the two armies the triumvirs conferred with their lieutenants and close advisers for two days, agreeing a broad outline strategy and plans to implement it. Antony and Octavian would take the field to avenge Caesar and wrest the Roman East from Brutus and Cassius, while Lepidus would govern Rome and all Italy; for this he would retain three of his legions and hand over three to Octavian and four to Antony, so that each had twenty for the coming war.

They divided between them the provinces not controlled by Brutus and Cassius; Antony kept Cisalpine and Transalpine Gaul, Lepidus Narbonese Gaul and Nearer Spain and added Further Spain, and Octavian took Africa, Sicily and the other islands. Though this division to some extent confirmed the status quo in that Antony retained Transalpine and Cisalpine Gaul, which the Assembly had voted him the year before, and Lepidus already held Provence and Nearer Spain, it also indicates that Antony was the senior partner. The Cisalpina was the key to Italy, and having surrendered Further Spain to Lepidus Pollio apparently took over the province as Antony's legate. Octavian was left with the task of ejecting Sextus from Sicily, where he had established himself in the west of the island, and possibly Cornificius from Africa Vetus which he had been appointed to govern by the Senate.

The self-appointed triumvirs then nominated the consuls for the next five years. Octavian agreed to resign his office for the remaining two months of 43, allowing Antony to reward Ventidius by making him Pedius's colleague. Plancus was confirmed as consul designate for the coming year, with Lepidus replacing Decimus. Perhaps to compensate him for the breaking off of his daughter's betrothal to Octavian, Servilius was nominated with Lucius Antonius for 41, and Pollio and Domitius Calvinus for 40. Domitius had been one of the most able of Caesar's generals, and with Lepidus one of the few from an old senatorial family; he was to be virtually the only one to hold high command under the triumvirate. Though he and Pollio were acceptable to Octavian as loyal Caesarians they were friends and supporters of Antony, and the selection of the consuls for these four years again emphasises Antony's pre-eminence. The five year period would be rounded off by Antony and Octavian taking office in 39, each for his second term.

As they laid their plans the triumvirs could not afford to ignore their watching armies. In a sense it was the soldiers who had brought about the reconciliation between Antony and Octavian, and now with their demands for revenge for Caesar and land for themselves were dictating the overall strategy. Collectively they were beginning to realise that they had made these three men who before their eyes were now ordering and dividing the Roman world, and who without them would be nothing. The triumvirs knew this well enough, and to satisfy the soldiers' hunger for land they named eighteen of the richest cities in the most fertile areas of Italy and called on them to provide the necessary land for resettlement. But perhaps neither they nor their soldiers appreciated the scope of the social revolution on which they were embarking and the scale of the reallocation of land, which would soon redress some of the ills of the peasantry.

A marriage tie as evidence of their good faith would bind the principals and meet the soldiers' demand for a guarantee that the agreement would last. Lepidus's son was already betrothed to Antony's daughter, and so a marriage was arranged between

Octavian, conveniently released from his engagement to Servilia, and Claudia, Fulvia's daughter by Clodius and Antony's step-daughter.

The terms of the whole agreement were set down in writing, signed by the triumvirs, and read out to the waiting armies by Octavian as consul; the soldiers greeted the announcement with relief and applause and then lost no time in starting on their own celebrations and reunions with their comrades across the river. With the soldiers satisfied and their attention diverted the triumvirs left the open dais and retired into one of the tents with their senior officers for a secret session. The questions they still had to resolve were how to finance the coming war and how to deal with their political enemies in Rome and Italy. Between them they had a total of forty three legions and the money to pay and maintain them on a war footing had to be found. The impoverished western provinces could barely maintain their six garrison legions. Brutus and Cassius were gathering in the taxes and tribute from the East, and from western Sicily Sextus was threatening Africa and Sardinia with his fleet. Thus Italy was left as the only possible source of revenue; but they could not hope to raise what they needed from direct taxes which had not been levied in living memory, and any attempt to do so would only alienate the ordinary citizens on whose support they relied. The real wealth of Rome and Italy still lay securely in the hands of comparatively few; some of them were Republicans and erstwhile supporters of Pompey, but many more were merchants, bankers and provincial landowners who had prudently eschewed politics.

The triumvirs' enemies were Republicans and ex-Pompeians who had now been joined by many of the younger generation from the noble families of Rome; they were led by Caesar's murderers, some of whom he had pardoned after they had fought for Pompey. It seemed to the triumvirs that Caesar's policy of clemency and pardon to his Roman enemies had contributed to his downfall and this was an error they were determined not to repeat. Octavian knew how the senators had proposed to treat him after Mutina; Antony and Lepidus were still bitter at the indignity of being declared public enemies by the Senate when they held high elected office and angry at the attacks on their families.

Thus they arrived at a single solution to the problems of financing the war and dealing with their political enemies, with Sulla's proscriptions providing both precedent and example; they would eliminate their enemies by proscribing them and fund the war with their confiscated property. It was neat and logical, and they congratulated themselves on recognising and avoiding the mistake which Caesar had made in pardoning his enemies. No doubt each privately recalled personal scores which could be conveniently settled, and inevitably their thoughts also turned to the rich whose wealth they coveted, even if they were not properly enemies.

Still on that island in the Lavinius the three Caesarian leaders, two of them Roman nobles from families of ancient Republican lineage and one the young heir to Caesar's name and fortune, sat down in cold blood to plan the deliberate campaign of licensed murder which would engulf and destroy what was left of the senatorial oligarchy and the Republic in a reign of terror, blood and treachery. In secret, abetted by their lieutenants, among them Plancus and Pollio, they proceeded to list the proscribed. Predictably the friends whom one of them wished to protect were the enemies of another, but so determined were they, individually and collectively, to make sure their enemies did not escape that they bartered their friends and relatives for the inclusion of those enemies.

Lepidus sacrificed his elder brother, Lucius Aemilius Paullus, perhaps without scruple or regret for it was he who had moved the ultimate decree against him; Paullus's son, Aemilius Lepidus Paullus, was also proscribed. To ensure that Cicero was listed Antony offered up his uncle, Lucius Caesar, who had seconded Paullus; here Octavian's reluctance was perhaps feigned, if not later invented, for there could be no place for Cicero in the future he envisaged for Rome. Octavian then named Gaius Toranius who had been his tutor and his father's friend, Plancus his own brother and Pollio his father-in-law.

This set the tone and perhaps was intended to emphasise the triumvirs' intent; in the event none of their relatives died except Pollio's father-in-law who was drowned at sea fleeing from Italy. Cicero was the only consular who was killed and he had opportunity enough to escape, but this time his indecision was to prove fatal.

It was Antony, supported by Lepidus, who proscribed Cicero, though it is not so much for this act of revenge, but rather for the exultation he and Fulvia showed at Cicero's death and the indignities they heaped on his severed head, that history has indicted him. Certainly Antony felt that he had ample justification: the Philippics had reached a new level of sustained personal abuse, and it had been Cicero who had organised the coalition against him at Mutina.

Cicero's reputation and the incalculable debt which Western civilisation owes to him derives from his liberal and humanist philosophy so ably expounded in his essays and treatises. His standing as a man of principle and the defender of Republican ideals has fluctuated with the political concepts of the time, its zenith when oligarchies similar to that of ancient Rome flourished in Europe and

America.

His contemporaries were often spell bound by his oratory, but they came to distrust him as a politician. They admired his literary talents and they recognised his integrity as a man of Republican principle, but they grew weary of his vanity and self-congratulation as he constantly harped back to his own achievements as consul. That a man of such genius should have been so inept a politician, so blind to the realities of his day, is difficult to appreciate from our distance in time which blurs the distinction between the man of letters and the man of affairs. It is evident from the comments of Brutus and Pollio that Cicero's hatred of Antony bordered on the paranoic and that they found this distasteful. For whatever Antony's faults, and they were many, he was not a man who inspired hatred in any of his other enemies. His peers did not condemn him for Cicero's death; what dismayed them was the ribald glee he displayed when Cicero's head was brought to him, what appalled them was the venom with which Fulvia drove pins into the tongue which had spoken the Philippics.

It is difficult to determine the part each triumvir played in the proscriptions. The first accounts were written during the long reign of Augustus, who in later life commended the works of Cicero to his grandson; it was politic for the writers to play down Octavian's part, though under his successors material less favourable to him was included. The sources available to the later ancient historians had already been confused by editing and propaganda. Some modern historians have seen a startling transformation in personality between the cold and ruthless young Octavian and the wise and benign Augustus, founder of the Principate and Empire, which stems in part from the modern convention of using different names. They have attempted to explain it by postulating a reluctant Octavian carried along by the blood lust of his older colleagues. When faced with clear evidence that it was Octavian who became the most pitiless and unprincipled of the three in carrying out the proscriptions they have pleaded his youth and suggested a complete later change of character.

But the truth is surely simpler, and at the same time more complex. Antony, impulsive and prone to overreact, Lepidus, ever mindful of his dignity and lineage, both had personal scores to settle, and no doubt they named their enemies with relish. But by birth and upbringing they both belonged to the old ruling oligarchy, as did Plancus if not Pollio, and they had no mind to destroy it. It was the cool and calculating Octavian who recognised the advantage to him in eliminating most of the two to three hundred members of that oligarchy whom the secondary sources agree were proscribed. Appian quotes a figure of 300 senators and 2,000 equites, but there is no other evidence to support either this or the assumption that Plutarch's figure of 200 to 300 refers only to senators.

The triumvirs ordered the proscriptions to be implemented at once, apparently choosing a method deliberately designed to cause terror and confusion. The older men in Rome remembered Sulla, and among them were some who had been proscribed and escaped. But Sulla was now to be outdone: as one of the triumvirs remarked, three men had more enemies than one. This time the property of the wives and families of the proscribed was also declared forfeit, and the reward of head money, 25,000 denarii for citizens and freedom for slaves, was shrewdly pitched to appeal to the baser instincts of envy, malice and greed.

When the execution squads arrived in Rome there was consternation among all who feared that their names might be on the secret list of proscribed. Though on that first night the city gates were closed to prevent the victims escaping, only four of the seventeen on the first list were killed. Pedius, in charge of Rome as consul, knew nothing of the triumvirs' intentions or how many they had proscribed. In defiance of their orders he tried to stay the panic which gripped the city by publishing the names of the seventeen and declaring they were the only ones to be listed. The next day he collapsed and died, according to Appian exhausted by his efforts to restore confidence and maintain order.

By the time the triumvirs reached Rome the senators and the wealthier citizens were in a turmoil of fear for their lives and property. On three successive days, each escorted by his praetorian cohort and at the head of a single legion, they made their separate formal entries into the city to the applause of the mass of the people, who were unaffected by the proscriptions and neither knew nor cared that they were witnessing the last bloody act in the death of the Republic. Perhaps there was reason in their lack of concern for it was they who survived, and themselves ensured that Rome would survive the Republic.

The Assembly was summoned on 27th November to pass the Lex Titia ratifying the setting up of the triumvirate and the powers of the triumvirs. That same evening the names of another 130 proscribed were posted on the rostra in the Forum, followed shortly by a further list of 150. In this manner, as a deliberate act of policy on the part of these three men, shrewdly calculated by at least one of them, and aimed both at their political and personal enemies and those whose only crime was their wealth, the oligarchy which had ruled the most powerful and long lived Republic of the ancient world came to its end; and in this welter of blood and treachery the Principate and a new oligarchy was conceived.

Appian describes the fate of the proscribed in some detail, with stories of how some slaves won freedom by betraying their masters and others sacrificed their lives to save them, stories of the hiding places, disguises and stratagems used to evade arrest, of how some met their deaths and others escaped, tales of darkest treachery and devoted self-sacrifice. The wealth of detail is itself a measure of the terror the proscriptions engendered. It is clear that, by the time Appian wrote, these tales had passed into the folklore which took the place of fiction in the ancient world.

But many did escape, and perhaps it was intended that some of them should, for then their property remained forfeit but no head money had to be paid. There were some whose wealth and connections put them at risk but who were not proscribed; Atticus was saved by the help he had given Fulvia, and he was to cover himself against a Republican victory by protecting Brutus's mother, Servilia. Lucius Caesar found refuge in the house of his sister, Julia, who outfaced his would-be executioners by offering her breast to their swords and reminding them that it had suckled Antony. But Octavian did not forget Selicius, who paid with his life for his vote to acquit Caesar's murderers.

Though himself proscribed Sextus now controlled most of Sicily; his army had trapped the praetor and governor, Pompeius Bithynicus, who eventually surrendered and joined him. Sextus used his fleet to rescue the fugitives from the proscriptions, and he soon had a considerable body of them with him including a number of senators.

Cicero escaped by ship, but then, a victim of seasickness and his own irresolution, he put back to land and went into hiding in one of his villas. In the end he was betrayed and met his death bravely, ordering his servants not to try and defend him. His head and the hand with which he had written the Philippics were cut off and brought to a jubilant Antony, who rewarded the centurion with a quarter of a million denarii; emulating Sulla's treatment of the victims of proscription he ordered the head to be displayed on the front of the rostra from which Cicero had so often spoken. Appian remarks cynically, but perhaps with truth, that more people came to view his severed head than ever listened to him alive. Later Antony had the head placed on his dining table, and it was then that Fulvia is said to have showed the dark side of her nature by running pins through the tongue. Such was their macabre revenge, such the end of the man of whom Caesar had said 'He threw wide the bounds of Latin genius'.

The public auctions of the goods of the proscribed failed to provide sufficient funds to finance the coming war; some refrained from bidding for the property of their friends while others feared the consequences if Brutus and Cassius won; Appian puts the shortfall at the enormous sum of 200 million denarii. The triumvirs were forced to turn to taxation to raise the balance. No woman had been proscribed and much private wealth was in the hands of women in their own right; a decree was published ordering the richest 1,400 to submit a return of their property so that a wealth tax could be levied, with heavy fines for undervaluation and generous rewards for informers whether citizen, freedman or slave.

The women petitioned Octavian's sister, Octavia, and Antony's mother, Julia, who were both sympathetic, and Fulvia who was not, and chose one of their number, Hortensia, to speak for them at the next formal tribunal in the Forum. There she addressed the triumvirs in forthright fashion, reminding them that many had already lost male relatives in the proscriptions and telling them that they might as well proscribe the women as attempt to levy such a tax. She recalled the sacrifices the women of Rome had made in the past and promised that they would do the same against a foreign enemy, but not in a civil war. Taken aback by this verbal assault the triumvirs ordered their lictors to clear the Forum, but when the crowd demonstrated in favour of the women they promised to reconsider the decree.

The following day they agreed to reduce the number to 400; instead they announced a similar tax on all men, foreigners, priests and freedmen as well as citizens, whose total assets exceeded 100,000 denarii, in the form of a levy of one year's income and a compulsory loan of 2% of their capital, to be enforced by the same system of fines and rewards to informers.

In this manner, under threat of the sword, enough money was raised to fund the war; but the proscriptions and the levy of such punitive taxes could hardly be repeated; graffiti had already appeared in Rome deriding Octavian as 'pater argentarius'. The revenues of the East remained in the hands of Brutus and Cassius; Sextus's fleet threatened the corn supply to Rome, and there was the constant danger that he would join forces with Brutus and Cassius and give them command of the seaways of the central Mediterranean.

The triumvirs had to act quickly, and not only on economic and strategic grounds; their soldiers, impatient for their promised rewards, were near to getting out of hand. When towards the end of December Lepidus and Plancus held Triumphs, supposedly for victories over Alpine tribes, their legions marched in procession along the Sacred Way to a cynical refrain of their own which derided their generals as triumphing not over the Gauls but their own proscribed brothers. There was little Lepidus, Plancus or the other Caesarian generals could do, for the soldiers had at last begun to realise that the ultimate power was theirs, that the triumvirs could be made to pay for their loyalty in booty and land; it was through these soldiers that the rural proletariat would soon repossess its rightful share of the wealth of Italy.

When on 1st January 42 Lepidus and Plancus took office as consuls their first act was the formal deification of the dead Caesar. This allowed Octavian to call himself the son of a god and he lost no time in doing so and in castigating the self-styled Liberators as the murderers of a god.

But there was little time for polemics or celebration and the triumvirs had to turn their attention to prosecuting the war. On their behalf Sextius in Africa Nova called on Cornificius to hand over Africa Vetus. Cornificius refused, declaring that he had been appointed by the Senate and cared nothing for the orders of the triumvirs. But in spite of his brave words Sextius defeated him in a short campaign and took over both provinces; the remnants of Cornificius's army escaped to Sextus in Sicily.

Octavian gave his friend, Salvidienus Rufus, the task of expelling Sextus from Sicily. But Salvidienus's ships and inexperienced crews found the strong tidal stream and the short confused seas in the Straits of Messina too much for them, and Sextus's fleet had no difficulty in repulsing their invasion attempt. Sextus failed to exploit his success, and Salvidienus managed to put back for repairs to Brundisium, where Antony and Octavian had concentrated their army.

Apart from the damage to Octavian's prestige this was a reverse the triumvirs could ill afford. As well as providing a refuge for the proscribed and a rallying ground for the Republicans, possession of Sicily allowed Sextus to dominate the Sicilian Strait with his superior fleet, threaten the triumvirs' communications with Africa and harass the southern coasts of Italy. If he acted in concert with Brutus and Cassius he could give them command of the north Ionian Sea and the Adriatic narrows, so that even if Antony and Octavian ferried their army across they would be cut off from Italy. With Antony's approval Octavian prudently rescinded the orders against two of the eighteen proscribed cities, Vibo and Rhegium, which faced Sicily across the Straits of Messina; he then set out to direct operations himself against Sextus.

CHAPTER X

Philippi

After rejecting the Senate's invitation to cross to Italy and ignoring Cicero's pleas Brutus left Dyrrachium. He sent a message to Cassius proposing a council of war at Smyrna, and towards the end of May he was on the march east along the Via Egnatia.

Cassius had used the twelve legions he had taken over in Syria to establish his authority throughout the Levant. He trapped Dolabella and his two legions in Laodicea, and Dolabella took his own life rather than surrender. Cassius appointed his own client princes in Syria, and in Judaea he extracted large fines from the Jews. He was preparing to march south to punish Cleopatra for allowing Allienus to come to Dolabella's assistance when Brutus's messenger reached him and he called off his expedition against Egypt.

At Abdera Brutus reviewed his army, and he then mounted a short punitive campaign against a rebellious Thracian tribe, as a result of which his soldiers hailed him as Imperator. He then crossed over to Asia Minor where he recruited more cavalry and auxiliaries from the central highlands and ordered further taxes to be levied from the Greek cities; only Rhodes and Lycia, relying on their status as friends and allies of Rome, dared to protest.

When news of Octavian's march on Rome and his seizure of power was followed, a month or so later, by reports of his agreement with Antony and Lepidus and the setting up of the second Triumvirate, Brutus knew that the Caesarians were bent on war and all hope of a compromise with Antony was gone. Earlier he had resisted Cicero's demands that Gaius Antonius should be killed, but now he instructed Hortensius, his legate in Illyricum, to execute him, allegedly as a reprisal for Cicero's death.

When Brutus and Cassius met at Smyrna it was for the first time since they left Italy the year before. Then they had been little more than fugitives: now they both commanded formidable armies, and between them they controlled the whole of the Roman East from the Adriatic to the Euphrates with all its manpower resources and material wealth. Some sources suggest that Brutus wanted to move west at once to meet the threat from the Caesarians, but Cassius's counsel prevailed and they decided first to consolidate their position in Asia Minor, raise further taxes to fund the war and deal with Rhodes and

Lycia. Though they must have been in touch with many of their supporters who had fled to Sicily, they apparently made no overtures to Sextus nor did they attempt to coordinate their plans with him.

The Rhodians sent envoys to Cassius to remind him of their treaty of friendship with Rome and of the years he had spent as a student at their university. But Cassius was unmoved: Rhodes had broken the treaty by aiding Dolabella, tyrants had usurped power in Rome, he and Brutus were the only true representatives of the Republic, and they would either obey his orders or he would compel them to do so by force of arms. He proceeded to make good his threat, defeating the Rhodian navy and then capturing the city with a seaborne assault. He executed fifty of the leading citizens and employed much the same system of rewards and informers as the triumvirs to extract 1,300 talents in taxes and fines.

In Lycia Brutus used similar methods, which he tried to conceal behind an outward show of moderation. He invested Xanthus, the principal city, but the citizens emulated their forbears who had resisted the Persian invaders, preferring death for themselves and the destruction of their city by fire to surrender; Brutus commented 'The Xanthians through their madness in rejecting my kindness have made their city their grave'. Appalled at the fate of Xanthus the rest of Lycia submitted, and Brutus fined the country 150 talents.

Sometime during 42 the triumvirs agreed to allow Cleopatra to appoint her son Caesarion, now four or five years old, as her titular co-ruler. This accorded with Egyptian practice, and for Cleopatra it meant that they at least recognized him as her son if not Caesar's. For them it may have been a concession to keep her loyal and prevent her from aiding Cassius and Brutus. After Cassius called off his projected attack on Egypt Cleopatra sailed herself with the powerful Egyptian fleet to support the triumvirs, perhaps at their request.

Brutus and Cassius had stationed a squadron at Taenarum under their admiral, Staius Murcus, to cover the sea approaches to the Peloponnese and forestall any such move. Reports reached Murcus that the Egyptian fleet had suffered serious storm damage at sea and had been forced to put back to Alexandria; this was confirmed by identifiable wreckage washed up on the southern shores of the Peloponnese. With the naval threat from Egypt thus removed, Murcus, apparently acting on his own initiative, sailed for Brundisium to deny the Caesarians passage of their army across the Adriatic narrows.

Antony was waiting at Brundisium while Octavian tried to recover Sicily, but he had already got a force of eight legions unopposed across the straits under command of Norbanus Flaccus and Lucius

Decidius Saxa. When Murcus anchored his fleet off the entrance to Brundisium Antony found himself blockaded as he had six years before when Libo had cut him off from Caesar. With his few warships he was unable to dislodge Murcus; he then mounted artillery towers on barges and used them to give covering fire while his transports ran the blockade, but this was only possible when a strong westerly wind allowed the beamy square-rigged transports to outrun Murcus's oared warships.

Antony called on Octavian for assistance from the fleet he was assembling on the south-west coast for the invasion of Sicily. So far Octavian had made little progress, and Sextus had such effective command of the Straits of Messina that Octavian had to pass his relieving squadron right round the west coast of Sicily; this took some considerable time. But as his ships slowly clawed their way up from Tarentum and neared Brundisium Murcus abandoned his blockade and sailed off, opening the passage out to sea for the Caesarian transports, which soon had Octavian's warships to escort them. Murcus tried to intercept the convoys, but Antony and Octavian ferried the rest of their army across the straits without loss.

To reinforce Murcus, Brutus and Cassius sent fifty warships and one legion under Gnaeus Domitius Ahenobarbus, whose father, Lucius, had died at Pharsalus. But he was too late; a few weeks earlier, even with the limited sea keeping capability of the oared warships of the day, he and Murcus could have made the crossing hazardous for the Caesarians. With Sextus's fleet and the expertise of his Greek admirals they could probably have closed the straits, allowing Brutus and Cassius to defeat Saxa and Norbanus in detail. But though he was firmly in control of Sicily Sextus again showed the reluctance to strike back at his enemies or to act in concert with potential allies which was typical of him, and in the end was to prove his undoing.

Though they would have welcomed the destruction of the Caesarians at sea Brutus and Cassius were perhaps not too concerned that they were across the Adriatic; if they could cut their supply lines from Italy, Illyricum and northern Greece could not possibly support an army of such a size for very long. This Murcus and Ahenobarbus proceeded to do, sealing off Brundisium again and establishing effective naval control of the straits.

On Antony's orders Saxa and Norbanus had thrust rapidly down the Via Egnatia to secure Thessalonica and cut off mainland Greece from the east; marching on to seize the Thracian passes beyond Neapolis, through which passed the only practical land route from Asia into Europe. The speed of their advance took Brutus and Cassius by surprise.

After the destruction of Xanthus and the surrender of Rhodes Brutus and Cassius had met at Sardis near Ephesus. A bitter quarrel between the two leaders was patched up, and during the late summer they crossed the Hellespont and concentrated their armies at the head of the gulf of Melas on the northern side of the Gallipoli peninsula. Here they held a ceremonial review; the forces of the client princes, consisting of 5,000 cavalry and a large body of infantry, parading before them in colour and pageantry, and the disciplined power of some 80,000 Roman infantry, organised in nineteen under strength legions and supported by 8,000 cavalry and 400 mounted archers, must have made them confident of victory. But to ensure the legions' loyalty they felt it prudent to give them generous bounties in advance, 7,500 denarii to every centurion and 1,500 to every soldier.

From Melas they marched west along the Via Egnatia, with the fleet under Tillius Cimber covering their seaward flank; his appearance offshore outflanked Saxa and forced him to withdraw on Norbanus, who was holding the Symbolum defile near Neapolis. From here the Via Egnatia turned inland over the coastal hills to Philippi; it then ran south-west, through the plain of the river Angites north of the Pangaeus range, and so to the Strymon valley and Amphipolis. An older road which the Persian invaders had used took a more direct route, leaving the Via Egnatia west of the Symbolum pass to run along the narrow Marmarica rift valley south of Mount Pangaeus and thence to Amphipolis.

With the help of local guides Brutus and Cassius passed part of their army through the densely wooded foothills north of the road to outflank Norbanus and emerge behind him on the Via Egnatia east of Philippi. However the two experienced Caesarian generals managed to extricate themselves by night, and they then withdrew down the old road back to Amphipolis. Here they fortified positions covering the city, whose walls were protected on three sides by the winding course of the river Strymon.

Brutus and Cassius halted astride the Via Egnatia west of Philippi, and here they were joined by Cimber who had disembarked his single legion at Neapolis, an indication that they had decided to stand and fight on ground of their own choosing. And they had chosen well: they were close enough to Neapolis to secure their sea communications with their supply base on the island of Thasos, and they controlled the Thracian passes and the only road back to the Hellespont. North of Philippi on its precipitous rocky outlier the mountains protected their right flank, and to the south there was a large area of marsh draining into a shallow lake. To advance down the Via Egnatia towards Amphipolis would invite a flanking counter thrust up the old route south of the Pangaeus. To stand at Philippi gave them the advantage of a naturally strong position with short and secure supply lines; it would also force the Caesarians to stretch even further their long and difficult lines of communication and supply, which already reached back more than 300 miles from Amphipolis to Dyrrachium.

Appian describes the Republican position as a little over two miles west of Philippi and based on two hills a mile apart, with Brutus's camp to the north of the Via Egnatia and Cassius's to the south and a feeder stream of the Angites running across their front; but, though the line of the road is known, Appian's description and distances cannot be related to the ground as it is today. They dug a ditch and raised a wall to connect their entrenched camps, with a stockaded gate on the road itself; the strength of these fieldworks would defeat any frontal assault the Caesarians might be rash enough to make and their flanks were secured by the marsh to the south and the steeply rising hills to the north. It seemed that all they had to do was to stand on the defensive, and the Caesarian army, cut off from its bases in Italy by the Republican fleet and with only the meagre supplies of northern Greece to subsist on during the coming winter, would surely disintegrate. Thus Brutus and Cassius evidently reasoned and there was merit in such a strategy, always provided they could rely on the loyalty and discipline of their legions in a waiting defensive role.

Octavian fell ill at Dyrrachium, but with the Adriatic closed behind them the Caesarians could not afford to wait; late summer was already turning to autumn, and they too knew only too well that Macedonia could not long provide enough supplies for their twenty legions; somehow the war had to be won before winter came. Leaving Octavian at Dyrrachium Antony set off with twelve legions down the Via Egnatia. Despatches from Saxa and Norbanus must have reached him; he would have known that they had withdrawn to Amphipolis, and no doubt he feared they would be unable to prevent the Republicans cutting off the Chalcide peninsula and debouching into the plain of the lower Vardar. He reached Thessalonica by forced marches, thus at least securing central Greece; a few days later he joined Saxa and Norbanus and their eight intact legions at Amphipolis.

He left one legion under Pinarius Scarpus to hold Amphipolis and marched on along the Via Egnatia with his two legates and the combined Caesarian army. Cavalry reconnaissance confirmed that Brutus and Cassius had halted at Philippi, but the strength of their positions must have come as an unpleasant surprise when Antony halted facing them a mile away. He had little choice but to entrench his camp as best he could. But to the watching Republicans the confident manner in which he set about doing so on the bare open plain, and his apparent assumption that the initiative was his, appeared audacious and menacing; it seemed to express contempt for them and their leaders as they waited on the defensive. Brutus was astonished by the speed of Antony's approach march, and Cassius at once began to extend his defences south to the marsh. Octavian arrived only ten days later; still too weak to ride he had been carried in a litter down 350 miles of the roughly paved Via Egnatia; his willpower had triumphed over his sick body to ensure that Caesar's heir was present when the final account was settled with Caesar's murderers.

Thus the stage was set at Philippi for the greatest battle ever fought between Romans, with the four most famous men of the time as the generals and the prize the Roman world. Every material advantage in supply and equipment lay with the Republicans; so too did the tactical advantage of the ground. But perhaps misled by the enthusiasm of the young nobles in their camp Brutus and Cassius had failed to gauge the mood of the legions or to realise that the battle cry of 'Liberty under the Republic' meant little to them. The soldiers' purses were heavy with the money already lavished on them and they had more booty from the pillage of Asia than they could carry. They were impatient to brush aside these impudent Caesarians with as little loss and inconvenience as possible, so that they could enjoy their spoils in Italy and there receive the grants of land and the further cash bounties of 1,500 denarii which Brutus and Cassius had promised them.

The Caesarians with empty purses and half empty stomachs had the magic name of Caesar, even though now it was carried by a sick youth in a litter, to remind them that they had Caesar to avenge. They remembered Pharsalus and knew that in Antony they had the most able general of the four; he understood them well enough to point to the booty and food which was theirs for the taking in the Republican camps, and to pose the stark alternative of hunger and death. Thus the advantage in morale lay with the Caesarians, always provided that Antony could bring on and win a battle before the onset of winter brought inevitable disintegration and defeat. Such was his anxiety to force the issue that on the morning after Octavian's arrival he drew up his army in front of Cassius's, with Octavian's facing Brutus, and offered battle. In case the Caesarians were desperate enough to try a frontal attack Brutus and Cassius formed up their own army behind their fortifications, but they had no mind to surrender their ground advantage and risk a battle when the enemy's every act confirmed their own reasoning that time was on their side. Brutus and Cassius had themselves appreciated the Caesarians' dilemma more accurately than some of their lieutenants, and they were determined not to have a battle forced on them. But among the senators and nobles in the Republican camp were many, who, like the soldiers, were confident of victory and impatient to return to Italy, and they became more and more critical of these waiting defensive tactics.

Though he knew the challenge would not be accepted Antony drew up his army every morning before Cassius's camp and offered battle; his soldiers' shouted taunts of cowardice raised their own morale and added to the frustration of the more impetuous of the Republicans. But his main purpose may have been to divert Cassius's attention from the southern flank; here he put his engineers to work on building a causeway through the marsh out of sight of the enemy, so that he could outflank Cassius and turn the Republican defences by cutting the Philippi Neapolis road.

Working mainly by night, at times within a mile of the enemy lines, the engineers completed the causeway in ten days, undetected by Cassius. On the night of 22nd October Antony passed several cohorts along it, and by dawn they were dug in threatening both the road and the rear of Cassius's left flank. Cassius retaliated by driving a counter work through the marsh to cut the causeway and isolate these newly won positions. Antony counter-attacked to open the causeway, but in doing so he exposed his left flank to Cassius's main camp.

It was this counter-attack which precipitated the first battle of Philippi. Octavian's army was drawn up facing Brutus's; from their higher ground Brutus's soldiers could see Antony's legions a mile away moving obliquely across their own front and Cassius's to counter-attack on the causeway. The sight of Antony's open flank proved too much for them and they advanced, apparently without orders from Brutus; they inflicted some casualties on Antony's left, but the main weight of their assault fell on Octavian's army and several of his legions gave ground in close and heavy fighting. Brutus then launched his cavalry on the northern flank, but they failed to keep contact with his infantry and Octavian's troops struck back at the gap with some success. Brutus held this counter thrust, and then at the critical moment when the enemy were off balance he threw in his reserve; Octavian's centre broke and fled in disorder and Brutus's infantry stormed into the Caesarians' camp. Still not recovered from his illness Octavian prudently absented himself before their final assault, warned, he said afterwards, by a dream.

Brutus had shown nerve and great tactical skill in seizing control of what had begun as a confused soldiers' battle and swinging it in his favour. Only his failure to turn his troops from looting to exploiting the victory they had won saved Octavian's army from destruction; as it was they lost 16,000 dead and wounded. In the dust and the

168

confusion it is unlikely Antony realised that a mile away Octavian had been routed and their camp sacked. Even if he had there was little he could do about it for he was committed to an attack across Cassius's front and had no choice but to press it home. This he did with vigour, breaching Cassius's line in the marshes and outflanking him along the causeway. He then halted his thrust, and before the enemy could counter-attack he struck northwards at Cassius's camp, leading the final assault in person.

Blaming Brutus for not coming to his aid, Cassius abandoned his camp and withdrew north-east with part of his army. But Brutus was desperately trying to regroup and exploit his victory before Octavian could reorganise his army, and he did not realise that Cassius had failed to hold Antony's attack. It was only later, when he was riding back in triumph to his camp with the three legionary eagles he had captured from Octavian, that he saw Cassius's camp was taken and sent troops to his assistance. They raised clouds of dust as they approached and Cassius sent one of his officers, Titinius, to find out whether they were friend or foe. He and his staff watched anxiously as Titinius and his escort rode to meet them, but as they closed the shortsighted Cassius mistook the welcome of Brutus's men and thought Titinius had been captured by Octavian's advancing troops. Convinced that Brutus too had lost the day he brushed aside the anguished pleas of his officers who begged him to wait at least until his fears were confirmed; drawing his dagger he handed it to one of his freedmen, Pindarus, and ordered him to stab him to death. He was dead when Titinius returned a few minutes later and he, in an agony of self-reproach, fell on his own sword. Thus Cassius died on his sixtieth birthday, struck down on his own order with the dagger which he had used to strike down Caesar. In death he denied Brutus the fruits of his victory over Octavian, for as soon as Antony realised the extent of the defeat Octavian had suffered he called off his pursuit of Cassius, evacuated the captured camp and withdrew to aid Octavian and recover their own camp.

So as the dust settled and the light of that October afternoon faded and darkness fell on the plain of Philippi the armies found themselves back where they had started that morning. Cassius had lost 8,000 dead and wounded, and Brutus spent much of the night reorganising the survivors and trying to restore some measure of order and discipline; to this end he gave them 1,000 denarii each to make good the money and personal property they had lost when Antony sacked their camp. The weather broke that night, and it was in a downpour of rain that Brutus drew up his army the next morning behind their entrenchments. The Caesarians marched out with Antony's triumphant legions alongside those of Octavian's which were still fit to fight, and offered to renew the battle.

But for the moment Brutus was even more determined not to move out from his fortified lines. He had taken many prisoners, and they must have confirmed that Octavian was still grievously ill and their army short of supplies. The Caesarians had also lost more men, and provided Brutus could hold his army together he was right to stand on the defensive and wait for hunger and the coming winter to allow him to complete their destruction. They were already dangerously short of food and forage, and the continuing rain added to their discomfiture by turning the plain into a morass of mud which froze at night; the poor agricultural lands of eastern Macedonia could no longer support them unless they dispersed on wide foraging expeditions.

On the day of the battle the Caesarians had suffered a serious reverse in the Adriatic, though the news took several days to reach the armies at Philippi. Domitius Calvinus had loaded urgently needed supplies at Brundisium and embarked reinforcements consisting of four legions, a praetorian cohort, a regiment of cavalry and some specialist units. He only had a few warships available as escort and he waited for a favourable wind to try and slip across to Dyrrachium undetected. But Murcus and Ahenobarbus with a fleet of 150 warships sighted the convoy, and as they closed the wind dropped leaving most of Domitius's ships wallowing helplessly at their mercy. The outnumbered escort surrendered and the Republicans set about burning and sinking the transports; Domitius himself escaped, but though they sold their lives dearly there was no escape for the veteran Martial legion or most of the reinforcements.

At Philippi Antony tried to repeat the outflanking tactics which had served him so well against Cassius, using no less than fourteen legions in an attempt to infiltrate through the marshes and turn Brutus's southern flank. But Brutus was alive to the threat, and again he showed tactical skill in rapidly deploying his reserve to counter Antony's every move and fortify new positions covering his flank. Foiled in this effort to outflank Brutus and unable to force a battle the Caesarians' plight was desperate. The torrential rains turned their camp into a quagmire and the dispirited soldiers huddled wet and hungry in their tents to escape the freezing wind. Antony was forced to detach one legion on a foraging mission to Achaea; to keep the initiative and bolster morale he continued to offer battle every day, though there seemed little hope of provoking Brutus into accepting.

But dry and well-found as Brutus's soldiers were behind their strong defences, all was not well in his camp. As his legions looked out across the muddy plain below them they chafed at the inaction,

170

unable to understand why Brutus held them back; they had routed Octavian and foiled Antony himself, and they were confident that they could sweep aside these tattered Caesarians who jeered at them so insolently and blocked their return to Italy. But the survivors of Cassius's army, still demoralised by their defeat at Antony's hands and their general's death, were ill-disciplined and unreliable with little stomach for another battle; Brutus judged that the Caesarian prisoners were spreading disaffection and he ordered some of them to be executed. Far from their homelands with winter approaching the client princes and their Asiatic auxiliaries did not take kindly to a waiting strategy, though it was probably for other reasons that Deiotarus's general, Amyntas, took the opportunity to change sides.

So the pressures mounted on Brutus, and it may be that the decision to fight was forced on him against his better judgement. Despite Plutarch's dramatic account to the contrary he had probably received reports of his admirals' victory in the Adriatic, and he was certainly well aware of the Caesarians' critical shortage of supplies. But it is not easy for any general to hold an army together in such circumstances. Aloof from his soldiers and preferring a consensus of his peers, Brutus had neither Antony's personality and military reputation, nor Octavian's purpose and confidence in his own judgement, to impose his will on his unruly Roman subordinates and the heterogenous allied contingents, which with the legions made up his army. But he may himself have decided that the moment had come to strike and destroy the Caesarians before winter forced them to disperse. In another bid to encourage his soldiers and keep them loyal he promised them Thessalonica and Lacedaemon to loot and pillage; it was a promise recalled long afterwards in Greece and held against his memory.

It must have been with surprise and relief that Antony and Octavian saw Brutus's army form up for battle one afternoon in mid-November. Octavian was still so ill that he had to be carried in a litter, but all that mattered was that he was there to invoke the name of Caesar. Antony hardly needed to remind the soldiers that they were fighting for their own survival, for this was plain to all of them. 'Revenge and survival' was a more emotive battle cry than Brutus's of 'Liberty under the Republic'; only for the leaders was this a battle to decide the fate of the Republic and who should rule the Roman world.

Eager to repeat their victory over Octavian's army Brutus's legionary infantry under Messala attacked on the northern flank, and there the two battle lines first clashed and closed in heavy hand to hand fighting. After a hard struggle Octavian's legions were slowly forced back; Brutus then committed his cavalry but they failed to break Octavian's line. Antony held his ground in the centre and probed

171

forward round the southern flank, repeating his tactics of trying to envelop Brutus's left and threaten his rear. Brutus had already weakened his centre when he reinforced this flank to hold Antony's attempt to infiltrate round it after the first battle, and sensitive to this renewed threat he moved his reserve to contain it. Whether Antony had planned the whole outflanking operation as a diversion, or whether he reacted instantly to seize the opportunity as it occurred, is not clear; but as soon as Brutus committed his reserve he held his flanking movement and launched a violent assault on a narrow front against Cassius's soldiers who were holding Brutus's centre. They broke and fled in disorder, infecting the rest of the army with their panic as Antony's troops poured through the gap. Brutus managed to withdraw with four intact legions, but Antony cut off his camp from the rear.

After Octavian's legions had absorbed the fury of Messala's attack and held Brutus's cavalry they counter-attacked. Advancing on the axis of the road they stormed the central gate and linked up with Antony to complete the encirclement of the main Republican defences. Ill and now exhausted, Octavian handed over his command to Norbanus. Antony launched the cavalry in two columns, one with the task of cutting the Neapolis road, the other to harass Brutus as he withdrew to the foothills north of Philippi.

A squadron of Antony's cavalry came up with Brutus and his staff. To confuse them and save Brutus from capture one of his friends, Lucilius, gave himself up, saying that he was Brutus and asking to be taken to Antony rather than Octavian. When he was brought before Antony Lucilius admitted that he had tricked his captors into thinking he was Brutus; he said that Brutus would never be taken alive, and that for himself he was prepared for whatever Antony might do to him. Antony told the disillusioned and indignant troopers not to worry about their mistake: if they had brought back Brutus he did not know what he would have done with him, but he did know that he would rather have Lucilius for a friend than an enemy. He then embraced Lucilius, who was to prove as true a friend to him as he had been to Brutus.

The night passed with Antony's cavalry covering Brutus and his four legions, and Norbanus investing the rest of the Republicans. In the morning Brutus told his officers he proposed to fight his way back to their old camp and thus reunite the army. But they refused to obey his orders, saying that they had no wish to tempt fate too far and perhaps lose their last chance of accommodation with the Caesarians. For Brutus, who saw himself as the saviour of the Republic from tyranny, this was not so much personal betrayal as evidence of their failure to understand what he had fought for and their willingness to accept servitude. Despairing of such men he took aside his shield bearer and two of his oldest friends from his student days, and one of them held a sword for him to run on. So Brutus died in his thirty seventh year, and so for the second time Caesar was avenged at Philippi.

In the two battles the Caesarians' total casualties were slightly more than those of the defeated Republicans. But many of the younger nobles from the famous families of the Republic died fighting for Brutus, like their fathers who had died for Pompey's cause; among them were Cato's son, Marcus, and Cassius's nephew, Lucius. Others escaped to join Murcus and Ahenobarbus or make their way to Sextus in Sicily. Fourteen thousand of Brutus's soldiers surrendered and were temporarily absorbed into the Caesarian army. Brutus's stepson, Lucius Bibulus, and Messala made their peace by negotiating the surrender of the base at Thasos, complete with all its supplies and war materials, and both joined Antony.

When Brutus's body was found Antony covered it with his own scarlet general's cloak, remarking that of all Caesar's murderers only Brutus's motives had been unselfish, only he had really believed that what they had done was a splendid and noble deed. He gave instructions for an honourable funeral, ordering the body to be wrapped in his own cloak for cremation and the ashes to be returned to Brutus's mother, Servilia. Octavian insisted that the head be first cut off and sent to Rome, there to be cast down at the foot of Caesar's statue. This macabre compromise over Brutus's body was typical of the attitudes of the two Caesarian leaders. So was Antony's summary execution of the freedman to whom he had given the orders for Brutus's cremation, when he discovered that he had stolen his cloak and most of the money for the funeral rites: and so too was his order for Hortensius, who had executed his brother, Gaius, to be himself executed at Gaius's tomb.

Some of the Republican leaders who had survived the battle took their own lives rather than surrender; among them was Livius Drusus, whose daughter, Livia, was to be Octavian's wife and lifelong partner in the Principate. According to Suetonius, Octavian showed a brutal cynicism in exacting his revenge on the Republican prisoners of rank: the plea of one for decent burial he referred to the vultures, and he ordered a father and son to draw lots as to which of them should die, and then watched with satisfaction as the father sacrificed himself and the anguished son committed suicide across his father's body. This may be true, for Dio drawing on different sources describes similar behaviour by Octavian after Lucius Antonius's surrender of Perusia a year later. But Suetonius's story that the prisoners at Philippi whose lives were spared were so disgusted with Octavian's conduct that as they were led away they saluted Antony as the victor and reviled Octavian to his face probably derives from later Antonian propaganda against Octavian.

The two leaders conferred at Philippi, and as now undisputed masters of all the Roman world except Sicily they proceeded to divide that world between them. Octavian's share was both the Spains, the islands of Corsica and Sardinia, and Sicily when he had expelled Sextus. Antony took Macedonia, Greece, the provinces of the East, and all Gaul except for the Cisalpina which was to become part of Italy. Lepidus, whom they did not pretend to consult, was to have the two African provinces provided that on his return to Rome Octavian was satisfied that reports that he had been secretly negotiating with Sextus were false; should they prove true Octavian, according to Dio, would take New Africa and Antony the old province of Africa Vetus; Appian has it that both would go to Octavian.

They also agreed that Antony would establish their authority throughout the East, reorganise the client states of Asia Minor and the Levant and call Cleopatra to account for any help she might have given Brutus and Cassius; in the East he would also replenish their war chest and restore the flow of taxes and tribute. Octavian, still not recovered from his illness, would return to Italy and there demobilise and resettle the time-expired soldiers. Between them the triumvirs had some forty legions, twenty eight of which had taken part in the Philippi campaign; it has been estimated that a quarter of the youth of Italy was under arms. Perhaps some 50,000 had served since 49/48 and were eligible for discharge; of these 8,000 volunteered to extend their service and were reorganised into elite praetorian cohorts. Octavian would thus be faced with finding land and money to resettle more than 40,000 soldiers. He and Antony decided to retain eleven legions from their combined armies, five for Octavian and six for Antony. Octavian agreed to lend two of his to Antony, who promised to replace them from his legate, Calenus's army in Gaul; this gave Antony eight legions and 10,000 cavalry for his task in the East.

The terms were set down in writing and signed and sealed by the two principals, who then exchanged the originals so that each could satisfy the other's supporters that the agreement was genuine. Antony was a man who would honour such a pact once it had been made: his mistake was to assume that Octavian would do the same. But it was the only practicable arrangement they could have reached, for Octavian was too ill to do other than return to Italy; there it would fall to him as Caesar's heir to redeem the promises made to Caesar's soldiers, and if the credit would be his, so too, Antony may have reflected, would the unpopularity arising from the inevitable further taxation and forcible appropriation of land. Much would depend on the flow of taxes and tribute to Rome from the East, and this Antony would control.

The agreement clearly shows that Antony remained the dominant partner, though in the longer term this division of the Roman world into East and West was to give Octavian de facto control of Italy and the central source of power. But as they went their separate ways from Philippi, after ordering a triumphal arch to be set up astride the Via Egnatia to commemorate their victory, Antony must have felt that his standing in Italy and the West was unassailable. His legates, Calenus, Ventidius and Plancus, held all Gaul with seventeen legions between them; his friend and supporter, Pollio, had seven more in the Cisalpina which he would govern until it was absorbed into Italy. In Rome he could count on powerful and broadly based support in the Senate, and his brother, Lucius, his experienced agent, Manius, and his loyal and politically minded wife, Fulvia, could be relied upon to guard his interests. The acclaimed victor of Philippi could enjoy the fruits of victory that winter in the congenial atmosphere of Athens with no need for a backward glance at his sick young colleague, who would be fully occupied with the task of demobilisation and his preparations to recover Sicily from Sextus.

Octavian was carried back along the weary miles of the Via Egnatia to a winter crossing of the Adriatic, now clear of marauding Republican squadrons. At Brundisium he became dangerously ill, and all Italy waited to see whether he would recover or die. When at length he did recover he travelled on to Rome; here Lepidus was able to satisfy him that he had not plotted with Sextus, and Octavian accordingly confirmed the allotment of the two African provinces to him.

Octavian had neither the money to pay the time expired soldiers nor the land on which to resettle them. They demanded that the land be found from the proscribed cities, which in their turn pleaded that in equity all Italy should share the burden, or that at the very least they should be paid for any land they were forced to provide. But Octavian had nothing to pay them with; when he sold the property of the defeated Republicans the proceeds fell far short of what he needed. The soldiers became insubordinate, the protests from the proscribed cities more vociferous, and frustration and fear of dispossession brought widespread outbreaks of mutiny and civil disorder throughout Italy.

PART 3

The Uneasy Alliance

CHAPTER XI

Cleopatra at Tarsus

Octavian's problems in Italy were far from Antony's mind as he settled his army into winter quarters in northern and central Greece and then set out for Athens. He entered the city, not as a Roman general preceded by lictors and fasces, but as a private citizen whom the fortune of war had made overlord of the East. The Athenians were quick to appreciate that, contrary to the usual run of Roman proconsuls, he genuinely liked the Greek way of life and hence to their way of thinking was a civilised man.

For Antony to dress as a Greek and be accepted by the Athenians, to attend their lectures and religious ceremonies and be initiated into the Eleusinian mysteries, to be applauded at the games and in return to lavish gifts on the city, was to find free expression of a part of himself which was stifled in Rome. Here in Athens he could indulge his hedonistic whims, his appetite for beautiful women and luxurious living, his taste for the company of actors and musicians, and find understanding and approval from the Greeks instead of the censure of the Roman establishment.

But beyond the culture and the flesh pots of Athens, as his staff were not slow to remind him, the provinces of the Roman East and the client states of Asia Minor and the Levant awaited his presence and his decisions on their reorganisation. And, as Antony himself had not forgotten, there was a debt of Roman honour to be settled beyond the Euphrates and in the settling of it much honour to be won. Since Caesar's death the Parthians had done little more than raid across the Euphrates. Even when Brutus and Cassius had shamed the name of Rome by sending Quintus Labienus, son of Titus Labienus who had defected to Pompey in 49, to seek help from Parthia, Orodes had not intervened; after the news of Philippi reached Labienus he stayed on in Parthia and took service with Orodes.

Early in the spring of 41 Antony left Lucius Censorinus with six legions in charge of Achaea and Macedonia and crossed over to the province of Asia with his remaining two legions. Ephesus, the provincial capital, welcomed him as a living god, the new incarnation of Dionysius; as he entered the city, garlanded in his honour with ivy and pinecones, the streets echoed to the music of harp, pipe and flute, and he was escorted in procession by women dressed as Bacchantes,

179

men as Satyrs and boys as Pans.

Though Ephesus, like the other Hellenistic cities of Asia Minor, was essentially Greek, contact with the East over several centuries had given it a character and an outlook very different from that of Athens. The client princes waiting on Antony, his Greek chamberlains and secretaries, and his companies of actors, musicians and dancers all fitted in with the eastern pattern of the court of an absolute ruler. Octavian now styled himself the son of the god Julius, and Antony, like Pompey before him, was hailed in Asia Minor as a living god. A surviving inscription from Ephesus refers to him as a god born of Ares and Aphrodite and come to save mankind; it is not certain whether it dates from this spring of 41, or from 37 when he again welcomed the divine role he was accorded as the new Dionysius.

But to the Greeks of Asia Minor Dionysius had many faces, cruel and avaricious as well as bucolic and benevolent. It was this other face which Antony showed when he summoned the Diet of Asia to meet at Pergamum and ordered the leaders of the Greek city states to pay ten years taxes in one year instead of the two Brutus and Cassius had allowed them. They protested, as well they might, for the Republicans had been ruthless and efficient in collecting taxes and food supplies, and the city treasuries and granaries were bare. Hybreas of Mylasa in Caria made the point for all of them by asking Antony to provide them with two harvests in this one year; he also reminded him that the client states and cities of Asia Minor had already raised the vast sum of 200,000 talents for him and suggested that if he had not received it he should ask his tax collectors for an explanation. At this Antony relented to the extent of reducing his demand to nine years taxes and giving them two years in which to pay.

He rewarded the cities and states which had suffered at the hands of Brutus and Cassius. He exempted the Lycians from paying taxes to Rome and promised them aid in rebuilding Xanthus; Tarsus and Laodicea were also excused taxation. He allowed the Rhodians to repossess the islands of Andros, Naxos, Tenos and Myndus, and he repaid Athens for her hospitality by returning Aegina and some smaller islands. He confirmed and extended the ancient rights of sanctuary belonging to the Temple of Artemis at Ephesus. A delegation came from Hyrcanus to plead for the Jewish hostages Cassius had taken in Judaea, and he ordered their release.

From Ephesus Antony continued his progress on through the client states whose rulers owed allegiance and tribute to Rome and now held their kingdoms by his favour. He was the semi-divine overlord from whom all power and authority stemmed, and he delighted in indulging his every whim. Troupes of musicians and dancers travelled with him and the inevitable knaves and confidence tricksters attached themselves to his retinue. Plutarch quotes Sophocles in describing Asia as laden with incense and echoing to the sound of music and the lamentations of wealthy families who suddenly found themselves penniless. In Magnesia Antony gave a man's house as a present to a chef whose dinner he had enjoyed. Plutarch recounts how Antony told his financial steward to give one of his friends a deciens, a Roman term for one million sesterces. Appalled at this extravagance the steward had it all laid out to show how much it was; Antony duly asked what the heaped piles of coins were for and was told it was the deciens he had ordered for his friend. Sensing the implied disapproval he could not resist the grand gesture with the remark 'It looks a paltry sum to me; I imagined a deciens was more than that; you'd better double it'.

In his reorganisation of Asia Minor Antony has been criticised for not replacing some of the client kings and princes with men on whose loyalty to his person he could rely more surely. But over the period of the late Republic the cautious and parsimonious Senate, always deeply distrustful of its overseas governors, had found it safer, and cheaper in manpower and resources, to impose law and order on the subject territories by means of indirect rule, maintaining minimal Roman forces only in the provinces which they had been obliged to take over and administer. Long experience had shown that the most practical way of doing this was to retain the existing feudal hierarchies and appoint rulers only from the local princely houses, using a system of rewards and threats to keep them loyal and ensure the flow of tribute to Rome. After Pharsalus Caesar continued this policy in Asia Minor, and now Antony did the same.

Nearly all the client kings had supported Brutus and Cassius, but they had had little real choice other than to do so. In the East the Republican cause had died with Brutus and Cassius at Philippi, and all that Antony required was that the loyalty of the client rulers to Rome should be channelled through him and their tribute paid to him; again they had little choice.

Antony had no hesitation in confirming Deiotarus on the throne of Galatia, which covered much of the north central plateau of Asia Minor and included part of the old kingdom of Pontus: he might have annexed Lesser Armenia, but his Galatian contingent under Amyntas had changed sides before the final battle of Philippi. Another delegation from Judaea reached Antony in Bithynia, this time with accusations against Herod, son of the dead Edomite chief minister, Antipater; but Herod came himself to answer them, and impressed with him Antony dismissed the charges.

From Bithynia Antony travelled on to Cappadocia where two claimants were disputing the throne; despite an affair with Queen Glaphyra, mother of one of them, Antony confirmed the other, Ariarathes, as king. Lesser Armenia and eastern Cappadocia were the buffer provinces bordering the upper Euphrates and in any conflict with Parthia their loyalty to Rome was vital; Antony probably intended that Deiotarus and Ariarathes should watch and balance each other as well as guard the river frontier with Parthia.

To avenge Carrhae and recover Crassus's lost eagles, to humble Parthia and stabilise Rome's eastern frontier was the present sum of Antony's ambition; he had Caesar's master plan for the invasion of Parthia, and he was derermined to implement it and win himself military renown matching Pompey's and Caesar's.

But before he could embark on any such operation he had to settle the future status of Egypt and her relations with Rome, and ensure that he could rely on her political and economic backing. In spite of Auletes's profligate spending Egypt was still the richest country in the East and the only one with the resources to supply his army and build the rest of the ships he needed to control the eastern Mediterranean; Pompey and Sextus had demonstrated what could be achieved with command of the sea, and Antony had already ordered 200 warships to be built in the yards of Asia Minor.

So he sent his subtle and devious personal agent, Quintus Dellius, to Alexandria to summon Cleopatra to attend him at Tarsus. The pretext was to call her to account for the help she had given Cassius by allowing Allienus to join him with the Roman army of Egypt, though Antony must have known that Allienus had marched north on Dolabella's orders and Cleopatra had sailed herself with the Egyptian fleet to support the Caesarians. But with all that he required of Egypt, and no Roman garrison to enforce his demands, Antony had to establish his authority there as quickly as possible. To this end, and to enhance his own standing in the East, it was politic that the Queen of Egypt should be seen to obey the summons of the Roman overlord of the East.

Realising what the result was likely to be, Dellius urged Cleopatra in her own interest as well as Antony's to leave for Tarsus at once. But conscious of her dignity as Egypt's Queen, and intensely proud of her lineage as heir to Alexander and the Ptolemies, she delayed her departure from Alexandria so that Antony arrived first at Tarsus. Plutarch's account, immortalised in English by Shakespeare, shows her through the wondering eyes of the watching Romans as she sailed up the river Cydnus to Tarsus. Her arrival was stage-managed with consummate skill, designed to impress Antony with the opulence and majesty of Egypt's Queen. If he was hailed as the new Dionysius she was Isis reborn, 'The Lady of All, All Seeing, All Powerful, Queen of the known World, Star of the Sea.' If she had perforce to come to Tarsus at his bidding, once there she would make sure that he came to pay court to her on Egypt's royal barge.

That evening Antony and some of his Roman officers dined on board as Cleopatra's guests. He had met her before, first as a young girl in Alexandria after Gabinius's restoration of her father, then as Caesar's mistress in Rome during the winter of 45/44. Athenaeus and Socrates of Rhodes describe the extravagant setting for the banquet: the walls hung with tapestries of gold and silver, the nets of roses above the table and the floor deep in their petals, the golden dishes decorated with precious stones which she presented to Antony and the lavish gifts she showered on his companions.

As Dellius had foreseen Antony was dazzled by her regal trappings and captivated by her as a woman. But he had summoned her to Tarsus for reasons of state and in order to get what he wanted from Egypt. That he and Cleopatra were two of the most striking and brilliant people of their time, fit partners one for the other, that their story in triumph and disaster would colour the history of the next decade, all tends to obscure the fact that this meeting at Tarsus was between two absolute rulers, each of whom needed much that only the other could give: Cleopatra, Roman backing and the continuing independence of Egypt with herself as Queen, Antony, the material assistance against Parthia which only Egypt could provide.

Though they soon mixed pleasure in each other with affairs of state it was in no sense a meeting of lovers. Antony did not fall in love with Cleopatra at Tarsus, nor she with him. Such a concept in itself was alien to the ancient world, a madness poets might indulge in but shunned by normal people, an affliction to be pitied in a friend and mocked in an enemy. Octavian's later propaganda, seeking to fasten the latent Roman dread of retribution from the East on the person of Cleopatra, tried to insinuate that at Tarsus she bewitched Antony to the extent of diverting him from his purpose and bending him to her will. As propaganda it was subtle and effective, combining as it did the need to discredit a popular leader and unite the Romans by exploiting their subconscious fear of a foreign enemy; but it was a travesty of the truth, for Antony was not such a man. He needed women, and he seems to have preferred them to be intelligent and ambitious, but his tastes were catholic, and if they could be indulged and fitted in with his other plans so much the better. If the ruler of Egypt whose help he needed chanced to be a woman who fascinated him, this was no more than a bonus he felt to be rightfully his. He was a man to grasp what fortune offered and ask no questions: here lay his weakness, for it seems that not until it was too late did he ask himself what Cleopatra sought of him beyond Egypt's independence with herself as Queen. History has posed the same question, but the answer is lost with her.

Eight years earlier Cleopatra had given herself to Caesar, and he had given her Egypt and her first-born son, Caesarion. But now Caesar was dead and the fate of Egypt was in Antony's hands; it was through him that she might aspire to restore the Ptolemaic empire to its former size and power. If after Philippi Octavian had come to the East her approach to him would probably have been different, but her purpose would have been the same; though whether, for the sake of her throne and Egypt's independence, she would have been prepared to sacrifice to Caesar's heir her claim that Caesarion was Caesar's son can only be conjecture.

But it was Antony who had come, and she was well enough satisfied with him. That, as Dellius had foreseen, he was taken with her merely helped to point her way. There is no evidence that she ever had any lovers other than Caesar and Antony; in her eyes both were fit partners for a Macedonian princess and Egypt's Queen, and from both there was much that she could hope to gain.

The most part of what is known of Cleopatra derives from pro-Augustan Latin sources. The Romans were to come to fear her as they had feared only Hannibal before in all their long history. They recalled the prophecies of the mad praetor foretelling the vengeance that would come out of the East and the banned verses of an unknown Greek in the Oracula Sibyllina predicting that a widow would humble Rome; that she would also usher in a Golden Age of reconciliation, peace and justice held no appeal for them. Octavian's propaganda tried to focus this immemorial Roman fear of the East on Cleopatra in order to unite Italy behind him in his coming struggle with Antony; to denigrate and vilify her was part of the pattern. Roman stories of her unpopularity in Egypt are in direct conflict with all the other evidence which suggests that her standing and her popularity, particularly among the indigenous Egyptians, was far higher than that of any of her predecessors; she was the first of the Ptolemies to speak Egyptian and the first to be identified with the ancient gods of Egypt, and she was the only Ptolemy against whom Upper Egypt never revolted but instead offered to rise on her behalf in her hour of need.

Attempts to depict her as a promiscuous wanton derive from the wish to cast doubt on Caesarion's paternity. Stories that she tried and failed to seduce Herod are almost certainly inspired by his jealousy of her and her hatred of him, and there is no evidence to support rumours of liaisons with the sons of Lucullus and Pompey. Allegations of

184

drunkenness probably stem from the Dionysiac ring she always wore and a misunderstanding of its significance: the subtlety of Dionysius's symbol inscribed on the amethyst stone of sobriety was beyond the grasp of most Romans.

At Tarsus she and Antony obtained much of what each wanted of the other: Cleopatra pledged Egypt's backing for the attack on Parthia and he promised Egypt's continuing independence with her as Queen. Enchanted by his royal mistress Antony took what she and the moment offered; it was perhaps because their bodies matched so well, as did their rank, that he did not recognise the will and ambition within her nor perceive her further purpose.

She succeeded in persuading him to agree to the execution of her half-sister, Arsinoe, despite the fact that she had claimed sanctuary in the Temple of Artemis, the ancient right which Antony himself had only recently confirmed. Arsinoe was accused of supporting Cassius, but Cleopatra had never forgiven her for her attempt on the throne of Egypt. On her insistence Tyre was required to hand over Arsinoe's chief minister, Serapion, and Aradus, a pretender who claimed to be Cleopatra's dead brother, Ptolemy XIIIth; both were executed.

Before she left Tarsus Cleopatra invited Antony to Alexandria that winter, and he promised to come after he had settled the affairs of Syria and Judaea. He deposed some of the petty princes in Syria, but he confirmed Ptolemaeus as ruler of Chalcis and Damascus, and Iamblichus as ruler of Emesa. His attempt to make Palmyra pay tribute was frustrated by the flight of the leading citizens and merchants to Parthia. He appointed Saxa as governor in Syria with two legions largely made up of ex-Republican troops.

In Antioch a delegation several thousand strong arrived from Judaea to petition Antony to remove Herod from office as tetrarch of Galilee. Irritated at the importunate way in which the Jews pressed their demands he dispersed them by force, and perhaps feeling they were more easily governed by a non-Jewish dynasty, he dismissed their complaints against Herod and confirmed his brother, Phasael, as tetrarch of Jerusalem.

So in the late autumn or early winter of 41, a year after Philippi, Antony arrived in Alexandria as Cleopatra's guest. Again he came as a private citizen, wearing Greek dress instead of Roman uniform and without the symbols of Roman power which had so incensed the Alexandrians against Caesar. To suppose that he came solely to renew his liaison with his royal mistress and while away the winter months in her palace is to mistake the strength of his purpose against Parthia. But Alexandria would provide a suitable enough winter headquarters, and here he would redeem Cleopatra's promise of support and translate it into the ships and supplies he needed.

These Cleopatra was prepared to provide, for though she was unwilling to open the treasury of Egypt to Antony for his Parthian venture she wanted to bind him firmly to her as the instrument by whom she might realise her dream of reviving the ancient glory of the Ptolemaic empire; only for this was she ready to stake the wealth of Egypt. Whether now or later her ambition included the eastern provinces of Rome, or even the heartland of Italy itself, is impossible to determine.

By now she knew, or thought she knew, that the best way to hold Antony to her was to entertain him by night and day with new pleasures and diversions. So through that winter she played and drank and slept with him, arranging hunts for his pleasure and dinners in his honour, and even going with him on wild escapades in disguise through the night streets of Alexandria. Plutarch tells of their companions, the gilded youth of Alexandria, and how they styled themselves the Inimitable Livers. He goes on to describe the magnificence of their banquets; according to one of his grandfather's friends, then a medical student in Alexandria, a number of identical dinners were prepared every evening and cooked at intervals so that one was always ready when Antony decided to eat.

Action against Parthia had to wait until spring brought the next campaigning season, but the ships could be built and preparations set in train while Antony dallied in Alexandria. Other affairs of state could wait on his pleasure as master of the East, and his pleasure was to enjoy his mistress and all she provided for his entertainment in this most cosmopolitan of cities. As triumvir and the victor of Philippi he was secure, and beyond Parthia he did not look for he was loyal to his pact with Octavian. His young colleague was welcome to his problems in Italy: the resettlement of the veterans, the disaffection of the dispossessed, the protests of the landowners, and his coming confrontation with Sextus. It was true that there had been a series of letters from Octavian and from Fulvia, Lucius and Manius, all full of contrary stories and counter accusations; and a deputation from the veterans had come all the way to Alexandria to put their complaints to him. But Italy was far away and their disputes seemed remote and unimportant; indeed the latest despatches had brought news of a reconciliation between Octavian and his brother, Lucius, who was consul. Soon the etesian winds would stop all sailings from Rome for the winter and end this stream of tedious and contradictory despatches. His position was unassailable: Censorinus held Macedonia and Greece and Calenus all Gaul, and in the New Year Pollio would be consul. Thus perhaps Antony reasoned when he replied to Lucius and Manius in vague temporising terms, telling them to do nothing unless his standing, his dignitas, was threatened.

CHAPTER XII

Perusia

Lucius Antonius and Servilius had taken office as consuls on 1st January 41. Lucius had been popular as a Caesarian tribune in 44, and the ineffective Servilius had been Caesar's colleague as consul in 48; his daughter Servilia was betrothed to Octavian in 43, but the engagement was broken off before the setting up of the triumvirate when Antony's step-daughter, Claudia, was betrothed to Octavian.

Lucius celebrated a Triumph over some Alpine tribes, voted by the Senate, according to Dio, on Fulvia's instructions. As Antony's wife and Octavian's mother-in-law this ambitious and intelligent woman now wielded considerable political power and patronage. It is probably her head which symbolises victory on a contemporary quinarius struck at Lugdunum, and if so this is the first coin portrait of a living Roman woman; it was certainly copied in Asia Minor with the intention of portraying the head of Antony's wife.

When Octavian returned to Rome in the New Year Lucius at first co-operated in observing the terms of the Philippi agreement, his impetuosity, according to Appian, restrained by Fulvia. Octavian sent Salvidienus Rufus with six legions to take over Spain from Gaius Carrinas, and the ex-centurion, Gaius Fuficius Fango, to relieve Sextius in the two African provinces. In Italy Octavian had neither the money nor the land for the discharge and resettlement of more than 40,000 time expired soldiers and they soon voiced their discontent at the inevitable delay. He could no longer plausibly blame Caesar's murderers and there was no foreign enemy against whom he could divert the mounting disaffection. Sextus was hardly a credible substitute, though it was his fleet, now augmented by Murcus's squadrons, which was interfering with the corn supplies, raiding the coasts of southern Italy and threatening Sardinia; Octavian's remaining four legions, now in the Capua area, were helpless against Sextus's command of the sea. When the spring came Ahenobarbus, operating independently of Sextus, won control of the Adriatic and began to harry the eastern coast of Italy.

But it was the size and complexity of the resettlement problem and the need for further land appropriation and new taxes which posed the most serious threat to law and order. Before Philippi Antony and Octavian had promised their soldiers 5,000 denarii each, the equivalent of twenty years pay, and now those who had not been at Philippi were demanding the same amount on discharge. The two triumvirs had also committed themselves to giving every soldier who had fought at Philippi a land grant on discharge of a third of a centuria, a generous enough allotment equivalent to sixteen hectares. The provision of land in Italy on such a scale required an extensive and lengthy scheme of expropriation, which was not made any easier by the soldiers' insistence that no relative of theirs or their dead comrades should be dispossessed.

As Octavian methodically set about implementing this programme, Appian describes how the boredom and frustration of the soldiers waiting in their camps erupted into widespread violence and mutiny on a scale unprecedented under the Republic and never to be repeated in the Empire. They had at last realised that it was they who had made the triumvirs and they were determined to force them to make good their promises. The legions had often dictated events to their generals and in the future they would make and break many emperors, but this was the first and last time in the long history of the Roman army that there was such a complete breakdown of internal discipline, with the middle ranking and junior officers losing all control of their men.

Marauding bands of armed soldiers terrorised the countryside, robbing, looting and seizing land for themselves. Octavian himself was threatened, and when he was late for a meeting to address some of the soldiers they killed a centurion who tried to protect him. The small freeholders and tenant farmers banded together to defend their land and property and sporadic fighting broke out all over Italy; when they realised the extent of the proposed land expropriations they directed their protests at Octavian and soon the whole country was near to open revolt against the rule of the triumvirs. Nor was this all: the establishment of colonies of veterans, Roman mercenaries as they appeared to the local inhabitants, in regions like Etruria and Umbria and on land belonging to proud and ancient cities which once had been tribal capitals, served to rekindle old passions and arouse new fears of domination from Rome and so threaten the fragile unity of Italy itself.

Octavian gained the gratitude and loyalty of the soldiers he managed to resettle, but those who had lost their land directed their rancour and bitterness at him. Virgil's family were evicted from their farm near Mantua, though he was protected himself by his friend and patron, Pollio. References by Horace, Tibullus and Propertius all testify to the plight of the dispossessed. Many of them made their way to Rome where they joined the urban mob in rioting on the streets. They put their grievances to anyone who would listen, and in Lucius they found a ready listener especially to complaints against Octavian.

Swayed by the tide of popular opinion Lucius as consul began to champion the old ideals of the Republic, though whether as a committed Caesarian he was sincere in this is open to doubt. What is clear is that he distrusted Octavian, who had come back a sick man from the victory Antony had won at Philippi, and instead of conveniently dying at Brundisium was now trying to undermine Lucius's standing as consul and reap the reward from the veterans which was rightfully his brother's.

Despite the new found Republican sentiments which Lucius was professing it would seem that he acted out of loyalty to Antony and concern for his own standing as consul. He assumed the cognomen Pietas and used the symbol of a stork on coins he struck during his consulate to emphasise his family solidarity with his brother. He and Fulvia were well content that the blame for all Italy's ills should fall on Octavian, but they were determined that he should not win an undue share of the credit for resettling the veterans; some of Antony's soldiers were in fact being given land grants in northern Italy and Plancus was resettling others near Beneventum.

As Octavian's resettlement programme got under way Lucius and Fulvia apparently recognised the longer term threat to Antony in Italy. They protested that Octavian was abusing his patronage by appointing his own nominees as leaders of all the new colonies and by giving preference to his own soldiers. Lucius perhaps overestimated the extent to which his own wide support throughout the country could be translated into action. The Antonian generals, Calenus with thirteen legions in Gaul and Pollio and Ventidius with eleven more in Italy, had received no instructions from Antony; all they knew were the terms of the agreement he had signed with Octavian at Philippi.

The suggestion that Fulvia deliberately stirred up trouble with Octavian in order to get Antony back to Italy because she was jealous of Cleopatra is mistaken in time: Antony had not yet gone to Alexandria, and she could hardly have known that he planned to do so. It also takes no account of her unassailable standing as his Roman wife against his foreign mistress.

The truth about Fulvia's motives is perhaps more mundane. She was concerned for her children's interests, and she was intensely loyal to Antony whom she had not seen since he left for Greece the year before. Octavian had returned with the agreement he and Antony had signed, and which now she and Lucius believed he was interpreting to his own advantage. It was they who were faced with Octavian, and they may well have thought, probably correctly, that they could see where his ambition was leading him more clearly than Antony could.

As their mistrust grew their relations with Octavian worsened. For his part Octavian suspected that they were secretly in touch with Antony and acting on his instructions; indeed Lucius and Fulvia tried to warn Antony in a series of letters, and Octavian sent two envoys, Lucius Cocceius Nerva and Gaius Caecina, to Syria to reassure him.

The dispute came to a head when Octavian despatched a force of cavalry south to Bruttium, ostensibly to counter Sextus's raids, but perhaps also to report on Lucius's dispositions. At any rate Lucius concluded that this move was directed at him and he retaliated by enlisting a bodyguard of Antonian veterans. As consul he already controlled several legions near Rome, and their officers and those of Octavian's legions, alarmed at the rift between consul and triumvir, arranged a meeting at Teanum to resolve their differences.

A reconciliation of a sort was staged. Lucius agreed to disband his bodyguard and he tried to persuade Calenus to hand over two legions to Octavian in accordance with the Philippi terms; he also agreed to ask Pollio to let Salvidienus pass through the Cisalpina on his way to Spain. Octavian conceded Lucius the right to appoint some of the leaders of the new colonies on Antony's behalf, although this was apparently not included in the Philippi agreement. He promised to give Antony's soldiers an equal share of the proceeds of future sales of Republican property and allot land only to those who had fought at Philippi, with equal treatment for all who had. It was further agreed that the triumvirs would not interfere with the consuls' prerogatives, and that there would be no more conscription in Italy by either side.

Lucius duly disbanded his bodyguard and Pollio allowed Salvidienus through the Cisalpina. Other than this nothing came of the meeting at Teanum for neither was prepared to trust the other. Calenus demurred at handing over the two legions without orders from Antony, and Octavian did not keep his promises to act impartially. On balance it appears that Lucius was probably justified in his allegation that Octavian was interpreting the Philippi agreement to his own advantage.

Relations between them continued to deteriorate, with Octavian consolidating his hold on the new colonies and Lucius gaining widespread support for the Republican sympathies he continued to voice in his attacks on the triumvirate. Both Appian and Dio believed that his new found enthusiasm for the institutions of the Republic was genuine; if it was it arose partly from his need to protect himself and his time-honoured office as consul. Certainly Fulvia cared nothing for the Republic: she realised where Octavian's ambition must lead, and with Lucius as consul and Antony absent in the East she saw an opportunity to contain, and perhaps to eliminate him.

Alarmed at the turn of events some of the senators sent envoys to

Lucius, who was at Praeneste with part of the consular army, and offered to mediate. Lucius was prepared to listen to them, but Manius harangued the officers of the legions and made a bitter personal attack on Octavian; he read Antony's letter to them, probably rephrasing it in more positive terms to say that they should fight if his standing was threatened. Then the veterans from two of Antony's legions who had been resettled in Ancona proposed a meeting between Octavian and Lucius at Gabii, half-way between Rome and Praeneste; but both doubted the other's good faith, and after a clash between advanced cavalry patrols Lucius refused to meet Octavian.

Consul and triumvir now openly prepared for war. Sextius had remained in Africa and Lucius ordered him to recover the two provinces he had handed over to Fuficius Fango. Octavian despatched couriers to recall Salvidienus, who had reached Provence, and he sent one legion to Brundisium to prevent any reinforcement for Lucius arriving from Censorinus's army in Macedonia. In the Senate he protested that he had no quarrel with Antony; Lucius retorted that the legion had been sent to Brundisium with the specific task of preventing Antony returning to Italy. Octavian sent Claudia back to Fulvia, averring that she was still a virgin and their marriage unconsummated; this was a calculated insult aimed at Fulvia rather than Antony. It seems an unlikely story, particularly in view of the perverse pleasure Octavian took in later life in deflowering virgins procured for him by Livia; but it may well have been true, for it would have been simple to refute and Antony's later propaganda never attempted to do so.

Octavian marched out from Rome with his army in order of battle, leaving Lepidus to hold the city with two legions. Two of Lucius's consular legions mutinied at Alba Fucens, but Octavian failed to get there before Lucius managed to repurchase their loyalty. Lucius then marched on Rome and infiltrated three cohorts into the city by night; they opened the gates, the garrison went over to him, and Lepidus fled to Octavian. Lucius promised to punish Lepidus and Octavian, and a delighted crowd hailed him as Imperator when he announced that on his return Antony would give up his triumviral powers and take office as consul.

With Lucius now holding Rome and commanding wide backing throughout the country, Octavian withdrew north into Etruria; here he could rely on local support and was better placed to meet Salvidienus. But there can be little doubt that with eleven legions between them the experienced Antonian generals, Pollio and Ventidius, could have defeated Salvidienus before he reached Octavian; faced with them Salvidienus might well have changed sides if subsequent events are any guide. Then, with Lucius holding Rome, the Antonians could have made short work of Octavian and Lepidus. Lucius as consul would have found himself in undisputed control of Rome, though whether as his brother's legate or as the restorer of the Republic no one could be sure. It seems likely that Fulvia and the Antonian generals would have made him defer to Antony, who, if Octavian and Lepidus had been eliminated, might well have resigned his triumviral powers and taken office as consul for a second term; the rest can only be speculation.

Ventidius was shadowing Salvidienus's return march; he was an able professional soldier, but he had risen from the ranks and now he looked to Pollio for a political lead. With no instructions from Antony Pollio hesitated, his loyalty to Antony and his distaste for Octavian balanced by distrust of the impulsive Lucius and reluctance to precipitate another civil war.

Lucius marched out from Rome with his six legions to block Salvidienus and cover Sentinum and Nursia, held by the Antonians, Gaius Furnius and Titisienus Gallus. But Salvidienus got to Sentinum first and captured and sacked the city. Titisienus was forced to surrender Nursia, where later Octavian was to take savage reprisals. Furnius and Titisienus escaped to Lucius, who managed to interpose his army between Salvidienus and Octavian. With Pollio and Ventidius closing in from the north Salvidienus seemed trapped. But he was saved by Octavian's lieutenant, Agrippa, who seized Sutrium on the Via Cassia to threaten Lucius's rear. Lucius withdrew north, apparently with the intention of joining Pollio and Ventidius; Octavian and Agrippa harassed his march up the valley of the Tiber, but they made no serious attempt to force a battle.

Lucius halted outside the ancient Etruscan city of Perusia, presumably to wait for Pollio and Ventidius and then take the offensive against Octavian and Salvidienus. But Agrippa and Salvidienus closed in on him, and when Octavian arrived Lucius was forced to withdraw inside the city. Perusia on its hilltop site was all but impregnable and Octavian did not attempt an assault; instead he started to build seven miles of continuous ditch and rampart to seal off the city. Lucius failed to prevent this, and with no provisions for a long siege he sent Manius to urge Pollio and Ventidius to come to his relief. Octavian detached Agrippa to block their approach march and strengthened his own lines with forts at regular intervals.

Fulvia also called on Pollio and Ventidius to relieve Lucius, and she sent Plancus to raise troops from the veterans he had been resettling near Beneventum. But Pollio and Ventidius were still without instructions from Antony; they advanced slowly towards Perusia, uncertain what to do in this conflict between his co-triumvir and his wife and brother. Their dilemma was made worse by Antony's quaestor, Marcus Barbatius, who had returned from the East after a dispute with Antony, and was giving out that Antony considered war against Octavian a threat to them both as triumvirs.

Before Pollio and Ventidius could themselves join forces they found Agrippa barring their separate approach roads to Perusia. They halted and after consulting one another they both withdrew back through the Apennine passes, Pollio in the direction of Ravenna and Ventidius towards Ariminum. Plancus had marched north with his two newly recruited legions, but after destroying a single legion of Octavian's in an encounter battle he halted at Spoletium and waited to see what would happen at Perusia.

There Octavian had the city closely invested and Lucius's supplies were already running short. Sling bullets from the siege have been found with graffiti scratched on them by the soldiers; some derided Fulvia or mocked Lucius's bald head, others bore lewd insults to Octavian; some invoked the name of the divine Julius or their imperator Marcus Antonius. Octavian himself took a hand in this war of words with scurrilous verses ridiculing Antony and his mistress Glaphyra, sneering at Fulvia and abusing Pollio, who commented that Octavian's obscenities did not merit a reply; it is to be noted that it was still Glaphyra, and not yet Cleopatra, whom Octavian pilloried as Antony's mistress.

Pollio and Ventidius conferred with Plancus, and apparently deciding that they could not leave Lucius to his fate in Perusia they joined forces and advanced to his relief. But when they found Salvidienus and Agrippa astride the Via Flaminia the Antonians halted at Fulginium, twenty miles from Persuia and close enough for their camp fires to be seen at night. Pollio and Ventidius wanted to brush Agrippa and Salvidienus aside, but typically Plancus advocated caution and his counsel prevailed. Pollio had nothing but contempt for him as a man, and he and Ventidius with their eleven legions had no need of his military talent or his two legions. But Plancus was a consular and politically the senior of the three, and Pollio was reluctant to fight without his agreement.

When the three Antonians failed to come any closer Lucius assumed that they had been defeated. In Perusia the civilian population was starving and the army little better off; Lucius decided that he must break out. Perhaps deliberately selecting New Year's Eve in the hope of catching Octavian's troops off guard he launched a series of night attacks, using improvised bridging equipment to cross the ditch and ladders to scale the investing ramparts; but after heavy hand to hand fighting his every attack was repulsed.

The siege continued through January and into February. Towards the end of that month, after the failure of another desperate attempt to break out, Lucius sent three envoys, Furnius among them, to ask Octavian for terms. Unable to take the city by assault Octavian promised quarter for all but his personal enemies; Lucius then met him between the two lines and offered to surrender. The next day Octavian received the formal surrender of Lucius's troops at a carefully staged ceremony designed to humiliate them; with his own army drawn up behind him he sat on a tribunal wearing the victor's laurel wreath as they laid down their arms before him. But the effect was spoiled and the reprisals he contemplated pre-empted by the soldiers on either side, many of them old comrades, who at once began to fraternise. Octavian had also planned to revenge himself on Perusia and reward his soldiers by giving the city over to them to pillage, but in this too he was thwarted by one of the citizens who set fire to his own house; the fire spread rapidly and the ancient city of Perusia perished in the flames.

Octavian arrested the members of the city council and executed all of them except one who had served on the tribunal which condemned Caesar's murderers. The tally of his personal enemies came to some 300 and these too he executed, dismissing pleas for mercy, according to Suetonius, with a curt 'You must die'; the story that he sacrificed them before Caesar's altar on the Ides of March probably derives from later propaganda.

He spared the rest of the inhabitants who had survived the siege and the fire, and Lucius himself he treated with honour. The vicious personal slanders, the accepted common currency of civil war, were conveniently forgotten. To have executed Lucius after he had asked for terms would surely have provoked an open break with Antony, and Octavian was still unsure what part, if any, he had played in the Perusine war; Pollio and Ventidius were camped only a few days march away and Calenus held all Gaul with another large army.

Lucius's surrender gave Octavian undisputed command of Rome and central Italy. During the siege one of Lucius's officers, Tiberius Claudius Nero, had got out of Perusia to raise a diversionary rebellion in Campania in the name of freedom under the Republic; with the fall of Perusia this revolt collapsed and he fled to Sextus in Sicily, taking with him his young wife, Livia, and their infant son, Tiberius, destined to be Octavian's successor as Emperor.

Pollio and Ventidius withdrew slowly with their eleven legions towards the Adriatic coast. Octavian's agents followed them bearing messages of good will and promises of cash rewards to the soldiers if they would change sides. But Pollio and Ventidius were both loyal to Antony and they had no difficulty in holding their soldiers' loyalty. Predictably it was Plancus who abandoned his two legions, and Agrippa persuaded them to join Octavian. Fulvia fled from Rome with her two sons, Marcus and Iullus Antonius, escorted by 3,000 cavalry; Plancus joined her near Brundisium and they took ship for Greece. Antony's mother, Julia, also left Rome and found refuge with Sextus in Sicily.

Octavian now controlled all Italy south of the Po, and on his return to Rome he was given a triumphant welcome. But elsewhere his cause had not prospered. Sextius had defeated Fango and retaken both African provinces. Sextus's admirals had captured half Sardinia from Octavian's legate, Marcus Lurius. Gaius Carrinas was defending Further Spain against Bogud of Mauretania, who had invaded the province at Lucius's bidding during the Perusine War. Censorinus held Greece and Macedonia for Antony, and from Gaul Calenus could threaten Octavian's communications with Spain; he had still not handed over the two legions. Pollio had reached Venetia and was reported to be negotiating with Ahenobarbus whose fleet dominated the Adriatic. Thus, in spite of his victory over Lucius, Octavian was ringed about with potential enemies. There was still no word from Antony, but if he was not already on his way it seemed certain that he would return when news of the Perusine War reached him in Alexandria.

It was essential for Octavian to prevent his enemies from joining forces against him. Julia was probably advocating to Sextus an alliance with Antony; and in an effort to forestall this Octavian sent Maecenas on a mission to Sicily in which Sextus's mother, Mucia, took some part and may have travelled from Rome with Maecenas; Octavian's proposal was that he should marry Scribonia, sister of Sextus's father-in-law, Scribonius Libo; she had been married twice before and she was old enough to be his mother, but he seems to have judged neither this, nor the resulting somewhat distant relationship with Sextus, a bar to an effective political marriage designed to stop him joining Antony. That he was about to use his father-in-law as an intermediary in negotiating with Antony did not deter Sextus from agreeing to the marriage, nor Libo from readily giving his consent as head of the family. For once Octavian had been outwitted by someone as unprincipled and devious as himself. Some time between March and June 40, the sources disagree as to whether it was before or after his visit to Gaul, he and Scribonia were married in Rome.

Octavian hurried to Gaul when Antony's legate, Calenus, died suddenly; his pretext was to claim the two legions which had not yet been handed over. Like the deaths of Pansa and Hirtius, Calenus's was so opportune that it gave rise to speculation as to whether it was from natural causes. With Pollio near Venetia there was no Antonian of sufficient standing to assume command of the army of Gaul, and Calenus's son handed over the whole army of thirteen legions to Octavian. He replaced the senior officers with his own men and appointed Salvidienus, in whom he had complete trust, to take over command.

He got Lucius out of the way by sending him to govern Nearer Spain with a handpicked staff on whose loyalty to his own person he could rely. Lepidus had taken his side in the Perusine War, and Octavian evidently felt it prudent to reward him and remove him from Italy before Antony returned: he sent him to recover the two African provinces. For this he gave him Plancus's two legions of Antonian veterans and the four Gallic legions which were most loyal to Antony, thus also getting them out of the way. When Lepidus arrived in Africa Sextius handed over his four legions, giving him an army of ten legions.

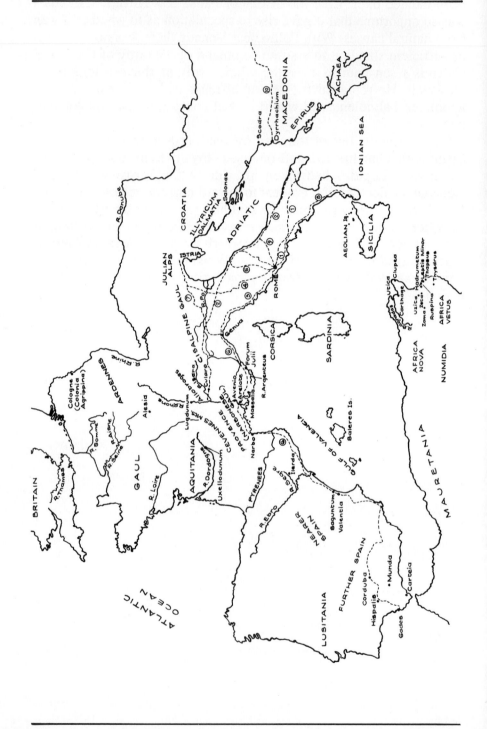

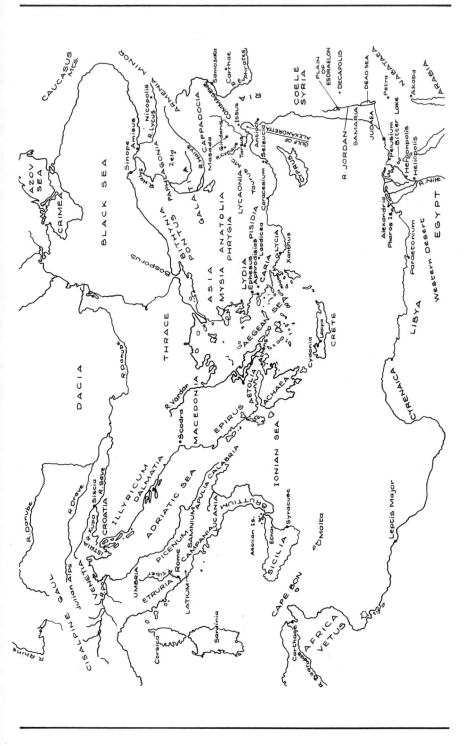

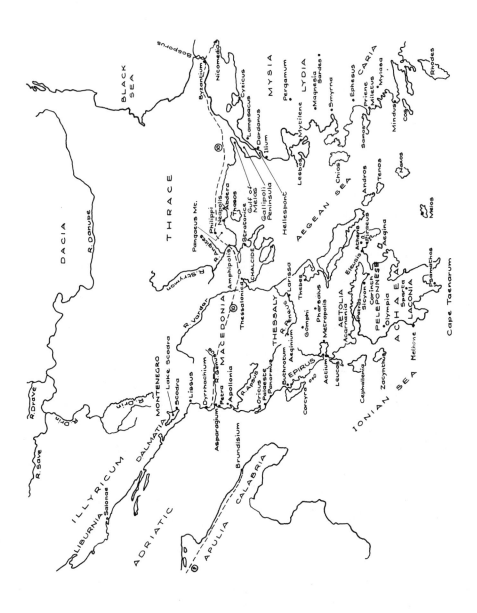

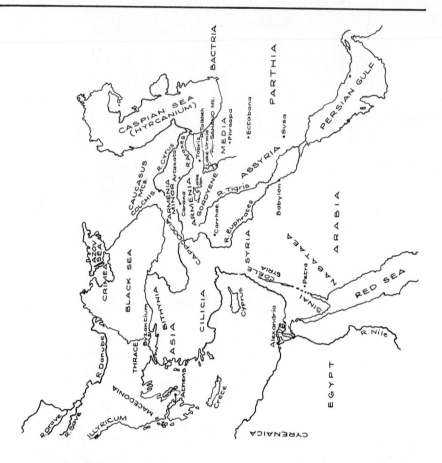

V (a) SYRIA, JUDAEA AND EGYPT.

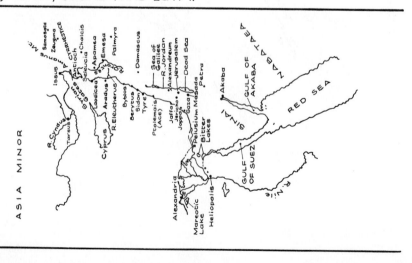

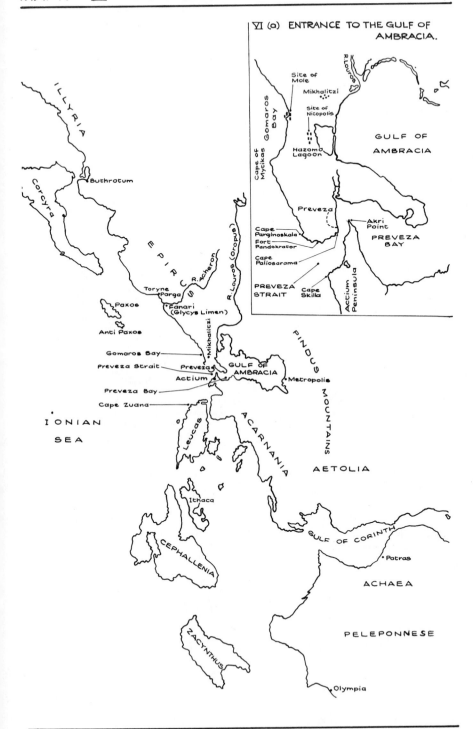

VI (a)   ENTRANCE TO THE GULF OF AMBRACIA.

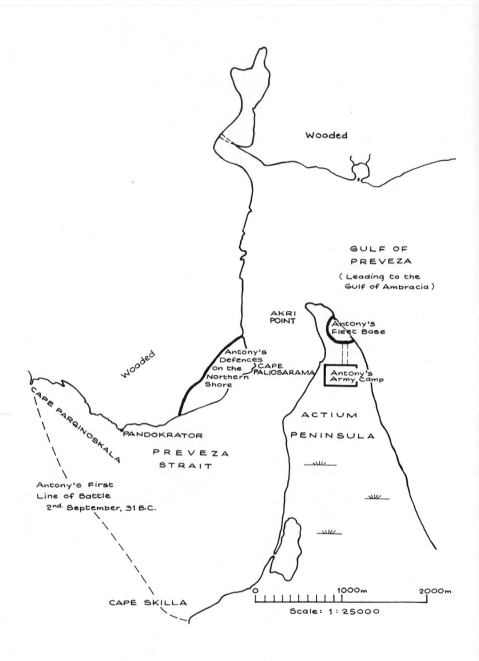

Wooded

GULF OF
PREVEZA
(Leading to the
Gulf of Ambracia)

AKRI
POINT

Antony's
Fleet Base

Wooded

Antony's
Defences
on the
Northern
Shore

CAPE
PALIOSARAMA

Antony's
Army Camp

CAPE PARGINOSKALA

PANDOKRATOR

ACTIUM
PENINSULA

PREVEZA
STRAIT

Antony's First
Line of Battle
2nd. September, 31 B.C.

CAPE SKILLA

0   1000m   2000m

Scale: 1 : 25000

CHAPTER XIII

Brundisium and Misenum

In Alexandria Antony knew nothing of the Perusine War and its outcome, nor of Fulvia's flight with their children to Greece. Appian makes it clear that the first he heard of what had happened in Italy was when he reached Rhodes or Cyprus in the late spring of 40. It was news of sudden disaster in Syria which made him leave Egypt hurriedly in February or early March. By then Cleopatra probably knew that she was carrying his child; she was not to see him again for more than three years.

With Octavian and Lucius embroiled in civil war in Italy and Antony safely out of the way in Egypt, Labienus recognised the opportunity for Parthia and persuaded Orodes to seize it. Early in January 40 Orodes's son, Pacorus, and Labienus launched a full-scale Parthian offensive with the recovery of Syria and the Levant as their objective. Saxa had no chance of withstanding them. Less than two years before his two legions had formed part of Cassius's army in Syria and many of the soldiers knew Labienus; after one defeat they went over to him and Pacorus added their captured legionary eagles to his trophies. Saxa managed to hold Apamea on the Orontes for a time, but after Labienus had spread disaffection among the defenders with arrow borne leaflets the city fell to the Parthians, as did the great centre of Antioch on the Orontes soon afterwards.

From Antioch Pacorus turned south into Syria and Labienus drove north to Issus at the head of the Gulf of Alexandretta; from there he swung west to force the Cilician Gates and fan out into central and southern Asia Minor where he caught up with Saxa and killed him. Cappadocia and Commagene welcomed the Parthians, Deiotarus's grandson, Castor, made no attempt to resist them in Galatia, and the other principalities and city states collapsed before them. Labienus met no serious resistance till he reached Lydia where Zeno the orator and his son, Polemo, defended Laodicea. But Mylasa and Alabanda fell and finally only Stratonicaea and Aphrodisias held out against him. Plancus, Antony's legate in the province of Asia, cravenly fled to the islands. Once again the Hellenistic kingdoms and the ancient Greek cities of Asia Minor suffered at the hands of a Roman general; it made little difference to them that this time it was a renegade mercenary, who on the coins he struck styled himself Parthicus Imperator.

After the fall of Antioch Pacorus was joined by Lysanias, who had succeeded Ptolemaeus as ruler of Chalcis. Soon all Syria was in Pacorus's hands except Tyre which held out behind its narrow isthmus. He then moved rapidly down the coast road, while his general, Barzapharnes, advanced inland into Judaea. The Jews welcomed the Parthian invaders; Antigonus, son of Aristobulus and nephew of the ruling ethnarch, Hyrcanus, gave Pacorus a thousand talents and five hundred captive Jewish women in exchange for the throne of Judaea.

For a time Herod and his brother Phasael managed to defend Jerusalem against the Parthians and their Syrian and Jewish allies, but then they were forced to withdraw into the citadel and abandon the rest of the city. Hyrcanus was deposed; according to Josephus Antigonus bit off his ear so that he could never again be High Priest, since by Jewish law only a whole man could hold that office. Phasael was lured into a trap and took his own life. But the resourceful Herod succeeded in escaping with the women of his family, among them Hyrcanus's granddaughter, Mariamme, to whom he was betrothed; he placed them in the safety of the precipitous desert fortress of Masada and rode on himself with a small escort to seek help in Petra. But the cautious Malchus favoured Parthia, and Herod left Nabataea and set out for Egypt to seek help from Antony.

But Antony was already on his way by sea to Syria; as he sailed into the harbour at Tyre he must have seen the lines of the besieging Parthians beyond the neck of the isthmus. Here he learnt the full measure of the disaster: in the short space of two months all Syria and Judaea had been lost and the eagles of Saxa's legions added to Crassus's captured at Carrhae; Cappadocia, Commagene and Galatia had welcomed Labienus and the Parthians, the Roman province of Cilicia had been ignominiously abandoned and the allied Greek cities of Lycia and Caria sacked and burned. From Ephesus to the borders of Egypt the whole coastline of southern Asia Minor and the Levant was in the hands of the Parthians. In terms of lost territory it was the most overwhelming defeat Rome had ever suffered in the East; that it was wholly unexpected only made it worse. Antony must have realised that the fault was his, not so much in his neglect to reorganise the client kingdoms on a sounder basis, as some historians have argued, but because he had failed to appreciate the threat from Parthia and had left Saxa with only two legions of doubtful reliability to keep the client princes loyal and help them defend the vast area from the Hellespont to the Euphrates and the frontiers of Egypt.

There was little Antony could do but promise relief to the hard pressed defenders of Tyre and sail on for Cyprus and from there summon reinforcements and organise a counter offensive. But when he arrived he learnt for the first time of the Perusine War and realised that he faced further disaster in the West as well as the loss of the whole Roman East. Deciding that any attempt to recover Asia Minor was for the moment impracticable he sailed for Athens, where at least he could expect the latest news from Rome.

Gathered to meet him were Fulvia, his mother, Julia, Plancus and Sextus's father-in-law, Libo. Fulvia had acted in what she thought were Antony's interests, but her complaints about Octavian must have sounded unconvincing against the sorry mismanagement of the Perusine War and its calamitous ending. Lucius was not there to support her or to defend himself, and appalled at the outcome Antony reproached her angrily and bitterly for the part she had played and refused to listen to her excuses. He had honoured the agreement he had made at Philippi with Octavian, and he felt that his wife and his brother had broken it in his absence without good cause; worse still they had failed, and in doing so had shattered his cause and put him morally in the wrong as well.

On Sextus's behalf Libo offered military co-operation against Octavian and proposed a formal alliance. However Antony was not convinced that Octavian was determined on war. He gave Libo messages for Sextus thanking him for giving Julia refuge and saying that if he was forced to fight Octavian he would be grateful for his proffered alliance, but if it was to be peace between them he would use his good offices to try and reconcile him with Octavian.

After a few days in Athens Antony, accompanied by Fulvia and Plancus, sailed for Italy with a fleet of two hundred ships, some newly built during the winter. Fulvia fell ill at Sicyon, and Antony left her there without having forgiven her for her part in the Perusine War. It was on passage from Athens to Italy that he received reports that Calenus had died and Octavian had taken over the entire army of Gaul. For Antony this was the first real evidence of a deliberate breach of the Philippi agreement by Octavian; perhaps for the first time he began to question his good faith.

It was probably when Antony put in at Corfu that he received a despatch from Pollio in the delta of the Po telling him that Ahenobarbus had offered his backing against Octavian. Ventidius had moved south down the Adriatic coast, and practical soldier that he was he sent messages warning Antony that Octavian had sent Servilius Rullus to reinforce Brundisium and giving details of ports to the north where he could cover Antony's landing.

Soon after leaving Corfu they sighted another fleet, and as they closed Antony's captain identified it as Ahenobarbus's; Antony ordered the rest of his own fleet to heave to and then sailed on with five ships to meet Ahenobarbus. Standing at Antony's side on his flagship Plancus begged him to heave to as well: here was an outlawed Republican, he said, who had been proscribed with Caesar's murderers and had fought for Brutus and Cassius at Philippi. Antony replied that he would rather die through a breach of good faith on Ahenobarbus's part than play the coward, and he ordered the captain to hold their course. There was no more the terrified Plancus could do as they rowed on to what seemed to him certain destruction. Then Ahenobarbus's flagship pulled ahead of the rest of his fleet, and as the two ships came within hailing distance Antony ordered his lictor in the bows to call on Ahenobarbus to dip his ensign. There was a moment of tension as they continued to close bow on; then Ahenobarbus sheered away, his oars came up in salute and his ensign dipped. He was rowed across to Antony, and on board he repeated the offer he had made to Pollio; the two fleets then sailed on in company to Ahenobarbus's base at Paloeis, where his two legions hailed Antony as Imperator.

In spite of Ventidius's advice Antony decided to sail with Ahenobarbus straight for Brundisium. Servilius closed the gates, but he could not prevent Antony from entering the harbour and disembarking his troops. Antony at once sealed off the city with a ditch and rampart and fortified the island of Santa Andrea and the approaches to the harbour, thus securing a foothold in Italy and a vital port.

Servilius continued to hold the city against him, and this seemed to Antony evidence that Octavian had decided to fight. For his part Octavian took Antony's unheralded arrival at Brundisium, and in the company of one of the proscribed who for the past year had been ravaging the Adriatic, as a hostile act. Thus the scene was set for a war which at this stage neither sought.

Antony deployed strong reconnaissance forces which captured Sipontum on the coast north of Brundisium. He called for assistance from Sextus who landed infantry and cavalry in Bruttium and laid siege to Thurii; Sextus also sent his Greek admiral Menodorus with four legions to Sardinia, and Octavian's legate, Lurius, surrendered with his two legions.

Octavian ordered Agrippa to raise troops from the veteran colonies and take the field against Antony's detachments in northern Apulia. Agrippa told the veterans they were being called up to defend southern Italy against Sextus, but when they discovered that Antony was also the enemy many of them refused to fight against their old general or their comrades in his legions and instead made their way home.

Appian may have exaggerated these desertions, but it is clear that they made Octavian realise once again that he could not rely on the loyalty of the Caesarian veterans in any conflict with Antony.

After being delayed by illness at Canusium Octavian reached Brundisium only to find that he could not get through Antony's lines, and he was forced to camp outside the city. Antony had sent an urgent call to Censorinus for some of the Macedonian legions; while he waited for them to arrive he tried to deceive Octavian by secretly embarking civilians on his transports in the harbour under cover of darkness and sending them to sea, to return the next morning dressed in legionary armour to impersonate the Macedonian legions. News came that Agrippa had recaptured Sipontum and Sextus had been repulsed from Thurii, and Antony redoubled his efforts to complete the siege engines and artillery he was building for the assault on Brundisium.

One evening as Antony sat with his staff at their evening meal reports came in from patrols that Servilius, who had been sent north by Octavian to raise reinforcements, was returning with 1,500 cavalry. Antony left his dinner unfinished and rode up the coast road with an understrength regiment of cavalry to intercept Servilius's force; he took them by surprise in their overnight billets, captured them all, and was back the next morning with his prisoners. It was no more than a successful minor cavalry operation, but the speed and resolution with which Antony carried it out had a disproportionate effect on friend and foe alike, reminding them that he was the victor of Philippi and the most formidable captain of the day.

While Antony was preparing to batter down the walls and storm Brundisium and Octavian was gathering his forces to save the city, news reached Antony that Fulvia was dead. She had died in Sicyon, unforgiven by him and without his blessing; he must have reproached himself bitterly, particularly now when her warnings about Octavian seemed only too accurate. If she and Lucius had been with him they would surely have urged him to settle with Octavian once and for all.

Everything was in Antony's favour: the Macedonian legions would soon reach Brundisium, for with Sextus's support and Ahenobarbus's fleet Antony had undisputed command of the sea: Rome and all central Italy lay at the mercy of Pollio and Ventidius. And if this was not enough, Octavian's trusted friend and general, Salvidienus, secretly offered to change sides and bring with him the army of Gaul; here was the opportunity to pay back Octavian in his own coin. One decisive victory which Antony could hardly have failed to win, and all Italy would rise rejoicing on his behalf.

But for Antony absolute power was not an end in itself. He did not yet appreciate that in the long term there could be no sharing of power on equal terms with a man such as Octavian. Nor was there anyone left to persuade him; Brutus was dead and now Fulvia too, Lucius was far away in Spain if not also already dead, and Cleopatra abandoned in Alexandria. For Antony there was no middle way: if he did not grasp what the fates now offered he stood to lose everything; hindsight makes this plain enough. There would be other chances, but this was to be the best of them all. It is perhaps not surprising that lacking Octavian's soaring ambition Antony could not read his purpose and so fell victim to his own nature.

He sent no order to Pollio to march on Rome nor to Ventidius to block Agrippa, no messages of reassurance to Salvidienus. He did not seize the opportunity so briefly offered, if indeed he recognised it; it was gone as soon as the two armies outside Brundisium started to fraternise, as Roman armies so often did in civil war. It began with Antony's praetorians reproaching Octavian's troops for taking up arms against the man to whom they all owed their victory and their lives at Philippi. Soon they were swopping stories and seeking out old comrades and men from the same district for news of home and family; letters were for the generals and nobles, not for the common soldiers many of whom could neither read nor write; Ahenobarbus's men who had fought for Brutus had been away from Italy for several years and must have been avid for news of their homes and families. Once this fraternisation had started there was little Antony or Octavian could do to stop it, and the longer it went on the less likely the two armies were to fight each other.

With the backing of the officers on both sides Cocceius Nerva attempted to mediate between Octavian and Antony. After delivering Octavian's letter to Antony in Antioch the year before Nerva had remained with him. Both leaders trusted him, and he was able to convince Octavian that Antony had known nothing of the Perusine War; he also assured Antony that Octavian had given no order to bar him from Brundisium and that Servilius had been forced to close the gates by the citizens who feared that Ahenobarbus would sack their city. Nerva reminded Octavian that Ahenobarbus had not been one of Caesar's murderers and had only been proscribed as a friend of Brutus's, perhaps wrongly incriminated on evidence unwittingly provided by Cicero. In the end he prevailed on Octavian to write to Julia and ask her as Antony's mother and a member of the Julian family to use her influence to bring about an understanding.

It was Antony who felt himself strong enough to make the first move by agreeing to talks; to show his good faith he asked Sextus to withdraw from the mainland, and he got Ahenobarbus out of the way

210

by appointing him to govern Bithynia. Pollio, acting for Antony, and Maecenas for Octavian, now joined Nerva, and with the help of officers from both the armies the three worked out terms for an agreement. It was at their suggestion that Octavian offered the newly-bereaved Antony his sister, Octavia, in marriage. Her husband Marcellus, consul in 50, had died earlier in the year leaving her with three infant children, a son, Marcus Claudius Marcellus, and two daughters both called Marcella; the younger of the two had been born earlier in 40. Octavian's regard for his sister was well known, and Antony accepted his offer as tangible evidence of good faith; certainly he could not have asked for a more beautiful, virtuous and accomplished bride than this young widow in her late twenties. In a world where the women of noble families accepted arranged marriages for political ends Octavia for her part could count herself fortunate in a second marriage to a husband such as Antony.

Antony and Octavian agreed that Lepidus should remain their co-triumvir and continue to hold the two African provinces. The rest of the Roman world they divided between them, Octavian taking the West and Antony the East. The boundary was carefully chosen to run through Scodra on the eastern shore of the lake and then north to the head waters of the river Drin, so that Illyricum belonged to the West and Macedonia and Epirus to the East. In theory Italy was to be common ground, but since Octavian would be in control Antony insisted on equal recruiting rights, though he must have known these depended on Octavian's goodwill.

Pollio was confirmed as consul for 40, and as his colleague Octavian appointed Caesar's general, the able Domitius Calvinus. Censorinus and Calvisius Sabinus, the two senators who had tried to protect Caesar when the conspirators struck him down, were nominated for 39. After his consulate Pollio was to command in Macedonia, and because there was tribal unrest on the northern frontier of the province Antony arranged that he would take over from Censorinus in the autumn of 40; for similar reasons Octavian wanted Domitius in Spain before the end of the year. Caesar's agent, Balbus, and Antony's lieutenant, Publius Canidius Crassus, were rewarded by being made consuls for the last few weeks of the year.

Antony was to be responsible for expelling Labienus and the Parthians from Asia Minor and the Levant, and this task he delegated to Ventidius. He appointed Plancus to govern the province of Asia, and Octavian agreed that Ahenobarbus's proscription should be rescinded. Octavian returned five of the legions from the army of Gaul to Antony. Before Philippi Antony had borrowed four legions from Lepidus, and these may have been set against four of the six Antonian legions Lepidus had taken to Africa; however Antony continued to claim four from Lepidus, possibly those Sextius had handed over to him.

These then were the terms of the Brundisium pact which can be dated by an inscription to early October 40. By the end of November all Antony's generals had left Italy, and it would seem he had decided that he could trust Octavian without reservations. As Plutarch says he was essentially straightforward himself, slow to perceive duplicity in others and quick to admit his own mistakes. He had acknowledged that Lucius and Fulvia had been at fault, he had come to an agreement with Octavian, and his marriage to Octavia would take place on their return to Rome; clearly he meant to keep his side of the bargain.

His mistake was to assume that Octavian intended to do the same, that he too would be content with half the Roman world. To judge Octavian by himself, to credit him with his own good intentions, was a naive and grievous error of judgement on Antony's part, and it was to cost him dear. Pollio may have allowed his desire for peace to override his distrust of Octavian's motives, but before Ahenobarbus left for Bithynia Antony had refused to listen to his warnings.

Octavian demanded the execution of Manius for the personal attacks he had made on him during the Perusine War; in an ill-judged gesture of goodwill towards his co-triumvir Antony cruelly sacrificed his loyal and trusted agent. Manius may have exceeded his instructions, but he had acted in Antony's interest, and for this Antony let him pay with his life.

The two armies celebrated the reconciliation between their generals with relief and enthusiasm, confident that if they stood together they could make them pay dearly in land and money. As the news of the agreement at Brundisium spread rapidly through Italy there was universal rejoicing. Peace was what the people wanted more than anything else, and now they sensed a real hope of lasting peace and even the long awaited Golden Age.

Carried away by this new mood of harmony Antony made another rash, impulsive and ill-conceived gesture by disclosing Salvidienus's offer to defect. A hint of such treachery was more than enough for Octavian; Salvidienus was summoned to Rome on some pretext, arraigned before the Senate and quickly condemned and executed. Antony may have feared that evidence of Salvidienus's offer might emerge at a later date to give Octavian grounds for accusations of double dealing; but this was a small risk to set against the secret knowledge that Octavian's trusted general was his man. Nor does Antony seem to have considered the inevitable effect of Salvidienus's exposure and execution on any other of Octavian's generals who might be tempted to change sides; rather he appears to have either disregarded or discounted the possibility of future conflict with Octavian. Fate does not easily forgive so profligate a squandering of advantage by those who play for such stakes; Antony had still perhaps to recognise how high they were.

In late October or early November Antony and Octavia were married in Rome, the glittering public ceremony performed amidst scenes of spontaneous rejoicing. Like the rest of Italy the people of Rome longed for peace, and the union between Antony and Octavian's sister promised this and more.

A decade of civil war had brought famine and misery to the towns and cities, and ruin to the agricultural economy of the countryside. As always in such times men had turned away from the old gods and the old ways to seek relief from their present troubles and hope for the future in a world of dreams and fantasy; out of the East came old prophecies and mystic new beliefs to meet this human need. Virgil captured the spirit of the time, the hope of a new Golden Age, in his 4th Eclogue, dedicated to his patron and benefactor, Pollio,

> Ours is the crowning era foretold in prophecy:
> Born of Time, a great new cycle of centuries
> Begins. Justice returns to earth, the Golden Age
> Returns, and its' first-born comes down from heaven above.
> Look kindly, chaste Lucina, upon this infant's birth,
> For with him shall hearts of iron cease, and hearts of gold
> Inherit the whole earth – yes, Apollo reigns now.
> And it's while you are consul – you, Pollio – that this glorious
> Age shall dawn, the march of its great months begin.
> You at our head, mankind shall be freed from its age-long fear,
> All stains of our past wickedness being cleansed away.
> This child shall enter into the life of the gods, behold them
> Walking with antique heroes, and himself be seen of them,
> And rule a world made peaceful by his father's virtuous acts.
> . . . Come soon, dear child of the gods, Jupiter's great viceroy!
> Come soon – the time is near – to begin your life illustrious!
> Look how the round and ponderous globe bows to salute you,
> The lands, the stretching leagues of sea, the unplumbed sky!
> Look how the whole creation exults in the age to come! . . .
> . . . Begin, dear babe, and smile at your mother to show you

know her –
This is the tenth month now, and she is sick of waiting.
Begin, dear babe. The boy who does not smile at his mother
Will never deserve to sup with a god or sleep with a
  goddess.

                                    translated C.Day Lewis

For two thousand years there has been speculation and controversy as to the identity of this boy who would be born to lead the world into the new Golden Age of peace and plenty. Pollio's son, Gallus, was to claim that he was Virgil's chosen one, and the secondary sources named another of Pollio's sons, Salonius, otherwise unknown to history. Some early and medieval Christian writers believed that Virgil had foretold the birth of Christ. Augustan propaganda was to suggest Octavia's son, Marcellus, who had been born in 42, and even Octavian's daughter and only child, Julia, born to Scribonia in 39. But concentrating on the present of that late autumn of 40, and taking into account the relief and hope engendered in the hearts and minds of the people of a ravaged Italy by the new accord between the two Caesarian leaders symbolised by Octavia's marriage to Antony, it seems likely that Virgil had in mind a son to be born to Antony and Octavia, and this view is generally accepted; in the event it was the elder Antonia who was born to Octavia in 39.

But the general mood of euphoria faded when Antony was unable to reconcile Octavian with Sextus, and it became clear that Octavian was determined to recover Sicily from him. Exasperated by Antony's failure to bring about an agreement Sextus used his sea power to step up attacks on the mainland from bases in Sardinia, which his admiral, Menodorus, had retaken after briefly losing the island to Octavian's legate, Helenus. Octavian had no fleet to challenge Sextus's command of the sea, and Antony had no mind to ask his ex-Pompeian admiral, Bibulus, to fight Pompey's son.

The price of corn rose sharply, and there was rioting in Rome with the urban mob demanding bread and peace. If Octavian would not come to terms with Sextus he had to provide himself with a fleet to break his hold on Italy. The Parthian invasion had abruptly halted the flow of taxes and tribute from the East, and Antony could not have financed a shipbuilding programme on Octavian's behalf even if he had been willing to do so. Octavian had no money, and to fund the coming war with Sextus he announced new taxes which included death duties and a poll tax on slaves. These coupled with the prospect of another civil war brought widespread disillusionment and despair; Antony was known to favour a compromise with Sextus, and the protests were directed at Octavian. There were demonstrations at the Plebeian Games in November, and the spectators applauded the statue of Neptune, tutelary deity of the house of Pompeius; troops had to be called in to control the riots which followed. Octavian was attacked and stoned by the crowd in the Forum and only rescued by Antony's timely arrival.

Mucia went to see Sextus in Sicily, and Antony made another attempt to mediate, sending him a conciliatory message and promising safe conduct to his envoys. Sextus responded by sending his father-in-law, Libo, who was now Octavian's brother-in-law. Desire for peace was so strong that popular opinion forced Octavian to endorse Libo's safe conduct, and the mob threatened to burn down Mucia's house unless Sextus called off his blockade.

Sextus was also under pressure to negotiate from a powerful section of his own supporters, notably the proscribed who saw a possible end to their exile and a return to their families and recovery of their property in Italy. Libo proposed a meeting of the three leaders.

Antony had consistently advocated compromise, and this had enhanced his reputation throughout Italy and strengthened his standing as the senior partner in the triumvirate. Though still smarting over the loss of Sardinia Octavian was forced in the end to bow to public opinion and negotiate with Sextus.

The three leaders agreed that their meeting should take place at the small port of Misenum near Puteoli. Sextus arrived there with his fleet, and while the rest of his ships anchored off shore he tied up alongside the harbour mole in his flagship, an imposing and superbly fitted out 'six', a decked warship with double manned oars at three levels. Antony and Octavian set up their camps on the shore, each with a personal escort of praetorians as well as cavalry and legionary infantry. The degree of distrust between Octavian and Sextus is shown by the painstaking, if bizarre, arrangements which their staffs made for the meeting; they built two platforms on piles driven into the sea bed, one nearer the shore than the other, the distance between them nicely judged to frustrate any sudden treacherous move across the intervening strip of water without obliging the principals to shout to make themselves heard.

This was the outlandish setting on the edge of the winter sea for the meeting designed to bring Octavian and Sextus together and divide the Roman world between them and Antony and the absent Lepidus. Watched by the Pompeian fleet and the two Caesarian armies, Sextus, no doubt wearing his blue admiral's cloak, was rowed across with his lieutenants to the platform further from the shore; there they took their seats with their backs to their anchored ships. Wrapped in their scarlet

215

generals' cloaks Antony and Octavian were presumably carried in upright chairs to the platform nearer the shore.

The weather, which the staff could neither control nor predict, was apparently fine and the sea calm. Sextus had expected to replace Lepidus as the third triumvir, but at this first meeting Octavian and Antony would agree only to end his exile; Sextus then retired to his flagship and the two triumvirs to their camps. Negotiations continued through their senior lieutenants, probably not across the gap between the platforms; this was for the principals, and though doubtless the conventions were observed, it was only sensible to continue the talks in comfort, with an opportunity for exchange of personal news and gossip when they broke off for food and wine. Eager though they too were to fraternise, the soldiers on shore and Sextus's men on their ships had perforce to wait.

Sextus's demands, perhaps put even more forcibly by his officers, were that Caesar's murderers should be accorded a safe place of exile, and all the rest of the proscribed should have their rights as citizens restored together with their homes and goods. This last the triumvirs were in no position to concede, even if they had wanted to do so, for nearly all the property of the proscribed had long since been sold; Antony himself was living in Pompey's house. In the end they agreed to buy back and restore one quarter of the forfeited property; they put this offer in writing and shrewdly sent it direct to the leaders of the proscribed, who, anxious to end their exile and perhaps glad to recover anything, accepted at once. Realising that he stood to lose most of his more influential supporters with little advantage to himself Sextus demurred, declaring himself betrayed by those whose cause he had espoused.

But under pressure from his wife and his mother he agreed to another meeting; this time it took place with the Pompeian ships moored alongside the breakwater at Puteoli, described by Strabo not long afterwards as the greatest port in the world. In the knowledge that, whatever he might say, the proscribed would accept the triumvirs' offer Sextus had no choice but to make the best bargain he could; for their part Antony and Octavian were prepared to make considerable concessions in order to persuade him to lift his blockade. In this more realistic spirit they soon reached agreement; Octavian would cede Corsica to Sextus and Antony the Peloponnese, and they agreed his title to Sicily, Sardinia and the rest of the smaller islands he was holding. Sextus undertook to call off his blockade and afford safe passage to all merchant ships trading to Italy; he also agreed that payment to Rome of the Sicilian taxes in corn should be resumed. The triumvirs promised to restore one quarter of the property of the proscribed and all that of the other refugees who had fled to Sextus, to pardon and manumit the slaves who had joined him, and to give his soldiers the same rights as their own. They also agreed to refund 70 million sesterces from Pompey's estate, and to allow Sextus the same right to hold the consulate through a nominee as they had accorded themselves.

The terms were set down in writing, signed and sealed by the three parties, and a copy was sent to Rome to be deposited with the Vestal Virgins. To bind themselves with a marriage tie a betrothal was arranged between Octavia's two year old son, Marcellus, now Antony's stepson as well as Octavian's nephew, and Sextus's infant daughter.

When the agreement was announced to the waiting fleet and armies there were wild scenes of rejoicing as the soldiers from either side and Sextus's sailors mingled together on the beach and began their own celebrations in the wine shops of Puteoli. The three leaders entertained each other in turn, Antony and Octavian dining first on Sextus's ship with their bodyguards standing behind them carrying concealed daggers. As food and wine mellowed them Sextus jested that he was playing host in his only home, the carina, or keel, of his ship, a punning innuendo aimed at Antony, who after Pharsalus had acquired Pompey's family home, known as the House of Ships, in the Carinae district of Rome.

The story may well be true, but Appian's account of another incident later that evening is perhaps apocryphal. Mendorus is supposed to have whispered to Sextus that if they slipped their cables he would have Antony and Octavian at his mercy, and the chance to avenge his father and brother and make himself master of the world. Sextus replied that it was a pity he had not done so without asking, but, since he had, Roman honour and the sacred laws of hospitality forbade it.

The next morning the three met again, and ignoring Lepidus and acting as if Sextus was the third triumvir they nominated the consuls for the next four years: Antony and Libo in 38, Octavian and Sextus in 37, the two Antonians, Ahenobarbus and Gaius Sosius, in 36, with Antony and Octavian again holding office in 35. After entertaining Sextus on the next two evenings at banquets in their own camps Antony and Octavian left together for Rome, their joint popularity as triumvirs suddenly restored in the general relief at the agreement.

Sextus sailed off with his fleet for Sicily, but the majority of the proscribed, among them Tiberius Claudius Nero with his wife, Livia, and their infant son, Tiberius, elected to remain in Italy. Sextus had won a considerable diplomatic success when in order to get his blockade lifted Antony and Octavian had effectively recognised him as their fourth partner; the terms themselves are a measure of the concessions they were obliged to make. But much depended on whether Octavian had ceded the islands in good faith and would honour the treaty any longer than it suited him; unlike Antony Sextus may well have recognised the danger of such an assumption, but once he had taken over Corsica and the Peloponnese he would be even better placed to reimpose his blockade of Italy should it prove necessary. Nevertheless his cause and his own credibility had suffered when so many of his more respectable and influential Roman supporters had stayed behind in Italy; the triumvirs' offer to end their exile was an astute move and did more than anything else to weaken Sextus's position. Antony evidently did not trust Sextus too far, for he sent Sosius to hold Zacynthus against any move he might make up the Ionian coast from the Peloponnese.

The news from Misenum reached Rome before the triumvirs. All the dark fears of civil war were suddenly lifted; Antony and Octavian were hailed as the saviours of the State and thanksgiving ceremonies were held in their honour. They remained in Rome through the spring of 39, acting together and for the most part in harmony; to please Octavian Antony agreed to become a priest of the new cult of the deified Julius. Despite her age Scribonia was carrying Octavian's child, and Octavia was proving a devoted stepmother to Antony's two sons by Fulvia, Marcus and Iullus; it was not long before she too knew that she was pregnant.

It was more than a year now since Antony had left Cleopatra in Alexandria and the twins she had borne him in 40 were nearing their first birthday. Her hand can perhaps be detected in Plutarch's story of an Egyptian astrologer, who had accompanied Antony to Italy, warning him that he was destined to be always outdone by Octavian when they were together. But in the eyes of Rome and all Italy Antony remained the senior partner in the triumvirate, and it was mainly to him that the old senatorial families and the new commercial interests gave their support; they still feared and distrusted Octavian as a revolutionary, while Sextus shorn of his Roman supporters seemed little more than an adventurer with a famous name and a taste for piracy, and Lepidus could safely be left out of the reckoning.

For once there was peace and concord throughout Italy; the towns prospered, and with a new season the countryside began to recover, and external trade quickly revived with Sextus honouring the Misenum pact. But in the mountains of central Spain Domitius Calvinus was engaged in a difficult campaign against the Cerretani; growing unrest in the province forced Octavian to go there and confer with Domitius, and with Agrippa who had taken over Salvidienus's army in Gaul. For Antony there was the recovery of all the Roman East beyond the Hellespont which had now been in Parthian hands for over a year.

CHAPTER XIV

Antony and Octavia in Athens

On 1st January 39 Censorinus took office as consul and celebrated a Triumph for his victory over the Parthini; but this southern Illyrian tribe continued to raid into Macedonia, and Pollio carried on the border war to contain them. In eastern Macedonia and Thessaly he campaigned against the Dardani to secure the Thracian passes and to remove any threat to the Via Egnatia, the only road to the Hellespont and the only overland route for the coming attempt to recover Asia Minor.

Antony gave Ventidius eleven legions, and most of the 10,000 cavalry he had retained after Philippi, for the task of expelling Labienus and the Parthians from all the Roman East. With Pollio's eleven legions, seven of them in Macedonia and four in Epirus, and the two which Ahenobarbus had taken to Bithynia, Antony had a total of twenty four legions, now numbered I to XXIV. He was apparently satisfied with this order of battle, for though he continued to claim four legions from Lepidus he did not raise any to replace them.

In the spring of 39 Ventidius crossed over with his army to the province of Asia. He had learnt his trade under Caesar and had earned his promotion in the field; given a military role with no political strings he was one of the most able and talented generals Rome ever produced. Faced now with the daunting task of recovering the Roman East he directed a mobile force under Quintus Poppaedius Silo to strike through Lydia into Caria and Lycia. Taken by surprise Labienus sent an urgent call for help to his Parthian allies and withdrew eastwards harassed by Silo's cavalry. Ventidius outmanoeuvred and outwitted him and forced him to abandon the greater part of Asia Minor without a battle. It was not until Labienus reached the southern slopes of the Taurus mountains that he halted to wait for the Parthian reinforcements; Ventidius came up with the advanced guard and joined Silo in covering him until the main body of the Roman army arrived.

Antony had given Ventidius several auxiliary regiments of slingers to counter the mounted archers who had won the day at Carrhae. But unknown to Antony and Ventidius pressure from the feudal barons had forced Orodes and Pacorus to discard the highly effective but plebeian archers and rely instead on the heavily armoured knights, or cataphracts, of the Parthian aristocracy as their main battle arm.

Pacorus was himself beyond the Euphrates, and when the relieving Parthian nobles arrived they disdained to regroup with Labienus; instead with hardly a pause the heavy cavalry rode on into battle, charging uphill against the entrenched Roman positions. Expecting to face the deadly dipping fire of the mounted archers, Ventidius must have watched in amazement and delight as the cataphracts delivered themselves into his hands. Before they came within range of the legions he ordered his artillery and slingers to open fire; the lead shot from the slingers penetrated the Parthian armour and broke up their formation. The first volley of thrown javelins brought them to a halt and threw them back down the hill in disorder. Ventidius launched his Gallic cavalry and the experienced Silo turned the Parthian retreat into a rout. Ventidius then advanced with his legionary infantry against Labienus, but unnerved by the debacle he had witnessed he too fled the battle; he was later captured in Cyprus and executed as a traitor and renegade.

Pursued by Silo's cavalry the Parthians did not halt their headlong flight until they reached the Amanic Gates, the narrow pass which carried the old road from the Cilician plain through the Amanus mountains to the crossing of the upper Euphrates. Here they stood their ground in a position of immense natural strength and Silo could not dislodge them; but when Ventidius arrived the legions made short work of storming the pass, and the demoralised survivors, relentlessly harried by Silo's cavalry, did not pause until they were safely across the Euphrates. The campaign was a brilliant feat of arms on Ventidius's part, a text book example of the co-ordinated use of infantry and cavalry in offensive mobile operations which had taken him from the Hellespont to the Euphrates. On the slopes of the Taurus and at the Amanic Gates he had inflicted two of the three most crushing defeats Parthia was ever to suffer from Roman arms; the third was to come also at his hands in the following year. In one short, decisive and economical campaign he had recovered the whole of Asia Minor and had swung the balance of power in the East back in Rome's favour.

Outflanked as they now were from the north the Parthians' position in Syria was untenable, and the last and most important bastion of Roman power in the East reverted to Ventidius without a battle. He then turned to Judaea where Herod had raised an army against the Parthian puppet king, Antigonus.

After his flight from Jerusalem and his rebuff from Malchus Herod had made his way overland to Egypt to seek help from Antony; but Antony had already left Alexandria and Cleopatra gave Herod a ship to follow him. He sailed to Rhodes, and, after building another ship there, he braved the winter passage to Italy and at last caught up with Antony in Rome. He arrived at an opportune moment after the agreement at Brundisium and lost no time in appealing to the two triumvirs. The patrician Marcus Valerius Messala Corvinus had joined Antony after being pardoned at Philippi; he had defended Herod against his Jewish accusers in Asia Minor and now he spoke for him in the Senate, supported by Lucius Sempronius Atratinus, one of Antony's admirals. Antony liked Herod for himself and he needed a strong pro-Roman ruler to replace Antigonus in Judaea; Octavian doubtless recalled the help which his father, Antipater, had given Caesar. But Herod was neither of the old priestly dynasty nor a Hasmonaean, and though he was betrothed to Mariamme, granddaughter of Hyrcanus and niece to Antigonus, the Jews would never accept him as High Priest and Ethnarch.

At Antony's direction and with Octavian's approval the Senate decreed that Herod would be king of Judaea, thus separating the civil and religious functions and departing from the Roman practice of selecting client kings from the ruling houses. As the newly appointed king this half-Jewish Idumaean had no hesitation or scruples in joining the triumvirs and the high Roman officers of state in sacrificing to Jupiter when the Senate's decree was formally placed on the Capitol. That evening Antony gave a banquet in his honour, and within the week he was on his way back to Judaea to claim his kingdom.

Ventidius did nothing to help Herod; according to Josephus Antigonus bought him off with a large bribe. This may be true, but it seems more likely that Ventidius was reluctant to commit Roman troops to a civil war in Judaea when Antigonus was popular with the Jews and the citadel at Jerusalem difficult to reduce without siege artillery. He probably extracted tribute from Antigonus, as he certainly did from Malchus, while he waited for instructions from Antony, who in his turn may well have wished to see Herod married to Mariamme before imposing him on the Jews by force of arms.

Ventidius left Silo in charge in Judaea and returned to Syria where he set up his headquarters for the winter at Antioch, with his army strung out on a long arc from the Black Sea coast to the upper Euphrates and thence through Syria to Judaea. When his despatches reporting the recovery of Asia Minor reached Antony in Athens late in 39 a festival was held to celebrate the defeat of the Parthians.

Antony and Octavia had come to Athens after the birth of their daughter, Antonia, in the late summer, and he was to make his headquarters there for the next two years. During that first winter he gave himself over to the Greek way of life as he had after Philippi; this time the difference lay in his happy and simple domestic life with Octavia. She had a deep interest in philosophy and together they attended lectures and debates. But it was as much for herself and her kindliness and goodness of heart as for her beauty and intelligence, or even the fact that she was Antony's wife, that the Athenians came to love and respect her and accord her the rare distinction of naming the Panathenaic festival of 38 in her honour.

To the newly recovered East Antony was an absolute ruler cast in the mould of the Hellenistic kings. Once again he was hailed as the new Dionysius who had saved Asia, and evidently he saw no incongruity in Octavia being acclaimed in Cleopatra's place as his semi-divine partner in the East. Coins were struck bearing their portraits, among them the cistophoric tetradrachm with Antony's head bound with Dionysius's ivy, and on the reverse Octavia's between two serpents emerging from the 'cista mystica'.

There were revels in Athens, and dancing on the Acropolis against a backdrop of flaming torches. A contemporary Athenian inscription commemorating a festival set up in Antony's honour and named after him refers to 'Antony the God, The New Dionysius'. But Seneca's story that in his role as Dionysius Antony symbolically married Pallas Athene and then demanded a million drachmae from the Athenians as dowry for their patron goddess is probably allegorical. During the two winters Antony spent in Athens there were stories of client princes and Roman governors kicking their heels in antechambers as they waited for audiences on affairs of state, while he devoted himself to the intellectual life of Athens. There may be some truth in them, but he selected his subordinates well and he was content to delegate authority to them; in return they gave him their unstinting loyalty. The reorganisation of the client kingdoms and the re-establishment of Roman administration in the recovered provinces was efficiently carried out, with Antony directing affairs from Athens and personally deciding whether to confirm or replace the client rulers. He has been criticised for not making more sweeping changes, both after Philippi and in the aftermath of the Parthian invasion, but this takes little account of the immediate problems or of the outstanding merit of the reorganisation he had completed by 36, to which perhaps the best tribute is the reluctance of his successors to alter it.

With the exception of the directly administered provinces, Asia, Bithynia and Syria, for Cilicia was now to disappear, Roman control of the East was based on indirect rule. Rome recognised the client states as friends and allies, protected them from external invasion and underwrote their rulers' thrones. In return they paid tribute and were expected to keep the peace in their realms and make their armies available in Rome's interest when the need arose. With neither the resources nor the inclination to engage in local wars the Roman policy of selecting rulers from the existing royal families had been a logical development. Loyalty to Rome, the will and capacity to resist her enemies, the ability to govern their own territories and to raise the taxes to pay the tribute were the paramount considerations in choosing them.

But having acted in concert with Octavian to raise Herod to the throne of Judaea, Antony now appointed two more rulers from outside the royal houses on whose loyalty and ability he believed he could rely. After the death of Deiotarus Galatia was divided into three parts, and of these he gave Pisidia and southern Phrygia to Deiotarus's general, Amyntas; Polemo, who had defended Laodicea with his father Zeno, was rewarded with Lycaonia and the mountainous western part of Cilicia. For his resistance to the Parthians Tarcondimotus was made ruler in Amanus, and Cleon who had led a guerilla campaign against Labienus in Mysia received Olympos in Lycia. Antony did not forget the Greek cities which had suffered for opposing the Parthians; Aphrodisias had already been specially favoured by Sulla and Caesar, and the new charter he now gave it, making it a free city with immunity from taxes, is preserved in the transactions of the Senate.

As well as Ahenobarbus's fleet now based in Bithynia and covering the approaches to the Hellespont, Antony had three more squadrons of some sixty ships each, one of which was stationed under Sosius's command at Zacynthus where he was well placed to watch Sextus in the Peloponnese and protect Antony's interest in any conflict between Octavian and Sextus.

Late in 39 or early in 38 Antony felt able to transfer his four legions in Epirus from there to Asia, presumably in readiness for the invasion of Armenia which he planned as the first phase of his attack against Parthia. The seven legions which remained in Macedonia under Pollio were in effect his strategic reserve; Pollio celebrated a Triumph for further victories over the Parthini, either in the autumn of 39 or 38. Antony reappointed Plancus to govern Asia, and according to Appian he sent Furnius to Africa to recover the four legions he claimed from Lepidus.

During the autumn of 39 relations between Octavian and Sextus worsened, and Octavian began to prepare for war. The treaty of Misenum had left him at a disadvantage: from bases in Corsica, Sardinia, Sicily and the Peloponnese Sextus controlled the seas for the whole length of Italy's western and south eastern coasts, and he could interrupt the corn supply at will. There is no evidence that he did so, though some of his admirals probably continued to make sporadic raids on coastal towns and attacks on merchant shipping. For Octavian the treaty of Misenum had served its purpose, and he was now determined to break Sextus's naval stranglehold on Italy.

His first move was to sever his marriage connection with Sextus; he divorced Scribonia with the excuse that he found her temper tiresome, choosing the very day she gave birth to Julia, destined to be his only child. He had met and fallen in love with the twenty year old Livia, now back in Rome with her husband, Tiberius Nero, who had been pardoned at Misenum. Perhaps for the only time in his life he let his heart overrule his head, and he decided to marry her at once despite the fact that she was carrying Nero's second child. Nero had no choice but to divorce her, and since her father had taken his own life after Philippi he gave her away himself at the marriage ceremony in January 38.

This marriage alliance between the young Caesarian leader and the ancient and patrician Claudian family provided some respectability for the new aristocracy which Octavian's patronage was to create, and which during his Principate would gradually replace the old Republican oligarchy. When Livia's second son, Drusus, was born a month or so later Octavian made much play of returning him to his father who had been found a post in Spain; but Nero died soon afterwards, and Octavian found himself the butt of an anonymous lampoonist as the father of three children, Julia, Tiberius and Drusus, three months after his marriage to Livia.

Octavian had transferred some troops from Gaul to southern Italy and he had brought round his newly built fleet from Ravenna. But he did not have sufficient forces available for an attack on Sicily and he could not call on more reinforcement from Gaul or Spain. Agrippa was engaged in operations to contain the German tribes on the Rhine. In Spain Domitius had repelled raids by Bogud, but he needed all his legions for the continuing campaign against the Cerretani; in Bogud's absence his brother Bocchus had taken over all Mauretania as Octavian's client.

Thus Octavian was not yet ready for war with Sextus, whom he feared might come to an understanding with Lepidus or even Antony. Perhaps to pre-empt this he called on his co-triumvirs for assistance: he asked Lepidus to prepare to land an army in Sicily, and naming a day he invited Antony to meet him at Brundisium to discuss his dispute with Sextus.

Then Menodorus secretly offered to defect and bring over Corsica and Sardinia to Octavian as well as his fleet and army of three legions. His approach may have been prompted by a sudden summons to

Sicily from Sextus and fear of sharing the fate of Murcus, whom Sextus had executed on suspicion of plotting against him; it is not clear whether Menodorus was already contemplating changing sides, and if he was whether Sextus knew.

It was too good an opportunity for Octavian to miss. He negotiated with Menodorus while he cast around for a pretext for war against Sextus which was plausible enough to carry the people of Italy with him in another civil war and avoid antagonising his co-triumvirs. But apart from repeating his charge that Sextus was encouraging the pirates to raid the coasts of Italy the grounds he chose seem obscure, even trivial: he alleged that the grant of the Peloponnese to Sextus had not included the taxes for 39, which apparently Antony had not collected and Sextus was now claiming. His motive may have been to try and involve Antony in the dispute and so ensure that at least he stayed neutral.

With Sextus dominating the Sicilian Strait Lepidus felt it safe, even prudent, to ignore Octavian's call. But Antony arrived at Brundisium on the appointed day, only to find Octavian not there and the city gates closed against him. It is possible that Octavian, as he later maintained, had simply been delayed, though he sent no apology to Antony and no instructions to his commander in Brundisium.

But to Antony, who had travelled from Athens at his behest, his absence was an affront and shutting the gates of Brundisium an insult. Angry and frustrated by his wasted journey, and suspecting that he had been deliberately slighted, Antony was in no mood to wait on Octavian's convenience. He left an abruptly worded message warning him not to break their treaty with Sextus and sailed for Athens, still furious at the unnecessary delay to his plans for attacking Parthia.

During the winter Pacorus had raised fresh forces for a counter-offensive in 38. He had not been with the defeated Parthian army, and he saw no reason to alter their tactics of relying on the armoured cavalry as the main arm. Reports of his preparations reached Ventidius, who was faced with the taxing problem of concentrating his army at the right place and time to meet the Parthian attack; with a deception plan of some subtlety he induced Pacorus to cross the Euphrates north of Zeugma, thus allowing him to concentrate his own army in Cyrrhestice.

The year before he had displayed his outstanding military talent in conducting and maintaining the momentum of the offensive which had won back Asia Minor. Now in defending a very long land frontier against a mobile and numerically superior enemy he showed acute strategical insight in choosing ground which obliged the Parthians to attack him at Gindarus. There on the slope of the mountain he entrenched and fortified a position of great natural strength, and one which Pacorus dare not bypass in a thrust directed either on Asia Minor or on southern Syria and Judaea.

According to later Roman tradition it was on 9th June 38, the anniversary of Carrhae, that Pacorus led his cataphracts in a ponderous uphill assault on the front of the Roman position. Once again the accurate fire of the slingers and legions brought their attack to a standstill, and they recoiled back down the hill in disorder; when Pacorus was killed they broke and fled. Silo exploited with the cavalry so effectively that only demoralised groups of fugitives escaped across the Euphrates, though some survivors found refuge with Antiochus, king of Commagene and Orodes's father-in-law.

Parthian control of eastern Syria had rested largely on Pacorus's personal relations with the local princes and their respect for him; on his death Ventidius had little difficulty in re-establishing Roman rule, and only the coastal city of Aradus held out for fear of Roman reprisals.

There were public celebrations when the news of Gindarus reached Athens and Antony was hailed as Imperator for the third time. To many in Rome as well as in the East it seemed that Carrhae had at last been avenged. For others, Antony and most of his officers and soldiers among them, this was but the prelude; not until a Roman army had crossed the Euphrates in strength to humble Parthia in her own homeland and recover the lost eagles would Crassus's and Saxa's legions be truly avenged.

Ventidius was far too able a professional soldier not to realise that the Parthians had twice played into his hands by committing their heavy cavalry to hopeless frontal attacks. He had come to the East prepared to counter their mounted archers with his slingers, and he must have appreciated that sooner or later they would heed the lesson he had taught them and recall the mounted archers. This would present him with a different tactical problem, and the answer might well be to supplement his slingers with mounted archers of his own.

After Gindarus he marched north to punish Antiochus for harbouring the Parthian stragglers; at the same time he may have intended to recruit some of the mounted archers for whom Commagene was renowned. It was also vital to control Commagene and its eastern border facing Armenia across the upper Euphrates, if Antony proposed to use Caesar's plan to attack Parthia from the north through Armenia.

Antiochus closed the gates of his capital, Samosata, and tried to buy Ventidius off with a bribe of a thousand talents. Ventidius invested the city and reported back to Antony; he made no attempt to assault its walls, but this could have been because he had no siege equipment. Josephus's account that he accepted Antigonus's bribe at Jerusalem has led to the assumption that he did the same at Samosata, but this may derive from a lack of understanding of Ventidius's character and background. Though he was now a consular he was not a Roman noble by birth, but a soldier of middle class Italian provincial origin who had risen to high command on his own merit; as a boy he had walked as a captive in Pompeius Strabo's triumphal procession. At Mutina, and again at Perusia, he had shown reluctance to act on his own initiative when political issues were involved. He was also well able to distinguish between the routine extraction of tribute from the client kings and matters of high policy such as their removal and replacement. The evidence indicates that he left all political decisions to Antony, and he may well have hesitated to depose either Antigonus or Antiochus without instructions from him.

When Ventidius's despatch from Samosata reached Antony in Athens he left at once for Commagene. Soon after his arrival Antiochus surrendered, though whether by negotiation or force of arms is uncertain; he is not heard of again, and Antony probably now replaced him with his brother, Mithridates.

Herod made the long and difficult journey to Samosata to appeal to Antony for military assistance against Antigonus, whom he acused of bribing Silo to do nothing. Antony ordered Sosius, who was with him at Samosata, to march south with most of the field army and depose Antigonus. Sosius placed two of his legions under Herod's command to return with him at once to Judaea. With their help Herod defeated Antigonus's army north of Jerusalem and closed in on the city; while he waited for Sosius and the main body of the Roman army he at last found time to marry Mariamme. Sosius did not arrive until the spring of 37, and then he had to bring up heavy artillery and siege engines to batter breaches in the outer and inner walls of the city. Antigonus's garrison put up a desperate resistance and it was not until August that the Temple citadel finally fell after a five month siege, and Herod at last was king of Judaea in fact as well as in name. He bought off the Roman troops from sacking the city and Sosius returned to Syria with his army, taking Antigonus with him as a prisoner; later Sosius struck a coin at Zacynthus to commemorate his capture of Jerusalem.

Ventidius returned to Rome; what passed between him and Antony before he left can only be conjectured. Plutarch has it that Antony was jealous of the brilliant victories his lieutenant had won, but this seems an unlikely story. Antony had set the seal on his own military reputation at Philippi, and it was hardly in his character to feel jealousy or envy of Ventidius, who had risen from obscurity and had served him, sometimes in adversity, with such unswerving loyalty and outstanding success; the denarii struck to commemorate the recovery of the East, the rarest of Antony's coins, bearing his head and Ventidius's name on the reverse, are perhaps evidence enough of this.

Other historians following Josephus have held that Antony sacked Ventidius because he was unwilling to countenance corruption on such a scale by his legates. But even if the charges of bribery were true this would appear an even more unlikely interpretation. Generous to a fault, and not over scrupulous himself with the money of others, Antony was scarcely the man to grudge his legates their rewards. Ventidius was one of the few generals of the time who never allowed his soldiers to loot and pillage; yet their loyalty and devotion to him shows that he in his turn did not neglect their rewards. Doubtless he could also distinguish between his own perquisites as Antony's general, and what was due to Antony himself.

The truth may be more prosaic: Ventidius had completed the task Antony had given him in throwing back the Parthians behind the Euphrates. Now it was for Antony to take Caesar's part and lead the invasion of Armenia and Parthia in person. Ventidius was in his sixtieth year and he had spent the last twenty years on almost continuous active service, first under Caesar in Gaul, then in the civil war, and finally as Antony's legate in Italy and the East; he may well have welcomed a return to Italy. In November 38 he celebrated a richly deserved Triumph, which was to be long remembered and recalled with nostalgia as the only Triumph ever awarded to a Roman general for victory over the Parthians. When he died not many years later he was given a state funeral.

CHAPTER XV

Tarentum and Sicily

Menodorus duly came over to Octavian bringing with him Sardinia and Corsica. Octavian received him with honour and enrolled him as a Roman knight of the equestrian order, but he was careful to place him under Calvisius who commanded the newly built fleet in Etruria. Sextus demanded his return, and when this was refused he ordered his other Greek admiral, Menecrates, to carry out reprisal raids on the coast of Campania. Antony's reported comment that if he caught Menodorus he would return him as a runaway slave to his master led Sextus to believe that Octavian could expect little help from Antony. In Rome Octavian publicly proclaimed that he was the injured party and invoked the terms of the Misenum pact to try to show that it was Sextus who was breaking it by encouraging the pirates to attack Italy and so precipitating war between them.

Despite his protestations Octavian had already made up his mind to eliminate Sextus and recover Sicily in 38. He now had 370 warships divided into two fleets, Calvisius's on the Etrurian coast and Lucius Cornificius's probably based at Brundisium; his plan was to concentrate them in Calabria and win command of the waters round north-eastern Sicily so that he could ferry his army across the Straits of Messina.

Calvisius slowly clawed his way south, his inexperienced captains hugging the coast to avoid both Sextus's warships and the worst of the weather. Octavian joined Cornificius at Tarentum and they brought the Adriatic fleet round to Rhegium; from there he sailed north through the straits of Messina to meet Calvisius. Sextus was at Messina but with only forty ships; he allowed Octavian and Cornificius to pass with the van of their fleet and then emerged to fall on their rear. Octavian was forced towards Cape Scylla where he found shelter inshore; Sextus attacked his anchored ships, burning and destroying a number of them, though many of the crews, Octavian among them, escaped ashore. Cornificius slipped his anchors and tried to counter-attack, but his ships were no match for the expertly handled Pompeians and he lost many more before the light faded and Sextus broke off the action.

Calvisius arrived the next morning to find the wrecks of Octavian's ships, some scattered along the shore, some still burning, and he anchored to protect the survivors. During the day the wind freshened from the south and Sextus put back to Messina. He and his Greek officers had read the signs correctly, for the weather rapidly worsened and as darkness fell a southerly gale was whipping up the narrow waters of the strait; during the night the wind veered south-west and increased to storm force. Menodorus also recognised the weather signs, and on his advice Calvisius made enough offing with part of the fleet to ride out the storm, though he had to use oars intermittently throughout the night to keep his ships head on to wind and sea.

By dawn the storm had completed the destruction of the greater part of Octavian's fleet, and his ships lay shattered in a tangled wreck of timber and gear strewn along the shoreline. With the help of the weather Sextus had triumphed; and declaring himself truly the favoured son of Neptune he sacrificed in thanksgiving to his patron god; but he made no attempt to exploit his victory. Dissatisfied with his subordinate role and despairing of Roman seamanship Menodorus rejoined Sextus, who took him back and gave him command of a squadron.

Octavian sent Maecenas at once to Rome to forestall any coup against him as a result of his defeat; he also took what steps he could to stifle the protests which were mounting against the war throughout Italy. But without a fleet he was helpless against Sextus, and later that year he sent Maecenas to Athens to seek help from Antony in the form of replacements for the ships he had lost.

As consul designate for 37 Agrippa returned to Rome in the autumn of 38. While he was governor of Gaul he had put down a rebellion in Aquitania and he had founded the colony which was to become Cologne; he had been the first Roman general since Caesar to bridge the Rhine and pacify the German tribes on the eastern side. But he declined the Triumph he had earned, declaring that it would be inappropriate in the light of Octavian's own misfortune. Instead he set to work at once on the task Octavian gave him of building the ships and training the crews for a new fleet to challenge Sextus's command of the sea.

Maecenas came back from Athens that winter with promises of help; Antony kept his word, and accompanied by Octavia and their children he sailed from the Piraeus in the late spring of 37 with a fleet of 300 warships. Tarentum was the agreed meeting place with Octavian, but Antony called first at Brundisium and for the third time he found the gates of the city shut in his face. Furious at this affront he sailed on round the heel of Italy to Tarentum; again Octavian was not there to meet him and again he sent no message to explain his absence. It is possible that Agrippa's return from Gaul had given Octavian renewed confidence and that he now regretted Maecenas's mission to Athens; it also appears that he suspected Antony of secretly negotiating with Lepidus and perhaps with Sextus as well.

Though Antony made no attempt to conceal his anger he waited at Tarentum, perhaps persuaded to do so by Octavia who was determined to do all she could to avoid an open breach between her husband and her brother. He also wanted to exchange some of his ships for the reinforcements he urgently required for the Parthian campaign, and while he was in Italy he needed time to contact his supporters, some of whom had not seen him since before Philippi.

When at length Octavian did reach Tarentum he was not only adamant that he wanted no help from Antony, but he even refused to meet him. Nerva, who had mediated at Brundisium, Fonteius Capito, described by Horace as Antony's friend without a flaw, and Maecenas all tried to persuade Octavian that his suspicions were groundless. But they failed, and it was left to Octavia to try to convince her brother that Antony was as blameless as she herself knew him to be; in the end she succeeded and another reconciliation was staged.

The terms of a new agreement were then worked out: Antony would lend Octavian 120 warships, probably the two squadrons commanded by Bibulus and Atratinus: in return Octavian promised him four legions. Antony gave his consent, apparently with reluctance, to Octavian making war on Sextus and calling on Lepidus for military assistance; he also agreed that Sextus be deprived of the offices given to him at Misenum.

The five years which the triumvirs had allowed themselves to restore the State had expired at the end of 38, and the triumvirate was now renewed for a further five years, though it is not clear whether this period was to run to the end of 33 or 32. It was agreed that two of Antony's supporters, Sosius and Ahenobarbus, would be consuls in 32, and that Antony and Octavian would themselves hold office in 31, both for the third time. As a token of their good faith a betrothal was arranged between Antony's eldest son, Marcus, and Octavian's infant daughter, Julia, and to seal the agreement Octavia gave her brother ten light warships known as phaseli and prevailed on him to give Antony 1,000 praetorians.

It was past midsummer by the time the negotiations at Tarentum were completed. When Ventidius returned to Italy Antony had given Publius Canidius Crassus command of the field army and the task of reducing Armenia as the first stage of the invasion of Parthia. Canidius's operations across the Euphrates were successful, but it was too late in the year for Antony to return to the East and lead the final assault on Parthia which would now have to wait until the following year.

Reassured by the massive scale of Agrippa's naval programme, Octavian too was content to wait until 36 to launch his attack on Sicily. He did not want Antony to stay too long in Italy, where his presence was bound to affect his own efforts to widen his support and unite the country behind him; and there was always the danger that if he suffered another defeat at Sextus's hands the whole country might turn to Antony. But this time he was confident of victory and he was determined that the credit for a final end to the civil wars should accrue solely to him, so that he could use it to consolidate his hold on Italy.

There can be little doubt that if Octavian and Antony had acted together in 37, with Lepidus to support them, they could have expelled Sextus from Sicily without difficulty. But neither was prepared to take their new accord to such lengths. Indeed it was perhaps now in the summer of 37 that Antony first began to realise that co-operation with Octavian as an equal partner was impossible. For six years he had kept the agreements which they had made on the setting up of the triumvirate and after Philippi and had renewed at Brundisium and now again at Tarentum, but at last it was becoming evident to him that Octavian had only done so when it suited his purpose; first there had been his arbitrary takeover of Calenus's legions, and now this attempt to involve him over the Peloponnese in his dispute with Sextus. Twice he had returned to Italy in response to Octavian's call for help, and twice he had been rebuffed. As a result he had twice deferred his own plans for the attack on Parthia, and now he was determined to waste no more time: to settle Rome's account once and for all with Parthia would prove him the true heir to Caesar's military genius and bring him renown far beyond any Octavian could win in an unpopular war against Sextus. But he appears to have given scant consideration to the advantages which Octavian, in sole control of Italy, could extract from a victorious end to the civil wars which had torn the country for more than a decade. Antony's support throughout Italy was still considerable and it does not seem to have occurred to him that Octavian could erode it.

Ever since that first meeting after Caesar's death Antony had felt ill at ease with Octavian; he had disliked and distrusted the callow youth who had somehow usurped the name of Caesar and who seemed to be forever trying to put him in the wrong and conceal his own double dealing by accusing him of duplicity. Whenever he had been at fault himself, even unwittingly as in the Perusine war, he had freely admitted his mistake, but this Octavian would never do. At last Antony began to realise that any means would serve Octavian's ends, though precisely what these ends were he had not yet divined; he had paid little heed to the oath which Octavian had sworn with hand outstretched to Caesar's statue. His failure to recognise where Octavian's ambition must lead him was the gravest error in one who shared with him the Roman world; but others too have given clear enough notice of their pursuit of absolute power and yet been ignored until it was too late, or all but so.

Then there was Octavia, and the unpalatable but inescapable fact that his wife, now carrying their second child, was Octavian's sister; nothing could alter this, though both of them must have hoped that their second child would be the boy who would bring substance to Virgil's dream. He had been happy enough with her in Athens, and she had shown herself a loving stepmother, not only to his own two young sons by Fulvia, Marcus and Iullus, but to Fulvia's other children by Clodius and Curio. At Tarentum she had acted in complete loyalty to him, anxious though she had been to avoid a breach with her brother. But she remained Octavian's sister, and at times he found it difficult to live with such a paragon of all the virtues, however beautiful and talented.

His mind turned more and more to the East and the invasion of Parthia which he had twice delayed on Octavian's account. He badly needed the four legions Octavian had promised, but there seemed little prospect of getting them until Sextus had been defeated. Though he wanted no part in this unnecessary war, for which Octavian was preparing with such energy and single minded purpose, it is not clear why he apparently made no attempt to exercise his right of recruiting in Italy.

While he waited in Rome he may have recalled the prophecy of the Egyptian astrologer: if he was destined to be outwitted in his dealings with Octavian perhaps it was because Octavian could not be relied upon to keep his word; but if co-operation with him was impossible the Roman world was surely big enough for both of them. Thus Antony may have reasoned in apparently deciding to go his own way in the East and let his co-triumvir do the same in the West; that only the whole Roman world might satisfy Octavian does not seem to have occurred to him.

He sailed for Athens leaving the pregnant Octavia in Rome with their children; Marcus may have been living with his grandmother, Julia. As the coast faded behind him for what was to be his last sight of Italy his mind was probably on Parthia and what lay ahead, rather than on the Italy he was leaving overshadowed by Octavian's preparations for another civil war.

All the evidence suggests that Antony did not foresee an open break with Octavian leading in the end to war between them. If he had he would hardly have left his two naval squadrons with Octavian against an unfulfilled promise of four legions; nor would he have agreed, however reluctantly, to Octavian using Lepidus's army against Sextus. And it seems unlikely that he would have left Octavia and the children in Rome.

It must have been with relief that Octavian saw him go; he foresaw the break between them clearly enough, and though he was not yet ready for it he wanted Antony out of Italy. First he had to reduce Sicily, for he could never be truly master of Italy while Sextus controlled the surrounding seas and provided a haven for his enemies and a constant threat to the corn supply from Africa. With the fleet Agrippa was building he was confident of victory, and he was determined that he alone should reap its fruits. When Sextus was defeated, then would be the moment to capitalise on the end to the civil wars and unite all Italy behind him. He appreciated that undisputed control of Italy would give him the central source of power, economic and political power as well as manpower; time itself would then be on his side.

Like Octavian, Agrippa was still in his middle twenties, but in Gaul and Germany he had revealed a talent for high command beyond his years. Now as he set to work with energy and enthusiasm to build the new fleet and train its crews he showed outstanding administrative capacity and original thinking. He came from an Italian provincial family which had played no part in the political life of Rome, but whose origins were probably not as obscure as his enemies liked to suggest. He has been described as a man born to be first who contented himself with second place, but this is perhaps too superficial a judgement; it was Octavian who inspired a life long devotion in men like him and Maecenas, and it is such as Octavian who are born to be first.

To build the ships capable of outfighting Sextus and to give their crews the will and skill to man them was a formidable task. Agrippa had no Roman naval tradition to draw upon, and not even a secure harbour on the south-west coast of Italy for his base. The destruction of Octavian's fleet in 38 had shown only too clearly that all the naval expertise lay with Sextus and his Greek admirals. In Rome it had become part of the accepted order of things that the Pompeian fleets should dominate the seaways of the central Mediterranean, and this was a psychological barrier Agrippa had to overcome.

He decided to build larger and heavier ships than Sextus's, strong enough to carry fighting towers and an extra complement of soldiers, with timbers able to withstand the underwater trident shaped rams of Sextus's faster and lighter ships. He fitted them with boarding bridges and developed the harpax, a catapult fired grapnel, to compensate for their lack of manoeuvrability. Octavian and Maecenas found the men and the money; men in the shape of 20,000 slaves given their freedom if they volunteered to man the rowing benches, money from taxes and from voluntary and involuntary gifts.

To provide a secure fleet base beyond Sextus's reach where he could concentrate his ships and train his crews Agrippa cut a canal from the open sea on the Bay of Baiae to the Lucrine lagoon, and another thence to the dark crater lake of Avernus, known in Roman mythology as the entrance to the underworld. The wide stretch of inland water thus created was an ideal training area for the new fleet; he built slips and barracks and named the new harbour Portus Julius.

But Sextus's fleet had a forward base on the island of Aenaria a few miles off Cape Misenum, and from here they picked off Agrippa's newly built ships as they rounded the cape on passage south from the shipyards to the Lucrine basin. Aenaria lies within sight of the mainland, and Sextus's squadron, 200 miles from Sicily, was exposed and vulnerable; but such was his command of the sea that Agrippa dare not risk an attack across this narrow strip of coastal water.

Instead he decided to cut a canal across the Misenum peninsula from Lake Avernus to the sea at Cumae so that his ships would not have to run the gauntlet of Sextus's squadron on Aenaria. His engineers had to drive a tunnel for the canal 900 m. under the foothills of Monte Corillo, but they completed the whole grandiose project with speed and precision, displaying remarkable ingenuity in overcoming the problem of silting at the Cumae entrance. The remains of these monumental works bear testimony to their skill and Agrippa's determination; they also pay tribute to the long arm of Sextus's seapower.

After a solemn religious ceremony in which the ships were blessed and libations poured to propitiate Neptune, the new fleet emerged from the Lucrine basin on 1st July 36, the day specially chosen as the first of the month which had been renamed in Caesar's honour. Octavian's plan was for a three pronged attack on Sicily, and on the same day Lepidus sailed from Africa and Statilius Taurus from Tarentum. Lepidus, who had recruited six more legions, was to land in the west of the island with all his sixteen legions and 500 cavalry; Taurus, who appears for the first time as one of Octavian's admirals, was to cover a landing by part of the army on the east coast of Sicily. Agrippa was to embark the main body of the army under command of Messala who had now joined Octavian, and land it on the north coast.

This co-ordinated attack by three fleets, one from Africa and the other two from bases on the opposite sides of Italy, had required careful and detailed planning. But with the available communications it was impossible to alter it at short notice to meet Sextus's reaction or the vagaries of the weather. As the three fleets converged on Sicily a storm developed with southerly winds reaching severe gale force. Taurus was able to turn back to Tarentum with the wind on his starboard quarter. Lepidus's armada of 1,000 transports escorted by a squadron of warships had no choice but to run on before the storm for Sicily. Though a few of his ships foundered, Lepidus successfully disembarked his main echelon of twelve legions and then moved slowly against Sextus's legate, Plinius Rufus, who with one legion and some auxiliaries held the city and port of Lilybaeum.

The storm caught Octavian near Cape Palinurus and he ran for shelter at Velia. But his captains and crews, trained in the calm of the Lucrine basin, had no experience of handling their ships in rough water. A shift in the wind put them on a lee shore, and they lost thirty ships with many more damaged as they tried to beach them to escape the seas.

For the second time Sextus's enemies had been scattered and wrecked by a sudden storm. Wearing a blue cloak in Neptune's honour instead of his general's purple he again made a symbolic sacrifice in thanks to the god of the Ocean. It was a gesture of some significance in the light of Octavian's own public and apparently fruitless libations to Neptune, and there were riots in Rome, where the religious and the superstitious were beginning to believe that Sextus was truly favoured by the god.

In spite of his numerical superiority Lepidus advanced cautiously against Plinius while he waited for the second convoy carrying his remaining four legions. For Octavian time was running short: it could well be disastrous if he was forced to watch impotently from the coast of Italy while Lepidus won all Sicily. Agrippa sent the survivors from the wrecked ships to Tarentum, where Taurus was short of crews, and then set to work to repair the damage to the rest of the fleet.

One of Sextus's Greek admirals intercepted Lepidus's second convoy in the Sicilian Strait and sunk the transports carrying two legions, but the other two escaped and landed safely. Sextus reinforced Plinius and tried to contain Lepidus with his cavalry under his only other Roman general, Titisienus Gallus. Although Sextus had eight legions they were largely made up of ex-slaves and Spanish and Greek mercenaries, and he was not strong enough to drive Lepidus and his fourteen legions back into the sea.

He still had complete command of the sea but he made no attempt to exploit his victory. He seems to have believed that he could continue to defeat Octavian's fleets at will whenever they threatened Sicily. Menodorus showed what could be done in a brilliantly executed raid in which he damaged a number of Octavian's ships in harbour; but this turned out to be no more than a somewhat bizarre way of demonstrating his naval talent prior to again offering to change sides. However it appears to have had the effect he sought, for Octavian accepted his defection from Sextus for the second time.

In the space of a month Octavian and Agrippa were ready again. Taurus moved his fleet to Scolacium, only a day's march across the peninsula from Vibo where Messala's army was concentrated. Agrippa seized the Aeolian Islands and Sextus moved round with his fleet from Messina to cover this threat to the north coast. The two fleets met off Mylae, where in 260 the Romans had won their first victory at sea over the Carthaginians. Some of Agrippa's heavier ships made effective use of the harpax to get to close quarters; once grappled to Sextus's ships their fighting towers and boarding bridges and their extra complement of trained soldiers gave them the advantage in what amounted to a series of individual land battles fought at sea. Directing operations from on shore Sextus gave the order to break off the engagement when he had lost thirty ships; most of his captains did so successfully by pulling back into shallower water where Agrippa's ships with their deeper draft could not follow.

Octavian had transported the army by sea from Scolacium to Leucopetra south of Rhegium on the eastern side of the straits of Messina, and he had sent Carrinas with three legions to Styllis. Believing that Sextus was fully engaged with Agrippa at Mylae, Octavian started to ferry the army across to Tauromenium. But Sextus sailed back through the straits and caught Octavian at sea, with three legions under Cornificius ashore near Tauromenium and the rest of the army still at Leucopetra; he scattered Taurus's fleet, and as darkness fell Octavian found himself adrift in an open boat with one companion, perhaps his friend, Gaius Proculeius. After a long row they managed to struggle back to the shore of the mainland; Octavian was exhausted and in despair, and that night he called on Proculeius to kill him but this he refused to do.

The next morning brought better news: Agrippa was not only ashore but had seized the walled city of Tyndaris on its rocky headland, and Cornificius had beaten back the Pompeian counter-attacks and was marching north across the slopes of Mount Etna to join Agrippa.

Messala and Carrinas were able to make an unopposed landing with the rest of the army and suddenly the balance had swung in Octavian's favour. With twenty one legions ashore, together with cavalry and auxiliaries, and Lepidus advancing from the west with fourteen more it could only be a matter of time. By the end of August Octavian and Lepidus controlled the whole island except for the north-east corner where they had Plinius and Titisienus bottled up in Messina.

The final battle took place at sea off Naulochus on 3rd September. After a long and hard fought struggle Agrippa's heavier fleet won the day. Sextus fled from Sicily with seventeen ships, leaving Plinius and Titisienus to their fate; Titisienus surrendered at once with the cavalry and Plinius then asked Lepidus and Agrippa for terms. Agrippa urged Lepidus to wait for Octavian's arrival, but Lepidus evidently felt that he had won most of Sicily and that the time had come to assert himself. He ignored Agrippa's plea, and when Plinius accepted the terms he offered he took over his legions. That night he gave Messina over to his soldiers to loot and pillage. With twenty two legions now under his command he decided next morning to challenge Octavian and demand all Sicily for himself.

When Octavian arrived with a small escort there was a dispute with Lepidus who threatened him and ordered him to leave his camp. But in such straits Octavian never lacked personal courage and he seized a chance to address some of Lepidus's soldiers. He knew exactly how to appeal to them; at this moment of victory the last thing they wanted was to fight fellow Caesarians and they listened to Octavian, contrasting his youth and courage with the uninspiring middle-aged Lepidus. Plinius's troops, afraid that Octavian might not ratify the terms of their surrender, were the first to go over to him, and they were soon followed by all the African legions. Isolated by this sudden and wholesale desertion of his army Lepidus was brought before Octavian and begged for mercy. Octavian summarily stripped him of his command and his triumviral powers, but he spared his life and allowed him to retain the office of Pontifex Maximus.

Whether Lepidus's downfall was due solely to this rash and uncharacteristic bid for power, or whether Octavian had in some way helped to contrive it, is uncertain. Once again the timing was remarkably opportune for Octavian; in the two months' campaign Lepidus and his army had played their part in turning defeat into overwhelming victory, and now as soon as it was won he was neatly and conveniently removed and his African provinces added to Octavian's.

Once the fighting had ended Octavian's own soldiers began to demand their discharge and to insist on grants of land and money instead of the honours and decorations he offered them; soon they became insubordinate and threatening. There were no less than forty five legions in Sicily, making a total with the fleet, cavalry and auxiliaries of some quarter of a million men under arms, and the dangers were only too evident. Though he ordered Sicily to pay an indemnity of 1,600 talents for supporting Sextus, once again Octavian had neither the land nor the money to satisfy all his soldiers. Again he resolved the problem by dividing them into two categories. Six years was now the accepted term of service, and he gave the 20,000 soldiers who had served since Mutina and Philippi their immediate discharge and grants of land and money; as the oldest soldiers they were the most troublesome and he shipped them back to Italy as quickly as possible. Once they were out of Sicily he presented the decorations which they had spurned to the rest of the army, coupling them with promises of further rewards and threats as to their future behaviour. Plinius's legions were disbanded and Octavian reneged on the terms of their surrender, returning the ex-slaves to their former masters or executing them.

Leaving Taurus to reorganise Sicily and take over the African provinces Octavian returned to Rome. There he was greeted with jubilation and thanksgiving for at last bringing the civil wars to an end. When he remitted some debts and taxes and promised a return to constitutional government as soon as Antony had defeated Parthia there was no limit to the adulation accorded him. The Senate voted him a home on the Palatine, a golden statue in the Forum and the powers of a tribune for life, the last carrying a useful immunity from prosecution. In his turn Octavian rewarded his lieutenants: Agrippa was given a golden crown decorated with ships' beaks, and although no vacancy existed, a place was found for Messala in the College of Augurs.

PART 4

Overlord of the East

CHAPTER XVI

Antony and Cleopatra in Antioch

Antony returned to Athens in the early autumn of 37. After the long drawn out negotiations at Tarentum, and the sombre mood of resignation to another civil war as Octavian intensified his preparations against Sextus, he must have been glad to have been back again in Greece. Away from Italy and Octavian life was simpler: he was in undisputed control of the Roman East, and he was determined to settle his account with Parthia without further delay.

He sent Fonteius Capito to Alexandria to summon Cleopatra to Antioch, where he had decided to make his headquarters. During the winter he would complete the political reorganisation of Asia Minor and the Levant which he had begun in 39; before he moved against Parthia it was essential to ensure the stability of the whole area by securing the loyalty and support of the client rulers and so safeguarding his supply routes and lines of communication. When he left Athens for Syria he took with him a wreath from Athena's sacred olive tree which grew on the Acropolis and a flask of holy water from the nearby spring.

After the fall of Jerusalem in July Sosius returned with the army to his province of Syria, leaving one legion, perhaps the Ist, as garrison in Judaea. Herod was now established as king and Antony was confident of his loyalty and his capacity to rule Judaea. Instead of choosing as High Priest his young brother-in-law, Aristobulus, whom he distrusted as the last male Hasmonaean, Herod appointed Ananel, a direct descendant of the priestly dynasty which had held the office before the Seleucids gave it to the Hasmonaeans. Herod's mother-in-law, Alexandra, was furious at her son being passed over and she appealed to Cleopatra, who, always ready to espouse a woman's cause and sensing an opportunity to embarrass Herod, agreed to help her.

Even more than a strong Judaea Antony needed the financial and economic resources of Egypt, and Cleopatra knew this well enough. She also knew that he had only to give Sosius the order to march and all he wanted of Egypt was his for the taking. But his personal relations with Cleopatra aside, this was a course Antony would only take in the last resort; as well as running counter to his policy of indirect rule, to take over Egypt posed immense logistic and administrative problems calculated to dissipate his forces and postpone the invasion of Parthia yet again. He could obtain what he wanted from Egypt through Cleopatra, or so he thought, and at the same time continue his liaison with his royal mistress; it seemed to him no more than his due as master of the East that he should satisfy his public and private needs through her person.

This time Cleopatra did not stand on her royal dignity but made haste to sail with Fonteius for Antioch; here she could re-establish her hold on Antony, whom she had not seen since the spring of 40, and present him with the twins she had borne him. If he needed Egypt's resources she had need of him to underwrite the independence of her kingdom and extend its boundaries. These were her objectives, and though her relationship with Antony dictated her method it remained secondary to her purpose.

How much Antony needed her as a woman is more difficult to assess, though hardly to the extent that Plutarch would have it as he describes her malign influence reaching out to embrace him as he neared the Syrian coast. The more widely held view is that Antony had to have a woman such as Cleopatra, above virtue and beyond beauty, and that now he fell in love with her to a degree that blinded him to all else and gave her a fatal hold over him. This derives from Octavian's later propaganda, and it ignores the fact that she had been Antony's mistress in 41 and since then he had not seen her. It also perhaps mistakes both the man and the contemporary evidence by following Octavian's line in seeking to portray Antony as a Roman no more, but a man bewitched out of his senses and enslaved as the helpless tool of the foreign queen who threatened Rome's existence.

It may be nearer the truth to take Plutarch's view of Antony's own philosophy of love and life and women: that a noble lineage such as his, sprung from Anton the son of Hercules, should be transmitted to posterity as widely as possible rather than by a single womb. He had already given this living substance through Fulvia, Cleopatra herself and Octavia, arguably the three most brilliant women of the time. Men as fortunate in their women as Antony are not given to question their fortune but to take it as a right; Italy and Syria were half the divided world apart, and what was more natural than to go from his beautiful and virtuous wife, mother of his children and mistress of his house in Rome, and in Antioch resume his liaison with his royal mistress who also was mother of his children.

Whether Antony married Cleopatra during the winter of 37 is uncertain. He made no move to divorce Octavia who remained his legal Roman wife; for a Roman citizen any form of marriage with a foreigner was invalid in Roman law. It seems possible, even likely, that he married Cleopatra in Antioch according to the ancient Macedonian rites of the Ptolemies; to do so may well have seemed to him both natural and expedient. If she was to assume Octavia's mantle as his partner in the East they must both be revered as semi-divine rulers, Dionysus and Aphrodite to the Greeks of Asia Minor, Osiris and Isis to the Egyptians. And their issue, the twins, Alexander and Cleopatra, whom he now saw for the first time, must take their rightful places in the dynastic hierarchy; he acknowledged them as his children and they were given the additional names, Helios and Selene. Alexander was thus linked with the Sun, which old prophecies foretold would give birth to the new Golden Age so eagerly awaited by many in the East and West alike, and with his mother's claim to be daughter of the Sun god. The names also gave notice to the new Parthian king, who styled himself Brother of the Sun and Moon, that he had no heavenly monopoly.

Broken by Pacorus's death Orodes had named another son, Phraates, as his heir. But late in 38 Phraates, who must have been aware of Antony's preparations against Parthia, decided that he could wait no longer to succeed to the throne and seized power by murdering his father and most of his half-brothers. Many Parthian nobles loyal to Orodes died in the coup, but some escaped, among them Monaeses, feudal lord of the Parthian border province between the Tigris and the Euphrates, who fled to Antony in Syria.

Rumours reaching Rome that Antony had married Cleopatra according to Ptolemaic law and custom caused little comment since such a marriage was invalid in Roman law. A few years later these stories were not even considered suitable material for propaganda, for had not Octavian's father, the divine Julius, himself taken Cleopatra as his mistress. It was the ten year old Caesarion, the result of this liaison of Caesar's who posed the threat which Octavian as Caesar's son and heir could not ignore.

Antony spent the winter preparing for the attack on Parthia and completing the reorganisation of Asia Minor and the Levant which he had begun in 39. Ariarathes X of Cappadocia was executed for the part he had played during the Parthian invasion, and Antony gave his kingdom to Glaphyra's son, Archelaus of Comana, but without the key frontier province of Armenia Minor lying between the upper course of the Euphrates and the river Lycus. Polemo's kingdom was split up, Lycaonia going to Amyntas of Galatia and western Cilicia to Egypt; instead Antony gave him Armenia Minor and Pontus as far west as the Halys river, and included part of Pamphylia in Amyntas's enlarged Galatia.

Antony presented western Cilicia to Cleopatra as the traditional Ptolemaic source of timber for the Egyptian shipyards, and he confirmed Caesar's return of Cyprus to Egypt. The rest of Cilicia, no longer a separate Roman province since 39, continued to be directly administered from Syria. Lysanias paid with his life for aiding the Parthians and Chalchis came under Egyptian rule, as did the non-Jewish part of the Decapolis which Pompey had detached from Judaea. Antony also transferred Coele Syria to Egypt, together with most of the Mediterranean seaboard north from Egypt proper to the old Ptolemaic frontier on the Eleutheris river. Tyre and Sidon were left as free and independent cities, and, though Herod had to surrender Joppa to Egypt, Gaza remained as Judaea's outlet to the sea.

Thus Antony effectively resurrected the empire of the earlier Ptolemies, at least in territory if not in sovereign power, and gave it to Cleopatra, some said as a wedding gift, but perhaps more practically as the southern cornerstone of his reorganisation of the Roman East. The only important difference was that then Judaea had been a Ptolemaic province and now it was an independent state, and Herod was no longer the fugitive tetrarch whom Cleopatra had helped for Antony's sake, but the ruler of this Jewish enclave she considered rightfully hers. She did all she could to persuade Antony to give her Judaea but this he refused to do, in itself hardly the act of a man so besotted that he could deny his mistress nothing. Josephus makes it clear that she went on pressing her claim; it was this continuing threat to his kingdom that aroused Herod's hatred for Cleopatra as much as the cession of the valuable date palm and balsam groves at Jericho, which was all that Antony would concede to her.

These date palms were famous for their prolific cropping, but it was the balsam groves that Cleopatra particularly coveted. Balsam was widely used in medicine, and it was also an important ingredient in the Egyptian manufacture of the oils and perfumes which were complementary to the eastern trade in herbs and spices largely controlled through Alexandria. Cleopatra leased the groves back to Herod, and he accepted this further affront, judging it preferable to an influx of Egyptian officials fifteen miles from Jerusalem.

Though not strictly a client king, Malchus of Nabataea felt it prudent to obey Antony's instructions to make over to Cleopatra the bitumen deposits at the southern end of the Dead Sea, together with a strip of land running down to the head of the Gulf of Akaba. As well as its uses in medicine and embalming, and as an insect repellent in vineyards, bitumen was the most effective material for caulking the timbers of ships and the Egyptian shipyards required a regular supply. Cleopatra leased the bitumen deposits back to Malchus, and, to settle

246

old scores with his neighbour, Herod agreed to collect the rent on her behalf.

Herod's uneasy throne was but newly won, and now as Antony's client he found himself the object of the bitter enmity of his patron's mistress. Faced with this delicate balance he showed resource and strength of character in his determination to remain ruler of an independent Judaea. He had had to cede the groves of Jericho, and he made the best he could of this bad bargain. But he stood firm over Judaea's vital outlet to the sea and resisted Cleopatra's every attempt to subvert his rule in Gaza. The surviving Hasmonaeans were a constant threat to him, and when to placate Cleopatra and Alexandra Antony invited Aristobulus to Antioch Herod pleaded his brother-in-law's youth and the dangers of the journey to keep him under his own eye in Jerusalem without offending Antony; later he had to give way and appoint him as High Priest in Ananel's place. He persuaded Antony to order the execution of Antigonus, whose presence as a prisoner in Antioch provided a rallying point for every disaffected Jew. Facing the Temple in Jerusalem he began to build himself a fortress palace which he named Antonias in Antony's honour.

In his settlement of the East Antony had played the part of kingmaker, giving substance to his own remark that Rome's greatness lay in the exercise of her power to bestow kingdoms rather than annex them. The framework he built was based on the three Roman provinces of Bithynia, Asia and Syria and the three most powerful client kings, Amyntas in Galatia, Polemo in Armenia Minor and Archelaus in Cappadocia, with Herod in Judaea to balance the new Ptolemaic empire which he would control through Cleopatra. With this blend of direct and indirect rule, and a minimal use of his own manpower resources, he brought stability to the Roman East and imposed his own overall rule on the whole of this vast area and its diverse peoples. The lasting worth of his reorganisation provides the best tribute to his political judgement and his strategical insight, qualities for which he has been given meagre credit.

The only provision which appears to lack any clear purpose was the cession of the Jericho groves to Cleopatra; but Antony knew that Herod was his man, and this was a sop to Cleopatra for his refusal to give her Judaea, a grievance which she believed that in time she could prevail on him to redress. Though she was to be proved wrong in this, she could take comfort and pride in the renascence of Egypt's empire, which in territory, with the one irritating exception of Judaea, now matched that of her Ptolemaic ancestors at the height of their power.

It is sometimes said that Cleopatra was opposed in principle to

Antony's expedition against Parthia and to the conquest of lands beyond the Euphrates; this is probably mistaken for she was always conscious of the fact that the Ptolemies were co-heirs to Alexander's empire. But her priorities were more realistic than Antony's: power and dominion were more important to her than the pursuit of military glory and the recovery of Rome's lost eagles. She saw earlier, and more clearly than he did, that Octavian posed the immediate danger, and she decided that the Egyptian treasury could be more profitably employed to build a fleet rather than fund the Parthian adventure.

It is impossible to say whether her ambition embraced the whole Mediterranean world; certainly the Romans believed that it did. They saw in her a personification of the widow whom the mad praetor and the banned Sibylline books foretold would come out of the East to shear Rome's hair. This despoina prophecy was widely believed in the East, and it was feared by many Romans who saw in it a sinister twist to their own belief that a world era was coming to an end and a new Golden Age was about to dawn. Thus they came to fear Cleopatra as once their ancestors had feared Hannibal; but he had posed a direct and tangible military threat to Rome's existence, and to the practical but superstitious Romans retribution inspired by the Fates for their despoilation of the East was intangible and so more menacing. In all Rome's long history no other foreign enemies aroused such fear as Hannibal and Cleopatra.

It may be that Cleopatra's habit of swearing the most solemn oaths by the day that she would mete out justice on the Capitol should be taken as a literal statement of intent, in the same light as Octavian's oath to Caesar's statue. In a sense it was she and Octavian who were the protagonists, for it was she who foresaw the coming struggle; whether she had already concluded that war between Antony and Octavian was inevitable, or whether she worked to make it so in order to further her own ends, is difficult to assess. Certainly she envisaged a new empire in the eastern Mediterranean reaching out to include Greece, Macedonia and north Africa, with Antony and herself founding a new imperial dynasty. It is possible that Caesar had once confided to her a secret vision of bringing East and West together in harmony and partnership. On her coinage she introduced a new system of regnal years with the Egyptian calendar year which began in the autumn of 37, the sixteenth year of her reign, becoming both sixteen and one; this may have been either to celebrate the rebirth of the Ptolemaic empire or her marriage to Antony, perhaps both. Now she had to steel his will and forge his purpose to match her own, and kindle in him the flame that was in her and once had burned so brightly in Caesar and in Alexander himself.

CHAPTER XVII

The Parthian Adventure

During the campaigning season of 37 Canidius invaded Armenia proper and defeated the king, Artavasdes, who to keep his throne agreed to transfer his allegiance to Rome and submit to Antony. Armenia had long been a client state of Parthia's, and through his upbringing and ties of common interest Artavasdes's sympathies lay with the Parthians; he was currently in dispute with his rival and namesake, Artavasdes, king of neighbouring Media and also a Parthian client. Canidius put the field army into winter quarters in Armenia and Artavasdes resigned himself to his new status as friend and ally of the Roman people. To celebrate the conquest of Armenia Antony struck denarii in Antioch early in 36 bearing the crown of Armenia on the reverse.

When Monaeses arrived in Antioch, supposedly as a fugitive from Phraates, Antony received him with honour, gave him lands in eastern Syria and promised him the throne of Parthia as well as the return of his own border province. Whether Monaeses's flight was feigned in order to discover Antony's plans for Phraates, and, if it was, whether Antony was deceived is uncertain; it may well be that in the aftermath of Phraates's coup Monaeses genuinely feared for his life.

Phraates had not had time to consolidate his hold on Parthia and he was already alarmed at reports of the scale of Antony's preparations. As lord of the western marches Monaeses held a key role in the defence of Parthia against an attack across the middle Euphrates; according to Dio, Phraates was so dismayed by his defection that he sent messengers after him offering to reward him and to confirm his title to his feudal lands if he would come back to Parthia.

With Armenia detached from Parthia and Phraates unprepared for war, and now deserted by Monaeses, Antony could probably have negotiated the return of the lost eagles and the surviving Roman prisoners as part of a frontier settlement based on the Euphrates and leaving Rome in control of Armenia. Apart from Armenia Rome had no real territorial ambitions beyond the river, and if Antony could secure the return of the eagles and the prisoners Roman honour would be satisfied and there would be nothing to be gained from invading Parthia.

But like Pompey and Caesar before him Antony seems to have

discounted the advantage to Rome in a long term settlement of her eastern frontier. Like them he sought the renown which could only be won by force of arms and the glory that would have been Caesar's had he lived to conquer Parthia; only thus would he be able to prove to the world, and perhaps to himself as well, that he had truly inherited Caesar's mantle.

Monaeses was apparently reassured by Phraates's overtures, or if all along he had been playing a part, he pretended to be. Antony agreed to his return to Parthia and sent envoys with him; Plutarch suggests that their mission was to deceive Phraates into believing that Antony wanted to negotiate. But he could hardly have hoped to conceal his true intentions for long and he would have done better to have held Monaeses; to allow him to return may have been the sort of gesture which appealed to Antony, but it was foolhardy and perhaps stemmed from over-confidence.

On Antony's orders Canidius marched north with the field army in the early spring of 36 to subdue the Iberians and the Albanians in the southern foothills of the Caucasus; he was to meet Antony in mid-June at Carana near the source of the Euphrates in central Armenia. These two tribes had made a practice of raiding across the northern borders of Armenia, but they scarcely presented a credible threat to Antony's communications even though he had chosen the northern route through Media for his attack on Parthia. Artavasdes may have exaggerated their raids to get Canidius away from his capital, Artaxata, where the cost of maintaining the Roman army was falling on the Armenian treasury. A quarter of a century earlier Pompey had conquered both tribes, and it may be that Antony merely wanted to emulate him so that he too could boast that he had taken Roman arms to the Caucasus and the Caspian. There does not seem to have been any sound strategical reason for the campaign, which was bound to delay the invasion of Media to a point that would make it dangerously late to attack Parthia that year; the risk outweighed the possible rewards to an extent which suggests that Antony may not have recognised them, such was his impatience and his overweening confidence.

He had decided to avoid the short direct line of advance which had taken Crassus across the desert from the Euphrates to defeat at Carrhae. Instead he would march up the river and follow the great sweep of its upper course north-east to Carana. Here around midsummer the whole expeditionary force would assemble, Canidius with the field army, Ahenobarbus with his two legions from Bithynia, the contingents from the client states of Asia Minor and Artavasdes with the Armenian army. From Carana Antony would advance east down the valley of the upper Araxes and invade Media from the north. Once he had reduced Media he would strike south to the Parthian capital of Ecbatana, and then on to Susa, only some hundred and fifty miles from the head of the Persian Gulf, thus cutting off Assyria and the rich province of Babylon between the two rivers from the rest of Parthia. His proposed timing is uncertain, but it seems likely that he planned to secure Media in 36 and mount the final attack on Parthia in the following year.

It was a bold and imaginative design and Antony gave out that it followed Caesar's master plan for the campaign of 44. The concept may well have been Caesar's, but in his detailed planning for such operations Caesar never neglected to secure his supply bases and communications and he always made sure that his army's weapons, training and equipment would give him the tactical advantage; he also recognised that everything would never go precisely according to plan, and he had the capacity to improvise which is one of the hallmarks of the great captains.

Antony may have had Caesar's notes and draft plans, but he had no experience in preparing and executing such a complex operation as the invasion of Media and Parthia from the north. He had proved himself an able and resourceful general in the field and he had shown personal resilience and exceptional qualities of leadership, particularly when all seemed lost; this, coupled with flexibility of mind, speed of reaction and an innate tactical sense, had made him perhaps the greatest of the few notable cavalry commanders Rome ever produced. Now he was to need something of Caesar's genius.

In the spring, accompanied by Cleopatra, Antony left Antioch for Zeugma, where the Euphrates reaches its nearest point to the Mediterranean at the head of the Gulf of Alexandretta. Cleopatra was four or five months pregnant, and after resting at Zeugma she set off on the long overland journey back to Egypt. On the way she completed her deal with Herod over the Jericho groves and Malchus's bitumen deposits; a measure of their commercial value is the annual rent which in both cases she fixed at two hundred talents.

Dio has it that the Euphrates crossings were so well guarded that when Antony left Zeugma in May he was forced to march up the west bank of the river. But at the latest his decision to concentrate at Carana must have been taken before Canidius moved out of winter quarters near Artaxata. By mid-June Canidius was back at Carana; even if, as is likely, the Albanians and Iberians offered little resistance, the distance he had covered across difficult and almost unknown country made the campaign a remarkable feat, however obscure its purposes. It was this Caucasian diversion which had obliged Antony to delay the assembly of the army at Carana until June, rather than dalliance with Cleopatra at Antioch as Plutarch suggests. It is not known when he received the news that Octavia had given birth in the spring to a second daughter, the younger Antonia, but it must have been before he left Carana.

Sixteen of Antony's twenty four legions were now concentrated at Carana. Of the remaining eight, one was in Judaea, and the other seven made up the army of Macedonia, its role to provide a strategic reserve and block any eastward move by Octavian. Ahenobarbus had brought his two legions 800 miles from Bithynia, and the provinces of Asia and Syria had also been denuded of Roman troops. To hold the vast semicircle from Macedonia through Asia Minor, Syria and Egypt to Cyrenaica with only eight legions was a measure of Antony's confidence in his reorganisation of the Roman East.

At Carana he carried out a ceremonial review of the army, which Plutarch describes as the finest Rome ever put in the field. With no drafts forthcoming from Italy the sixteen legions were under strength, totalling some 60,000 Roman infantry. The cavalry, composed of Gallic, Spanish and Galatian regiments, was 10,000 strong. The contingents from the client states, mainly light infantry with some slingers and mounted archers, numbered 15,000 and were commanded by Polemo. Artavasdes himself brought 6,000 Armenian cavalry and 7,000 infantry.

As well as the light artillery, which was an integral part of every legion, there were heavier pieces of artillery and among the siege engines a massive battering ram twenty five metres long; these were needed for the reduction of city walls in country where there was likely to be no suitable timber for building them on the spot. The entire baggage train comprised three hundred vehicles.

Plutarch describes how this forward concentration of Roman military might at Carana caused a ripple of alarm to spread out beyond Parthia and across central Asia to Bactria and India. Antony anticipated no more difficulty in defeating the Parthians in Media and in their homeland than Ventidius had experienced in expelling them from Asia Minor and driving them back behind the Euphrates. The size and strength of his army as it passed before him in review order must have made him even more confident.

Probably he expected that the Parthians would again rely on their armoured cavalry and he had enough slingers to counter them. The disaster at Carrhae was still fresh in Roman memory, but the Parthians' use of mounted archers, with a well organised replenishment system for their arrows, which had led to Crassus's defeat had largely been forgotten. If Ventidius was still alive he was far away in Italy, and neither Canidius, Ahenobarbus, nor Plancus's nephew, Titius, who was Antony's quaestor, had any battle experience against the Parthians; thus there was no one of rank to remind Antony that they might recall their mounted archers and to urge him to take more mounted archers and slingers of his own.

Artavasdes was to command the Armenians in person, and Antony seems to have thought that the king's presence with the army would be enough to keep Armenia quiet and loyal. This might be so if all went according to plan, but prudence dictated that a Roman garrison should be left in Armenia and some members of Artavasdes's family sent to Antioch as sureties for his good faith. Antony's neglect to do either again points to over-confidence, and it was to cost him dearly and many of his soldiers their lives.

It was early July before the army left Carana and marched east down the valley of the upper Araxes. Phraapa, the Median capital, lay nearly four hundred miles to the south-east, beyond the great inland lakes of Van and Urmia, and fifty miles further by the circuitous northern route Antony had chosen. It was already late enough in the year for an invasion of Media, let alone Parthia, and Antony probably planned to winter in Media after taking Phraapa.

As soon as the army left the valley of the Araxes and headed south into the hills north-east of Lake Urmia they were in Media's mountainous northern province and advancing through unknown hostile territory. But they saw no signs of the enemy as they came down on to the plain between the lake and the mountains to the east rising sharply to the 3700m peak of Mount Sahand. On the dusty rockstrewn tracks the huge siege engines and the heavy artillery could not keep pace with the marching legions. Chafing at the delay Antony allowed his impatience to provoke him into a grave blunder; he decided to press on himself to Phraapa with the main body of the army and let the heavy equipment and the loaded wagons of the baggage train follow at the best speed they could make. He left Oppius Statianus in command with two legions, some of the auxiliaries under Polemo, and Artavasdes and his Armenians as escort.

Though the cavalry screen had failed to detect any enemy the army was in fact being shadowed by Parthian and Median reconnaissance groups. On his return Monaeses had not only been restored to favour, but Phraates had appointed him to command the 40,000 strong Parthian field army in Media; the Median king was at the head of another 10,000 mobile troops. He and Monaeses can hardly have believed their good fortune when they realised that Antony had divided his army into two echelons.

To make sure that this was no Roman trap they waited until Antony was far enough ahead with the main body before they fell upon the hapless and unsuspecting baggage train. Oppius managed to get a courier off to Antony as he formed up to meet the attack, but Artavasdes discreetly disappeared taking with him all the Armenian contingent; thus denuded of cavalry and outnumbered by five to one the two legions and Polemo's auxiliaries fought desperately, but it was only a matter of time before they were overwhelmed. Polemo was taken prisoner, but 10,000 were killed, among them Oppius who died fighting sword in hand. The Parthians captured the two legionary eagles and set fire to the siege equipment and wagons.

When Oppius's courier caught up with Antony he was nearing Phraapa. He at once sent back a strong force of cavalry, but all they found were the smouldering wrecks of the baggage train and the vultures picking at the bodies of their dead comrades. Antony laid siege to Phraapa, but he could make no impression on the walls without his artillery and battering rams and there was no timber available to build replacements. The Parthian field army remained outside the city, and though they avoided battle they continued to harass the Romans. To take Phraapa Antony would have had to wait for his siege equipment in any case; all he could have done before they arrived would have been to prepare their earth and timber firing platforms. As it was he had risked and lost his entire baggage train for nothing, and Artavasdes's desertion had compromised his forward bases in Armenia and his vulnerable and tenuous communications with Syria.

The summer was nearly gone, and with the Roman army helpless and dangerously exposed before the walls of Phraapa the initiative passed to the Parthians. Confident now that time and the season were on their side they were determined to avoid any set piece battle which would favour the legionary infantry, and instead use the superior mobility and firepower of their mounted archers to wear down the invaders.

In an attempt to break the deadlock and bring on a battle Antony took a large force made up of ten legions, three praetorian cohorts and all his cavalry on what he hoped the Parthians would think was a foraging expedition in strength. They shadowed the Romans and when they were a day's march from Phraapa they tried a surprise attack which failed. The next morning Antony struck camp as if to continue the march, but he had issued secret orders for battle. The Romans marched off in column of route, and as they passed the main body of the Parthians drawn up in a crescent formation on the flank Antony gave the signal and his cavalry suddenly wheeled and charged. Taken by surprise the Parthian archers recoiled. Antony

254

threw the legions into the attack, but the Parthians continued their tactical withdrawal to such good effect, that after the Roman cavalry had pursued them for twenty miles and the infantry for six, all they had to show were thirty prisoners and a head count of eighty dead. The next day Antony had some difficulty in fighting his way back to his lines outside Phraapa. He continued the siege, but he was short of supplies and the Parthians took an increasing toll of his foraging parties. The city was resolutely defended, and his improvised siege equipment had made little impression on the walls. The garrison succeeded in demolishing some of the siege works when the Romans abandoned them in the face of determined sorties; Antony punished the units concerned with decimation.

But as the summer passed the Parthian commanders in their turn became anxious lest the siege went on into the autumn and winter; they feared that the feudal ties which held their army together would not be strong enough to stop many of the soldiers returning to their homes in Parthia for the harvest, leaving the Romans to tighten their investment and reduce Phraapa by starvation.

Phraates offered a truce if the siege was lifted, and as a result Antony withdrew from his close investment of the city and demanded the return of the lost eagles and the surviving prisoners. Phraates took the opportunity to destroy the Roman siege works and then rejected Antony's demands, offering him instead an unimpeded withdrawal from Media.

By now it was late September and in northern Media winter came early. Unable to take Phraapa or bring on a battle, with his supplies running short and no winter clothing for his soldiers, Antony had little choice but to try and extricate the army as best he could. Already he had delayed too long: even if Phraates kept his word not to interfere with the withdrawal it would be difficult enough to get the army back across the Araxes to the doubtful safety of Armenia before the first snow came, let alone to winter quarters in Syria.

When camp was struck for the last time and the legions were ready to march out on the first stage of their long retreat Antony was in such despair that he called on Ahenobarbus to make the general's customary speech. But as soon as they were on the march his mood changed, and once again he drew deep on some inner reserve of strength to lift and inspire his soldiers. They forgot, and perhaps he too forgot, that it was a series of mistakes on his part which had brought them to their present pass; instead they blamed Artavasdes for his treachery and Phraates for avoiding a pitched battle, and looked to Antony for deliverance.

Except for the loss of the baggage train and Oppius's two legions and the defection of the Armenians the army was more or less intact when they left Phraapa. On the advice of a Mardian tribesman who had proved his loyalty when the baggage train was overrun Antony chose a different route through closer country, avoiding the open hills where the enemy archers were most effective. For the first two days the Parthians contented themselves with shadowing the retreating army, but the Mardian guide warned Antony that despite his promises of safe conduct Phraates had no intention of allowing them to escape from Media. He was soon proved right, for when the Parthians thought they had lulled the Romans into a false sense of security they set up an ambush ahead on their line of march. The Mardian noticed that a stream had been diverted and was able to warn Antony of the trap. Volleys of arrows from the Parthian archers hidden on the flanks took their toll, but the slingers outranged them and forced them back; they rallied and returned to the attack, but this time the Roman cavalry charged and dispersed them.

The tactical lesson was not lost on Antony; he deployed strong flank guards as well as his advanced and rear guards, giving each of them a detachment of slingers in close support. He kept his cavalry concentrated, with the task of keeping the enemy archers out of range and strict orders not to carry their counter-attacks too far. For the next few days these tactics not only kept the Parthians at a distance but enabled the Romans to inflict enough casualties to make them chary of pressing home their attacks.

But the Araxes was still three weeks march away, and if they were to get back to Armenia they would have to beat off every attack by a mobile enemy confident that victory was within his grasp. Antony would have to hold the army together while they fought their way in worsening weather over difficult terrain with only the supplies they could wrest from the sparse lands of northern Media, and at the end of this bitter road the dubious haven of Armenia. Such a fighting retreat is the most exacting of all military operations, demanding the highest standards of morale, discipline and leadership; other armies, some commanded by the great captains of history, have disintegrated under conditions less arduous and hazardous than those which now faced Antony.

After a time the Parthian soldiers became discouraged by their failure to break the discipline of the retreating Romans, and more and more reluctant to continue this seemingly fruitless pursuit which was taking them ever further from their homes in the warm south, ever deeper into the wild inhospitable country east of Lake Urmia where the winter winds were already blowing across the bare hills.

Then one of Antony's officers, Flavius Gallus, encouraged by their defensive successes believed he saw the chance to hit the Parthians hard enough to make them call off their pursuit. He persuaded Antony to give him some cavalry and auxiliary infantry, and with them he took up a defensive position behind the rearguard commanded by Canidius. When the Parthians attacked him, instead of trying to draw them within range of the slingers and then on to the legions Gallus stood his ground. He ignored orders from Canidius to rejoin the rearguard, and he refused to obey Titius when he went back to repeat the order; soon he was cut off and surrounded. As an able professional Canidius doubtless disapproved of the entire operation, and instead of using the whole rearguard to extricate Gallus he sent back a series of detachments each of which was defeated in detail as it reached the battle.

When Antony realised what was happening he hurried back himself with the IIIrd Gallica Legion and forced the Parthians to withdraw. But by the end of the day the Romans had lost 3,000 dead, and the 5,000 who had been wounded posed an all but insuperable problem; Antony refused to abandon them and the last of the baggage was jettisoned so that the surviving pack animals and vehicles could carry those who could not march. Antony's concern for the wounded and the knowledge that his intervention with the IIIrd Legion had saved the whole army from disaster raised morale and stiffened the soldiers' resolve. His wry humour and the way he shared their hardship won him the devotion of these tough but simple men, and they blindly put their trust in him; though he was not to fail them, it was a crisis which he and Canidius should never have allowed to develop and this they must both have known.

The losses they had inflicted on the Romans gave the Parthians new heart just when it had seemed that there was nothing more they could do to disrupt the retreat and turn it into a rout. All at once they sensed victory, and they concentrated 40,000 men for what they were now convinced would be the final battle, bringing up the Parthian royal guard so that Phraates would be present in spirit at the destruction of the invaders, since by long custom the kings of Parthia never commanded in the field.

Antony dared not risk being caught on the march by a mobile Parthian army of this size, and he had no choice but to stand and fight. He considered wearing a dark cloak to impress the army with the gravity of their position when he made his pre-battle speech. But his staff dissuaded him, and in his scarlet general's cloak he began by praising the units which had rescued Gallus's men, singling out the IIIrd Legion for special mention. He went on to reproach those who had not pressed home their counter-attacks, and when they begged him for any punishment he considered fitting he knew that he had made his point.

Then in front of the whole army he prayed to the gods of Rome that if the Fates were about to call on him to pay for his former good fortune, then they should call on him and him alone, and grant the army victory and a safe deliverance. The listening soldiers must have known that in their present peril Antony would not lightly make such a public prayer to the immortal gods; it was something that those who were to survive would remember and recount to their children's children, and it seems likely that it was from them that Plutarch heard it.

Their hearts and spirits were lifted by Antony's concern for them, and when the Parthians moved in confidently for the kill they were met by well directed fire from resolute troops grimly rejoicing in having their elusive enemy at last within range of their javelins. These were still the disciplined iron legions the Parthians feared and they pulled back to regroup after they had had the worst of the battle, allowing the Romans to resume their march.

According to Dio it was during the retreat that Antony perfected the testudo, or tortoise, as a defence against the high trajectory dipping fire from the enemy archers; to meet this the legionary infantry formed a number of tight squares with the auxiliaries inside, interlocking their shields to form walls and a rounded roof like the shell of a tortoise. When they first used the testudo and the Parthians saw the front rank drop on one knee to form the lower part of the shield wall they thought that at last the legions' will to fight was faltering, and they pressed home their attack only to be thrown back at close quarters by javelin and sword.

So through the month of October the army marched north across the bare, bleak, barren uplands, shadowed and harrassed by the mobile Parthian columns who again and again forced them to deploy and stand and fight. But the legions broke their every attack and when the cavalry had forced them back the army formed up again to continue the march. The bitter wind cut through their tattered summer uniforms and chilled their weary, hungry bodies. The meagre harvest had long since been gathered, and it was difficult for the staff to find enough grain for the army and for the soldiers to grind what little there was; many of the small portable grindstones, part of the legion's equipment on a scale of one to eight men and normally carried on its transport, had been lost or abandoned when the baggage vehicles and pack animals were put to carry the wounded. The price of a modius of wheat grain reached fifty denarii, more than two months' pay, and loaves of the despised barley bread sold for their weight in silver.

There were many cases of dysentery and food poisoning as the half starved soldiers chewed roots and ate unknown plants, some causing hallucinations and loss of memory.

At last they came to an open plain stretching away before them, probably the one which borders the south-eastern shores of Lake Urmia. Antony was tempted to take the easier going it offered, especially as the Parthians were tending to keep their distance. But the enigmatic Monaeses sent his cousin, Mithridates, to warn Antony secretly that the whole Parthian army was massing to cut them off on the plain and to advise him to keep to the mountains east of the lake. The Mardian guide thought that this might well be true, and though Antony distrusted Monaeses's motives he rewarded Mithridates and chose the route which avoided the plain and took them across the rocky and confused western slopes of Mt Sahand. Water was hard to find in the hills and some of the few wells they came across were contaminated: many of the soldiers had lost their water flasks and to allay their thirst Antony ordered the army to march by night and rest by day, but the Parthians matched their night marches and attacked at dawn when they were entrenching their camp.

Then Mithridates appeared again to say that the Parthians would stop at the next river; it seems probable that their generals were under orders not to carry the pursuit beyond this river, possibly the Talkheh which runs through Tabriz into Lake Urmia. During the last night's march before they reached the river a rumour ran through the army that the rearguard had been overrun; discipline at last broke down and some of the soldiers began looting the few remaining supplies. For a moment Antony despaired, and he made one of his staff swear to run him through if he gave the order. Then the Mardian guide announced that he could smell the river ahead and reports arrived that all was well with the rearguard.

Again the Mardian proved right and that morning they came to the river. Antony deployed his cavalry to cover the crossing and began to ferry the wounded across. As soon as the leading Parthian troops saw the river they unstrung their bows, calling to the Romans that they would not impede their crossing and saluting them for their courage and fortitude. But Antony did not trust them, and for the six days it took to reach the Araxes the army continued to march in tactical formation ready for immediate action. At the point where they came to the Araxes the river was deep and fast flowing, but they found a ford and the whole army crossed without incident. At last on the further bank there was respite from the threat of sudden attack and all at once the tension was gone; the soldiers wept as they embraced each other and knelt to kiss the alien soil of Armenia.

After they had rested for a few days on the banks of the Araxes Antony reviewed the army. He had lost 20,000 infantry and 4,000 cavalry, more than half of them from disease. The retreat from Phraapa had taken twenty seven days, and they had fought eighteen separate battles in each of which they had held and beaten back the Parthian attacks. It was a feat of arms which ranks with the few great fighting retreats in history, and Antony is rarely given the credit he deserves for its conduct, perhaps because it was his own blunders which had put his army in such straits. Though at the last they had failed to destroy the Romans the campaign was a triumph for Phraates and his generals, an object lesson in defensive strategy and the tactical use of mobile forces to contain and wear down a numerically superior invading army and eventually force it to retreat.

Now that they were back in Armenia Antony's soldiers urged him to take his revenge on Artavasdes, whose defection they blamed for their defeat. But this he would not do, for if he was to get the army safely back to winter quarters in Syria he needed all the help he could get from Armenia. So the settling of the Roman account with Artavasdes was deferred, and Antony ignored his desertion of Oppius and instead treated him as a friend and ally.

From the Araxes he ordered a courier and escort to ride with all speed for Egypt carrying a letter to Cleopatra asking her to meet him at Leuke Come in Syria with food, winter clothing and money for the army. He had been without reliable news of the outside world for four months, and even if the Parthians did not retaliate with an immediate attack on Syria he could not tell what might happen when reports of his defeat in Media began to filter through to the Roman East. His choice of the fishing harbour of Leuke Come for his rendezvous with Cleopatra is significant: it was small and unimportant enough to give her a reasonable chance of seizing it from the sea if Syria was lost or in revolt.

Ahenobarbus and Canidius were to bring the army back to Syria; their long winter march across the mountains and over the snow-bound passes of eastern Anatolia was to cost no less than a further 8,000 casualties from disease and exhaustion. Antony's reason for ordering it, instead of putting the army into quarters in Armenia ready for another attack on Media in the spring, was that he feared a Parthian counter-offensive directed across the middle Euphrates on to a defenceless Syria. Leaving Ahenobarbus and Canidius in command Antony set off from the Araxes with a small cavalry escort to ride to Leuke Come. On the way reports reached him of Octavian's defeat of Sextus in Sicily and the downfall of their co-triumvir Lepidus.

CHAPTER XVIII

Proconsul and Dynast

It was perhaps towards the end of November when Antony reached Syria; he must have been relieved to find that the Parthians had made no move across the Euphrates and that from Macedonia to Egypt the Roman East was quiet. Throughout December he waited for Cleopatra at Leuke Come. After the months of action in Media and the long ride back from the Araxes these weeks of enforced idleness came as an anticlimax; he started to drink heavily, and his anxiety and frustration showed in his constant visits to a vantage point from which he could scan the southern horizon for a sight of Cleopatra's sails.

He had much to reflect upon while he waited; although his worst fears had not been realised and his command of the East remained unchallenged, he knew well enough that despite the despatches he had sent to Rome claiming victory in Media it was the Parthians who had been the real victors. They might not have defeated him in battle, but he had lost a quarter of his army and this figure was to rise to more than a third by the time Ahenobarbus and Canidius had struggled back to winter quarters in Syria. Already he may have come to regret that he had not left at least part of the army to hold down Armenia.

He could not make good his losses in Roman infantry unless he could persuade Octavian to release the four promised legions now that Sextus had been expelled from Sicily. It is known that Octavian wrote to Antony at Leuke Come outlining plans for his campaign in 35 against the Illyrian tribes in Dalmatia because Antony replied offering his assistance. Probably Octavian also tried to explain his removal of Lepidus from the triumvirate and called on Antony to deal with Sextus who had fled to the East. It is possible too that he again tried to detach Antony from Cleopatra; at some point in 36 after the birth of the younger Antonia Octavia had travelled to Athens taking with her all the children except Marcus, but early in the winter she had returned with them to Antony's house in Rome.

With the defeat of Sextus and the eclipse of Lepidus Octavian was now in undisputed control of Italy and the two African provinces, as well as Gaul and Spain together with all the islands. But though Rome rejoiced at the end of the civil wars Octavian still had to tighten his hold on Italy and widen his support if a unified country was to look to him as its natural leader; for this he needed time.

The army had to be trained for what lay ahead, and there could be no better training than a frontier war in Dalmatia against the Illyrian tribes who were constantly raiding into north-east Italy. The people would be reassured to see the army again operating in its traditional role of preserving peace in Italy by securing the frontier against a foreign enemy. And there were sound strategic reasons, both for completing the consolidation of the northern frontier on the great semicircular mountain barrier of the Alps from the Maritimes in the west to the Julian Alps in the east and for bringing more of the eastern coast of the Adriatic under Roman control.

Octavian was not yet ready for the final break with Antony, and the campaign would also provide a useful excuse for not sending him reinforcements. He must have received reports of what had really happened in Media, but he accepted Antony's despatches at their face value and ordered victory celebrations to be held in Rome. Among the honours voted by the Senate to the two triumvirs were the setting up of their statues in the Forum and the right to dine with their wives and children in the Temple of Concord; the latter was perhaps prompted by Octavian as a veiled threat to Antony, reminding him that Octavia was his wife and that his children were with her in Rome.

Antony's letter reached Cleopatra safely in Alexandria; whoever carried it on that long and gruelling winter ride from the Araxes to Egypt did not tarry on the road. That autumn Cleopatra had given birth to her fourth child, her third by Antony, a boy whom she named Ptolemy Philadelphus after the greatest of her royal ancestors; but it was the time it took to assemble the ships and to collect and load the supplies for Antony's army which caused what little delay there was before she left for Syria.

She sailed from Alexandria on the dangerous passage north in the face of the prevailing winter headwinds. It was probably sometime in January when she arrived with the stores and clothing Antony had asked for, though significantly with no large sums of money. He may have been waiting impatiently, but it is a tribute, both to the astonishing speed and endurance of his unknown courier who could not have left the Araxes much before mid-November and to Cleopatra's energy and sense of urgency, that she reached Leuke Come before the end of January.

The army was reclothed and re-equipped from the stores Cleopatra had brought. But all the money that Antony could scrape together to give his soldiers came to no more than a hundred denarii a head. Though this was not a derisory sum, amounting as it did to nearly half a year's pay, it was notably small, particularly coming from Antony, when set against the hardships they had suffered, the booty from

Armenia they had been forced to abandon and the personal possessions they had lost. Only part of the money he distributed came from Cleopatra, but he gave out that it had all been provided by her.

In the early spring of 35 Octavia again sailed for Athens, this time with supplies for Antony's army, and reinforcements of 2,000 praetorians and the seventy surviving ships from the 120 he had lent to Octavian. It is difficult to tell what lay behind this move; Octavia herself was almost certainly acting in good faith and in her husband's interests, determined to bring him what help she could in the shape of all the men and stores she could extract from her brother; she may also have hoped to detach him from Cleopatra. Octavian's part is more obscure: he appreciated Antony's need for reinforcements well enough and the praetorians may have been a token gesture to satisfy Octavia; but it is possible that he used his sister as his unwitting tool, nicely calculating the minimum she could be persuaded to take, and contriving to keep it small enough to appear perfunctory, even insulting to Antony, and so make him react precisely as he did: this was to write to Octavia telling her to send on the men and stores from Athens but to return herself to Rome.

Much or little can be read into this letter of Antony's. His mind was still on Parthia, and for the moment he had no thought of re-establishing his headquarters at Athens; there is no evidence that Octavia planned to stay there, as it seems likely that on this trip she left her children in Rome. Though it was probably not a deliberate rejection of Octavia it shows how constrained Antony was by the fact that she was his Roman wife, while in the eyes of the East his wife was Cleopatra. He and Octavian might have divided the Roman world but it remained one entity grouped round a common sea; Antony's role as the triumvir and Roman magistrate who ruled the East would become more and more difficult to reconcile with the part he was to play as co-founder of a new Hellenistic dynasty.

Whether or not he was genuinely angry at Antony's treatment of his sister Octavian made the best possible propaganda use of it; conceivably he may have felt remorse for exposing her to such a slight in order to serve his own ends. He demanded publicly that she should leave Antony's house, but this she refused to do, declaring that she would continue to care for his children and look after his clients and his interests as best she could and for as long as he wished her to do so. According to Plutarch she begged Octavian not to plunge the Roman world into another civil war on her account, if he had not already made up his mind to do so for other reasons. Her position as Octavian's sister and Antony's wife was delicate and invidious, yet in the exchange of abuse which was to come nothing was ever alleged against her by either side, at least nothing that has survived. For this reason, and because of her loyalty to Antony and her enduring love for his children, history has dwelt on her forbearance and goodness of heart, making her stand out across the centuries like a beacon of light in the darkness of her time: it may well be a fair and accurate judgement though this is by no means certain. But the very fact that she continued to care for Fulvia's children and keep Antony's house damaged his standing in Rome because the people came to reproach him more and more for wronging such a loyal and virtuous wife.

While Antony was in Media Herod took the opportunity to get rid of Aristobulus. He had continued to keep his own mother-in-law, Alexandra, under house arrest in Jerusalem, and she tried to smuggle herself and Aristobulus out of the city hidden in coffins. Soon after the failure of this escape attempt Aristobulus was drowned in what Herod maintained was an accident. Alexandra again appealed to Cleopatra, who sensing a chance to get rid of Herod again took her part. To satisfy Cleopatra Antony summoned Herod to Laodicea to account for Aristobulus's death, but he accepted his explanation and dismissed the charges against him of complicity. The only concession he made to Cleopatra was to require Herod to cede Gaza to Egypt, thus depriving Judaea of her last vital outlet to the sea.

In the late spring Antony left Syria and went to Alexandria with Cleopatra. By then reports were beginning to come through from across the Euphrates that Phraates and Artavasdes of Media had quarrelled over the division of the booty captured from the Romans; a break in Phraates's coin issues in 35 may point to internal disturbances during that year. Encouraged by this news Antony began to plan another offensive against Parthia, though first he had to reassert his authority over Armenia.

Soon after arriving in Alexandria Antony had to decide what to do about Sextus. After escaping from Sicily he reached Cephallenia with his seventeen ships; here he ordered his remaining followers to disperse and save themselves. He sailed on himself to Asia Minor to appeal to Antony, who he was confident would repay the sanctuary he had given Antony's mother in the winter of 44; and Antony might well have felt bound in honour to do so despite Octavian's likely reaction. He was still loyal to their pact, but if he foresaw even the possibility of war with Octavian prudence dictated that at the least he should give Sextus refuge in the East where the name of Pompey was still honoured. It was an alliance between Antony and Sextus that Octavian feared, for though it might provide a plausible excuse for war it could only be a renewal of civil war against Roman enemies. To unite Italy behind him in a struggle with Antony for the Roman world Octavian needed a foreign enemy, and he may have already cast Cleopatra for that part.

But it was not in Antony's character to make contingency plans against his colleague; rather he would keep to the terms of their agreement for as long as he could against all the mounting evidence of bad faith. Admirable though such qualities may be, there can be no place for them in one who aspires, however reluctantly, to supreme power.

But Sextus himself solved this dilemma for Antony, if dilemma it was. In the spring of 36 he put into Lesbos where he heard that Antony was already on the march against Parthia. He stayed there till the summer when rumours reached him that Antony had been defeated and killed in Media; he at once crossed to the mainland of Asia Minor, apparently with the intention of proclaiming himself as Antony's successor.

Plancus had left the province of Asia to take over Syria, and he had been succeeded by Gaius Furnius who had no instructions as to how Sextus was to be received. Reports reached him that Sextus was recruiting an army, and he moved east to shadow him with what forces he could muster. Sextus called on Thrace and Pontus for support and sent an embassy to Parthia, an ill-judged move in the absence of confirmation that Antony was dead.

When Sextus heard of his safe return from Media he sent envoys to him in Egypt, unaware that his mission to Phraates had been intercepted by Antony's army in Syria. In Alexandria they put Sextus's case to Antony, reminding him of the refuge he had given Julia and stressing the threat from Octavian to both of them. Antony gave them a sympathetic hearing, until at an unfortunate moment for Sextus despatches arrived from Syria reporting the capture of his envoys to Parthia. Even then, though Antony ordered Titius to take the field against Sextus, he told him to treat him as a friend if he submitted.

Sextus embarked the infantry and the small force of cavalry he had raised and sailed to Nicomedia in Bithynia; here he landed and burnt his ships, presumably to impress on his troops that there could be no going back. He then marched west to Lampsacus on the Hellespont where he tricked the city into opening its gates to him. He had now recruited three legions, and though he failed to take Cyzicus in Mysia he had the better of an inconclusive battle with Furnius, who called on Amyntas of Galatia for help. Titius then arrived with several legions and the seventy ships Octavian had returned to Antony, and after he and Furnius had joined forces they moved against Sextus. Realising that Sextus was fast becoming no more than an outlaw with a price on his head three of his senior officers deserted to Titius and asked to be allowed to make their peace with Antony. With them came Libo, Sextus's own father-in-law, and two of Caesar's surviving murderers, Turullius and Cassius of Parma; Titius accepted them and they all joined Antony.

Sextus then offered to surrender to Furnius and Amyntas, but he refused to treat with Titius whose life he had saved when Titius was proscribed. After the failure of an attempt to burn Titius's ships, Sextus was pursued and captured by Amyntas who handed him over to Titius. After some delay Titius had him executed at Miletus, whether on his own initiative, or on orders from Plancus or from Antony, is uncertain. Antony had given Plancus his personal seal and had delegated overall power to him as his deputy in Asia Minor and Syria, and it is likely that Plancus authorised Sextus's execution. But it was Titius who for the rest of his life in the eyes of the Roman people was to bear the odium for the murder of the last of Pompey's sons.

The reports of Phraates's dispute with Artavasdes of Media proved accurate, and fearing for his life and his throne the Median king sent envoys to ask Antony for an alliance, releasing Polemo as a token of his good faith. His approach was totally unexpected: suddenly he was offering all that Antony had fought for the year before and failed to win, a secure base for a new attack directly on Parthia, and furthermore he was doing so as a suppliant out of fear of Phraates. Antony at once decided to join Artavasdes on the Araxes and march with him against Parthia.

But first he had to re-establish effective control of Armenia, and he was reluctant to commit the army to this task until he knew that Sextus had submitted or that Titius had defeated him. He sent Dellius to Artaxata to summon Artavasdes of Armenia to Alexandria, there to make his formal submission in person. But in spite of all Dellius could do Artavasdes prevaricated, distrusting Antony's intentions and fearing a coup in his absence from Armenia.

So because of Sextus's foray into Asia Minor and the failure of Dellius's mission to Artaxata the campaigning season of 35 was lost, and despite the new alliance with Media Antony was obliged to defer the recovery of Armenia and the renewed attack on Parthia. But Sextus had been executed by July at the latest and there seems to have been nothing to have prevented Antony from going to Rome in the late summer or autumn. There were compelling reasons for such a visit; now would have been the time to encourage his still considerable body of support in Italy with his presence, and to insist in person on his right to recruit replacements for the 20,000 soldiers he had lost, a right which Octavian had agreed at Brundisium and reaffirmed at Tarentum and which he would have been hard put to deny him.

But Antony did not go; he had returned twice to Italy at Octavian's request, and once of his own accord after the Perusine War. Then he had left Cleopatra in Alexandria and she had not seen him again for three and a half years. Now she must have feared that if he went back he might again come to terms with Octavian, who would surely insist on Octavia's rights as his Roman wife; doubtless she did all she could to persuade him to stay in the East.

Antony seems to have felt that, though co-operation with Octavian might be fruitless or even dangerous, he could still safely go his own way in the East if he let Octavian do the same in the West. However this was no good reason for letting his support in Italy wither and die, nor for resigning his right to recruit there by default. But if he went to Rome he would certainly be faced with making the choice between Octavia and Cleopatra; if he did not go it could be deferred. The time would come, sooner rather than later, when he would have to choose between them, but as yet he did not perceive that such a choice was inevitable; when events forced it on him there would be no real choice.

The Roman East was his, but unless he was prepared to depose Cleopatra and bring Egypt under direct rule he needed her support as much as she needed his. He could not get reinforcements from Italy without Octavian's consent, and this was unlikely to be forthcoming unless he renounced Cleopatra for Octavia. His dilemma was rooted in the basic incompatibility between his role as triumvir and the position he was fast assuming, whether by accident or design, as co-founder of a new dynasty in the East; it was aggravated and made more immediate by the fact that his Roman wife was Octavian's sister.

He still did not anticipate an open breach leading to war, but he was certain that if he returned to Rome Octavian would find some way of cheating him and evading any agreement they might make. This distaste and distrust of Octavian was to lead to his tacit surrender of Italy.

Sometimes it is assumed that Antony preferred Cleopatra's wit and intelligence to Octavia's beauty and domestic virtues, but this is perhaps too subjective a judgement; that Octavia was Octavian's sister and Cleopatra Egypt's queen were more compelling factors. It was Antony's fortune to have loved two such women; it was his misfortune that he could neither resign himself to the future Octavian envisaged, nor mould the future to the pattern he and Cleopatra would design. It is this personal dilemma of Antony's, interwoven into the struggle for the Roman world, which has captivated the imagination of posterity for two millennia.

In the autumn of 35 Antony began a new ship building programme in the Egyptian yards; this has been taken to indicate a switch in his strategic planning from a renewal of the attack on land bound Parthia to preparation for war with Octavian. But after Sextus's defeat Octavian had a huge fleet at his disposal, and Antony's ship building may have been designed to reinforce his defensive naval capability in the central Mediterranean. Sosius had returned to his station at Zacynthus and Antony had garrisoned Crete and Cyrenaica; his legates, Lucius Lollius in Crete and Marcus Crassus, grandson of the triumvir, in Cyrenaica, both struck coins which did not carry the Roman title of their offices, an omission perhaps presaging the Donations.

It has been argued that the comparative rarity of some of the legionary denarii which Antony began to strike late in 35 or early in 34, both to honour and pay his army, shows that he moved six experienced legions from Macedonia to the East and replaced them with six new legions, and further that this indicates that his priority remained the attack on Parthia. But this argument is invalidated if the rare denarii for Legions XXIV to XXX are not genuine, and numismatic evidence now suggests that they are not.

CHAPTER XIX

Octavian in Illyria and
The Alexandrian Donations

Octavian did not waste the campaigning season of 35. Historians have paid little attention to his campaigns in Illyria in 35, 34 and 33, perhaps because they were both unspectacular and successful. But they welded his army into a tough and efficient fighting machine, and they put an end to the tribal raids on north-eastern Italy by pushing back the frontier to a more easily defended mountain barrier. They also helped to increase his support in the country: what had once been a revolutionary party could now be seen to be carrying on the government in much the same way as in the days of the Republic, using the army on the frontiers to preserve peace in Italy.

For a hundred years the Dalmatian islands and a narrow coastal strip of the mainland had been administered from Rome as the province of Illyricum. As in Cilicia the tribes of the hinterland had not been pacified and Roman control had never extended north to include the Istrian peninsula and so link up with north-east Italy. There had been recent tribal raids on Tergeste and the important port of Aquileia, and the new colony at Pola had been destroyed; the coasts of Istria and northern Dalmatia were infested with pirates who gave their name to the fast Liburnian warships.

In the spring of 35 Octavian opened the campaign in the north-east with a two pronged drive from Aquileia. One was directed east on Emona and the valley of the upper Save; the other, which he led in person, was to cut across the base of the Istrian peninsula and then advance east over the Kapela mountain range to the valley of the Kupa which joined the Save at Siscia. The fleet under Menodorus's command was to operate along the Istrian coast in close support of the army during the first phase.

The tribes fought desperately to defend their homelands in the densely forested mountains, but Octavian's offensive reached all its objectives and secured Croatia as far as Siscia and the line of the Save. The fleet played its part, clearing the pirates from the islands south of Corcyra Nigra and Melite and mounting a series of amphibious operations to subdue the narrow coastal plain.

At Metulum the Lapudes made a last stand to defend their tribal capital; they turned captured artillery on the Romans, countermined their siege works and threw back their scaling ladders. The legions wavered till Octavian and Agrippa rallied them and in person led the final assault to storm the stockaded hilltop town. Leaving garrisons in Croatia Octavian marched on down the Kupa to link up with the northern column advancing down the Save and then invest Siscia, which fell after a thirty day siege during which Menodorus was killed. The campaign was an example of what coordinated planning and the disciplined power of the legions could achieve in virgin densely wooded mountainous country against a fierce, courageous and resourceful native enemy. The colony at Pola was re-established and new ones were founded at Emona and Tergeste.

It was not until the autumn of 35 that the news of Sextus's death reached Octavian in the field. He must have been relieved, for he had feared that Antony might spare Sextus or even join forces with him. He ordered celebratory games to be held in Rome, but Pompey was still remembered by the mass of the people with affection and respect and they made it clear that they did not consider the death of his son good cause for rejoicing, though much of their disapproval was directed at the absent Titius. Octavian then tried to take advantage of the popular revulsion against Sextus's execution by contrasting it with his own lenient treatment of Lepidus.

During the winter Fufius Geminus successfully defended Siscia against a local uprising, and in the early spring of 34 the army advanced inland from Salonae. During that year and 33 the whole area between the rivers Cetina and Krka was conquered; in it lay the pass where Gabinius had been ambushed in the winter of 48/47, and his lost eagles were now recovered. Octavian's generals, Statilius Taurus and Marcus Helvius, crossed the river Neriena into Montenegro and penetrated south almost as far as Scodra and the river Drin, the dividing line between East and West agreed at Tarentum. Thus, in these three years, Octavian secured the whole eastern seaboard of the Adriatic from Istria to Scodra, together with much of the hinterland which was to form part of the enlarged province of Illyricum. In conquering western Croatia he gained control of the Ocra pass and the important trade route leading through it east to the Danube basin and the great plain of central Europe. In the north and north-west his generals stabilised the frontiers of Italy on the line of the Alps.

These three years also did much to improve Octavian's standing and establish him in the eyes of the people as the natural and accepted leader. With peace in Italy a fresh start could be made to repair the shattered economy in town and countryside alike. Octavian did his best to emphasise this return to more normal life with a number of reforms: some taxes were reduced, debts dating back to before the civil war were cancelled, and the civil powers of magistrates were extended.

During the decade of the 30s Octavian's and Antony's marshals both used the spoils of their foreign campaigns to vie with each other in an uncoordinated spate of public works, largely the restoration and completion of old buildings and the construction of new ones, which would make the grandeur, if not the merit, of Rome's architecture commensurate with her power and prestige as the capital of the empire.

Octavian restored and added to the complex of buildings known as Pompey's theatre, and in 36 he dedicated the foundation of a new temple on the Palatine to his patron god, Apollo. On a site by the Circus Flaminius he began the Porticus Octavia, thus called, he said, to commemorate the Octavius who had built an earlier colonnaded building on the site, though Suetonius says that he named it in honour of his sister, Octavia; in it he displayed Gabinius's eagles to remind all who passed by that it was he who had recovered them. Later in his life he would boast that he had found Rome a city of brick and left it a city of marble. But though the new buildings were on a grandiose scale their architecture was uninspired, neglecting all innovations such as those made possible by technical advances in the use of concrete. In more practical vein Agrippa repaired the Aqua Marcia and began the great new Aqua Julia to augment the city's water supply; but apart from this nothing was done to improve the lot of the people in the multi-storied tenement blocks of the old quarter which housed the majority of the population of the city.

After celebrating his Triumph Sosius built a temple to Apollo on the side of the river facing the Tiber island, and Ahenobarbus dedicated a shrine to Neptune to commemorate his victories at sea. Then it was the turn of Octavian's generals: the Regia, which stood between the Temple of Vesta and the Sacred Way and housed the religious records and the offices of the Pontifex Maximus, had been damaged by fire, and on his return from Spain Domitius Calvinus undertook its restoration. After triumphing for his victory in Africa Statilius Taurus began a huge new stone amphitheatre on the Campus Martius; after his Spanish Triumph Marcius Philippus built a temple to Hercules and the Muses, and Lucius Cornificius one to Diana. During his consulate in 34 Paullus Aemilius completed the Basilica Aemilia begun by his father in 55, which Pliny described as one of the most beautiful buildings in the world.

But behind the military pomp and the great new stone buildings all was not well, nor was Octavian's hold on Italy as firm as it might appear. Rome was not yet the accepted capital of a unified Italy, though the alien veteran colonies planted widely throughout the country were a reminder to the once proud and independent cities that Rome was now the seat of government. Nor were Rome and provincial Italy united behind Octavian; the Senate, its ranks swollen to a thousand members, might have a majority who owed their positions to him and preferred subservience and the advancement of their own interests to the exercise of sovereign power. The commercial affairs of the equites prospered, and though many of the great noble families had disappeared from public life some of the survivors of the old aristocracy had come to terms with Octavian and with commerce.

But there were others who remembered with nostalgia the free institutions of the Republic and forgot the corruption in the elections and the law courts of the late Republic. Expediency and self-interest now curtailed freedom of speech in the courts and the Senate and freedom of expression for poets and writers. The magistrates were appointed for shorter periods so that a greater number of Octavian's supporters could be rewarded and his authority more widely extended through patronage; in 38 there were no less than sixty seven praetors.

Many of the upper classes turned from what they saw as the empty charade of political life to find refuge in the study of philosophy or the practice of agriculture on their country estates. More and more foreign cults were established in Rome, and Agrippa's expulsion of astrologers, fortune tellers and magicians in 33 could not prevent men turning to occult practices and strange religions from the East.

Varro lived on in honourable obscurity; Sallust, once a partisan of Caesar's, turned in disgust from what he considered the erosion of the old Roman values and virtues, and retired to devote himself to writing history. The last of the poets like Catullus and Lucretius who had found freedom under the Republic to express their passionate and sincerely held philosophy of life were dead, though Catullus's poetry and Lucretius's strictures on the ill men did in the name of religion were to live on; their work had done much to unify Italy by giving her a common literary heritage. The new generation of poets, Horace, Virgil and Cornelius Gallus, looked to their patrons, Maecenas, Pollio, and Octavian himself, for inspiration and a lead into the new Augustan age which they were to redeem and adorn.

On 14th January 34 Antony assumed office as consul by proxy, and on the same day he laid it down in favour of Atratinus who had commanded one of the squadrons he had lent to Octavian. In the spring he left Egypt to settle with Artavasdes of Armenia by force of arms, and Cleopatra accompanied him to the Euphrates crossing; from there he invaded Armenia at the head of the field army and Artavasdes withdrew before him back to Artaxata. Antony called on him to surrender the city and the Armenian treasury and then managed to capture him with his wife and two younger sons, according to Octavian perfidiously arresting him after a parley under a flag of truce; this may have been a propaganda counter to Antony's equally unsubstantiated allegation that Octavian had secretly encouraged Artavasdes to resist. Artavasdes's eldest son, Artaxes, fought on until he was defeated and fled to Parthia.

Antony sent Artavasdes and the rest of the Armenian royal family as prisoners to Alexandria together with a large quantity of booty. To cement his new alliance with Media he transferred a strip of Armenian territory to Media and proposed a betrothal between the king's daughter, Iotape, and Alexander Helios. He gave Lesser Armenia to Polemo and made the rest of Armenia proper a Roman province, leaving Canidius to set up the provincial administration, control the influx of Roman traders and businessmen, and put the army into winter quarters.

After leaving Antony on the Euphrates Cleopatra set out on a slow royal progress back to Egypt. First she visited the ancient Greek city of Apamea and from there she went on to Damascus, a free city and the important western terminal of one of the overland caravan routes from the East; these ceremonial calls on old strongholds of the Seleucids gave public notice of her claim to be their heir as well as heir to the Ptolemies. From Damascus she travelled on to inspect her own newly acquired lands in Coele Syria on her way to Judaea.

Both Cleopatra and Herod had good cause to distrust each other; Herod because of the loss of the Jericho groves and the cession of Joppa, and now Gaza, to Egypt, and because he knew only too well that Antony's insufferable royal mistress was bent on making Judaea a Ptolemaic province; Cleopatra because Antony's friendship for the insufferable Herod and his Jewish enclave had so far proved stronger than her own influence over him. But when Herod entertained Cleopatra in the Antonias, his new fortress palace on the corner of Temple precinct, each was restrained by recognition of the other's special ties with Antony despite their own mutual antipathy.

Josephus has it that Cleopatra tried to seduce Herod either to discredit him with Antony, or simply because by nature she was wanton and promiscuous; he further suggests that the chaste and continent Herod was only restrained by his close friends from having her murdered. This story is certainly untrue: whatever else they might be Cleopatra and Herod were both realists, and they would have feared Antony's reaction. Josephus's account of Herod's concern for his honour is unlikely enough, and his portrayal of Cleopatra probably derives from Octavian's propaganda which consistently sought to depict her as a scheming and dangerous royal whore. There is in fact no evidence at all that she ever gave herself to anyone other than Caesar and Antony, and with them her first objective was to advance her own political ambitions.

In the autumn of 34, after returning from Armenia, Antony staged what Dio describes as a kind of triumphal procession through Alexandria. Envoys from the client states and cities of the East carried golden crowns which they presented to him in celebration of his victories. Detachments from his legions marching in the procession bore the letter 'C' on their shields in Cleopatra's honour. Artavasdes of Armenia walked with his wife and two younger sons, symbolically shackled with gold and silver fetters, followed by Armenian prisoners of war and floats displaying captured booty and war material; he showed considerable moral courage in refusing to bow down before Cleopatra or address her other than by her name.

Wearing the robes of Dionysus instead of the uniform of a Roman general Antony rode in a chariot pulled by four white horses; it is almost certainly this occasion that Velleius Paterculus refers to when he describes Antony riding in procession through Alexandria in a Bacchic chariot, wearing the buskins and golden robes of the god, his head wreathed with ivy and the sacred thyrsus in his hand. Velleius emphasises the religious aspect of the ceremony, and strange though it would have seemed to Roman eyes the sight of a victorious general dressed as Dionysus, the god who personified victory, was familiar enough to the Alexandrian crowds.

The plan of ancient Alexandria is described by Strabo and others, but it cannot be precisely related to the modern city that now overlays it. Only the site of the Caesareum is known, and the only remaining relic above ground is Pompey's pillar which is believed to have been erected on the site of the Serapeum in the time of Diocletian.

The procession probably started from the Palace quarter and wound round the edge of the Great Harbour to enter the city by the Gate of the Moon on to a tree lined avenue thirty metres wide; this was known as the Street of the Soma from the mausoleum where Alexander's body lay in a golden coffin, and was deliberately set on a NNW/SSE alignment to catch the cool prevailing summer breezes off the sea. At the central crossroads the procession turned into the colonnaded Canopic Way, the main axis of the city which ran for nearly four miles from the Gate of Canopus in the east to the western gate by the Eunostos Harbour. The route will have passed the Law Courts and the Library, the packed grand stand of the Paneium, an artificial hill shaped like a fir cone, and the city's civic centre, the vast Gymnasium which also housed the University.

The procession ended in front of Cleopatra enthroned high above her people before the Temple of Serapis, the god whom the earlier Ptolemies had created out of an amalgam of Zeus and Asclepius and of Apis and Osiris to fuse the religions of Greece and Egypt and preside over their new empire.

Antony dismounted from his chariot and climbed the 200 steps to the temple on the hill. Inside the propylaeum a double ring of columns encircled the temple itself under its circular gilded dome; the floor was of marble and the walls were hung with gold, silver and bronze sheets. Antony sacrificed and gave thanks to the god, whose huge ivory and gold statue stood at the east end with a sceptre in the left hand and the right resting on Cerberus, here depicted with the heads of a lion, a wolf and a dog.

It would seem unlikely that Antony deliberately staged a Roman triumph in Alexandria as his enemies were quick to allege. For a Roman general to do so in a foreign capital was almost without precedent for it not only amounted to treason and an act of rebellion, but it was also a blasphemy against Jupiter on whose altar on the Capitol all triumphators laid their laurel wreaths in homage to the god who was the fount of Rome's temporal and spiritual power; to hold such a ceremony in Alexandria was to deny Rome herself and all her patron gods. It is significant that neither Velleius nor Plutarch accuse Antony of any such act of impiety, though as well as being nearest in time they were both critical of his relationship with Cleopatra and this was an opportunity that they would hardly have missed.

What Antony failed to appreciate, or perhaps chose to ignore, was the ease with which such a ceremonial procession in Alexandria, for which the earlier Ptolemies had provided ample precedents, could be represented by his enemies as a sacrilegious parody of a Roman triumph.

His reconquest of Armenia and the setting up of a new Roman province might well have been celebrated in Rome, had it not been for the unprecedented and even more spectacular ceremony that he and Cleopatra staged a few days later which became known as the Donations. The great colonnaded Gymnasium, some 200 metres in length, held a vast concouse of Alexandrians when Antony and Cleopatra took their seats on golden thrones set on a raised silver dais. Cleopatra wore the traditional robes of the goddess Isis, and Antony was again dressed as Dionysus whom the Egyptians identified with Osiris, Isis's heavenly partner. Below them on four thrones sat the thirteen year old Caesarion, and their own three children, the twins, Alexander Helios and Cleopatra Selene, and the infant Ptolemy

Philadelphus. Though as Ptolemy XV Caesarion was titular co-ruler of Egypt with his mother, the placing of his throne below hers and Antony's but above those of his half-brothers and sister indicated his standing.

Antony addressed the crowd, announcing that the ceremony was being held to pay tribute to the deified Julius Caesar. He then proclaimed Cleopatra as Queen of Kings, Caesarion as King of Kings and Caesar's legitimate son, and Alexander Helios, who wore Median royal costume with the peacock feathers of Persia in his hat, as King of Armenia and overlord of Media and all the lands from the Euphrates to India, thus including Parthia in his domains. He went on to present Cleopatra Selene to them as Queen of Crete and Cyrenaica, and the two year old Ptolemy Philadelphus, a tiny figure in Macedonian royal costume, as King of Coele Syria and overlord of all the kings and princes of Asia Minor from the province of Asia to the Euphrates.

Behind the pomp and pageantry, beyond the claims of dominion over lands not yet won, there can be discerned a long-term design carefully calculated to fit together in space and time. As rulers of Egypt and joint heads of the new Ptolemaic empire Cleopatra and Caesarion were accorded the titles of Queen and King of Kings; under them Cleopatra's two sons by Antony were to be the overlords of all the East with the Euphrates as their common boundary.

This then was the pyramid of power they designed; they needed time to put it together. Antony took no title for himself since he was at once the architect and Cleopatra's semi-divine partner, the kingmaker who conferred on his children their royal degrees. He was also the Roman triumvir who ruled the East. In these two roles, joined together in Antony's person, lay the anomaly; he could be the founder of a new Hellenistic dynasty and he could be the Roman magistrate who ruled the East, but he could not be both at one and the same time and place; he seems to have believed that he could step from one to the other as it suited him.

The political concept behind the Donations was comprehensive and grandiose, formulating as it did a long term settlement of the East by establishing a hereditary hierarchy. It made no overt territorial claims beyond the dividing line Antony and Octavian had agreed, but in effect it gave notice of intention to divide the Roman world permanently and unite the eastern half under a dynasty which would rival Rome in power, wealth and territory; as such it was unlikely to prove acceptable to whoever ruled in Rome.

But it was Antony's public assertion that Caesarion was Caesar's legitimate issue which carried a personal threat to Octavian, particularly as it appeared gratuitous and bore no evident relation either

276

to the Donations, or to Caesarion's position as Ptolemy XV which Antony and Octavian had together approved in 42. It was a claim that Antony must have known Octavian could not and would not tolerate since it challenged his standing as Caesar's son and heir. It is also not clear how Antony proposed to substantiate it in Roman terms, for he had no evidence to support it; he could hardly ignore the fact that at the time of Caesarion's conception and birth Calpurnia was Caesar's wife, and there is nothing to suggest that Caesar took part in any form of marriage with Cleopatra under Egyptian or Macedonian law.

It seems likely that Antony made the claim purely for Alexandrian consumption, probably on Cleopatra's insistence that her son and co-ruler must be publicly recognised as legitimate. She may have argued that since Caesar was now deified and she herself the daughter of the Sun god, their issue must be divine and hence legitimate. It is also possible that Antony merely said that Caesarion was Caesar's son and this was exaggerated into a question of legitimacy in order to rebut it more effectively. It is far from certain that Antony intended to make a direct challenge which struck at the roots of Octavian's authority; he may well have again failed to realise that his actions in Alexandria could not be divorced from their effects in Rome.

During November reports of the Donations reached Octavian in Dalmatia where he was recovering from a wound; he returned to Rome at once. It may have been Antony's assertion of Caesarion's legitimacy rather than the Donations which made him decide that the time had come for the final break; if he did it was on consideration of political and military expediency rather than emotion.

For some time Octavian had realised that he would have to fight Antony in order to win the supreme power on which his heart and mind were set. The last years had redressed the balance between them; the campaigns in Illyria and Dalmatia had made Octavian's army into a formidable fighting machine and had given his fleet valuable experience in combined operations. In Italy he had tightened his hold on the machinery of government and widened his support in the Senate, and the commercial and business interests now looked to him to give them peace and stability. The veterans in their colonies were among his most reliable supporters, and in the main they were still young enough to provide a vital reserve of trained manpower.

But the great mass of people of Italy wanted peace above all else. The war with Sextus had been unpopular enough, though at its end Octavian had won much acclaim with his declaration that at last the civil wars were over and with his pledge of a return to constitutional government. He could not go back on these promises and hope to muster enough support for another war against a Roman enemy, certainly not against his own colleague in the triumvirate who was respected by the whole army and was currently fighting Rome's battles in the East. Italy however could perhaps be united behind him in a war against a foreign enemy who menaced Rome herself; he had cast Cleopatra for this role, and the Donations presented him with the opportunity of depicting her as a plausible threat and dismissing Antony as a tool in her hands.

The conquest of Armenia and the setting up of a new Roman province, together with the unexpected alliance with Media, were of great strategic importance to the whole Roman world. If these gains could be held it meant that the eastern frontier was settled at last, for, with Armenia under Roman administration and Media an ally, Parthia would never dare risk an attack across the Euphrates on Syria and the Levant. It seemed that Antony had achieved political stability in the Roman East where even Pompey had failed. Now he had an opportunity, as Pompey had once had, to consolidate what he had won and negotiate an agreement with Parthia from a position of strength and on terms which could surely have included the return of the Roman prisoners and the lost eagles. But his mind was still set on emulating Caesar and winning the renown that might have been his.

As well as its strategic importance Armenia offered lucrative markets to Roman traders and merchants, but the establishment of the new province was received in Rome with official silence. There were no public celebrations or thanksgiving ceremonies as there had been for the spurious victory over Media two years before, not even a token acknowledgement of what had been won by Roman arms; it was as if Antony was no longer Rome's proconsul in the East.

On 1st January 33 Octavian took office as consul, laying it down in favour of Volcacius Tullus in order to return to Illyricum and direct the final stages of the campaign. There were to be no less than eight consuls that year: Fonteius Capito and one other Antonian, and five nominated by Octavian to honour some of his lieutenants and increase his support among the consulars, soon to reach thirty in number. Before he left Rome Octavian publicly attacked Antony for the first time in the Senate; it was premeditated, for he took the precaution of surrounding the Curia with armed men, evidence in itself of Antony's continuing support among the senators. He rebuked him for his relations with Cleopatra and ridiculed his claim that Caesarion was legitimate; he accused him of giving away Roman territory to foreign rulers and blaspheming the gods of Rome by holding a triumph in Alexandria. It was this speech which marked the start of Octavian's war of words with Antony.

Antony replied with counter charges: Octavian had deprived him of his rightful share after the capture of Sicily and had failed to consult him before deposing Lepidus: he had only returned half the ships he had borrowed and he had not honoured his pledge to give Antony's veterans equal treatment with his own in resettling them in Italy. Though the ancient sources do not mention it Antony must have referred to the four legions which he maintained that Octavian still owed him.

Antony also wrote privately to remonstrate with Octavian, and a verbatim excerpt from his letter has survived in Suetonius's Life of Augustus:

'Why this sudden change?' Antony asked 'Because I lay the Queen? She's my wife. It all began nine years ago. Do you only lay Drusilla? Good riddance to you if by the time you read this you haven't laid Terulla and Terentilla, Rufillia, Salvia Titisensia and the lot of them. What does it matter where and how you get your rise?'

Much has been read into this letter, from inferences that Antony was drunk when he wrote it to sexual analysis in Freudian terms based on the repeated use of the crude but colloquial four-letter verb ineo. Scholars have disputed the secondary meaning of the noun uxor, some arguing that in this context it does not mean wife; and since there were no question marks in written Latin others have suggested that, in the context of a series of staccato sentences, 'Uxor mea est' means, not 'She is my wife', but 'She isn't my wife, is she?'.

It is perhaps more accurate, and certainly more rewarding, to accept it at face value and savour both its timeless human qualities and the revealing glimpse of the man who wrote it, his mood of irritated frustration and the hint of genuine surprise in the light of Octavian's well known sexual appetite, at least as catholic as his own and certainly more deviant. Whatever else can be made of it this letter hardly reads like one written by a great lover who thought the world well lost for Cleopatra; as Antony himself once remarked, such a man has lost his soul to another's body.

It appears that Antony did not take Octavian's outburst in the Senate too seriously, for early in 33 he left Alexandria to launch the long delayed invasion of Parthia. It has been suggested that he only went to meet Artavasdes of Media in order to reassure him, and to explain that the attack on Parthia would have to be postponed again because of the danger from Octavian in the West; this however would seem unlikely since he and Canidius took the whole field army to the Araxes. As token of his good faith Artavasdes returned the two legionary eagles captured from Statianus; he and Antony arranged the formal betrothal of Artavasdes's daughter, Iotape, to Alexander Helios, and she was sent to Alexandria, perhaps as insurance for Artavasdes' continuing loyalty.

Despatches from Rome finally caught up with Antony on the Araxes. Among them was Octavian's official reply to his complaints about Sicily and Lepidus and the missing reinforcements. The tone of Octavian's letter in which he repeated the accusations he had made in the Senate was abrupt and bitter. He said that Lepidus had been deposed for abusing his triumviral powers and that Antony was welcome to half of Sicily in exchange for half of Armenia; he added that he would surely have no need of reinforcements after his victories in Media and Parthia, where he could also presumably find land for his veterans.

With these despatches letters almost certainly came from Antony's supporters in Rome, among them Ahenobarbus and Sosius the consuls designate for 32, warning him that Octavian seemed determined on war, stressing the threat to Antony's position in Italy and urging him to act before it was too late. It may be that Cleopatra added her voice in letters from Alexandria, for she saw Octavian as a more dangerous enemy than Parthia. These reports from Rome probably deliberately exaggerated Octavian's readiness for war in an attempt to force Antony to recognise the long-term threat, though no doubt fears for their own safety also coloured his friends' letters.

Octavian was still not ready to move against Antony. From a purely military point of view he could strike south with his army from Illyricum, though he would have to take account of Antony's garrison in Macedonia, as far as is known still six or seven legions strong. He could probably ferry another army across the Adriatic narrows, though whether he could supply it against Antony's command of the north Ionian Sea was open to doubt. But financial and above all political considerations for the moment made such a military venture impracticable. Once again he did not have enough money, and to attempt to raise more taxes to fund another civil war would be dangerous, perhaps suicidal. To unite Italy behind him in such a war he had to show Antony as the aggressor, or better still as the agent of a foreign aggressor who threatened Rome.

If Antony chose to ignore the threat and proceed against Parthia there was little Octavian could do. With Antony engaged on humbling Parthia and avenging Carrhae he could not conceivably have carried Italy with him in an unprovoked attack on Macedonia and Greece, which might well have rebounded on his own head. If the attack on Parthia succeeded, and with Armenia a Roman province and Media an ally the conditions for its success were never more favourable, the balance of prestige and power would swing firmly, perhaps decisively, in Antony's favour.

All this Octavian probably appreciated well enough, while Antony's friends in Rome may have been too close to events they could not control, and consequently too anxious to stress the dangers to the leader whom they had not seen for six years and was now at the other end of the Roman world. After the long and difficult journey from Rome the timing of the arrival of Octavian's letter must have been fortuitous, but his acute political brain can be discerned weighing the military and political possibilities against Antony's likely reaction.

Thus the moment of decision came for Antony as he stood on the banks of the Araxes, this time with Media as his ally and fourteen legions poised to launch the long overdue assault on Parthia which for the past five years had been his most cherished ambition. Cut off from Alexandria as well as from Rome by huge distances and months in time, there was no way in which he could check the reports of Octavian's intentions and his readiness for war. To cross this furthest frontier of Rome and invade Parthia would be to isolate himself still more in time and space.

It may have been the warning of his supporters, and the abrupt tone of Octavian's letter as much as the contents, which made him decide that the danger in the West was too immediate to ignore. It was in Antony's character to trust others too far and too long, and then, when at last he perceived that his trust was misplaced, to react swiftly and without thought of the consequences. He had tried to co-operate with Octavian, and when this had proved futile he had tried to co-exist with him; now he suddenly seems to have concluded that co-existence was as impracticable as co-operation.

He made up his mind quickly as he had at Mutina, deciding that once again Parthia must wait, this time until the issue between him and Octavian had been resolved. Perhaps he should have shrugged off the threat from behind him, made the Araxes his Rubicon and struck south through Media into Parthia. But once he had resigned himself to the fact that he was going to have to fight Octavian he may well have thought that the sooner he did so the better, before his irreplaceable Roman legionary infantry had wasted further away. With his fiftieth birthday past it cannot have been easy to turn his back on Parthia: he was not to know that such an opportunity would never occur again, either for him or for Rome.

But once the decision was taken he acted to implement it without delay. He ordered Canidius to take the army on the long march back to the Mediterranean coast, and he sent instructions for the fleet to concentrate in western Asia Minor and for his headquarters to be set up at Ephesus. After reassuring Artavasdes of Media as best he could, he sent out orders, as Plutarch puts it, to all the kings and princes of the nations and the city states, from Syria to the Mareotic Lake and from Armenia to Illyria, summoning them to join him with their quota of men and war material in the province of Asia.

PART 5

The Actium Campaign

CHAPTER XX

The Trumpets Sound

In response to Antony's call to arms the forces of the client states began to assemble in western Asia Minor during the autumn of 33. Among the kings and princes who brought their own contingents were Amyntas of Galatia, Archelaus of Cappadocia, Tarcondimotus of Amanus, Mithridates of Commagene and Deiotarus of Paphlagonia; Artavasdes of Media and Malchus of Nabataea sent token forces and Rhoemetalces of Thrace was to join the army when it crossed to Greece. In all the allied contingents numbered some 25,000 infantry and 12,000 cavalry. Bogud, deposed by his brother Boccus as co-ruler of Mauretania, fled by sea to Antony when Octavian refused to reinstate him on Boccus's death.

After two months on the march from the Araxes Canidius reached the province of Asia in November and put the field army into winter quarters; one, or perhaps two, of its fourteen veteran legions may have been left behind as the garrison of Syria under Lucius Calpurnius Bibulus, grandson of Cato. Cleopatra arrived with the Egyptian fleet in a Syrian or Cilician port; here Antony joined her and they sailed on together to Ephesus. Herod got there soon afterwards, probably by sea, having left his troops to make the long overland march from Judaea. But Cleopatra refused to have him with the army and persuaded Antony to order him to take the field against Malchus, who had defaulted on two annual payments of rent for the Nabataean bitumen deposits he had been obliged to cede to Egypt. At the same time she sent secret instructions to Athenion, her general in Coele Syria, telling him to make sure that Herod gained no decisive advantage over Malchus. Before he left Ephesus Herod privately urged Antony to kill Cleopatra and annex Egypt; he may have been moved by jealousy and spite, but he also saw more clearly than others the dilemma Antony would face if she stayed with the army.

The fleet numbered 300 transports and 500 warships, the latter organized in eight squadrons, one or two of which were detached on station at Zacynthus, Corfu, and probably Cephallenia, off the Ionian coast of Greece. Some of the ships were newly built in Asia Minor, and Turullius had earned notoriety and general execration by felling Asclepius's sacred groves on Cos to furnish their timbers. Cleopatra contributed 200 warships and more than half the transports; against

Octavian's Rome she was willing to stake all Egypt's resources including the immense sum of 20,000 talents which she provided for the war chest. The fleet was about the same size as the one Caesar had concentrated for his second invasion of Britain; neither the Channel nor the Mediterranean would see such an armada again for two millennia.

During the latter half of 33 relations between Octavian and Antony worsened, and their exchanges, mainly in the form of speeches by Octavian, manifestos from Antony, and pamphlets written by their supporters, became more embittered as they moved rapidly from recriminations between triumviral colleagues to personal abuse and the scoring of propaganda points.

The triumvirate was due to end on the last day of 33, assuming that the five-year term of renewal in 37 ran from the first day of that year; it has been argued that it began on 1st January 36 and so only ended on the last day of 32. Antony was to continue to style himself triumvir, apparently maintaining that his appointment only ended when he laid down his office. Long afterwards Octavian wrote in his Res Gestae, his own brief account of his life's work, that he had held triumviral powers for ten years, implying that the second term ended on 31st December 33. This time there was to be no reconciliation leading to a second renewal.

It was just such a reconciliation that Cleopatra feared, for Octavian would assuredly insist that Antony returned to Octavia, still his wife in Roman law since he had made no move to divorce her. This would inevitably mean the loss of Cleopatra's newly won empire and the ruin of her dynastic plans for her children, perhaps even the end of Egypt's independence. So she refused when Antony suggested that she should return to Alexandria until the war was over, evidently feeling that she could not risk letting him out of her sight again.

With the triumvirate due to expire at the end of 33 it must have seemed to Antony that, with two of his supporters as consuls in 32, there would be an opportunity to reassert his authority in the Senate and in Rome. Like Pompey before him he now sent a formal statement of his acts to Ahenobarbus and Sosius for ratification by the Senate, setting out in it the details of his reorganisation of the East and the Donations; he also emphasised the benefits accruing to Rome from the acquisition of Armenia as a new province and offered to resign his triumviral powers at the same time as Octavian.

When the two consuls designate read Antony's statement and realised that he had included the territorial provisions of the Donations they knew that there was no possibility of the Senate ratifying them, and they feared that to read out in public details of his gifts of lands and titles to Cleopatra's children would only cause an upsurge of feeling against him. When they took office on 1st January 32 Octavian was away from Rome, whether by chance or design is uncertain. Ahenobarbus believed that peace, and through Antony the restoration of the Republic, were still possible, and in his inaugural speech he took a moderate and cautious line. But after defending Antony the less politically experienced Sosius made a violent attack on the absent Octavian, moving a vote of censure on him which was promptly vetoed by a tribune.

Octavian had himself made some play of laying down his triumviral powers, and with the New Year it could be argued that strictly he was no more than any other consular. But he remained consul designate for 31 and his person was invested with a tribune's immunity from prosecution which had been voted him for life after Naulochus; most important of all he could call on the army and the veterans to outmatch any forces the consuls could raise. Like Cicero when faced with constitutional niceties he was ready to invoke a higher authority than the Senate, and unlike Cicero he could back what he declared to be the greater good of the State by force of arms.

He returned to Rome at the head of a force of armed veterans and summoned the Senate to meet. He took his seat with the two consuls, but his supporters crowded round him making no attempt to conceal their daggers, and his soldiers made sure they could be seen as they took up positions surrounding the building. After defending his own actions he went on to castigate Sosius and Antony; the two consuls and Antony's other supporters were so intimidated by the daggers inside and the armed men outside that not one of them ventured to reply. Octavian then named a day for the next meeting, announcing that at it he would lay before the Senate further evidence incriminating Antony.

Once again Octavian had shown himself ready and able to use force to overawe the Senate and have his way. Faced with what amounted to an armed coup, and in fear for their lives, Ahenobarbus and Sosius judged it hopeless to oppose Octavian and decided to flee to Antony before the next meeting. Constitutionally they needed the formal authority of the Senate to leave Italy but Octavian did not try to detain either them or the three to four hundred senators who elected to go with them. That a third of the thousand senators were prepared to leave their families behind in Italy and put their careers and their property at risk is a measure of their distrust of Octavian and their support for Antony. There must have been others who felt the same but for one reason or another were not prepared to flee the country. Thus it would seem that although he had not set foot in Italy since 37

Antony still had the backing, active or passive, of nearly half the Senate.

Octavian made all the capital he could out of what he called his magnaminity in allowing them to leave. In one sense he must have been glad to see his enemies declare themselves and go, for without them it would be easier to coerce the rump of the Senate. He could replace Ahenobarbus and Sosius with his own men, and with some show of legality, since they had left without the Senate's leave; to placate what was left of the old oligarchy he chose kinsmen of Messala and Lucius Cornelius Cinna, both members of ancient and noble families. But the number of senators who fled must have caused him misgivings and again have made him realise the need to tighten his grip on Rome and use his patronage to create a new aristocracy which in time would merge with what remained of the old.

The influx of several hundred senators suddenly freed from the constraints of life in Rome brought a further diversity of views and opinions to Antony's camp. Among his heterogeneous band of leaders there were already ex-Pompeians and die-hard Republicans, young nobles bearing famous names and political opportunists of obscurer lineage, many of them exiles who had not seen Italy for a decade. Some, loosely attached to Antony by chance or hope of preferment, would seek pardon from Octavian, among them Oppius and Fonteius Capito, the Cocceii cousins, Dellius who had already deserted Dolabella and Cassius, Atratinus who had commanded one of the squadrons lent to Octavian and had held office as consul in 34, and Brutus's kinsman Marcus Silanus. Others would remain with him bound by ties of friendship or because they wanted no part in Octavian's Rome; among these were Sextus's relatives, his nephew Gnaeus Cornelius Cinna and his half-brother Marcus Aemilius Scaurus, who had both joined Antony in 35: Messala's half-brother Lucius Gellius Poplicola, consul in 36 and brother-in-law to Atratinus: Antony's stepson Scribonius Curio, and one of the Caecilii Metelli: the admirals Marcus Octavius, Quintus Nasidius and Marcus Insteius: Gaius Furnius, once Caesar's and Cicero's friend and Plancus's legate in Gaul, who governed Asia in 36 and 35 and is known to have resisted all Octavian's overtures: and Caesar's surviving murderers Turullius and Cassius of Parma, who could expect no mercy from Octavian.

Among Antony's legates who were not with the army at Ephesus were Quintus Didius, governor of Syria after the death of Bibulus in 32: Lucius Pinarius Scarpus, Caesar's great-nephew and co-heir with Octavian, who commanded the four legions Antony had stationed in Cyrenaica to cover Egypt against any attack from the African provinces: Crassus's grandson, the young Marcus Licinius, who by now had taken over command in Crete.

Plancus was the most senior of them all. As governor of Syria he had been Antony's deputy in 35, and in Alexandria he had played courtier to Cleopatra; his closest associate was his nephew, Titius, who had been Antony's quaestor in Media. Ahenobarbus detested the time-serving Plancus and their enmity added to the discord between the leaders. The staunchly Republican Ahenobarbus still believed that war could be averted and the Republic saved. If war came he was ready to fight because he distrusted Octavian and all he stood for. He was bound to Antony by old ties of friendship as well as the betrothal between his son and Antony's daughter and he believed that Antony would restore the Republic. But he was not prepared to fight against Rome on Cleopatra's behalf; when he arrived at Ephesus he had been appalled by her all pervading influence and the atmosphere of an oriental court which she had brought to Antony's headquarters; fresh from Rome he realised only too well the damage her presence would do to Antony's cause in Italy and he urged him to send her back to Egypt.

But Cleopatra again refused to go, pointing out that Egypt had found nearly half the fleet and that her treasury was financing the war. She appealed to Canidius and he took her part, arguing that the Egyptian contribution entitled her to stay with the army and stressing the benefit of her intellect to their war council; he also warned Antony of the effect her departure at the behest of some of the Romans would have on the morale of the Egyptian crews and the Asiatic auxiliaries. Ahenobarbus's supporters promptly accused her of bribing Canidius, but whether she had or not there was some reason in what he said on her behalf.

In all the lands bordering the eastern Mediterranean countless people, encouraged by ancient prophecies, had dreamed of the coming of a new world era when they would be freed from Roman rule and Roman exploitation. Since the renascence of the Ptolemaic empire, and in particular since the Donations, their hopes had centred on Cleopatra in the belief that she and Antony were destined to lead the crusade that would throw off Rome's yoke, and through Antony fashion the equal partnership between Rome and the East which would usher in a new Golden Age. Throughout the East Antony's philhellenism and his identification with Dionysus had won him respect and semi-divine authority. The Alexandrians used to say that he kept his serious face for Rome and his humorous one for them, and he was perhaps the only Roman whom the Egyptians ever really liked or trusted. But Antony without Cleopatra was Dionysus without

Aphrodite or Osiris without Isis, and thus no more than the Roman overlord of the East; if she returned to Alexandria the morale of his Egyptian, Asiatic and Hellenistic leaders and their troops would suffer in what they would see as no more than another Roman civil war.

This was the same dilemma which had long threatened Antony; now at Ephesus its horns were closing in on him and he was finding it increasingly difficult to try to act as Roman general and Hellenistic dynast at one and the same time and place. Faced on the one hand with Ahenobarbus's hostility to Cleopatra, and on the other by the advocacy of his most able and trusted general and the very real threat to the morale of his eastern allies, the latter a factor seldom taken into account, Antony either could not or would not insist on Cleopatra returning to Egypt. This deepened the division between the leaders, and most of those who could expect no accommodation with Octavian sided with Cleopatra; her opponents formed a Roman faction backing Ahenobarbus, and some of them even suggested that he took over command, though here they mistook their man. Plancus and Titius quarrelled with Cleopatra, but this was a personal dispute which did nothing to settle their differences with Ahenobarbus.

In the spring of 32 Antony and the leaders of the army crossed to Samos where he had arranged for a festival of the arts to be held in honour of Dionysus. Plutarch describes the packed theatres, the competing choirs, the client kings vying with one another in the lavishness of their banquets, the whole island echoing to the music of string and flute, and goes on to deplore this unseemly junketing while the rest of the world lamented the coming war. But Antony was perhaps following Alexander's example and the festival may have had an underlying religious significance designed to bind the loyalty of the client kings with a solemn ceremony to honour Dionysus. It may have been now they took their oath of loyalty to Antony, who in return pledged himself to fight on to victory without thought of reconciliation with his enemies.

To reward the performers for their services Antony established the guild of dramatic artists and musicians in permanent quarters at Priene. He made over to Cleopatra the famous library at Pergamum with its 200,000 book scrolls as a replacement for the library accidentally destroyed by fire in the Alexandrian war, and he authorised the shipment of a number of works of art from Asia Minor to Egypt.

During May Antony left Samos accompanied by Cleopatra to rejoin his headquarters which had moved to Athens; from there he issued orders for the army and fleet to concentrate in Greece. The transfer by land and sea of upwards of 80,000 men, together with all their arms, equipment and artillery, and the horses for the large cavalry arm, was a complex operation and it took his staff two months to complete it. Although there had been no declaration of war and Octavian had made no move across the Adriatic, the concentration of Antony's army and fleet in Greece perhaps indicates that he had finally accepted that war was inevitable.

He now had to decide on his overall stragegy, if he had not already done so. He has been taken to task for not carrying the war to Octavian in 32, but such criticism is mistaken. It is true that Octavian was not ready in 32 and was alarmed at the scale and speed of Antony's preparations. It is also true that the political balance in Italy was likely to tilt further away from Antony, and that with the two consuls presently in his camp it was to his advantage to fight that year if it was practicable to do so.

But with Octavian making no move the only way Antony could bring him to battle was by invading Italy, or possibly Sicily. To attempt this with Cleopatra at his headquarters and a large Asiatic contingent in his army was to play into Octavian's hands and unite Italy against him. In military terms such a combined operation was a hazardous undertaking requiring the early seizure of a port; units of Octavian's large fleet were already based at Brundisium and Tarentum, the only two suitable invasion ports in south-east Italy, and in Agrippa Octavian had a competent admiral who had proved himself at sea against Sextus.

Thus Antony had no real choice but to fight in Greece, and therefore at a time of Octavian's choosing. Twice before he had been one of the victors in a struggle for the Roman world fought out on the mainland of Greece at Pharsalus and Philippi. As Octavian's colleague he had crossed the Adriatic from Italy to meet Brutus and Cassius advancing from the East with their supply routes and lines of communication running back down the Via Egnatia through Thrace to the Hellespont and Asia Minor. Now it was Antony who was coming from the East, but although he held Greece and Macedonia he intended to rely on his powerful fleet to supply his army by sea from Egypt and Asia Minor.

Across the Ionian Sea Octavian was concentrating his army and fleet in southern Italy. Illyria was quiet as were the western provinces, Gaul under Gaius Carrinas and Spain under Calvisius Sabinus. But the flight of the consuls and senators had shown that Italy was far from united at the prospect of another war against a Roman enemy, particularly one like Antony who posed no credible danger; nor was there enough money in the Roman treasury to fund such a war.

Alarmed by reports of Antony's preparations and fearing that he might be forced to fight in 32 Octavian set to work to raise the money he needed. Acting on Maecenas's advice he imposed sweeping new taxes backed by the threat of armed force; they included a 25% income tax on citizens which had only once been levied before, and an unprecedented wealth tax on freedmen of one-eighth of their property over 200,000 sesterces. The announcement of these proposed taxes caused widespread protests which led to rioting and civil disorder throughout the country.

Antony's agents in Italy made good use of the ample funds he had put at their disposal in exploiting the unrest and disrupting the Italian economy. They used aureii and denarii bearing Antony's head in a well organised campaign of large scale bribery, and Octavian had to dissipate some of the new tax revenues in counter bribes. In his commentary on Virgil Servius mentions that Antony still had the use of a mint at Anagnia in central Italy and adds that some of the coin struck there bore Cleopatra's name. Antony's contemporary denarii with Cleopatra's head and titles in Latin on their reverse are from unidentified mints, and Grant has suggested that they may have been struck at Anagnia, perhaps from dies cut in Athens, Ephesus or Antioch to avoid the bulk transport of coin.

The introduction of these coins of Antony's into Italy must have embarrassed Octavian, though if Cleopatra's head with her titles in Latin did in fact appear on Roman coins circulating in Italy, for all the world as if she were the personification of Rome, they may have proved a two-edged weapon, causing alarm to many and giving substance to Octavian's allegations about the range of her ambition.

For Octavian had now stepped up his propaganda against her into a sustained and carefully orchestrated campaign of vilification rivalling Cicero's in the Philippics, and perhaps unsurpassed in history until recent times. No vice, natural or unnatural, was omitted from the barrage of accusations against her and her entourage of eunuchs, handmaidens and sorcerers. In an attempt to make all Italy believe that there were no bounds to her ambition, no limits to the retribution she had sworn to exact from Rome, Antony was portrayed as no longer a free agent but an instrument of her insatiable lust for power.

Though as always it was the victors who wrote the history, and the Latin sources which have survived, Cleopatra has emerged curiously unscathed, her reputation untarnished, perhaps even enhanced, by this onslaught of words.

Cicero's charges against Antony of drunkenness, debauchery, the keeping of low company and other such un-Roman traits were refurbished and embellished. Antony evidently thought them potentially damaging enough to rebut in a pamphlet 'De Sua Ebrietate', which, though lost, is vouched for in a reference by the younger Pliny. For his part Octavian must have considered the claim that Caesarion was Caesar's legitimate son serious enough to employ Caesar's old friend, Gaius Oppius, to refute it in another pamphlet.

Messala, a patron of the arts and once Antony's friend, now applied his own literary skill to ridicule Antony in a series of pamphlets, accusing him in one of them of outdoing even Cleopatra in depravity by using a golden chamber pot. With like distaste Calvisius, the proconsul of Spain, described at second hand the outrageous attentions Antony had paid Cleopatra at Ephesus such as anointing her feet in public and breaking off official business to write her love notes. Plutarch quotes these stories but remarks that few believed them; bizarre as they may seem they fell into the general pattern of Octavian's propaganda.

Expediency and what the people could be induced to believe were Octavian's only criteria. His propaganda was not without effect, at least among the more gullible; like all good propaganda it could be true, and what was untrue could not readily be disproved for it was five years since Antony had been in Italy. His reorganisation of the East could plausibly be exaggerated into the wholesale disposal of Roman territory and contrasted with Octavian's treatment of Mauretania, which on Bocchus's death he had made into a third African province. As well as appealing to the chauvinistic instincts of the Roman people this move was popular with the commercial interests who benefited more from the exploitation of new provinces than from trade with allied states. Eight years later Octavian was to allow Mauretania to revert to its old status as a client kingdom.

In the Donations and in Cleopatra's presence with the army Antony had given Octavian a credible target and an opportunity to play on the subconscious fears of the Roman people; Antony could be dismissed as no more than Cleopatra's tool, besotted with love, befuddled with drink and drugs, no longer a Roman general and the very shadow of the man the legions remembered.

Antony replied in kind and in good measure to this stream of calumny from Rome. As Cicero's target in the Philippics he was well versed in the exchange of personal abuse, which, undeterred by the antiquated law of libel, had been the stuff of Roman politics in the late Republic. Charge could be met with counter charge: if Octavian called Dionysus a cannibal despite the fact that most accounts had the young god as the victim rescued from the Titans' cauldron, and if his supporters gleefully pointed out that Hercules, patron god of the Antonii, had himself been bewitched and enslaved by a woman in the person of Omphale, Queen of Lydia, Antony could retort that Octavian's Apollo was by name the destroyer. If Antony had married his eldest daughter, Antonia, to Pythodorus, a rich Greek from Tralles, Octavian had broken the betrothal of his daughter, Julia, to Antony's son Marcus, and instead had offered her for his own political ends to a barbarian chieftan, Cotison of Dacia. If Octavian scorned Antony's literary style as florid and Asiatic, Antony could ridicule Octavian's contorted handwriting and his halting Greek.

Antony also taunted Octavian with his obscure and ignoble origins, alleging that his grandfather was a ropemaker and freedman from Thurii, and dubbing him 'The Thurian'; this was a nickname apparently given to Octavian's father, Gaius Octavius, for his part in putting down a local slave uprising, possibly in the same sardonic sense as Antony's grandfather had been called Creticus. In fact Gaius Octavius had been the first of his family to enter the Senate, and probably only premature death had denied him office as consul and the consequent enobling of his family. Cassius of Parma took up his pen on Antony's behalf, and like Messala prostituted his literary talent, for he was a poet in his own right, by deriding Octavian as the grandson of a baker and a moneychanger.

But like Octavian Antony was on firmer ground when there was an underlying stratum of truth on which to build his charges. All the world knew that he had led the Caesarians to victory at Philippi, and to stories that he had only taken part in the pursuit he could retort that Octavian had abandoned their camp and skulked in a marsh till the battle was won, adding for good measure that he had also lain prostrated by fear at the bottom of his ship while Agrippa won the day at Naulochus.

Poor health coupled with Octavian's inexperience as a general gave some credibility to such accusations, echoes of which were to find their way into the pages of Seneca, Tacitus, Suetonius and Plutarch. It was true enough that Octavian was an unlucky as well as an inept commander; indeed this may have been why he made such play of asserting that his luck and his guardian spirit always enabled him to best Antony in their personal disputes. But frail health and lack of experience in the field did not make him a coward; only the power of his indomitable will over his sick body got him to the field of Philippi where he was so ill that he could hardly stand, while at Naulochus he was probably prostrate with seasickness and anyway had the wisdom and courage to delegate command to Agrippa.

But there were some aspects of Octavian's character which provided even more fertile grounds for innuendo, and in attacking his morals there was no lack of material. There is evidence, apparently not deriving solely from Antony's propaganda, that behind the facade of Roman virtues which Octavian was later to extol, and even to attempt to enforce by law, his private life, though in some ways austere and frugal, in others was already vicious and depraved. An anonymous lampoon about his role in the so-called Feast of the Divine Twelve was familiar to Suetonius, as was Antony's allegation that Octavian had played the part of Apollo at this banquet which burlesqued the twelve principal gods. If true this amounted to blasphemy against his patron god, and were it not for the evidence of the lampoon which Suetonius quotes Octavian's participation would have seemed unlikely, if only on grounds of prudence. In the same way the Club of Inimitable Livers which Antony and Cleopatra formed in Alexandria would probably have been dismissed as an extravagant fantasy of Octavian's propaganda were it not for epigraphic evidence, complete with scratched graffiti parodying Antony and Cleopatra as Inimitable Lovers.

But corroborating evidence is the exception, and both sides mixed truth with untruth to give untruth an air of truth and make it impossible even for the ancient historians to disentangle one from the other.

Antony's accusations that some of Octavian's friends behaved like slave dealers in procuring the wives and daughters of respectable Roman citizens for his naked inspection have an air of truth in the light of Octavian's well documented proclivity for adultery and in later life for deflowering virgins. But charges attributed to Antony that Octavian only won adoption from Caesar by submitting to his homosexual advances may have derived from Fulvia's and Lucius Antonius's propaganda in the Perusine War; there is no other evidence to support them.

It is often only the ultimate victor who can edit the contemporary records from which history is later written. After Actium poets like Horace and Virgil continued to support Octavian, not in slavish obedience to the Princeps but because as Italians rather than Romans they rejoiced in the new peace and unity his rule brought to Italy. In the aftermath of civil war Virgil's family had been evicted from their farm near Mantua. Horace had the courage to admit that as a young man fighting for Brutus at Philippi he had thrown down his sword and fled from the battle; later he was to show courage of a different order when he declined Octavian's offer to make him his private secretary.

Pollio's history of his own times which he himself had helped to make is lost, as are the relevant books of Livy, the greatest Roman historian; their work was certainly more objective than the secondary sources which have survived, though some of these draw on both of them. Always eager to point a moral Plutarch pairs Greek with Roman in his parallel Lives, Demetrius Poliorcetes with Antony as cautionary examples of what can befall great men. Perhaps prejudiced by the suffering of his own great-grandfather, Nicarchus of Chaeronea, as one of Antony's press-ganged porters he is less sympathetic to him than he is to the subjects of his other biographies and he takes some contemporary writers to task for treating him too kindly, making it clear that such more favourable accounts did once exist.

The record was not in part redressed until Antony's descendants wore the purple, first his great-grandson, Gaius Caligula, then his grandson, Claudius, followed by another great-grandson, Nero. By then it was too late to sift fact from fiction even when there was a will to do so, and imperial displeasure at anything critical of the divine Augustus could not be safely discounted until the Julio-Claudian dynasty ended with Nero's death in AD 68. Plutarch was then a student in Athens, Tacitus a boy of eleven or twelve growing up in provincial Gaul, and Suetonius was not born until the following year; echoes of Antony's propaganda as well as Octavian's were to find their way into their works.

It was early summer when Antony and Cleopatra left Samos for Athens. The Athenians had always liked Antony, judging his philhellenism to be genuine and looking on him as a patron of the arts and of their own city. Now they welcomed him warmly as well as receiving him with the compliments due to the Roman overlord of the East.

For some time past there had been close and friendly ties between Alexandria and Athens instead of the rivalry which might have developed between the two foremost centres of art and learning in the Mediterranean. For this reason, and because Cleopatra was a scholar and linguist in her own right, they also welcomed her as a friend as well as formally receiving her as Queen of Egypt. Athens was not a Hellenistic city like Ephesus, but the spiritual and cultural capital of all Greece, and the setting up of Cleopatra's statue among the gods on the Acropolis was an honour not lightly accorded by the Athenians.

A few years before they had taken Octavia to their hearts and they still revered her memory, as must quickly have become apparent to Cleopatra from the wealth of inscriptions in her honour. For the first time she was confronted with the shadow of Octavia's presence, and she must have realised that not only in Italy but in the eyes of many Greeks she was still Antony's wife, and her own position anomalous. It was important that like the rest of the East all Greece should acknowledge her as Antony's wife as well as his royal partner in their struggle against Octavian. It was even more important that when victory was won she should enter Rome as Antony's consort, with Caesarion as their heir apparent in the East.

During that summer and autumn Antony's friends in Italy were actively campaigning on his behalf. One of them, a certain Geminius who is otherwise unknown to history, travelled to Greece as their spokesman to urge Antony not to allow himself to be deprived of his Roman offices and declared a public enemy. But Cleopatra believed that he was secretly acting for Octavia, and she did all she could to circumvent and humiliate him. Things came to a head at a dinner party when he was asked to explain his mission. He told Antony in front of Cleopatra that he would prefer to discuss it when they were all sober, but drunk or sober he could at least say that all would be well if he sent her back to Egypt. This enraged Antony, but it confirmed Cleopatra's suspicions and she retorted that it was lucky that he had told the truth without having to be tortured to extract it. Many of Antony's leading Roman supporters were scandalised that a freeborn Roman should be threatened with torture, and the incident increased their hostility to Cleopatra and their resentment of her presence with the army. A few days later Geminius cut short his visit and returned to Italy.

In Athens Cleopatra at last persuaded Antony to divorce Octavia, and on his orders the weeping Octavia was formally escorted from their house in Rome. With her she took the children, their own two daughters, her son and daughters by Marcellus, and Iullus, Antony's younger son by Fulvia; his elder son Marcus had probably joined him by now in Greece.

So Cleopatra suceeded at last where Octavian had failed; for four years he had tried to persuade Octavia to leave Antony's house but she had steadfastly refused, insisting that she was Antony's wife and would keep his home, care for his children, and serve his interest as best she could, for as long as he wanted her to do so.

Furious at this insult to his sister Octavian wrung every propaganda advantage from it that he could: here was Antony's lawful wife, whom despite her virtuous forbearance he had so deeply wronged suffering the final indignity of being turned out of his house, here was tangible proof of Cleopatra's malign hold on him. It was effective, for all Rome could see it was true; that in her plight Octavia still continued to care for Antony's children touched the sentimental Romans and in their eyes exacerbated the injury he had done to such a loyal and virtuous wife.

It may have been Antony's divorce of Octavia which prompted Plancus and Titius to change sides. Among his contemporaries the faint-hearted Plancus had an unenviable reputation for duplicity and deceit; Velleius describes him as diseased with treachery and venal to all men and in all things. But he had already shown that he had an instinct for survival and a talent for picking the likely winner. For Octavia or Cleopatra he cared nothing; in Alexandria he had been one of the most obsequious of Cleopatra's flatterers, earning the strictures of the staider Romans when he played the part of the naked sea god, Glaucus, to entertain her at a dinner party. His choice of this moment to desert suggests that he considered Antony's cause unlikely to prosper now that his divorce of Octavia made it clear that Cleopatra would remain with the army.

To insure his welcome by Octavian Plancus made certain that he had information of value to impart. As a member of Antony's war council he could reveal what he knew of his plans. But of far greater import was the news that Antony had made a will which he had deposited with the Vestal Virgins; Dio is alone in saying that it was in the safe custody of a friend in Rome. Plancus had apparently witnessed and sealed the will and he told Octavian that the contents were likely to be controversial. A hint was enough for Octavian and no trust too sacred to violate if expediency pointed the way; he brushed aside the protests of the Chief Vestal and forced her to deliver up the will.

It seems likely that Antony had in fact lodged a will with the Vestal Virgins, the traditional depositary: if he had not done so it would have been simple to call on them to deny it. But if the provisions were those which Octavian read out to the Senate, and other than his word there is no evidence that they were for he would allow no one else to read them, it seems unlikely that Antony would have put such an opportunity in his way.

For the first time a silent, startled Senate heard what purported to be Antony's written assertion that Caesarion was Caesar's legitimate son and heir; this was followed by details of legacies to his children by Cleopatra and a direction that after a funeral procession through the Forum his body was to be sent to Alexandria for burial. Some of these clauses might well have formed part of a will made in Alexandria and witnessed by Plancus at the time of the Donations, but it seems unlikely that such a will would have been deposited in Rome since testamentary legacies to non-citizens or foreigners were invalid in Rome law. If the will was genuine it must have been made before Antony decided on war, for if he lost and died there would be no public funeral procession in Rome and if he triumphed and lived no need for one. It was the clause about burial in Alexandria that offended public opinion in Rome.

The provisions Octavian read out were so precisely what he needed to substantiate his allegations against Antony that it has been suggested that he invented the whole affair, but this would have been relatively easy to disprove. It is possible Plancus knew that Antony had made a will in Alexandria and perhaps another separate will naming his sons, Marcus and Iullus, as his Roman heirs, and consequently deposited in Rome. Octavian would hardly have violated the sacred custody of the Vestal Virgins unless he was reasonably sure that some will of Antony's was there; then what Plancus had divulged of the more damaging clauses of the Alexandrian will, perhaps Caesarion's paternity and the burial arrangements, could readily be inserted into the Roman will.

But it is impossible to arrive at the truth. What is certain is the propaganda value to Octavian: here was evidence that Antony had abandoned Rome for Egypt, and from this it could be argued that he intended to transfer the capital to Alexandria, an abiding Roman fear ever since the rumours that Caesar had planned to do so.

Lone voices were raised in the Senate protesting that it was shameful to use a man's will against him while he was still living. A vicious tirade from Plancus attacking Antony was cut short by a praetor, Lucius Coponius, when he called Hercules to witness that Antony seemed to have committed every sort of crime before Plancus finally decided to desert him.

The disorders which had arisen earlier in the year as a result of Octavian's new taxes had died down; as Dio observes with insight when such a once and for all tax has been paid the outcry against it evaporates and it is soon forgotten. Octavian now felt strong enough to declare war, not on Antony or any Roman enemy, but on Cleopatra; he did so with all the ancient ritual and ceremony, leading a procession to the temple of Bellona and there driving a bloodied spear into the ground. As consul designate for 31 he declared Antony unfit to hold office as his colleague and publicly stripped him of all his other Roman titles.

He called for an oath of loyalty to his person, not only from the Senate and the army, but from the leading citizens in every town and city throughout Italy. Later he was to claim that it was freely given as a spontaneous and voluntary expression of support for him; but this was no more true than it ever has been for any revolutionary leader who called for such an oath, and there is no doubt that his agents used widespread coercion and intimidation.

The legions accepted it willingly enough, as did his veterans in loyalty to their patron who was Caesar's heir. Of the senatorial families and the landowners and merchant bankers, those who could not or would not come to terms with Octavian had already joined Antony. For their own preservation those who had stayed took the oath to the man who had the power to give or take away career, property and life itself, and was clearly prepared to exercise it; their clients followed their example. The property owning middle classes and the leading families in provincial Italy also took the line of least resistance; many favoured Antony, but peace and prosperity were more important to them than who ruled in Rome, and Octavian's continuance in power preferable to the disruption which civil war would inevitably bring to Italy.

Octavian's agents would tolerate no prevarication from those who wished to stay neutral, and they were cajoled or threatened into an open declaration of support. Only the city of Bononia and its surrounding district were excused on the grounds that this was Antony's own fief bound to him and his family by feudal ties, and here Octavian made much of his forbearance.

He left Maecenas in charge of Rome to guard against any coup in his absence and took the drastic but effective step of ordering every senator to join him with the army. The only Roman of rank who declined to take the oath or accompany Octavian to the war, and remained neutral and a free man in Italy was Pollio, Antony's friend and old comrade in arms. He was a man born out of his time, a man of moral courage and upright character whose intellect and independent spirit could see through all the posturing and deceit, and who deplored the damage another civil war would do to Rome and all Italy. When Octavian solicited his support, according to Velleius he replied:

> 'My service to Antony is too great, his kindness to me too well known; I shall stand aside from your dispute and be the victor's prize.'

CHAPTER XXI

The War in Greece

During the autumn of 32 Antony moved the field army into winter quarters in the Peloponnese and on either side of the Gulf of Corinth, as part of the forward strategy he had evidently decided to adopt; one result was to make the army even more dependent on supply by sea from Egypt and Asia Minor. Plutarch implies that he deployed nineteen legions in Greece; nothing is known of the location or movements of the legions of the Macedonian garrison, some or all of which presumably now formed part of the field army. Events were to show that he had no troops in Epirus and probably none in Acarnania.

Accompanied by Cleopatra and her court and most of the senators Antony set up his headquarters at Patras on the southern shore of the Gulf of Patras which leads into the Gulf of Corinth. From here he continued to broadcast promises that he would lay down his offices and restore executive power to the Senate and people within six months of gaining final victory over Octavian. Coins which he struck at Patras repeated his claim to the consulate of 31 in Latin, and on their reverse bore Cleopatra's head and her titles in Greek.

He deployed the fleet to cover the sea lanes round the southern and western coasts of Greece, establishing a chain of naval stations from western Crete to the Peloponnese and thence up the Ionian coast as far north as Corfu. Bogud held the fortified harbour town of Methone on the south-western peninsula of the Peloponnese; to the east Atratinus probably commanded in Laconia with a naval station at Psamathos near Cape Taenarum, the central promontory of the Peloponnese and the southernmost point of the Greek mainland.

Though the ancient sources do not mention them probably Cephallenia and certainly Sosius's own island fief of Zacynthus, both lying off the Ionian coast and commanding the inshore channels and the approach to the Gulf of Patras, formed part of the chain; Nasidius covered the entrance to the Gulf itself. Further to the north there was another fleet station on the mountainous island of Leucas which dominates the southern approach from the Ionian Sea to the Ambracian Gulf; here on the Actium peninsula, which forms the southern side of the narrow entrance to the gulf, Antony established his main fleet base, with perhaps half or more of his ships of the line tied up or beached inside Akri Point. Further north on the coast of

Epirus there were no harbours offering adequate protection from onshore winter gales, and his northernmost squadron was based on Corfu.

From Patras Antony made a reconnaissance up the coast beyond Corfu; here again there were no suitable harbours before Caesar's old port of Oricum, sixty miles to the north. As a naval base from which to cover the Adriatic narrows Corfu was too far to the south, but in any event the seakeeping capability of the warships of the day made it impossible to mount an offshore standing patrol in winter. As Pompey's admirals had discovered the only effective way of sealing off Brundisium was to seize the island commanding the entrance. In 48 Caesar and Antony had demonstrated that it was feasible to ferry an army from Brundisium across the Adriatic straits in winter. Interception at sea was a matter of good intelligence and luck, but the Republican admirals had shown that it was possible when they destroyed the Caesarian reinforcements during the Philippi campaign. Antony was aware of all this from his own past experience. But he seems to have made no attempt to deploy his fleet to interfere with Octavian's crossing; it was as if he was offering him unimpeded passage, and it is conceivable that this was his intention.

He may have underestimated what the battle experience gained in Illyria had done for the morale and military efficiency of Octavian's army, for he seems to have been confident that his veteran legions and his own talent as a general would enable him to prevail on land. Certainly a single decisive victory in the spring of 31 could have made him undisputed master of the Roman world.

He must have appreciated that the size and complexity of the logistical task made it impracticable to supply his army and fleet on a war footing in western Greece for an indefinite period. There was also the problem of holding together the diverse elements of his army in a long drawn out campaign and maintaining their morale and discipline. His legionary infantry would follow him, always provided they sensed victory and a triumphant return to Italy to enjoy its fruits, but unless that victory was quickly gained the Eastern allies might prove less reliable. He seems to have been convinced that Octavian had neither the funds, nor the supplies and material resources, to sustain a long campaign in Greece; it may well be that he judged it to his advantage to invite him to cross with his army and then cut him off by sea and defeat him on land.

Antony knew that after a series of humiliating defeats at Sextus's hands Agrippa had built Octavian's fleet into the formidable fighting force which had won the day at Mylae and Naulochus, and he knew that its well-found ships were now manned by experienced crews and commanded by competent seamen. He had also taken note of the tactical superiority Agrippa's heavier ships had given him against Sextus's lighter, better handled and more manoeuvrable fleet. But he probably anticipated that Agrippa would use his 400 available warships to cover the crossing from Italy and then to operate along the coast in close support of the army.

Antony had built his ships to match Octavian's in size, reinforcing them against ramming with iron-bound timber baulks. The story that Octavian's ships were significantly lighter, faster and more manoeuvrable is largely a myth which grew up after the battle of Actium. In both fleets the lighter warships were 'twos' or biremes, undecked galleys with two levels or banks of single-manned oars, and 'threes', or triremes, with three levels of single-manned oars. The ships of the line on either side were 'fives', or quinqueremes, decked warships with the lower two or three levels of oars double-manned, and some 'sixes' with their oars double-manned at three levels. In all cases the ratings refer to the number of fore and aft files of rowers on each side of the ship and not to the number of levels or banks, which even in the bigger polyremes never exceeded three, though these of course had more than two rowers to an oar. The number of rowers in each fore and aft file, and hence the length of the ships, did not vary significantly with the ratings, though the beam and the height of the deck above the water line varied with the number of files and rowers.

After his reconnaissance up the coast of Epirus Antony returned to Patras, apparently content to wait on events. The whole of the East was firmly under his control, with only local insurrections in Mysia and Berytus to disturb the peace in Asia Minor and the Levant. Apart from some disaffection in Sparta, where Lachares had been deposed and executed for piracy, Greece too was quiet though there were disturbances in Lappa and Cydonia in western Crete.

Late in 32 or early in 31 Octavian sent his friend, the poet Gaius Cornelius Gallus, as a legate of equestrian rank to hold the African provinces against any forward move by Pinarius Scarpus, Antony's general in Cyrenaica. Like the East, the western provinces, Spain, Gaul, Illyria and the islands, remained quiet; it was as if the whole Roman world had paused to await the outcome of the coming clash.

Octavian had considerable forces available in Italy for the war. From these he selected sixteen legions, some 80,000 heavy infantry if they were nearly at full strength, and 12,000 cavalry, and concentrated them near Brundisium; it is a measure of his confidence that he judged this comparatively small army sufficient for the task, though to some extent its size must have been restricted by considerations of supply and transport by sea. The fleet with Agrippa in overall command was based at Tarentum and Brundisium.

If it is assumed that the nineteen legions to which Plutarch refers made up the heavy infantry in Antony's army, and, if he had picked those legions with the highest proportion of experienced troops, he may have had about 60,000 legionary infantry of Italian origin. Like Octavian he had 12,000 cavalry, but unlike Octavian's essentially Roman army with a normal complement of auxiliaries, Antony's with its allied contingents was both larger and more diverse in its composition.

Many historians have criticised Antony for adopting this forward strategy, which forced him both to rely on supply by sea and to deploy part of his fleet to protect these supply lines, and for then standing on the defensive and making no attempt to dispute the passage of Octavian's army across the Adriatic. But there is no evidence that he intended to maintain this forward defensive stance beyond the winter of 32/31; indeed the choice of Actium as his main fleet station suggests the opposite, for it possesses a superb natural harbour for offensive fleet operations in the North Ionian Sea but lies too far to the north simply to defend the Peloponnese.

The entrance to the Ambracian Gulf between Cape Paliosarama and the western side of the Actium peninsula narrows to less than half a mile and so was easy to defend; inside, the wide inland waters of the Gulf, some 250 square miles in extent, provided shelter in all weathers and barred any direct approach by land from the north and north-east. But the Actium peninsula and the southern shores of the Gulf were flat, marshy and inhospitable, infested with mosquitoes and snakes, lacking an adequate supply of fresh water, and only accessible by land over mountainous tracks from the east and south. Thus for a fleet of any size Actium was only suitable as a base for a limited period, and even then command of the seaward approaches was vital if it was not to become a trap.

Apart from his choice of Actium there is no evidence as to Antony's plans for 31 had the initiative not been wrested from him by Agrippa. But to have remained passively on the defensive was out of character and it is unlikely that he planned to do so once Octavian had crossed with his army.

Much has been written about the campaign of 31 and the battle of Actium by both ancient and modern historians, but the surviving contemporary evidence is meagre in the extreme: some coins struck by Octavian and by Antony's legates, Pinarius Scarpus and Turullius, the stone remains of Octavian's jetty on Gomaros Bay and the monument he built at Mikalitzi, one of Horace's Odes and three of his Epodes, among them the IXth, tantalising in its ambiguity and on which widely differing reconstructions of the battle have been based.

The Augustan poets and historians were more concerned with the result than with the details of the campaign or even how the final battle was won. But it had to be a famous and dramatic victory, worthy of Octavian's Rome, and it quickly became part of the folk lore surrounding the birth of the Principate and Empire. A few years later Virgil was to write in the Aeneid:

> On one side Augustus Caesar, high up on the poop,
> is leading
> The Italians into battle, the Senate and People
> with him,
> His home gods and the great gods: two flames
> shoot up from his helmet
> In jubilant light, and his father's star dawns
> over its crest.
> On the other side, with barbaric wealth
> and motley equipment
> Is Antony, fresh from his triumphs in the East,
> by the shores of the Indian
> Ocean; Egypt, the powers of the Orient and
> uttermost Bactria
> Sail with him; also – a shameful thing –
> his Egyptian wife.

> translated C.Day Lewis

Velleius Paterculus, born c. 19 BC, followed the Augustan pattern in uncritical adulation of Octavian and unqualified abuse of Antony and Cleopatra; he is often derided as a third-rate historian, but at least he had the insight to comment that the campaign had been won and lost before the battle of Actium was fought.

Nicolaus, the Greek from Damascus who was tutor first to Antony and Cleopatra's children and then to Herod's, later had access to Octavian's state and private papers in Rome, but in his Life of Augustus he barely mentions Actium, and Suetonius in his Twelve Caesars only gives it a single sentence. References in the epitomes of Orosius and Florus are all that survive from the relevant lost books of Livy.

Plutarch and Dio are the only secondary sources who cover the campaign in any detail. It was more than a hundred years later when Plutarch wrote his Life of Antony, and, though he appears to have drawn on the account of an eye witness of the battle for some details,

305

he either could not or did not attempt to disentangle the facts from the legend which by then already surrounded Actium; Orosius and Florus quote figures for naval strengths which tend to corroborate Plutarch. Dio wrote his history 250 years after the event and his account is confused.

Both Plutarch and Dio describe at some length the supernatural omens and portents which preceded the campaign, and though they may have invented some of them as a required dramatic prelude to great events there can be little doubt that others, like similar stories about the battles of Pharsalus and Philippi, had been handed down from generation to generation and were widely believed. Plutarch describes how Antony's stautes sweated and at Athens Dionysus's was toppled in a storm, how at Patras Hercules's Temple was destroyed by lightning and at Actium swallows nested in the stern of Cleopatra's flagship, the Antonias. Dio tells of an owl and an ape invading temples in Rome, and of how the lava flowed from Etna and a two-headed serpent terrorised Etruria.

Both have it that Octavian proposed that he or Antony should withdraw their army a day's march from the coast to allow the other an unopposed landing, and that then within five days they should settle the issue by battle. This, and the story that Antony responded with a challenge to single combat, may derive from contemporary rumours which became legends.

What is certain is that early in 31, between late February and the middle of March, before the normal sailing season opened and while Antony's army was still in winter quarters, Agrippa mounted an audacious assault on Methone from the sea. Leaving Tarentum with perhaps three squadrons and their fighting complement of three legions he sailed undetected across 300 miles of open water despite the enemy held coast of Ionia to port, and then captured Methone. The operation was boldly conceived and brilliantly executed: the stunned defenders were overwhelmed and Bogud himself was killed. It is doubtful whether Antony and his staff had even taken the possibility of such a move into account; it was something Sextus's Greek admirals might have attempted, though only as a hit and run raid. But it soon became clear that Agrippa intended to hold Methone; five years earlier his capture of the Aeolian Islands had unlocked the door to Sicily and the lesson had not been lost on him. These two amphibious operations demonstrate his original thinking and his strategic grasp of the use of sea power, and they rank him with the great captains in naval history; they also mark a new dimension in Roman naval warfare.

It has been suggested that he selected Methone because it was only

306

forty five miles from Sparta where Lachares's son, Eurycles, was ready to declare for Octavian; but Psamathos was even closer and Atratinus was also waiting to defect when opportunity served. It is more likely that Agrippa chose Methone because its natural strength made it easy to defend from the landward side, and because it was here that Antony's transports on passage from Crete or Egypt made their landfall before they turned north up the western coast of the Peloponnese.

When reports reached Antony that Agrippa was fortifying Methone the threat to his supply routes by sea and to his whole position in the southern Peloponnese must have been evident; but he made no move to eject him. This may have been because under cover of Agrippa's attack Octavian ferried his army across from Brundisium escorted by 230 warships. The main body landed unopposed on the narrow coastal strip below the Acroceraunian Mountains, perhaps at the small port of Panormus some ten miles south of Palaese where Caesar had landed in 48.

From here Octavian ordered the army to move south by forced marches; he continued on himself down the coast with the fleet and perhaps three legions. The Antonian squadron had withdrawn from Corfu, and as soon as Octavian discovered the island was undefended he sailed through the Corfu channel and seized the small port of Toryne, modern Parga, and Fanari at the mouth of the river Archeron, known then as Glycys Limen, or Freshwater Harbour; here he disembarked the rest of his troops and set up a base for his fleet. He then marched on south with the army, sending one naval squadron to reconnoitre and if possible seize the entrance to the Ambracian Gulf.

News of Agrippa's capture of Methone must have been received at Antony's headquarters first with disbelief and then with dismay. But Octavian's crossing had long been anticipated and awaited with confidence; the only elements of surprise seem to have been the speed of his advance down the coast and the failure of Antony's intelligence and his naval patrols to give him any warning until the enemy fleet debouched from the Corfu channel and seized Toryne. It must have taken two days for reports to reach Patras, and following quickly as they did on the fall of Methone they caused consternation at Antony's headquarters, particularly as the army was still scattered in winter quarters; according to Plutarch, Cleopatra tried to allay the general alarm by facetiously asking what the fuss was about when all that had happened was that Octavian was sitting in a ladle; Toryne means this in Greek and perhaps describes the shape of the harbour.

Antony at once sent out orders for the army to concentrate at Actium, but it would be at least a week before the first troops got there and two or three more before the concentration was complete. Until then the fleet would be unable to take the offensive; depending on their size and rating the warships of the day carried a crew, including rowers, of between two and three hundred, and twenty to forty marines, but before they could fight they had to ship their full complement of between eighty and one hundred and twenty soldiers.

Agrippa had achieved surprise with the timing and direction of his attack on Methone and now Octavian had done the same with the speed of his advance down the coast of Epirus. Antony had been caught unawares with his army still in winter quarters and he now had to concentrate it at Actium to protect his fleet and provide its fighting element. To winter army and fleet so far apart in time as well as in distance was a cardinal error perhaps arising from his confidence that it was he who would dictate events; as it was Agrippa and Octavian had stolen the initiative and were forcing him to react.

Antony set off at once for Actium with his staff and Cleopatra and her attendants. When he got there he found that Octavian's squadron had tried to seize the entrance, but had been repulsed by the defences his captains had built on the northern shore; then, two or three days before his arrival, Octavian and his army had reached Mikhalitzi some five miles to the north.

Mikhalitzi lies on a sandy escarpment at the southern end of a low range of foothills facing south and commanding the mile wide isthmus between the open sea on the Bay of Gomaros and Mazoma Lagoon at the north-western corner of the Ambracian Gulf. Though no more than 175 metres at its highest point, the escarpment not only overlooks the isthmus itself but provides a panoramic view over the Gulf to the distant mountains of Acarnania, across the sea to the islands of Paxos and Antipaxos and down the coast from Gomaros Bay to Cape Mytikas.

Further to the south the sheer cliffs of Leucas can be seen on a clear day, but the Actium peninsula and the Preveza Strait, which leads into the Bay of Preveza and thence into the wide inland waters of the gulf, are hidden by rising ground beyond the isthmus in the centre of the Preveza peninsula.

This peninsula divides into two arms, one protruding south-east and partly cutting off the Bay of Preveza from the inner Gulf, the other running south from Cape Mytikas to form the northern side of the entrance channel on which modern Preveza stands, perhaps on the site of ancient Berenicia founded by Phyrrus. Less than half a mile away across the Preveza Strait the Actium peninsula runs north to Akri Point which protrudes into the Bay of Preveza. Antony's main fleet base was just inside this point and not far from the temple of Actian Apollo.

To defend the seaward approaches his captains had built towers and artillery positions on either side of the entrance, and it was these which had repulsed Octavian's squadron and saved Antony's fleet from being bottled up inside the Gulf; the comparatively short range of the artillery of the day makes it likely that these defensive works were near Fort Aktion, and on the opposite shore to the west of Cape Paliosarama. The same sites were later used by the Venetians whose forts guarding the entrance against the Turks can be seen today.

Octavian's position at Mikhalitzi was well chosen. Its natural strength was enough to deter Antony from an uphill frontal assault and so give Octavian the option of deciding whether or not to accept battle. Supplies and reinforcements could be landed from the sea only a mile away on the Bay of Gomaros, though this was an open sandy beach and could only be used in good weather. But there was no water at Mikhalitzi: the nearest sources were springs a mile away to the south across the isthmus on what was to be the site of Nicopolis, and the river Louros or Oropus which ran into the Ambracian Gulf a few miles to the north-east. To protect his beachhead and supply route Octavian began to construct parallel defensive walls from Mikhalitzi down to the Bay of Gomaros; here he built a jetty, the remains of which can still be seen two miles north of Cape Mytikas.

While Antony was waiting for his army to arrive the advantage lay with Octavian: he offered battle but Antony refused and contented himself with defending the northern shore. Octavian ordered another attack on the entrance from the sea. To support his defences Antony moved some of his warships into Preveza Bay with rowers from the other ships wearing armour to impersonate the missing soldiers. Though there is no evidence as to the course or scale of the battle Octavian's attack was again repulsed. It could have been the victory for which Antony was hailed as Imperator for the fourth time, though equally this may have been as the result of one of the later land battles.

This reverse prevented Octavian from interfering with the concentration of Antony's army at Actium, which was probably completed by the end of April. Antony then moved the main body across the strait and took up a position south of the isthmus which denied Octavian access to the spring. Here he offered battle and this time it was Octavian who refused: he could get water from the Lourus, and by now he must have known that Agrippa was established at Methone and beginning to capture some of Antony's supply ships.

Antony could hardly have failed to recognise the threat to his sea lanes, but instead of trying to expel Agrippa from Methone he did all he could to bring Octavian to battle. He sent a large cavalry force commanded by Rhoemetalces and Deiotarus on the hundred mile ride round the inland shores of the Ambracian Gulf with the task of denying Octavian access to the Louros and cutting him off from the north-east; this he hoped would oblige him to accept battle on the isthmus. At first all went well: the cavalry forced a crossing of the Louros and established themselves between Octavian and the river. But Statilius Taurus, and Titius, rewarded with the consulate for his desertion, led Octavian's cavalry in a determined counter-attack which threw the Antonians back behind the river. Rhoemetalces and Deiotarus took the opportunity to desert with their own contingents. When he was brought before Octavian Rhoemetalces began a tirade of abuse against Antony, but Octavian cut him short with the terse comment that while he liked the fruits of treachery he disliked traitors.

Perhaps encouraged by this evidence of the looseness of the ties which bound the client princes to Antony, Octavian sent columns east to challenge Antony's hold on Rhoemetalces's kingdom of Thrace and to encourage Cotison, his own Dacian ally on the Danube. Although other writers have suggested an earlier date Dio says that it was after Octavian made this move, and therefore probably during May, that Agrippa captured the naval base on Leucas and then won control of the whole island.

The potential strategic advantages from this latest coup by Agrippa were considerable and he exploited them to the full. Leucas dominates the seaward approach from the south to the mouth of the Gulf; with Fanari to the north already in his hands he was able to tighten his grip on the approaches to the entrance. He could also deny Antony's transports the channel between Ithaca and Leucas and force them to make the longer passage outside Cephallenia. The massive bulk of Leucas, with its cliffs rising precipitously for 300 metres and its summit peaks at over 1,000 metres, towers above the coast and the flat Actium peninsula to the north. The knowledge that it was now in enemy hands must have had a demoralising effect on Antony's army and fleet at Actium; and clearly it was not beyond the capacity of the man who had connected Lake Avernus and the Lucrine Lagoon to the sea and tunnelled through the Misenum peninsula to dredge the channel across the mudflats which separated the north-east corner of Leucas from the mainland and pass his ships through it.

But Agrippa was far too able a strategist not first to consolidate his grip on the coast of the Peloponnese between Methone and Leucas. This he did by defeating Nasidius in the Gulf of Patras and capturing Patras. The loss of Antony's winter headquarters was another damaging psychological blow, and as a result his supply ships had to make the even longer and more hazardous passage outside Zacynthus as well as Cephallenia. Agrippa's squadrons penetrated right up to the head of the long and narrow Gulf of Corinth to seize, though not to hold, the isthmus and the ruined city of Corinth itself. From his initial assault on Methone Agrippa's naval operations in the Ionian Sea are the first classical example of the use of seapower to dictate the course of a land campaign.

Antony's fleet was now trapped at Actium and his control of central and western Greece was threatened, while in Sparta Eurycles was in open revolt. His transports had to run the gauntlet of Agrippa's patrolling warships and he was soon seriously short of supplies. The alternative land routes from his supply depots in central Greece degenerated into no more than rough tracks over the mountains of Aetolia and Acarnania and they could not carry even the barest needs of some 160,000 men at Actium; with the cavalry and auxiliaries the army must have been more than 80,000 strong, and if there were no more than 350 warships at Actium their crews would have numbered over 80,000.

This shortage of supplies added to the difficulty of maintaining morale and discipline. As May brought in the hot Mediterranean summer hygiene and waste disposal for this number of men cooped up on the northern shore and on the unhealthy stagnant marshland of the Actium peninusla became critical; malaria was soon widespread and outbreaks of dysentery which ran rapidly through the crowded camps were hard to control.

But the position was by no means hopeless. Antony's great fleet was largely intact and one decisive victory on land or sea could well decide the issue; then Agrippa's stranglehold on the Ionian coast could be prised loose. But time was no longer on Antony's side and such a victory had to be won before conditions at Actium deteriorated too far; the maintenance of the army's morale and its will to fight were all-important.

At Mutina and during the retreat from Phraapa Antony had shown a rare talent for inspiring his soldiers and lifting them back from impending disaster. But then he had been leading essentially Roman armies whose officers and soldiers believed and trusted in him. Now at Actium there were too many jealousies and quarrels among too many nobles and would-be leaders, too many voices advocating widely differing courses of action. The army and the fleet were in the main a disparate collection of contingents drawn from all over the East; their loyalty and their will to fight rested on their assessment of the chances of victory rather than on any unity of purpose. The Gallic cavalry and the hard Italian core of the legions were still devoted to him, but even their ranks had been diluted with recruits from the eastern provinces. Like Artavasdes of Armenia in the Median campaign Rhoemetalces and Deiotarus had shown that some of the client princes could not be trusted; if Octavian appeared to them the likely winner others would seek to make their peace with him in the knowledge that the earlier they did so the more likely they were to keep their thrones.

Some of the senators with their minds on their families and property in Italy were beginning to regret their hasty flight. Unused to the discomforts of life in camp, prolonged incarceration at Actium was not improving their spirits; they still preferred Antony as one of themselves and someone they could understand to the revolutionary young autocrat who bore Caesar's name though none of his charm, but this was in the belief that Antony would win. They were prepared to accept Cleopatra as his wife or his mistress, it mattered little to them which, and also as the client queen who was their paymaster, but many of them resented the prominent part she played in their council of war and above all her influence over Antony.

The suave Dellius earned her displeasure, or pretended that he had done so, when he complained of the rough Greek wine they were drinking and contrasted it unfavourably with the best Falernian Octavian's page boys were enjoying. Ahenobarbus had consistently opposed her presence with the army and now some of the senators again suggested that he should take over command from Antony and send her back to Egypt; this time even Canidius added his voice, apparently fearing that she might prevail on Antony to risk everything on a battle at sea. Others like Turullius and Cassius of Parma continued to support her. This dissension between the leaders soon percolated down to the officers of the army, the legionary legates, the military tribunes and the centurions on whom morale and discipline depended. Cleopatra must have realised the danger, but for her there was no way back and she had no choice but to pin her hopes of victory on Antony. She continued to show admirable personal courage, strength of character and steadfastness of purpose befitting her station as Queen and absolute ruler of Egypt.

Then Ahenobarbus became seriously ill, perhaps with malaria or dysentery; despairing of Antony's cause he had himself rowed secretly across the Gulf in a small boat to Octavian's lines. He may have realised that he was dying and have wished for his family's sake to make his peace with Octavian. Antony tried to make light of this desertion by his most trusted friend, remarking that Ahenobarbus could not wait to get into the arms of his mistress in Rome; and despite Cleopatra's strongly voiced objections he insisted on making the grand gesture of sending his baggage and servants after him. But Ahenobarbus was not to see Rome or embrace his mistress again, for

312

a few days later he died in Octavian's camp; a Republican aristocrat, like Pollio born out of his time, it was perhaps as well that he could not know that his great-grandson and Antony's would be the Emperor Nero.

Silanus, and Crassus in Crete, also changed sides at about this time, as did Atratinus in Laconia perhaps when Eurycles raised a revolt in Sparta; Octavian welcomed and pardoned them all. In an attempt to deter further desertions Antony executed a senator, Quintus Postumius, and Iamblichus prince of Emesa apparently on evidence provided by his brother. Only three consulars, Canidius, Sosius and Poplicola were now left with Antony at Actium.

As the summer wore on Agrippa's ships took an increasing toll of Antony's transports and conditions at Actium worsened, with food and forage running short and malaria and dysentery rife. As well as rations for 160,000 men Antony's staff had to find forage for 10,000 cavalry horses, and they were forced to porter more and more supplies overland from central Greece; Plutarch describes how his great-grandfather was pressganged into service.

Wastage and disease had depleted the rowers for the fleet, and though Antony had boasted that he would not lack for them while a single able-bodied man remained in Greece any such replacements were necessarily untrained; they were also conscripts rather than the volunteers who, contrary to tradition, normally manned the rowing benches as paid crewmen in the warships of the day, probably because experience had shown them to be more reliable in battle. It was possible to manoeuvre and fight a warship with as few as one trained man to each oar, though this entailed some sacrifice in handling efficiency. Penned in at Actium with little opportunity for training and none for exercise in open water the battle fitness of the fleet must have suffered more than that of the army; some of the ships were unseaworthy and the story of swallows nesting in Cleopatra's flagship is perhaps true and revealing.

Foiled in his attempt to force a battle by land it seems Antony decided that at all costs he must extricate his fleet. He sent Dellius and Amyntas with a force of all arms to raise reinforcements in Macedonia and Thrace and sustain his ally, Dicomes of the Getae who was an enemy of Cotison's; probably he also aimed to counter Octavian's incursion into Thrace and to bolster up his own authority in northern Greece. Then a few days later he marched east himself with the main body of the army. Dio's story that after sending off Dellius and Amyntas he suddenly decided to follow them for fear they would desert is possible but unlikely; written with hindsight and knowledge of their later desertion it perhaps telescopes two separate events into

313

one.

For while they and Antony were away from Actium Sosius tried to break out with the fleet. It would seem that this was part of a prearranged and coordinated plan whereby Antony advanced east to cover any move Octavian might make round the Gulf and Sosius broke out with the fleet, possibly for a later rendezvous on the eastern coast of Greece.

Sosius emerged from the Preveza Strait under cover of a sea mist, no doubt using it to conceal the passage of his ships through the narrows. Where the Strait widens out into the open sea he suddenly ran on a squadron under Tarius Rufus lying at anchor, presumably with the task of blockading the mouth of the Gulf; taken by surprise and outnumbered Tarius tried to flee. Sosius was pursuing him in poor visibility when apparently by chance he met Agrippa cruising offshore with the main fleet. This time Sosius had the worst of the encounter battle and was forced to put back to Actium. Tarcondimotus, ruler of the land-locked principality of Amanus, was killed, suggesting that the fleet was manned at least in part by auxiliaries and that most if not all of the legions were with Antony.

When he heard that Sosius had failed to break out Antony led the army round the northern shore of the Gulf in a last attempt to force a battle on land. There is no evidence that Octavian moved out from Mikhalitzi to meet him but an engagement of some sort took place, probably east of the Louros; Antony was in command himself, but Amyntas succeeded in deserting with his 2,000 Galatian cavalry.

Unwilling to sacrifice the fleet Antony returned to Actium. Perhaps to stop more desertions he withdrew most of his troops from the northern shore to the already overcrowded Actium peninsula, leaving detachments to hold the defences covering the entrance.

It was now only too clear that unless he acted quickly the legions themselves might lose their will to fight. As in most of the civil wars there were no real political or ideological differences between the Roman officers and soldiers on either side. Regimental spirit, the hope of reward, and Antony's personal qualities as their general had kept the legions loyal to him and would continue to do so as long as they believed that he could bring them victory. But if they came to judge that his cause was hopeless, and that there was nothing he or they could do to retrieve it, then they would not fight on against a Roman enemy from whom they could expect quarter. Past experience had shown that it was safer and more profitable to bargain for terms as a disciplined legion capable of fighting on under its own officers. So far it had not come to this, but the dangers must have been apparent to Antony.

In contrast the morale of Octavian's army and fleet was high, for now they scented victory. At some stage Octavian sent a despatch to Rome describing Agrippa's victories at sea and Amyntas's desertion with his Galatian cavalry. It may have been this report which prompted Horace to write in the IXth Epode:

'With snorting steeds two thousand Gauls desert to us,
With Caesar as their battle cry,
And backing water, ships among the foeman's fleet
Lie skulking in the harbour walls.'

translated Michael Oaksey

Whether he wrote this now, or on receipt of the news of the battle of Actium as Tarn and others suggest, is a matter of dispute; much turns on the precise meaning of sinistrorsum in relation to the movement of Antony's ships. Horace may even have written it at a later date and deliberately made it appear contemporary with the events he describes. But his reference to two thousand Gallic cavalry can only refer to Amyntas coming over to Octavian, and it seems likely that the next line refers to Sosius being forced back into harbour by Agrippa after attempting to break out, and not to the subsequent battle of Actium.

CHAPTER XXII

The Battle of Actium

By now it was mid-August, and on the Actium peninsula there can have been little relief for Antony's soldiers from the burning sun and the blown dust, from the flies and the all pervading stench of rotting refuse. Supplies were dangerously low, disease was rampant, and there was a constant trickle of deserters. The fleet was in worse shape than the army for its ships had lain idle since the previous autumn. Somehow Antony had to extricate army and fleet from the trap which Actium had become, and to do so while they were still able and willing to fight. To do nothing was to risk losing the fleet without a battle, and perhaps the army as well through disintegration by mass desertion.

He called a council of war attended by Cleopatra and her Egyptian captains as well as by his own senior Roman officers and leading supporters, among them Canidius, Dellius and Sosius, and the admirals Poplicola, Insteius and Octavius; all were agreed that to remain on the defensive at Actium was to invite disaster. There were only two real courses open; either to sacrifice the fleet, burning the ships to prevent them falling into Octavian's hands, and withdraw the army across the mountains of central Greece to Thessaly and the Aegean coast, and if necessary eastwards down the Via Egnatia from Thessalonica to Thrace and the Hellespont; or alternatively to break out with the fleet, which would mean embarking some third of the legionary strength as its fighting complement, and withdraw the rest of the army overland for a later junction perhaps in the northern Aegean or even Asia Minor.

Most of the Roman officers were confident that they could defeat Octavian on land if they could only bring him to battle, but they recognised Agrippa's prowess at sea and feared the outcome of a naval battle. Canidius as the senior and most experienced general maintained that it would be folly to split the army and gamble part of it at sea, pointing out that Octavian's army had been specially trained to man the fleet which had defeated Sextus whereas their own soldiers had no experience in fighting from ships; he argued that the army must be kept intact, even if needs be at the expense of the fleet, so that Antony might use his talent as the most able general on either side to bring them victory on land, adding, somewhat inconsequentially, perhaps in Thrace with Dicomes's help. He and the other Roman officers must also have reminded Antony of the uncommitted legions in Syria and Cyrenaica and the vast untapped resources of manpower and material he still controlled in the East.

However Cleopatra was determined not to abandon the fleet. She and her naval captains stressed the time, effort and money that had gone into building the ships and training their crews, and she insisted that the fleet must be saved; tamely to burn the ships would not only mean surrendering all hope of ultimate victory for several years, but would also make this plain to friend and foe alike. No doubt she appealed to Antony's innate optimism by stressing that although they had failed to force a battle on land there was always the possibility of swinging the whole course of the war in their favour with one victory at sea, provided that the fleet remained in being.

But when both sides had had their say the decision was Antony's, and his alone. Compared with the hazards of the fighting retreat from Phraapa withdrawal of the whole army from Actium promised to be a relatively simple operation despite the mountainous terrain of central Greece. But in Media every Roman soldier had been aware that his own survival depended on the army holding together against a treacherous foreign enemy from whom no quarter could be expected. Now they faced a Roman enemy known to be ready, even anxious, to offer terms, and if they withdrew across Greece they would be turning their backs on their promised homecoming to Italy only a day's sail away across the Ionian sea.

Antony remained confident that if he was at their head the legions and the Gallic cavalry would follow wherever he led them. But to withdraw the whole army meant the ignominious sacrifice of the great fleet he had built to challenge Octavian. As Cleopatra had pointed out this would have a disastrous effect on their standing and authority throughout all the East, and it was true that it would take at least two years to build and train another fleet; by then he would be in his middle fifties, and there was no telling what Agrippa might accomplish in the meantime with undisputed naval command of the eastern Mediterranean.

Nasidius might have lost part of his squadron when Agrippa defeated him in the Gulf of Patras. Some of the ships at Actium were unseaworthy and there was a shortage of trained rowers, but the core of the fleet remained intact including the small number of heavier ships of the line he had built to outfight Octavian in the same way as Octavian had outfought Sextus. Agrippa might have had the better of it when Sosius tried to break out, but if he took command he could surely extricate most of the fleet and perhaps even inflict a defeat on

Agrippa which would turn the tables on Octavian and trap his army in Epirus.

Thus Antony may have reasoned in deciding that he could not and would not abandon the fleet. Whether he had accepted that he could not win the war in 31 and must therefore save the fleet for the following year's campaign, or whether he had any real expectation of gaining an overwhelming victory at sea, can only be conjectured; it would have been out of character if at least he had not taken the latter possibility into his reckoning.

How much Cleopatra influenced him is hard to judge; perhaps little if at all, for his was the only decision which kept alive any real hope of eventually defeating Octavian and at heart he was a gambler and an optimist. Whatever his secret objective may have been he gave out to the army and the fleet that he had made up his mind to fight the battle which would bring them final victory, and to fight it at sea. Perhaps to have said otherwise would have been to sap their will to fight; but if his primary object was to save the fleet there was also danger in not taking his ships' captains into his confidence.

Soon after the decision was taken Dellius went over to Octavian; in the past he had deserted Dolabella and then Cassius, both in their hour of need. When he reached Octavian's camp he explained that he had feared assassination at the hands of Cleopatra's agents. Probably the truth of it was that he had already concluded that Octavian would win and picked this moment when he could insure his reception; Dio says that he disclosed Antony's plans, while Velleius remarks that he was at least consistent in his treachery.

Dio's account of the battle of Actium is vivid and detailed, but it is also confused, probably because he did not himself understand its course; it owes much to his own imagination in embellishing the legend that had already grown up, a legend which the tradition of a great battle demanded. His long and supposedly verbatim pre-battle speeches by Antony and Octavian are no more than what he thought they might or should have said.

Plutarch's account appears to derive from two separate sources. The traditional one has Antony, swayed by Cleopatra, staking their all on a battle at sea despite the protests of his Roman officers, only to be betrayed by her flight and in his turn betraying his army and fleet by following her. The other source seems to derive from the evidence of an eyewitness, sometimes thought to be a deserter from Antony because he clearly disapproved of the decision to fight at sea; in recounting what he saw he appears to have preserved some vital facts without understanding their significance.

Two of the largest and most powerful fleets the Mediterranean had ever seen were engaged in the battle; the stake was the Roman world, and the result was the birth of the Principate and centuries of Imperial rule from Rome. It is small wonder that the ancient historians largely ignored the preliminary campaign and concentrated on making the battle worthy of its outcome. Perhaps because of this some modern writers have over-reacted in arguing that Antony's sole object was to save his fleet; this may have been so, but, if it was, not one of them has attempted to explain why he did not begin to pass his ships out through the Preveza Strait at first light, when in fine weather during late August or early September he could expect a good offshore breeze in the hours after dawn, an ideal sailing wind to clear the northern tip of Leucas before standing away to the south. It may be that Octavian's intelligence from deserters and from his observation posts facing Antony's defences on the northern shore was good enough to allow Agrippa to be waiting outside with his main fleet; but unless he was there it seems that there was little he could have done to prevent the escape of the bulk of Antony's fleet, especially if its leading squadron engaged any standing offshore patrol.

The likely weather conditions, the coastal topography and the relative strengths of the two fleets were factors which Antony must have taken into account; these and the facts which Plutarch preserves can help in deducing Antony's intention and the course of the battle.

In anticyclonic conditions of late summer the winds in the Ionian Sea follow a general daily pattern, though even today their precise timing, strength and direction cannot be predicted with total accuracy. Around dawn the cooling mass of the mainland generates an offshore wind which dies away in the forenoon with the strengthening sun. After a period of calm an onshore wind springs up from the west and then veers north-west and hardens throughout the afternoon. This wind pattern can hardly have altered and must have been well known to both sides.

If Antony's only object was to save what he could of his fleet, and if, for whatever reason, he decided not to make use of the dawn offshore wind it would seem preferable to have waited until the early afternoon to emerge from the Preveza Strait, and then to fight if necessary to make enough offing and use the freshening north-westerly to clear Leucas; but this he did not do.

Events were to show that Agrippa was reluctant to come too close inshore, probably because his numerical superiority would then be offset by the constriction of the coast as it funnels in towards the Preveza Strait; with Antony's fleet effectively bottled up Agrippa had been able to concentrate most of his 400 available warships. How many ships Antony had at Actium is uncertain. Tarn suggests that it was as many as 400 out of his original 500, that he was able to man nearly all of them, and that Plutarch's figure of 230 refers only to the right wing which Antony and Poplicola commanded. Most other modern historians have taken Plutarch's 230 as referring to Antony's total battle strength; Orosius gives this as 170 and Florus as under 200, and if these figures omit the fifty to sixty ships of Cleopatra's own squadron they tally well enough with Plutarch's.

It would seem unlikely that Antony could have had many more than 350 warships at Actium. If some were unseaworthy and others could not be manned through lack of rowers, and if as Plutarch says he burned all the Egyptian ships except for one squadron and some transports, then the figure of 230 for Antony's battle strength including Cleopatra's squadron is perhaps the best estimate.

If the Egyptian ships with their fighting complement of Greek mercenaries are again deducted Plutarch's total of 20,000 for the legionary infantry, perhaps five understrength legions, which Antony embarked gives an average of 110 per ship, a credible figure if, as he indicates, Antony retained all his heavier ships; the 2,000 archers he mentions were probably not evenly distributed but confined to the bigger ships with suitable fighting towers.

The approach to the Preveza Strait funnels in from the general NNW–SSE run of the coast between Cape Skilla on the western shoulder of the Actium peninsula and Cape Parginoskala, $1^3/_4$ nautical miles to the NNW. If Antony intended to fight a fleet action this was a sound tactical line with the rocky shores at either end providing protection for the flanks against a numerically superior enemy. Allowing sea room of 20 metres per ship, made up of overall width from oartip to oartip of 10–12 metres and 8–10 metres of open water between ships, and deducting some 100 metres for the offshore rocks, this meant that he could deploy 170 ships abreast in line of battle and hold one squadron in reserve.

The tactical advantage of the Skilla-Parginoskala line depended on the enemy's willingness to join battle on it; if Antony's main concern was to save his fleet its disadvantage lay in the fact that the left of the line off Cape Skilla would not be able to make good the required course of 220° True to clear Cape Zauna on Leucas under sail until the wind reached north-west. The war ships of the day could not sail much closer to the wind than eight points, or 90°, and on such a heading their single square-rigged sails gave them no more than two or three knots. Their best point of sailing was with the wind astern, when in favourable conditions they could reach eight knots or more. Under oars alone they could make five or six knots on a calm sea, the biremes and triremes up to seven or more for a limited period with a fit and well trained crew.

These ships of the line were a decked development of the earlier oared galley, of fairly light construction in comparison with the transports but reinforced with heavier timbers to carry their fighting platforms and protect their sides against ramming; in contrast to the tubby sturdy transports they were very long for their beam. Excavation of the foundations of covered sheds at the Piraeus in which the Athenian triremes of the 5th and 4th centuries were slipped and stored indicates a maximum beam with outriggers of six metres and an overall length of forty five metres. Pictograph evidence suggest that there was no fundamental design difference between these Greek triremes and the Roman warships of the 1st century BC. A length/beam ratio of 7 or 8/1 necessitated reinforcement with transverse ribs and longitudinal timbers or wales. The keel was carried forward to take the underwater bow ram, usually in the form of an iron trident sheathed in bronze; the decorated prow or beak was also finished in bronze. The single mast was stepped forward of amidships, but the heavy square sail and its cumbersome running gear were normally left ashore before battle.

Archers and slingers as well as the normal complement of soldiers were carried on the larger ships, some of which had fighting towers fore and aft; from these they could either fire straight down, or with a dipping trajectory and an effective range of up to 100 metres. Small artillery pieces fired stone shot and some were used for throwing Greek fire, an incendiary mixture probably based on saltpetre and bitumen. Grapnels and boarding bridges were standard equipment, and Agrippa had developed the harpax, a catapult operated grapnel thrower with a range of thirty metres.

These then, the coastal topography, the wind pattern and the relative strengths of the two fleets were the factors which determined Antony's plan and the course of the battle. If his aim was to save the fleet including some of the transports his timing relative to the likely winds was critical. There is little tidal rise and fall in the Mediterranean and normally the current in the Preveza Strait does not exceed one, or at the most, two knots in either direction. But strong winds acting on the huge expanse of inland water in the Ambracian Gulf can sometimes combine with the tidal flow through the narrow entrance to produce ebb and flood streams of up to four knots; these depend more on the wind and weather conditions than the tides and cannot therefore be predicted. In fine weather the tidal flow was not a major factor, though if possible Antony would have chosen to move his ships out at slack water or on the ebb.

Whatever the secret details of his plan may have been it seems certain that he did not intend to return to Actium, for contrary to the established practice he ordered sails to be shipped, brushing aside his captains' protests by saying they would need them to pursue the beaten enemy since he was determined that none should escape.

Like Octavian Antony had built two walls to link his fleet inside Akri Point with the army's camp in the centre of the peninsula. Octavian discovered that he was in the habit of walking down unescorted to his ships and sent agents to waylay him; but they ambushed the wrong man and Antony escaped.

Thanks to Dellius and other deserters Octavian's intelligence was excellent and reports soon reached him that Antony had ordered sails to be carried. As a result he considered allowing Antony's fleet to get well clear of Actium, presumably so that they could not return to harbour, and then closing in from the rear to destroy them. But Agrippa did not mean to carry sails himself, and he objected that if Antony was given enough searoom to clear Leucas it might prove impossible in certain weather conditions to bring him to battle. Octavian wisely accepted this advice; he had already made up his mind to delegate overall command to Agrippa and to direct the battle himself from a liburnian.

Antony burned his unseaworthy ships and those he could not man, among them most of the Egyptian ships except for Cleopatra's squadron and some transports. According to Plutarch he sacrificed his lighter ships thus accentuating whatever disparity in size of ships there already was between the two fleets. The clouds of smoke billowing up from a hundred burning ships could not be hidden from Octavian's observation posts or from Agrippa's offshore patrols; but the war chest was loaded in secret on to Cleopatra's flagship and other transports. Canidius was left in command of the army with orders to watch the battle, and if it went against them to withdraw eastwards.

By 28th August Antony was ready; gales are rare in the Ionian Sea in late August, but on that day the weather broke with strong onshore winds producing a heavy breaking sea. The storm took four days to blow itself out, and then the 2nd of September dawned fine and clear with a calm sea. It must have taken some time to embark his legionary infantry, but with the sun rising across the Ambracian Gulf behind them Antony's ships began to move out round Akri Point and pass through the Preveza Strait. At its narrowest point off Akri the channel is only 200 metres wide, and it will have been several hours before all his ships had cleared the Strait.

There is a bar between Fort Pandokrator and the shoals off Cape Skilla; today there are at least three metres of water over it for a distance of about 1,500 metres south from the Fort, and the deep modern dredged channel cuts through it. Though the shoals, the bar, the sandy bottom and the level of the sea itself may have shifted and altered over the centuries the depth of water on the bar seems to have been enough for Antony's ships, the heaviest of which would not have drawn much more than three metres.

On his way down before dawn from Mikalitzi to board his liburnian the story goes that Octavian met an old man driving an ass and stopped to ask his name. Perhaps recognising him the old man replied that his name was Fortunate and his ass's Victor; Octavian took this as a good omen and after the battle he raised a bronze statue of the old man and his ass on the spot where he had met him.

Agrippa was already at sea with the main battle fleet. He had embarked elements of eight legions and five independent cohorts on his 400 ships, a total of between 30,000 and 40,000 legionary infantry. His second in command was Lucius Arruntius who had fled to Sextus in 43, but later had joined Octavian. Tarius Rufus was left ashore in command of the army which he moved to a vantage point on the cliffs. Across the Strait Canidius drew up Antony's army so that they too could watch the battle from the western side of the Actium peninsula. Seldom in the course of history have two opposing armies been spectators at a naval battle which would decide their own fates and the fate of their world.

As they emerged from the Strait Antony's ships took up their battle stations in line abreast with the left squadron under Sosius protected by the Cape Skilla shoals; Octavius and Insteius commanded the squadrons of the centre, with the Egyptian squadron in reserve behind them. Poplicola took the right of the line off Cape Parginoskala; even from here he would not be able to use the wind to make good the course of 210° True, which he needed to clear Leucas, until it was within a point of NW.

A mile to seaward Agrippa also formed up his fleet in line of battle, but he made no move to close. Antony's crews laid on their oars, paddling a few strokes every now and then to hold their line. Antony transferred to a tender and had himself rowed from ship to ship encouraging the soldiers and urging the captains to keep station; watching from his liburnian Octavian thought for a moment that they had dropped anchor, so steady was their line.

Plutarch conveys something of the drama and tension as the two great fleets lay motionless, facing each other across a mile of open water, each waiting for the other to move. The sun glinted on the soldiers' armour and the beaks of the ships, and after a time the offshore breeze died away and the sea became a flat calm. From onshore the two armies, also separated by a mile or so of water, watched and waited in silence.

Still Agrippa made no move to close the gap; to have done so would have been to surrender his numerical advantage when the initiative was his, and sooner or later the enemy would have to come to him. It is possible that Antony was merely waiting for the wind to spring up from the west and veer towards the north. But the fact that he deployed his fleet between Capes Skilla and Parginoskala so early in the forenoon and held this line so long suggest that he hoped to entice Agrippa in to meet him. If Agrippa had moved in and had had the best of the battle Antony must have known that his own ships would have had no chance of picking up the wind to help them escape under sail until well into the afternoon. All the evidence indicates that he had resigned himself to having to fight his way out; his timing also suggests that he had not given up hope of a decisive victory if he could fight on the line he had chosen.

But this depended on Agrippa, and it soon became clear that he did not intend to close. Shortly after noon Antony's left began to move forward; according to Plutarch they did so without orders because the captains and crews were confident of victory and impatient at the delay. This may have been so, but it could equally have been part of a prearranged plan, for, if Agrippa held off, Antony had no real choice but to attack; the alternative was to put back to Actium. And it was Sosius's ships on the left which might need the extra searoom before the afternoon was out; Marcus Lurius's squadron was facing them, and Octavian ordered him to back water and draw Sosius further away from the protection of Cape Skilla and out into the open sea.

Antony was with Poplicola's squadron on the right facing Agrippa. Having failed to bring on the battle on the line of his choosing it may have been now that he resigned himself to saving what he could of the fleet. His ships moved forward on the right, either to keep station with Sosius or as the second phase of his plan. The centre squadrons were slow to conform and Plutarch's description of the two fleets in crescent formation may arise from this.

But Agrippa did not give way as Lurius was doing: instead, as soon as Antony's right was clear of Cape Parginoskala, he extended his line to the north, either to counter a similar move by Antony or more probably to use his advantage in numbers to turn this flank. As a result Antony's slower moving centre was stretched and weakened. It is not clear how closely his ships in the centre and the south engaged, but Cleopatra's squadron and the transports certainly stayed out of action behind them.

Thus the two fleets met first on the northern flank, and here the heaviest fighting developed. As the two battle lines clashed there was an opening exchange of fire with the artillery hurling stone shot and incendiaries, the archers and slingers firing down from their towers, and the soldiers crouching behind their shields ready to repel boarders or board themselves. Agrippa made no attempt to ram the reinforced sides of Antony's ships; instead his tactics seem to have been to try and lay two or even three of his ships alongside each of Antony's and board them from both sides. Antony's ships tried to grapple on one side and keep their attackers at a distance on the other so that they could bring to bear their individual advantage in the number of soldiers they carried.

The rowers toiled on their oars, and the helmsmen swung the great steering blades in response to shouted orders from the captains in their efforts to smash each other's oars and outriggers and protect their own as they closed. The catapult fired grapnel lines snaked out, and where they found their target they were either cut away at once or rapidly hauled in. Once grappled the boarding bridges came crashing down and the soldiers swarmed across on to the enemy ships or desperately defended their own. Soon the two lines of battle had merged and broken up into a series of ship to ship actions.

The Egyptian squadron and the transports lay motionless on the calm sea. In front of them and away to the south many of Antony's ships were still not closely engaged. But where he and Poplicola faced Agrippa the battle was soon close and fiercely fought. A few ships were already burning with their crews trying to put out the fires. But most of them were grappled together in twos and threes and drifting slowly out of their captains' control. The soldiers fought hand to hand across the heaving slippery decks, struggling to keep their foothold as the swell lifted the ships and ground them against each other. Below decks the rowers could only wait and pray as they listened to the clash of arms and the pounding of feet above their heads.

Many of these individual ship to ship actions were savage and prolonged, particularly when quarter was neither asked nor offered. The fighting flowed backwards and forwards across the decks, for when the attackers had taken half or more of the enemy ship they could no longer bring their numbers to bear and the defenders resisted even more desperately since few could swim and none could hope to survive in the sea for long in armour. The rowers who provided the motive power could expect to be spared if their ship was taken and some of their oars were still intact; if not they too would not last long in the water unless they could cling to wreckage.

A new supply of incendiaries brought up on Octavian's orders started more fires; some rebounded on the attackers when they failed to cut the enemy loose and fire swept both ships, forcing the crews to try and save themselves by jumping into the sea. A light breeze sprang up from the west and fanned the blazing ships. Soon a pall of smoke hung low across the water and was carried slowly by the wind towards the shore where it hid the fighting ships from the watching armies. They could still hear the cries and the shouted orders, the clash of swords on armour, the groan of timber grinding against timber and the crack of splintering oars; peering anxiously through the smoke they could see sudden flames leaping up to silhouette individual ships, but they could not distinguish them nor tell which side was winning.

Locked together in their separate battles it was difficult for the crews of the fighting ships to judge how the whole battle went. In fact after two hours or more neither side had gained any clear advantage. By now the wind had gone round towards the north-west and strengthened to thin the clouds of smoke which lay across the sea. Suddenly the Egyptian squadron could be seen making sail; then as they picked up the wind they threaded their way through the fighting ships and stood away on a south-westerly course.

It was this precipitate and apparently unexpected flight which all the ancient historians, Plutarch and Dio among them, took as evidence of Cleopatra's cowardice and treachery. They portrayed her as fleeing from the battle Antony was fighting on her behalf just as it reached its crisis. But her move was probably part of a prearranged plan to be put into operation on a signal from Antony when the wind served, and then only if they had not already won a decisive advantage. It has been objected that it was impossible for the Egyptian squadron simply to have sailed away through the embattled fleets and that therefore the ancient accounts are either wrong or omit some critical factor; but this shows a misconception of the nature of sea battles before the invention of gunpowder. For a disciplined and uncommitted squadron whose ships were commanded by experienced seamen it was a relatively simple manoeuvre, particularly in the smoke and confusion after two hours of battle had broken up the two fleets into a number of separate engagements.

Antony's ships which were grappled to the enemy could not break off the action; his own flagship was one. He transferred to another ship of the line and ordered her captain to hoist sail and follow the Egyptian squadron. At the same time he signalled Poplicola's squadron to conform and almost certainly repeated this order to the rest of the fleet.

Although the centre and left were not so closely engaged and by now had sufficient searoom to clear Leucas only thirty or forty ships followed him. Some, disabled, on fire, or grappled to the enemy, could not extricate themselves, some may either have not seen the signal or misunderstood it. But many others who could have obeyed did not do so. It seems that this was the price Antony now had to pay for not taking his ships' captains into his confidence; it was a price he could ill afford. Probably only Cleopatra, Canidius, and the admirals who commanded the squadrons, Sosius, Poplicola, Insteius and Octavius, had been privy to the details of his secret contingency plan.

All that the rest of the fleet could see was a number of ships raising sail and following in the wake of the Egyptian squadron; at the same time they could make out Antony's own flagship closely engaged in the thick of the fighting, and many of the captains must have assumed that he was still on board. Bewildered by this sudden dramatic turn it is no wonder that they hesitated, particularly when Sosius made no move to conform. What was clear was that this inexplicable flight of some hundred ships meant that the battle was lost. At first many of his soldiers and crews could not believe that Antony had abandoned them. When at last they realised that he had followed Cleopatra they felt that he had betrayed them and that now was the moment to surrender or to put back to Actium and ask for terms. Many of them did so; Sosius certainly survived to be pardoned by Octavian on Arruntius's plea, though nothing is known of the fate of Poplicola, Insteius and Octavius, who at this point pass from history.

So the story arose that Antony had been betrayed by Cleopatra, and in his turn had betrayed his embattled fleet. That a man with a reputation such as Antony's, who had again and again displayed high qualities of personal courage and leadership in rallying his men when all seemed lost, should act so completely out of character and for no evident reason when the battle he had long sought for the mastery of the world was so finely balanced had to be explained if it were to be in any way credible; it was all conveniently put down to Cleopatra's cowardice and the spell she had cast over him. That she, to whose courage and steadfastness even the Romans paid reluctant tribute, should cravenly flee the battle was not explained; it was enough that she was a woman and the feared and hated foreign queen who had sought to cast her spell on Rome itself.

Plutarch and Dio accepted this tradition and adapted their accounts to fit it. They described Antony's ships fighting on in worsening weather for several hours; no doubt some did so, but it seems that most of them neither followed Antony nor fought on. Some raised their oars in surrender, while others, probably Sosius among them, put back to Actium; for them this was no more than a prudent preliminary to making their peace with the victor. For Antony it was treachery and the final betrayal which spelled the ruin of his cause.

With his sails ashore Agrippa made no attempt to pursue the hundred ships which had escaped. This was left to Eurycles who had sails with him and his father's death to avenge. Octavian could not understand how Antony's fleet had disintegrated so quickly when the battle had been at its height, and he could not believe that his victory was so complete. He remained at sea all through the night cruising off the entrance to the Gulf in his liburnian, perhaps in itself an indication that the fighting in the centre and the south had not been close and that a considerable number of Antony's ships had returned to Actium undamaged.

As they sailed south in company Cleopatra signalled Antony to transfer to the Antonias. But when he came aboard he refused to speak to her or to anyone else and instead made his way to the bows where he sat alone, shocked and brooding. Later that evening Eurycles closed with them, and Antony roused himself to take command and face his pursuers. There was a shouted exchange with Eurycles who sheered off; but he managed to capture two of Antony's heavier ships and then stood away north with his prizes.

Antony returned to his silent vigil in the bows, and there he remained for the three days it took them to reach Taenarum. That he had saved a quarter or a third of his fleet was of no consolation against the sight, etched on his memory, of the others who could have followed him but instead had preferred to surrender or seek refuge in Actium. That for the first time his own Roman soldiers had deserted him in battle seemed grounds enough to him for despair; certainly from this moment on he was a broken man.

CHAPTER XXIII

The Bitter Aftermath

The comparatively small total of 5,000 which Plutarch gives as Antony's casualties tends to confirm that many of his ships had never engaged the enemy very closely, particularly if the figure included rowers, when it is equivalent to the total complement of fewer than twenty ships of the line. Though the number of ships which fell into Octavian's hands undamaged or only slightly damaged is uncertain, it is known that there were enough to provide the nucleus of the new imperial fleet which covered the western Mediterranean from Forum Julii in Provence. It seems likely that Antony lost less than forty ships in action.

In purely military terms the outcome provided no good reason for despair. After being outmanoeuvred and trapped at Actium he had chosen to fight at sea, and outnumbered by nearly two to one he had succeeded in extricating some hundred ships when he might well have been forced back on to a lee shore and lost his whole fleet. The rest of his legions and 10,000 cavalry were intact, with the able and loyal Canidius to conduct their withdrawal. Apart from the field army he had at least six more legions in the East, possibly as many as eleven, and he still controlled all the resources of Asia Minor, Egypt and the Levant. It seems tolerably certain that the reason for his despair was that he felt he had been betrayed, not by Cleopatra, but by the bulk of his fleet whose will to fight he had misjudged and that he recognised that the consequences were likely to prove fatal to his cause.

Although close to Eurycles's Sparta and less than fifty miles from Methone Taenarum was still held for Antony, and they waited here for stragglers from the battle to catch up with them; these brought news that though the rest of the fleet was lost Canidius was holding the army together.

Antony seems to have shaken off his mood of dark depression, and Cleopatra's attendants succeeded in bringing them together again. She was anxious to get back to Egypt before news of the outcome of the battle reached Alexandria; they decided to make for the north African coast where she could find out if there had been a revolt against her in Egypt and Antony could take over command of his four Cyrenaican legions.

First he offered some of his friends a ship, complete with her cargo of bullion and treasure from the war chest, and told them to make good their escape in it; but touched by his generosity and his concern for their safety they refused to desert him. In the end he persuaded them to head for Corinth, giving them a letter to his steward with instructions to hide them until such time as they could make their peace with Octavian.

From Taenarum he sent a message to Canidius confirming his orders to withdraw the army through Greece to Asia Minor. Canidius had already begun the long march when envoys from Octavian caught up with the army and offered terms. He could not stop his soldiers from listening to them and soon they were negotiating in earnest, demanding as their price for surrender the same pay and bounties as Octavian's army and the same land grants and gratuities on discharge.

Their morale and discipline must still have been high and their fighting potential unimpaired for Octavian agreed to all that they asked. Once again he had neither the land nor the money to satisfy his own legions let alone Antony's, but this was unimportant. The main body of his own army was still on the other side of the Ambracian Gulf, and it was vital to detach Antony's legions from Canidius before he could get them back through central and northern Greece to Asia Minor. Once they had laid down their arms any terms which Octavian had been obliged to concede could easily be amended.

Perhaps anticipating the possibility of such double-dealing and encouraged by the envoys' evident anxiety to reach agreement six of the legions refused these apparently generous terms. Prompted by past experience in the civil wars and moved, not by loyalty to Antony or Canidius, but by intense professional pride in their own legions the officers and soldiers insisted that Octavian must himself publicly agree to incorporate all six legions into his own army and allow them to retain their own officers and their own legionary eagles and titles.

Octavian demurred at this: unlike the promise of equal treatment it would be difficult to renege on such an undertaking made in person and in public, and in north-west Greece alone he already had sixteen legions of his own with at least as many again in Italy and the western provinces.

But the officers and men of the six legions solidly persisted in their demands, and after the talks had dragged on for seven days without any apparent weakening of their resolve Octavian gave in and agreed to what they asked. There is some evidence that he kept his word and that all six were among the twenty eight legions he retained as the regular establishment of the new imperial army. The IIIrd Gallica, the Vth Alaudae and VIth Ferrata certainly survived, and though the Vth was transferred from the Rhine to Dacia and lost in AD 86 the other two served on for centuries, the IIIrd on the Danube and the VIth as part of the garrison of Syria.

The story that Canidius basely left his army to its fate so that he could effect his own escape is probably no more than a slanderous invention of Octavian's propaganda which fitted neatly enough into the ancient accounts. It is true that he refused to surrender and instead made his way to Alexandria, but whether Octavian was unwilling to pardon him and he knew this is is uncertain; he may have acted purely out of loyalty to Antony and in so doing have sealed his own later fate at Octavian's hands.

Before they sailed on Antony may have received reports that the army was negotiating with Octavian's envoys; but it seems unlikely that he and Cleopatra stayed more than a few days at Taenarum and it is not known when or how he heard that they had agreed terms.

Antony and Cleopatra made their landfall with what remained of their fleet at Paraetonium, a small desert outpost on the coast 170 miles west of Alexandria. They probably chose it for the same reason as Antony once had chosen Leuke Come for his rendezvous with Cleopatra after the retreat from Media: if there had been a revolt in Egypt the circular natural harbour could readily be seized from the sea, giving Cleopatra the opportunity to find out what had happened in her absence while Antony contacted Pinarius Scarpus and the four legions in Cyrenaica.

Relieved to discover that all was quiet in Egypt Cleopatra sailed on for Alexandria, prepared to crush any revolt which the news of Actium might provoke. She entered the Great Harbour with her ships dressed overall as if in celebration of victory. Once ashore she lost no time in pre-empting any move against her by arresting the potential ringleaders and executing some of them; defeat had not weakened her resolve that she and her children should continue to rule in Egypt.

Antony remained at Paraetonium with his own squadron of forty or fifty ships. According to Plutarch he went ashore and wandered aimlessly round the desert with two attendants, a Greek named Aristocrates, and the Lucilius who had impersonated Brutus at Philippi and since then had served Antony as faithfully as he had Brutus. In fact he was probably waiting impatiently for the return of the couriers he had sent to Scarpus.

How the news of Actium reached Scarpus and whether he heard it before or after Antony's arrival at Paraetonium is uncertain. Reports may have been brought by a ship escaping from the battle, or they could have filtered through from the African provinces held for Octavian by Gallus. It is possible that the first Scarpus heard was from Antony's own messengers. If this was so they paid for it with their lives: after refusing to allow them any contact with his legions Scarpus arrested and executed them, and then declared for Octavian. Plutarch says that Antony tried to kill himself while he was at Paraetonium, and if he did it was perhaps when he heard of Scarpus's defection.

The news that Octavian had triumphed at Actium spread rapidly from Italy through the western provinces. Apart from allowing Eurycles his gesture Agrippa made no attempt to pursue Antony. He and Octavian were more concerned with securing the surrender of the ships which had put back to Actium and preventing Canidius from escaping with the army. When this had been done Octavian was content to gather the political fruits of his victory and deal with the urgent problems which faced him nearer home; without army or fleet Antony posed no immediate danger.

The most pressing question was what to do with the legions in north-west Greece; with the surrender of Canidius's army there were twenty nine or thirty of them as well as 25,000 cavalry and the survivors of the five legions Antony had embarked. After the defeat of Sextus and the downfall of Lepidus Octavian had faced the same problem with forty legions concentrated in the north-east corner of Sicily; now he adopted a similar solution. Those of his own legions which he intended to retain would remain under military discipline, and for them his promise of reward from the legendary riches of Egypt would suffice. The rest of his legions, and all Antony's except for the six whose continuing existence he had conceded, would be disbanded. All their soldiers who were over a certain age and of Italian origin would be returned to depots in Italy, there to await demobilisation and resettlement when he was able to procure the necessary land and money; Antony's recruits of eastern origin were thus excluded. The remaining soldiers from the disbanded legions would be drafted as reinforcements for the legions he was retaining.

The dangers were only too apparent: to try and levy more taxes or forcibly acquire more land would certainly provoke civil disorders in Italy, but failure to satisfy the soldiers awaiting demobilisation was potentially an even greater risk. Octavian could not afford to wait until the taxes and tribute from the East began to flow again to Rome. The only untapped source of gold and bullion in the quantity he needed lay in the vaults of the Egyptian treasury; if he could possess himself of this he could pay off all his veterans and at least pay for the land he expropriated on their behalf.

First he had to secure Greece, and with the surrender of Canidius's army the country lay ready and waiting for him to take over. After the formal celebration ceremony at which his troops hailed him as

Imperator for the sixth time he went straight to Athens, where one of his first acts was to order grain from Antony's depots to be distributed to the starving Greeks. While he was there he made a gesture of goodwill to the Athenians and perhaps satisfied his own curiosity by being initiated into the ancient rites and mysteries of Eleusis. Thus far he was prepared to make a show of philhellenism, always provided that the Greeks accepted political subordination to Rome. But he was determined to prevent the cults and religions of Asia Minor and the East from infiltrating the West and contaminating Italy.

In contrast Antony had been drawn to the Greek way of life, and he had been ready to accept the eastern religions and identify himself with their gods. He had come to recognize the aspirations of the nations of the East and to understand their resentment at Roman domination. This had made it easier for Octavian to play on Roman fears of retribution from the East and concentrate these fears on the person of Cleopatra. She and Antony had seemed, perhaps unconsciously, to offer the East a new Golden Age based on an equal partnership with Rome and the West; Octavian's victory at Actium was destined to postpone this until Rome herself declined and Byzantium took her place in the eastern Mediterranean. The intervening centuries of peace and stability under Rome's imperial rule moulded the future shape of western European civilisation, but it was Byzantium that kept alive the legacy of Greece and Rome for the young nations of the West.

But now reports reaching Octavian from Asia Minor told of Antony's authority collapsing as it had in Greece, with the client rulers scrambling to make their peace with the victor in the hope of keeping their thrones. From Athens Octavian crossed to Samos where he set up his headquarters for the winter. Despatches from Rome told of continuing unrest among the soldiers awaiting demobilisation, and of a plot to assassinate him when he returned to Italy which Maecenas's agents had uncovered. The ringleader was Marcus Lepidus, son of the triumvir and Brutus's nephew. With no immediate danger to Octavian Maecenas had allowed the conspiracy to develop until he had enough evidence to arrest and execute Lepidus; his wife, Servilia, took her own life by swallowing a live coal, but no action was taken against his father, the one-time triumvir, who in retirement still held the office of Pontifex Maximus. The existence of such a conspiracy must have been an unpleasant reminder to Octavian of the underlying opposition in Rome and the continuing strength of Republican sentiment.

Although Maecenas came from a wealthy and noble Etruscan family he had refused public office in Rome, preferring to work behind the scenes in Octavian's interest; consequently he ranked only as a knight and had no official standing. To reinforce his authority and to control the veterans in their depots Octavian sent Agrippa back to Italy. He authorised him and Maecenas to open his official letters and despatches before they were laid before the Senate, and also to amend them as they thought fit in the light of the current circumstances in Rome; to this end he gave them each a ring bearing a duplicate of the sphinx device which was his personal seal.

At Samos the principal prisoners were arraigned before him. Later he was at pains to emphasise the forbearance he had shown and the Augustan writers were to extol his clemency. But Dio says that he had many of them executed, levied fines on others and even spared some; amongst the latter was Sosius, pardoned on Arruntius's plea. It is possible, though it can only be surmise, that Arruntius pleaded that Sosius had not pressed home his attack and had surrendered instead of following Antony; if this was so he must bear much of the blame for Antony's defeat.

Sextus's half-brother, Marcus Scaurus, was condemned to death but later reprieved on the intercession of his mother, Mucia, whose help in his earlier negotiations with Sextus Octavian recognised; it may also have been due to her intervention that her grandson and Pompey's, Gnaeus Cornelius Cinna, was pardoned. Despite his father's services to Caesar, Fulvia's son and Antony's stepson, Scribonius Curio, was executed. Two of Octavian's younger officers, Caecilius Metellus and Gaius Furnius, interceded to save their own fathers who had been taken prisoner. But Aquillius Florus and his son had both fought for Antony and according to Dio Octavian ordered them to draw lots to decide which of them should die; before they could do so the son offered his neck to the executioner to save his father, and watched by Octavian the grief stricken father died by his own hand across his son's body. Suetonius records a similar incident after Philippi, though then it was the father who sacrificed his life and the son who killed himself over his father's body. Remembered as they were long afterwards these two macabre incidents must have made a lasting impression in a society which especially valued and honoured paternal and filial ties; they also shed some light on a dark corner of Octavian's character which in later years he was at pains to conceal.

As well as exercising what Velleius praised as clemency to the prisoners of rank Octavian rewarded the client princes and the cities which had helped him by their early defection. Rhoemetalces was confirmed as ruler of Thrace. In Crete Cydonia and Lappa were made free cities, and Lappa which had been partly destroyed as a reprisal was promised aid for rebuilding. Sparta's territory was enlarged and the city was honoured by being appointed to organise the Actian

Games; dedicated to Apollo this festival was to be held every four years to celebrate Octavian's victory, and it was accorded the same standing as the Games at Olympia.

It may have been while he was at Samos that Octavian issued instructions for work to begin on the monuments he planned to commemorate the battle of Actium. The decorated bronze beaks were taken from ten of Antony's ships, one from each class up to the huge dektere, or 'ten', and dedicated to Apollo at his temple on the Actian peninsula. In this and in the coins he struck Octavian perhaps sought to draw a parallel between Actium and the naval victories of Demetrius Poliorcetes over Ptolemy I off the south coast of Cyprus and those of his son, Antigonus Gonatas, over Ptolemy II at Cos and Andros; after these battles Demetrius raised a statue of Nike on the prow of a warship and Antigonus dedicted his flagship to Poseidon. As well as defeating the second Ptolemy it had been Antigonus who in 272 finally overcame Pyrrhus, another hated enemy of Rome. Ironically it was Demetrius whom Plutarch was to couple with Antony in his parallel Lives of Greeks and Romans.

Where his tent had stood at Mikhalitzi Octavian planned and later raised a grander and more lasting memorial: a crescent shaped wall of huge blocks of squared and dressed stone was built into the side of the hill and the prows of some of Antony's ships were fastened to its face as a platform for an open air shrine to Apollo. By the springs beyond the isthmus to the south he ordered the founding of a new city to be called Nicopolis, the City of Victory, perhaps also in emulation of Demetrius's foundation of Demetrias. The new city was designated as the site for the Actian Games; it was to be populated with discharged veterans and people forcibly removed from the nearby towns and cities, among them Ambracia which Pyrrhus had founded.

The ship memorial at Apollo's temple on the Actium peninsula was soon to be destroyed by fire; only a few years later the geographer and traveller, Strabo, searched for it in vain. But at Mikhalitzi the massive wall with the slots cut in it to take the timbers of Antony's ships stands there today, and from it can be seen the extensive ruins of Nicopolis across the isthmus.

But these were no more than ideas in Octavian's mind, or at the most notes for a directive, when an urgent despatch from Agrippa reached him at Samos: though the soldiers waiting demobilisation had been dispersed in depots throughout Italy the delay in discharging and resettling them had put them in such a dangerous mood that only Octavian's presence could prevent a mutiny which might lead to anarchy and civil war.

Navigation in winter between the Aegean and Italy was so

hazardous that all normal movement by sea stopped between November and March; that Agrippa asked Octavian to return to Italy is a measure of the gravity of the threat and the veterans' insistence that they would deal with him alone. Octavian must himself have recognised the urgency for he left by sea at once, and in spite of storms he reached Brundisium a week or so later; there the menacing attitude of the soldiers' leaders who had gathered to meet him showed that Agrippa had not exaggerated. Their behaviour was in marked contrast to the sycophantic flattery of the senators and the other leading citizens of Rome who had travelled to Brundisium to welcome him and so safeguard themselves, in much the same way as some of their fathers had gone to greet Caesar on his return from Spain.

Octavian did what he could to pacify the soldiers' leaders, and once again he managed to divide them by making different offers to different categories. He gave what money he had to his own veterans who had served since Mutina or Philippi, together with land expropriated from private estates in Italy forfeited by Antony's supporters. To others he gave land grants in new colonies at Dyrrachium and Philippi or cash advances against their gratuities; he tried to satisfy the rest with promises that they would be paid in generous measure as soon as the East was his. To emphasize that he simply did not have sufficient funds for them all he offered to auction his own personal property and that of his closest friends, a gesture which may have had some effect and certainly cost him nothing since none dared to take him up.

To raise further taxes in Italy was out of the question; only a month or so before a fresh wave of protest had forced Maecenas to remit the outstanding quarter of the special capital tax on freedmen. Dio says that they were as delighted with this concession as if they had been given the money instead of excused from paying it; a comment drawn from his own experience as a provincial governor which breathes life into his narrative and points to a quirk in human nature exploited by governments through the ages, and is as valid today as when he wrote it.

Thus Octavian managed to satisfy his own veterans to whom he owed so much and who were the boldest and most vocal in their complaints because they knew that they had made him and so feared him least. Deprived of their moral support the rest had no choice but to accept his word that they would be rewarded from the spoils of Egypt. He had staved off a mutiny, but with the political and economic fruits of victory almost within his grasp it must have been a forcible reminder that all he had worked for with such single-minded purpose since Caesar's death might still be lost, such was the mood of the soldiers and the desperate straits of the Italian economy, unless he could get hold of the Egyptian treasury intact and without overmuch delay.

Some thirty days after his arrival he left Brundisium, and he was soon back in Samos having hauled his ship across the isthmus of Corinth to avoid the winter passage round the Peloponnese. He was still uncertain of Antony's whereabouts, and in his turn Antony only learned of Octavian's hurried journey to Italy at the same time as he heard that he was back in Samos.

PART 6

Requiem in Egypt

CHAPTER XXIV

Octavian: Master of the World

After waiting at Paraetonium for some weeks Antony gave up any hope of winning back the Cyrenaican legions and sailed for Alexandria. There he found Cleopatra firmly in control of Egypt and engaged on several plans to preserve the Ptolemaic dynasty from Octavian. Broadly there were three courses open to her and Antony: to continue the war, to attempt to negotiate, or to abandon Egypt and escape beyond Octavian's reach.

Antony could take command in Asia Minor and Syria and if necessary withdraw through Judaea to hold Pelusium in strength, relying on the Sinai Desert to force Octavian into the coastal bottleneck. Beyond the delta the Western Desert provided a major obstacle to any advance from Cyrenaica unless Gallus and his army of Africa took the coast road, and this could be readily defended with a comparatively small force covering one of the natural defiles. Much rested on how many of the client princes remained loyal, and this largely turned on the attitude of Antony's legate, Didius, who held Syria with at least one and probably two legions. Armenia was already lost: during the Actium campaign Artaxes, backed by Phraates of Parthia, had overrun the new province slaughtering every Roman he could lay hands on, officials, traders and soldiers alike.

Soon after her return to Egypt Cleopatra executed Artaxes's father, Artavasdes, who had been held prisoner in Alexandria since 34. She sent his head to his old enemy and namesake Artavasdes of Media, in a move designed to hold him to his alliance with Egypt; his infant daughter, Iotape, was still in Alexandria as the betrothed of Alexander Helios.

Cleopatra considered sailing to Spain and there establishing herself in the central mountains like Sertorius and Pompey's sons; but the plan she favoured in the last resort was to found a new Hellenistic kingdom beyond Arabia, perhaps between the Persian Gulf and the Indus delta. When Antony arrived from Paraetonium she was already in the process of transferring part of her fleet to the Red Sea. The ships could readily be moved from Alexandria to the mouth of the Pelusiac branch of the Nile and thence upriver. From near Heliopolis a canal ran to the Bitter Lakes, and from there Ptolemy II had completed another canal to Heroonopolis on the Gulf of Suez, but it was silted up and too narrow and shallow for the transports Cleopatra needed to carry her treasure and supplies. Her engineers built a trackway for this last stage and succeeded in hauling the ships twelve miles overland, presumably in cradles mounted on rollers or wheels.

Antony apparently did nothing to assist her in this enterprise; according to Plutarch he considered it unnecessary as he did not yet know that Canidius's army had surrendered, unlikely though this would seem. The other evidence suggests that he was still sunk in apathy and had resigned himself to whatever the Fates might bring.

The contemporary sources for the winter of 31 and the spring of 30 are meagre and confused, and the main secondary accounts are those of Plutarch and Dio. Plutarch's sequence of events is clearly at fault; later, when he appears to draw on the lost memoirs of Cleopatra's doctor, Olympos, he preserves some valuable material and at the same time becomes more sympathetic to her.

Dio elaborates his theme of Cleopatra's betrayal of Antony in describing how she deceived him in her later negotiations with Octavian; but this account is suspect in that both Horace and Virgil, who would surely not have omitted any such further evidence of her treachery, make no reference to this. Instead, as the danger to Rome receded and final victory for Octavian became assured, they both began to acknowledge her courage and fortitude. Antony's lethargy and his lack of resolution added to the dangers which faced her, but other than Dio's there is no real evidence that she ever tried to deceive or betray him.

Antony made no attempt to reassert his authority in Asia Minor, nor did he order Didius to withdraw the garrison of Syria to reinforce the Egyptian army which Cleopatra had deployed to defend the eastern frontier. He may have realised that such an order would not have been obeyed and that it was too late to rally the client princes, though numismatic evidence indicates that some of the states and cities of Asia Minor were still coining in his name late in 31, and possibly even early in 30 while Octavian was in Samos.

That he took no action at all to rally his supporters or even to defend Egypt is a measure of the inertia which held him in the abyss of despair. Instead he had a small pavilion built at the end of a jetty in the Great Harbour and went to live there as a recluse, cutting himself off alike from his own officers and from Cleopatra and affairs of state in the nearby palace; he called it the Timoneum after Timon, a notorious Athenian misanthrope. This too reflects his state of mind; he felt that he had been betrayed by a series of desertions and that it was pointless to oppose Octavian since whatever he attempted would be frustrated by further desertions. But it was hardly the moment to try and create solitude out of the loneliness of betrayal.

Thus the flame that once had burned brightly enough in Antony to warm and inspire others flickered and died when they deserted him, and he drew back into himself. In his philosophy there was a time to live and a time to die, and it seems that it was only reluctance to abandon Cleopatra which held him back from taking his own life.

Now that he had surrendered hope he might stand irresolute between life and death, but Cleopatra had no one else to whom she could turn except this shadow of Antony. And if he was not prepared to abandon her to Octavian nor was she prepared to abandon him, perhaps because she had come to love him in a way she had never done during that first winter in Alexandria.

She had given herself to Caesar to secure the throne of Egypt, and she had come to love him as a young girl, even though she be a Ptolemaic princess, loves such a man as Caesar in his middle life. As a woman and a queen she had given herself to Antony to retain her throne and to further her own ambition; they had come to love each other as two such partners may without sacrificing their own identities or their separate purposes. Certainly, in Antony's own words, neither lost their souls to the other's body. That such a loss is to be envied and admired is no more than a later concept of medieval chivalry. To the Greeks and Romans it was an affliction, and indeed it remains so to some civilisations of our own time, an affliction that Octavian's propaganda tried to attribute to Antony with some success. Shakespeare's only source for his 'Antony and Cleopatra' is believed to have been North's version of Plutarch's Lives from a French translation of the original Greek. He took Plutarch's story of the noble Antony deprived of his Roman birthright and ruined by his passion for Cleopatra, discarded its moral theme and refashioned it with genius into what is more a tragic lyrical love poem than a play. Far removed in time from imperial Rome and freed from the constraints of prudence in his cycle of plays on the lives of the English kings, Shakespeare saw the pomp and circumstance of empire as no more than froth and tinsel. For him Antony's greatness lay in his sacrifice of the world for love; half a century later Dryden echoed him with his title: 'All for Love, Or the World Well Lost'.

It is perhaps only after Actium that the depth and strength of Cleopatra's love for Antony can be discerned, born as it had been out of self interest, nurtured by private happiness and tempered by triumph and disaster on the world's stage. Perhaps more enduring than the theme of the world well lost for love is this bond between them which was the real target for the accusations levelled at Cleopatra.

It was now that she tried to imbue Antony with some measure of her own strength and spirit and so call him back to the present and the threat of the immediate future. She was determined to do all she could to defend her kingdom and save her dynasty. If Antony would not take up arms again she could only try and negotiate with Octavian in the hope that she could buy him off from annexing Egypt and persuade him to allow one of her children to rule as a Roman client. Even if this failed, as seemed likely, it might serve to win time while she and Antony prepared either to fight or flee.

First she had to bring him back to life from the Timoneum. With another than Antony she might have appealed to the Roman virtues of stoicism and duty. As it was she tempted him to return to the palace with the lure of a fantasy world of revelry in which they might while the winter away with feasting and festivities. In an attempt to face and discount the reckoning which the new year must bring the club of 'Inimitable Livers' was dissolved and replaced by the 'Inseparables in Death'; to join this new court circle their friends pledged themselves to die with them. Thus she managed to entice him back to life, but she failed to steel his will and forge his purpose anew.

A lavish public ceremony was staged to mark the coming of age of Caesarion and Antyllus and the celebrations went on for several days with public banquets and festivals. Caesarion, now sixteen and already Cleopatra's co-ruler as Ptolemy XV, was formally enrolled in the ephebes according to the Macedonian custom of the Ptolemies. The white 'toga virilis' of Roman manhood was conferred on Antyllus, who was probably fourteen. Cleopatra may have wished to give notice to the Egyptians that as her co-ruler they now had a king who was an adult. Antony's motives for including his eldest son in this official coming of age are less clear; it is possible that Antyllus demanded it of him. It has been said that this formal recognition of Caesarion and Antyllus as adults was hardly the best way to divert Octavian's attention from them, but he would probably have acted as he did whether they were officially of age or not.

Throughout Egypt all remained quiet. Cleopatra had identified herself with the ancient gods of the Pharaohs, and in Upper Egypt she was accepted and even revered as no other Ptolemy had ever been. The people rallied to her, offering to rise against the threat of Roman invasion. This she forbade, but she began to collect treasure and bullion from all over the country and gather it together in the palace at Alexandria.

Reports from Asia Minor and Syria told of further wholesale desertions prompted by Didius's decision that the time had come for him to change sides; to prepare the ground he prevailed on Malchus, who still cherished his old grudge against Cleopatra, to descend on the Gulf of Suez where he destroyed the fleet she had assembled there with so much labour.

Throughout the whole of Asia Minor only one group remained loyal to Antony; bizarrely these were the gladiators who had been training at Cyzicus to fight in the games to celebrate his victory over Octavian. They decided to join him in Egypt and succeeded in fighting their way through Galatia and Cilicia. But Didius trapped them in Syria after persuading Herod to close the Judaean border. They refused to surrender and sent messages to Antony pledging their support and asking for his help. Finally, when no word came from him, they accepted terms from Didius allowing them to settle in a suburb of Antioch. Later Messala deceived them and split them into small groups by telling them they were to be enlisted in the army, and as Dio puts it they were disposed of in some convenient manner.

Antony may not have been in Alexandria to answer their call for help as Gallus invaded Egypt from Cyrenaica at about this time. Antony took a squadron of warships and a strong force of infantry to hold him at Paraetonium while he attempted to win back Scarpus's four legions; but as he approached their camp to parley Gallus used trumpeters to drown his words and then repulsed his attack. When some of Antony's ships entered the harbour Gallus trapped them by raising a chain boom he had sunk across the entrance. After losing forty ships and achieving nothing on land Antony returned to Alexandria, leaving Gallus in control of Paraetonium with the desert road to the delta open and undefended.

Alarmed by reports that Herod was co-operating with Didius, Antony sent his Greek Syrian secretary, Alexas, to Jerusalem to make sure that Herod at least remained loyal. But always a realist, and with an abiding hatred of Cleopatra, Herod had already decided that Antony's cause was hopeless and was considering how best to make his peace with Octavian. His first move was to eliminate Hyrcanus as a possible alternative client ruler of Judaea: this he did by accusing him of treasonable correspondence with Malchus and executing him. He banished his mother-in-law, Alexandra, to the fortress of Alexandreum and sent his own mother and sister with his wife, Mariamme, and their children to the all but impregnable desert citadel of Masada where they would be safe from seizure as hostages by either side. Then as soon as he heard that Octavian had left Samos in the spring he sailed to Rhodes to meet him.

He entered Octavian's presence wearing his royal robes, but bareheaded and carrying in his hand the crown of Judaea which he offered to Octavian. According to Josephus he made no apology for the part he had played as Antony's friend; instead he promised Octavian that given the opportunity he would prove as good a friend to him as he had been to Antony. His candour and his dignified bearing impressed Octavian who knew well enough that he was perhaps the only man who could rule the Jews and at the same time keep Judaea loyal to Rome. With his own hand he took the crown and placed it on Herod's head.

Herod had persuaded Alexas to come with him and himself seek pardon. But despite all Herod's pleas Octavian refused; he held Alexas to blame for turning Antony against Octavia and he ordered him to be taken back to his native Laodicea for execution.

Herod accompanied Octavian to Ptolemais Ace where he expressed his gratitude with a present of 500 talents; he arranged entertainments in Octavian's honour and organised supplies and accommodation for the Roman army. While he was at Ace Octavian rewarded Berytus with special privileges for the lead the city had taken in revolting against Cleopatra during the Actium campaign; he also ordered Tarcondimotus's son in Amanus and Iamblichus's brother in Emesa to be deposed.

Antony and Cleopatra now tried to come to terms with Octavian, but the course of these negotiations is far from clear. Dio's account, uncorroborated by contemporary sources, seems little more than an imaginative reconstruction designed to fit in with his theme of Cleopatra's betrayal of Antony, while Plutarch's chronology is confused.

Presumably acting in concert they sent envoys to Octavian with separate proposals on three occasions. Through another Greek secretary, possibly Hipparchus son of his steward in Athens. Antony offered to withdraw from public life and live as a private citizen in Athens. Cleopatra, acting according to Dio without Antony's knowledge, sent Octavian a golden crown and sceptre; like Herod's this was a symbolic gesture placing the throne of Egypt at his disposal in the hope that if he was not prepared to confirm her as queen he would allow one of her children to succeed her, and thus save Egypt from annexation and direct rule from Rome.

Octavian did not reply to Antony. He sent word publicly promising Cleopatra lenient treatment if she renounced the throne of Egypt and ordered her army to lay down its arms. But he intimated to her privately that Antony's death or expulsion from Egypt was the price for her throne. His first objective was undoubtedly the seizure of the Egyptian treasury, and his aim was probably to divide Antony and Cleopatra and make her uncertain as to his intentions.

For her part Cleopatra does not appear to have appreciated

Octavian's pressing need for money nor realised that nothing less than all the wealth of Egypt would satisfy him. She sent him presents of gold vessels and bullion with the promise of more to come, though she can scarcely have believed that he could be thus bought off. Antony wrote again reminding him of their partnership as triumvirs and offering to take his own life if Cleopatra was spared.

Dio says that Antony handed over Turullius to Octavian; if he did it was a shameful act of treachery for ever since Sextus's death Turullius had been one of his principal lieutenants. But as well as being out of character it seems an unlikely story, if only because Turullius as one of the last of Caesar's surviving murderers would never have put himself in Octavian's hands of his own free will, and Antony could scarcely have arrested him in Alexandria and sent him as a prisoner.

Again Octavian did not answer Antony and again he sent vague temporising messages to Cleopatra. Undeterred they apparently decided to send one more embassy, evidence in itself of the world of make-believe in which they were living, unable to come to terms with the inevitable and deluded by the absolute power they still exercised in Egypt into believing that Octavian could be bought off or diverted from his purpose by appeals to past friendship. At a loss to find trustworthy envoys who were willing to go they chose Antyllus and their children's Greek tutor, Euphonius; his predecessor in the post, Nicolaus of Damascus, had joined Herod.

If Antony did send his eldest son, and it is again only Dio who says that he did, his motives are obscure. He may have sought to appeal to Octavian through Antyllus who was Octavia's stepson and had once been betrothed to Octavian's own daughter, Julia. According to Dio Octavian took the gold and sent Antyllus back without any reply; but it seems unlikely that Antony would have risked sending him, and if he had that Octavian would not have held him either as a hostage or to protect him for Octavia's sake.

Cleopatra continued to gather together all the treasure which could readily be removed from the palaces and temples of Egypt; among it Plutarch lists gold, silver, emeralds, pearls, ebony, ivory and cinnamon. She collected it all in the two-storied mausoleum which for some years she had been building for herself on the edge of the Great Harbour in the Locias palace quarter near the tombs of the Ptolemies and Alexander himself.

Reports reaching Octavian told of her piling wood against the mausoleum and preparing it for firing with tow and pitch. To prevent her from destroying the treasure he sent a trusted Greek secretary, Thyrsus, with further vague promises and threats designed to confuse her. Antony's suspicions were aroused by Thyrsus's behaviour and the friendly reception Cleopatra gave him: he had him flogged for his impudence and sent him back with a message telling Octavian he could do the same to Hipparchus if he wished.

By midsummer Octavian's army was approaching the Egyptian frontier but Antony made no move to take over from Cleopatra's general, Seleucus, who was defending the key frontier city of Pelusium. When Octavian attacked Seleucus surrendered after no more than a token resistance, acting according to Dio on secret instructions from Cleopatra; Plutarch confirms that there were rumours to this effect. Dio has it that she sacrificed Pelusium because Thyrsus had convinced her that, if she did so, she could expect favourable terms from Octavian.

But if this was so she would surely have found some other way of concealing the truth from Antony, and at the same time repudiating Seleucus in public, other than by condoning the execution of his wife and children. The whole story of the surrender of Pelusium and the death of Seleucus must be taken with caution; Tarn has shown that Dio's later account of Cleopatra's attempt to trick Antony into taking his own life must be suspect, since if it were true it follows that her own attempt at suicide when surprised by Gallus and Proculeius must have been feigned; this however is contrary to the contemporary evidence of Horace and Virgil, who not only fail to corroborate Dio but begin to pay unwilling tribute to Cleopatra's constancy as well as to her courage.

The fall of Pelusium opened the way for Octavian across the northern delta. At about this time Cleopatra sent Caesarion to Upper Egypt in the care of his tutor, Rhodon, with instructions to take ship for the East from a Red Sea port. Coordinating his movements with Octavian, Gallus advanced slowly along the desert road to Alexandria and set up his camp near the Hippodrome. On the last day of the month of July his leading troops covered by a screen of cavalry approached the eastern gate of the city.

Rousing himself at last Antony rode out at the head of a regiment of cavalry, routed Octavian's advanced guard and pursued them as they fled in disorder back to the Hippodrome. There he shot leaflets into their camp promising 6,000 sesterces to each man who changed sides, but Octavian read them out himself to his soldiers, ridiculing Antony as he did so. Antony returned to the city in triumph, and still in his armour he presented one of his troopers who had distinguished himself in the battle to Cleopatra; she rewarded him with a golden helmet and breastplate but that very evening he deserted to Octavian. Antony's confidence was temporarily restored by his own success in leading the counter-attack and he sent a message challenging Octavian to single combat; the only response was a terse suggestion that he could surely find a better way to die.

That afternoon Antony issued orders for battle by land and sea on the following day. At dinner he called for more wine, telling his servants that only the Fates could tell whether by the next evening they would be waiting on Octavian and his officers while he lay dead on the field of battle. When some of his friends wept at his words he told them that he did not want to involve them in the fighting, since he could not hope for victory and only sought an honourable death for himself.

Plutarch describes an aura of impending doom which seemed to gather over the city when all was quiet later that summer evening. At around midnight the silence was broken by the singing of a choir accompanied by music from every kind of instrument. The sound of voices could be heard as if from a festive procession winding its way from the centre of the city towards the eastern gate. There the music died away again, and once more silence lay on the city. Those who heard the invisible choir and the voices of the revellers believed that it was Dionysius abandoning Antony and Alexandria. This story of Plutarch's follows the ancient legend of how the gods leave a doomed city before its fall. The modern Alexandrian poet, Cavafy, took it as the theme of a poem in which he enjoins Antony not to mourn what might have been, not to deny the evidence of his senses, but to accept it as his farewell to the city he loved.

The next morning, by the current Roman calendar the first day of Sextilis which was later to be renamed August in Octavian's honour, Antony drew up his army on the high ground outside the Canopic Gate. From here he watched his fleet put out from the Great Harbour, the ships packed with soldiers and cleared for action. They rowed slowly to meet the enemy fleet, but, instead of the usual exchange of fire and manoeuvering for position as they closed, their oars came up together as if on a signal. Octavian's ships raised their own oars to accept the surrender and the two fleets came together; after a time they moved on as one towards the entrance to the Great Harbour.

The whole army had witnessed this mass surrender by the fleet. The cavalry were the first to ride off towards Octavian's line of battle with their swords sheathed and their lances raised, and they were soon followed by some of the auxiliaries. Octavian advanced to the attack and for a time Antony's legions resisted half-heartedly; then some surrendered and the others broke and fled.

Denied the death he had looked for in battle by this last desertion Antony rode back to the city, crying out in his despair that Cleopatra and the fleet had betrayed him. He made his way to the palace, but she

349

had either anticipated the outcome or already had news of it for she had hurried to the unfinished mausoleum with her two attendants, Iras and Charmian; there they had shut themselves in and barricaded the ground floor door. Dio's story that she sent a messenger to tell Antony that she had taken her own life is almost certainly untrue; but he may well have heard rumours arising from her taking refuge in the mausoleum and he evidently believed that she was dead.

As his servant, Eros, helped him to take off his armour, Antony, according to Plutarch, exclaimed:-

'Cleopatra, I am ashamed that I have shown less courage than you; I will join you soon.'

Long ago he had made Eros swear that if the need arose he would help him to die. Antony now reminded him of his oath and told him that the time had come to keep his word. Eros drew his sword and raised it as if for Antony to run on; then he suddenly reversed it and fell on it himself. Antony cried out:-

'That was well done; you have shown me what I must do, even if you had not the heart to do it.'

He drew his own sword and tried to drive it two-handed into his chest but the blade slipped and entered his stomach, and he fell bleeding and unconscious. After a time the bleeding eased and he recovered consciousness; he implored his other servants to finish him off but they ran in panic from the room, leaving him twisting and turning in agony and calling for help.

Garbled reports of what had happened soon reached Cleopatra in the mausoleum and she sent a secretary who was outside to investigate. When Antony realised that she was still alive he insisted on being taken to her. The door of the mausoleum was so effectively barred and barricaded from the inside that it could not be opened. At Cleopatra's direction Iras and Charmian lowered some builder's ropes from the upper window. Antony was placed in an improvised sling and the three women began to haul him up. Plutarch appears to call on an eyewitness's account in describing the conscious but mortally wounded Antony reaching out his arms to Cleopatra as he swung helplessly below her; the three women, their faces contorted by the strain, struggled to the limits of their strength to pull him up while the onlookers encouraged them and tried to lend them strength.

At last they got him high enough to slide through the window and into the room where they laid him on a couch. When Cleopatra realised that he was dying she gave way to her grief, smearing his blood on her face and crying out to him as her lord and master.

Antony did his best to calm her and asked for a glass of wine. He begged her to look to her own safety, though not at the price of her honour, and advised her to put her trust in Gaius Proculeius, one of Octavian's officers. This is perhaps a fictional insertion to fit in with later events, for there is no known reason why Antony should have recommended Proculeius, an officer of equestrian rank on Octavian's staff and Maecenas's brother-in-law.

He told her not to grieve at his own fate, but rather to count him fortunate in winning honour and glory as great as any man had ever won, adding that he was content to die a Roman, honourably vanquished only by another Roman; this last may well be an invention by friends designed to rehabilitate his memory in Rome. Seneca refers to an unnamed contemporary poet who quotes Antony's last words as:-
'Whatever I have given, that I still have.'

Only Cleopatra and her two women can have known what passed between her and Antony, though it is possible that both Plutarch and Seneca's anonymous poet drew on the memoirs of her doctor, Olympos, who visited her shortly afterwards. What is certain is that Antony died in the arms of the woman he loved, and who at the last loved him. Now she was indeed alone, incarcerated with Iras and Charmian and the dead Antony in her own mausoleum piled high with the treasures of Egypt and ready for firing as her funeral pyre.

CHAPTER XXV

The Last of the Ptolemies

When Antony was carried from the palace to the mausoleum one of his freedmen picked up his blood-stained sword and took it to Octavian in the hope of being rewarded for this evidence of Antony's death. According to Plutarch, Octavian went into his tent and wept at the news. Then he called his staff together and read out to them the letters he had written to Antony, emphasising their moderate and conciliatory tone and contrasting them with those Antony had written to him. It would seem unlikely that he had with him in the field copies of his correspondence with Antony over the years, though he may well have used the moment to stress his past forbearance. But he was hardly the man to grieve for Antony as once Caesar had grieved for Pompey and Antony for Brutus; if he retired to his tent it may have been to conceal his relief rather than his grief.

He was more concerned with the living Cleopatra and the treasure in the mausoleum. All resistance had collapsed with Antony's death and Octavian entered Alexandria later on the same day. He sent Proculeius at once to Cleopatra; while it is conceivable that she had asked for him, his arrival so soon after Antony's death suggests that the story of Antony's recommending him to Cleopatra was indeed a later addition.

Proculeius talked to her through a grating in the barred ground floor door, urging her to take heart and put her trust in Octavian and her person in his hands. For her part she insisted that her children must be spared and one of them allowed to succeed her. Probably Proculeius's instructions were to seize her if he could, and in the meantime to make sure that she did not set fire to the mausoleum and destroy the treasure. As he parleyed with her through the door he was assessing ways of breaking in and taking her alive.

He reported to Octavian who sent Gallus back with him the next morning. As Octavian's legate commanding an army Gallus could negotiate with more authority. While he was speaking to Cleopatra through the grating, and so diverting her attention, Proculeius brought up a ladder and he and two of his men climbed in through the first floor window. As they ran downstairs one of her women screamed a warning to Cleopatra who was still talking through the door to Gallus. She swung round, and seeing Proculeius pulled a dagger from her belt; but before she could use it on herself he threw his arms round her and snatched it away. He then shook out her clothes and searched her for concealed poison, telling her all the time that she had nothing to fear.

Thus Octavian secured the treasure intact and now held Cleopatra a prisoner in her own mausoleum. He put one of Proculeius's Greek freedmen, Epaphroditus, in charge of guarding her, telling him to let her have any comforts she asked for but to make sure that she did not take her own life. He allowed her request to supervise the preliminary embalming of Antony's body and gave orders that he should be buried with honour; the funeral probably took place two or three days after his death.

Octavian made his formal entry into the city with the philosopher, Areius, his adviser on Egyptian affairs, at his side. The Alexandrians were summoned to the Gymnasium and when Octavian mounted the tribunal they prostrated themselves before him. But he told them in his halting Greek that they had nothing to fear; he promised to spare their city out of regard for Areius and because of his respect for its founder, Alexander. He pardoned their leaders, fining the more prominent citizens and imposing a wealth tax of two-thirds of their property on the richest; he used some of the proceeds to give each of his soldiers 1,000 sesterces as compensation for not sacking the city.

With the treasure so conveniently gathered together by Cleopatra in his hands and all the wealth and resources of the country at his disposal Octavian could afford to be generous in rewarding his soldiers and satisfying his veterans. All that he had striven and schemed and fought for at last was his. At the age of thirty two he was now the undisputed master of the Roman world, and that world awaited his orders; during the rest of his long life he was to devote his considerable political and administrative talents to organising and ruling it.

But first there was the problem of what to do with Cleopatra, held under guard probably with her three younger children; Caesarion had last been heard of making his way up the Nile in a bid to escape to the East. Octavian had no intention of allowing Cleopatra or any of her children to continue the Ptolemaic dynasty even as clients of Rome.

Antyllus was betrayed by his tutor, Theodorus, and sought refuge in the temple Cleopatra was building to Antony, later to be completed as the Caesareum and dedicated to Caesar. He was dragged from the sanctuary by soldiers acting on Octavian's orders and summarily executed outside the temple. Theodorus was accused of stealing the precious stone Antyllus was wearing round his neck, and despite his protestations of innocence he was crucified.

Long afterwards Octavian was to write in his Res Gestae that he pardoned all who asked for pardon; but there were some he could not pardon. The last survivors of Caesar's murderers, Cassius of Parma and Turullius, were condemned to death; as a gesture to the people of Cos, and to Asclepius whose sacred groves Turullius had felled to furnish timber for Antony's ships, he was returned there for execution. Canidius paid with his life for his loyalty to Antony, and as a posthumous insult to a brave and able soldier Velleius wrote that he died without dignity. Ovinius, a Roman senator who managed Cleopatra's textile mills, was also executed.

But Octavian was reluctant to order the execution of a woman, a practice hardly ever resorted to by the Romans even in the most bitter of civil wars. Widely worshipped as the reincarnation of Isis, Cleopatra's death at the hands of the feared and hated Romans could well provoke the popular uprising in Egypt which she herself had forbidden. He knew well enough what passion the name of the murdered Caesar could arouse, and he had no mind to present Egypt with a divine martyr. Nor could he risk exiling her, as one day he would exile his own daughter and granddaughter, for wherever he chose her living person would inevitably provide a focus for disaffection in Egypt and throughout the East.

To take back the proud Queen, who had arrogantly threatened Rome itself, to walk as a subdued and humbled captive before his chariot would add lustre to his Triumph; and no doubt the idea appealed to his vanity and his senses. But his cold and logical mind would have quickly marshalled the reasons for not doing so: he had united Italy in a holy war against her and the threat from the East which she personified, but once that threat had been removed the people of Rome might not take kindly to being reminded that they had gone in fear of a woman. He would recall too how the fickle crowds were moved to pity and protest at the sight of her sister, Arsinoe, walking in Caesar's triumphal procession. Cleopatra had once been Caesar's mistress as well as Antony's Egyptian wife and partner in the war: her statue still stood where Octavian's divine father had placed it in the temple he had built to honour Venus, patron of the Julian family. At the end of his Triumph the attitude of the people might make it almost impossible to have her strangled in sacrifice to Jupiter as was the Roman custom for vanquished kings and princes. Then the question of what to do with her would remain, and perhaps become even more difficult to resolve. Much as it might have satisfied him to have a shackled Cleopatra walk before his triumphal chariot the risks were all too evident.

So it would be convenient if she would take her own life, always provided that there was no overt Roman complicity. Distraught at Antony's death, and in despair at finding herself a prisoner and losing the treasure which was her only bargaining counter, Cleopatra refused to eat. But Octavian wanted no stories that the Romans had starved her to death and he made her break her fast with threats of the consequences to her children if she persisted. She was determined that she would not be preserved to grace his Triumph, but she still seems to have clung to the hope that he would allow one of the children to succeed her. Plutarch implies that she continued to be held prisoner in the mausoleum, but according to Dio she was removed under guard to the palace and if this was so it may have been now that she was transferred.

If Octavian had intended to take her to Rome he would hardly have made Epaphroditus her chief gaoler; nor would he have allowed Olympos and Egyptian court officials unsupervised access to her. Instead he would surely have mounted a military guard commanded by a Roman officer he could trust. As it was, while ensuring that he could not be held responsible, he appears to have given her every opportunity to take her own life; but this she did not do.

Both Plutarch and Dio say that a meeting took place between Cleopatra and Octavian, though no contemporary source mentions this. It is difficult to understand what he had to gain from such a meeting other than perhaps to satisfy his own curiosity, and he had almost certainly already met her in Rome after Caesar's return from Spain in 45. He had much to lose: he had deliberately played on Roman fears that Antony would move the capital to Alexandria, fears that had originally been aroused by rumours about Caesar's intentions during the winter he spent in Egypt, and in Rome these fears were very real. Caesar himself had succumbed to her wiles and Antony to her ambitions; the less Octavian had to do with her the better.

Plutarch and Dio may have believed stories of such a meeting to be true since they provided the logical dramatic climax. Dio's description of the wanton and promiscuous Cleopatra trying to move the upright and unbending Octavian with feminine guile and tearful appeals to Caesar's memory reads like a fictional exercise. But it is impossible to say whether such a meeting between the first of the Roman emperors and the last of the Ptolemies ever in fact took place. If it did no reliance can be put on Plutarch's and Dio's accounts, and what passed between Cleopatra and Octavian can only be conjectured.

After nearly a week Octavian grew impatient. He sent one of his staff officers, Publius Cornelius Dolabella, son or kinsman of the consul of 44, to Cleopatra; he told her that Octavian would leave Egypt shortly and hinted that he proposed to take her with him. Whether or not she believed this she evidently decided that the time had come for her to die.

The sequence of events is complicated by errors in the current Roman calendar, which since Caesar's reform had already slipped two days behind the historical Julian calendar; by the latter Antony died on the third day of August. Skeat has suggested that Cleopatra's death came nine days after Antony's on the tenth of Sextilis by the current Roman reckoning, the seventeenth of the Egyptian month Mesore, and that Octavian's official reign in Egypt began on the first day of the following month, Thoth, the Egyptian New Year's Day; this would account for the notional eighteen days rule by Cleopatra's children which was apparently inserted in the records by Egyptian officials after the Roman annexation in order to eliminate any interregnum. Others have argued that the interval of nine days is too short for the known events.

The ancient sources all agree that different accounts circulated as to how Cleopatra chose to end her life; one was that she had secreted poison to rub into a skin laceration, another that a snake was smuggled in to her. But clearly she had already made her preparations. The effects of various poisons were known to Egyptian medicine and science; the story that she had experimented on criminals to find the most painless poison can be discounted, for she had no need to do so since this was well known. Galen mentions that the bite of a cobra was sometimes used in Egypt as the most humane method of execution.

Loosely guarded as she was, probably by design, and with access through her doctor to the Alexandrian school of medicine, she had no difficulty in putting her plan into effect. The account which came to be accepted was that a snake, or pair of snakes, was smuggled in to her concealed in a water jar or a basket of figs. This story may have gained credence because her effigy carried in Octavian's Triumph wore a replica of the crown of the Ptolemies with its intertwined snakes. Propertius and others who watched the procession perhaps misinterpreted the symbolism and from it assumed that she had died from the bite of a snake; in fact the Egyptian cobras from the delta of the Nile had been the heraldic protectors of the Pharaohs for thousands of years and the Ptolemies had adopted their device. But Cleopatra was intensely proud of her lineage and it may well be true that she chose the bite of a royal cobra.

First with Octavian's leave she went to Antony's tomb to pour a libation. Plutarch probably invented the verbatim account of her cry from the heart to the dead Antony. But she did not go unescorted and someone may well have heard her prayer that she and Antony who had not been divided in life might be together in death. If this was reported to Octavian he did nothing to prevent her from taking her own life.

She wrote to him asking to be buried with Antony, and dissembling the contents of the letter she gave it to Epaphroditus to send to Octavian. Instead of using a courier he took it himself, afterwards declaring that he had been deceived at the time by her composure and serenity; it may well have been that with her mind made up to die, and the chosen means to hand, she seemed to him happy and free of care. Nevertheless if his instructions were to preserve her alive it appears strange that he should have left her alone with Iras and Charmian and unobserved by the guards outside.

When Octavian read the letter he knew that he had had his way. The story that he at once sent for the pselli, famed for their power to suck out snake venom, is probably true since it would have been too easy to refute; but it does not explain why he sent for them before he knew how she had chosen to die.

Iras and Charmian helped her to dress in her state robes and placed the crown of Egypt on her head. Then according to the accepted story she took the two cobras to her person and provoked them with a pin until they struck.

When Octavian's men arrived they alerted the guards and burst open the door. Cleopatra was lying dead on a gilt couch; at her feet Iras lay dying while Charmian, hardly able to stand herself, was straightening the crown on Cleopatra's head. One of the guards shouted angrily:-

'Is this well done?'

'It is very well done' Charmian replied. 'And right and
proper for a Queen who is the heir of so many Kings.'

With this she too collapsed, her last words a fitting epitaph for Cleopatra; it is not known what poison she and Iras had taken in order that they might not outlive the mistress they had served so faithfully.

Octavian granted Cleopatra's wish to be buried with Antony and ordered that statues of Iras and Charmian should be set up outside the mausoleum. Now only Caesarion remained as a possible threat. But as they fled south his tutor persuaded him that Octavian might after all allow him to rule Egypt, and while they waited, perhaps for the latest news from Alexandria, he was betrayed and captured. It seems unlikely that Octavian needed Areius's advice that there must not be too many Caesars in deciding that Caesarion must die; the divine Julius could have no other son but Octavian, and there could be no future for a youth whom half the world believed to be Caesar's son.

Octavian had neither the time nor the inclination for sightseeing and he did not linger long in Egypt. He did visit Alexander's tomb where he inadvertently broke the nose off the embalmed body, but he refused to inspect the dead Ptolemies or enter the temple of Apis, remarking that he had not come to see the bodies of dead kings and was accustomed to worship gods not animals.

There was much to be done: the Roman East had to be reorganised, and then he could devote himself to reshaping the whole Roman world. First there was Egypt; it was too rich in natural resources, too important strategically as well as economically, and above all too distant in time from Rome to warrant making it another province, with the ever present risk that some over-ambitious governor might persuade the Egyptians to revolt. Octavian had probably already decided that the country would be annexed and administered as his own personal fief; he chose Gallus as his prefect. Gallus's subsequent conduct amply justified Octavian's fears: he raised statues of himself all over Egypt, cut self-laudatory inscriptions on the Pyramids, mounted a military expedition into Upper Egypt without authority from Rome and made a treaty with Ethiopia. In the end he was recalled in disgrace and committed suicide.

Augustan writers were to praise Octavian for saving the Roman East from Cleopatra's grasping hands and from Antony's spendthrift policy of giving away Roman territory. The truth is different: Cyprus and Cyrenaica reverted to direct Roman rule, but Octavian made no other changes in the basic framework Antony had established consisting of the three provinces of Asia, Bithynia and Syria and the four major client kingdoms; Amyntas of Galatia, Archelaus of Cappadocia, Polemo of Pontus, and Herod of Judaea all retained their thrones and were to prove themselves capable rulers as well as loyal friends and allies of Rome. This is a tribute both to Antony's judgement, and to Octavian's wisdom in recognising the worth of these arrangements and in refraining from any attempt to recover Armenia or confront Parthia.

Although Octavian took no action against Artaxes of Armenia he refused to return his brothers, retaining them as hostages in Egypt because of the massacre of Roman citizens in Armenia; he also allowed Tiridates, Artaxes's defeated rival for the throne, to live in exile in Syria. He gave Lesser Armenia to Artavasdes of Media to counter any threat from Armenia, and he returned the king's daughter, Iotape, who had been betrothed to Alexander Helios.

Antony's three children by Cleopatra were sent back to Rome and Alexander Helios and Cleopatra Selene walked in Octavian's triumphal procession. Octavia took charge of them and brought them up with her own children; that she cared for Cleopatra's children is evidence enough of her goodness of heart, and perhaps also a measure of her abiding love for Antony. Cleopatra Selene was married to Juba's son, who as Juba II became the client king of Mauretania when in 25 Octavian allowed that province to revert to its old status. Their son Ptolemaios succeeded to the throne in AD 23, and was murdered in Rome in AD 40 on the orders of his cousin, Caligula. Little more is heard of Alexander Helios and Ptolemy Philadelphus who lived with their sister after her marriage. Iullus, Antony's younger son by Fulvia was with Octavia, and it was perhaps on her insistence that Octavian gave him his proper share of Antony's Roman estate.

It was nearly two months before news of Antony's death and Octavian's annexation of Egypt reached Rome; the seizure of the Egyptian treasury prompted an immediate fall in the current rate of loan interest from 12% to 4%. In the Senate Cicero's son was invited to read the despatch reporting Antony's death. Now that he was dead the senators took their revenge: they decreed that his birthday should be deemed an unlucky day, and they ordered his name to be erased from all inscriptions and public buildings and his statues to be cast down and destroyed. There is epigraphic evidence that this was done: even Antony's grandfather's name was partly chipped away from an inscription commemorating the hauling of his ships across the isthmus of Corinth. This may have been simply a mistake, or possibly the result of another order forbidding the use of the names Marcus Antonius in conjunction; by decree there were to be no more Mark Antonys. The destruction of Antony's statues must cast doubt on the modern identification of some as being of him.

Cleopatra's gilded statue was allowed to remain where Caesar had placed it in his temple to Venus, and there is evidence that it was still standing there in the third century AD; in Egypt one of her friends, Archibius, paid Octavian 1,000 talents to save her statues from being thrown down.

Herod did not change the name of the Antonias, the fortress palace he was building in Jerusalem to overawe the Jews and dominate the Temple itself. Several communities in Asia Minor continued to use the name of their old patron, as did individual soldiers and freedmen who had adopted it when enfranchised or manumitted. Antony's daughter by his cousin and first wife, Antonia, had married Pythodorus, and their daughter, Pythodoris, married two of the client kings in turn, Polemo and Archelaus; her son by Polemo was named Marcus Antonius Polemo. In Rome Iullus grew up to marry his stepsister, Marcella, Octavia's daughter by Marcellus; he was consul in 10 and governed Asia in 7/6, but in 2 he was condemned to death for adultery with Octavian's daughter, Julia, and took his own life.

It was through his daughters by Octavia, the two Antonias, that Antony's blood ran on in the Julian Claudian emperors until their dynasty came to an end with Nero's death in AD 68. The elder of the two, usually known as Antonia Major, married Lucius Domitius Ahenobarbus, son of the Ahenobarbus who died before Actium; their son Gnaeus was Nero's father, and their daughter, Domitia Lepida, was the mother of Messalina who married her cousin Claudius and bore him Britannicus. Claudius was himself Antony's grandson, for Antonia Minor married Livia's youngest son, Drusus, and their sons were Germanicus and Claudius. Germanicus married Agrippina, daughter of Agrippa and Octavian's daughter, Julia; their son Gaius, the Emperor Caligula, was thus both Antony's and Octavian's grandson. He was succeeded by his uncle Claudius, also Antony's grandson; after Messalina's death Claudius married his niece, Julia Agrippina, daughter of his brother Germanicus and Agrippina, and Nero's mother through her previous marriage to Gnaeus Domitius Ahenobarbus. Nero was thus Antony's great-grandson through Antonia Major and his great-great-grandson through Antonia Minor, as well as Octavian's great-great-grandson through Julia, and Ahenobarbus's great-grandson on the male side.

Thus Antony's blood ran down through this complex tangled lineage to mingle with Octavian's and Livia's, Octavia's and Ahenobarbus's, in the Julian Claudian emperors. In this manner he was to play his part in the first century of imperial Roman rule which Octavian's victory had begun, instead of in the equal partnership between East and West which he and Cleopatra had briefly seemed to offer.

It has been widely said and commonly accepted that it was well for the world that Octavian triumphed since he laid the foundations from which the nation states of Europe would emerge. And this is true, in that for four centuries Rome brought peace and unity to the Mediterranean world and held back the mounting pressures from the migrating tribes of northern Europe and central Asia. But essentially it is the view of those same nation states who were the heirs of Rome, and it must be asked for whom Octavian's victory was fortunate. The price was also four centuries of political and economic exploitation and the imposition of an increasingly sterile Latin culture which had already come to its full flowering in the late Republic.

It was through Constantine that the direct heirs of Greece in the Hellenistic civilizations of the eastern Mediterranean fused with that of Rome; it was Byzantium that held the ring for western Christendom for a thousand years and made possible the renaissance of the western nation states. Thus it could be argued that Octavian's victory postponed this partnership of East and West.

Research may have thrown more light on the history of the time, but little consideration has been given to what might have been if Antony and Cleopatra had been the victors at Actium. Such speculation may be fruitless, but it is a reflection on man himself if the vision of harmony and concord between the nations from the Atlantic to the Euphrates is to be dismissed as no more than an unrealisable dream. The Jews had prophesied that Cleopatra's victory would herald a new Golden Age and the birth of the Messiah; who can tell what the old and the new religions might not have achieved in such a world, who can say that our present human lot might not have been happier. For Shakespeare, Antony's greatness lay in the sacrifice of his birthright for love, and he reshaped Plutarch's Life into the most moving of his tragedies, the story, as in Dryden's title, of a world well lost for love. It may be that the future will see a different tragedy on a wider human stage.

Antony and Cleopatra still lie together deep in some hidden vault under the site of the mausoleum which once stood on the edge of the Great Harbour. High above them the life of Alexandria goes on, vibrant, teeming, cosmopolitan, alive with light and noise and colour, in essentials little changed from that of the city they knew and loved, the city which once was theirs and now protects their resting place. Let them sleep on together in peace undisturbed by the robbers of tombs, for theirs was no ignoble a dream. In our minds they live on, for their story belongs to all of human time, to time past and time future as well as to our own present.

Let the last words be Antony's:

'Whatever I have given that I still have.'

APPENDIX

Roman Personal Names

Every Roman citizen had at least two names, the praenomen, or personal name, and the nomen, or name of the gens, or group of families linked by a common name and a common ancestor. Many men, though not women during the Republic, had a third name, the cognomen: this was sometimes a nickname or inherited family nickname, sometimes the name of a sub-division of the family group. In theory women had two names, but the feminine of the family name was often used to the exclusion of the personal name, especially among the upper classes. On marriage women did not take their husbands' names.

Examples:-
(a) Gaius Julius Caesar
    praenomen: Gaius
    nomen: Julius, indicating the Julian family
    cognomen: Caesar, indicating the Caesarian branch of
                   the Julian family

(b) Marcus Antonius
    praenomen: Marcus
    nomen: Antonius, indicating the Antonian family
    cognomen: none

Antony's three Roman daughters were all called Antonia; though probably they had personal names these were not used outside the family, and are not known to history.

Within the family the praenomen was normally used, among friends either the nomen or praenomen, and on formal occasions the praenomen with either nomen or cognomen. As in any society the pattern and custom in the use of personal names evolved and altered over the centuries, particularly during the Empire.

The Oxford Classical Dictionary has a useful article on Roman personal names.

Roman Units

1. Distance

The Roman mile was 1000 paces each of five Roman feet (each 296 mm); it was divided into 8 stades each of 125 paces.
.1 Roman mile = 1522 metres or 1665 yards

2. Area

1 iugerum   = $^5/_8$ acre
1 iugerum   = $^1/_4$ hectare
200 iugera = 1 centuria
200 iugera = 50 hectares
200 iugera = 124 acres

3. Weights

The Roman pound, the libra, was equivalent to 327 grams, or a little less than $^3/_4$ of an English pound.
The talent was originally a measure of one man's load, and the Greek standards varied between equivalents of 26 and 38 kilograms. It was divided into 60 minae, each on the lighter standard approximately equivalent to one English pound.

4. Measures

The Roman sextarius was equivalent to .55 litre or approximately one English pint. For dry measures a modius consisted of 16 sextarii, equivalent to approximately two English dry gallons. For liquid measures the amphora was used as the bulk unit and for calculating the cargo capacity of ships; it contained approximately 26 litres or 5.7 English gallons.

Numbering of the
Ptolemies

The Ptolemy Kings of Egypt used additional names instead of numbers to distinguish themselves from their predecessors. There is a divergence among historians over the numbers given to the later Ptolemies. This arises because Ptolemy Neos Philopater is usually, but not always, included as Ptolemy VII. The more generally accepted practice of including him has been followed here, so that Ptolemy Auletes, father of Cleopatra, is Ptolemy XII; his sons, Cleopatra's brothers or half-brothers, are Ptolemy XIII and XIV, and Caesarion, Cleopatra's son by Caesar, is Ptolemy XV.

Cleopatra, mistress of Caesar and wife of Antony, is always herself numbered as Cleopatra VII, but there is again a divergence over the numbering of the earlier Cleopatras. This arises because it is not certain whether the Cleopatra Tryphaena, here numbered VI, who briefly ruled Egypt 58-57 after the expulsion of Auletes, was his eldest daughter and hence Cleopatra's sister or half-sister, or whether she was one and the same person as the Cleopatra Tryphaena, here numbered V, the sister whom Auletes married, and hence the mother or stepmother of Cleopatra, acting as regent after his expulsion. The Cleopatra Tryphaena whom Auletes married was certainly the mother of Berenice and probably of Cleopatra. The name of Auletes' second wife, mother of Arsinoe and Ptolemy XIII, is not known. Here it is taken that Cleopatra V was Cleopatra's mother and Cleopatra VI her eldest sister.

Money

It is probably misleading, and certainly of only transient relevance to attempt to convert the money which the Romans used into present day terms. In the late Republic the principal coins were the silver denarius and the copper, bronze or brass sestertius and as; the gold aureus was not in general use, though Caesar used his spoils from Gaul to strike a number of issues in gold, and there were more in the Imperatorial period to 30 BC. No coin smaller than an as has ever been found on a Roman military site of the period.

The denarius, roughly equivalent to the Greek drachm, was effectively revalued from 10 as to 16 between 133 and 122 BC; this was made official in 85. The sestertius, in which the Romans continued to reckon large sums, was worth 4 as, and there were 4 sesterces to the denarius.

In the middle 40s Caesar doubled the basic legionary pay to 225 denarii a year. In his prosecution of Verres in 70 Cicero implies that wheat grain cost something over 6 sesterces a modius (roughly six kilograms).

Inflation and debasement of the coinage did not become a serious problem until later in the Empire, and the following figures from inscriptions at Pompeii in the 1st century AD can be used as a rough guide to the price of bread and wine in the previous century:-

1 modius of wheat . . . . .30 as
a measure of ordinary wine . . . . .1 as
a measure of good wine .2 as
a measure of best wine .4 as

Martial mentions 20 as and Columnella 60 as as the price of an amphora (roughly 26 litres) of wine of unspecified quality.

The talent of gold or silver was originally a Greek term for the load one man can carry, the lighter and more common standard being roughly equivalent to 26 kilograms. As a monetary unit the more normal talent of silver is sometimes taken as the equivalent of 6000 drachmae.

During the late Republic the approximate bullion exchange rate was 1 to 10 for gold to silver and 1 to 50 for silver to bronze.

Perhaps the best short appraisal is 'Money and Exchange in the Roman World', Michael Crawford, J.R.S. 1970.

Antony's Coins

Antony's coin issues start after Caesar's assassination in March 44 when he was 39, and they form a continuous series until the battle of Actium in 31 BC and his death a year later. They illustrate his fluctuating fortunes and graphically demonstrate the transition in fourteen short years from a man in the early prime of life to the prematurely aged, heavy jowled, bullnecked portraits of 31 BC. These coins, together with the unique series of legionary issues, honouring every one of his individual legions, are a subject in themselves. See Seaby, Roman Silver Coins, Vol. I, and J.M.C.Toynbee's Roman Historical Portraits.

Coins illustrated: (Page xxiv)

ANTONY: Denarius, c. 44 BC
Obverse: Antony's head between vase and lituus (an augur's staff), veiled and bearded in mourning for Caesar. Perhaps the first coin struck after Caesar's death.
B.M.C. 4178.
Seaby, Antony, 74.

ANTONY: Denarius, c. 42 BC
Obverse: Antony's head, bearded. This coin commemorates the victory at Philippi.
B.M.C. 4293.
Seaby, Antony, 4.

ANTONY: Denarius, 41/40 BC
Obverse: Antony's head with lituus behind.
Legend: ANT. IMP. III. VIR. R.P.C.
(Antonius Imperator Tresviri Reipublicae Constituendae: triumvir for the reconstitution of the Republic). Reverse shows the prow of a ship, a star of 14 rays and the legend:
CN. DOMIT. AHENOBARBUS IMP.
This coin marks the reconciliation of Antony with Ahenobarbus.
B.M.C. 112.
Seaby, Antony, 10a.

ANTONY and AUGUSTUS: Denarius, 40/39 BC
Obverse: Antony's head with star below.
Legend: M. ANTON. IMP. III. VIR. R.P.C.
This coin was probably struck by Antony to mark his reconciliation with Octavian at Brundisium.
B.M.C. East 121.
Seaby, Antony and Augustus, I.

ANTONY: Denarius, 36 BC
Obverse: Antony's head.
Legend: ANTONIVS AVGVR COS. DES. ITER. ET TERT.
(Antonius, Augur, Consul designate again, and for the third time)
The reverse of this coin shows the Armenian tiara with bow and arrow and bears legend:
IMP. TERTIO III. VIR. R.P.C.
This coin refers to Antony's attack on Media and Parthia in 36.
B.M.C. East 172.
Seaby, Antony, 19.

ANTONY: Denarius, 31 BC
Obverse: Antony's head.
Legend: M.ANTONIVS AVG. IMP. III. COS. TERT.III. VIR. R.P.C.
(Augur, Imperator four times, consul three times, triumvir).
Reverse: shows Victory.
This coin refers to the victory he promised his army and fleet at Actium.
B.M.C. East 228.
Seaby, Antony, 81.

Other Coin Portraits from Roman Denarii

Coins illustrated: (Page xxv)

CAESAR: Denarius, c. 44 BC
  Obverse: Laurelled head of Caesar; behind crescent between P. and
  M. (Pontifex Maximus).
  Legend: CAESAR IM. P.M.
  One of the last coins struck before Caesar's assassination.
  B.M.C. 4152.
  Seaby, Caesar, 22.

BRUTUS: Denarius, c. 43/42 BC
  Obverse: Brutus' head.
  Legend: BRVT. IMP. L. PLAET. CEST.
  This coin celebrates the assassination of Caesar. Lucius Plaetorius
  Cestianus was the moneyer responsible. The reverse shows the
  Cap of Liberty between two daggers and bears the legend: EID
  MAR (Ides of March).
  B.M.C. 68.
  Seaby, Brutus, 15.

ANTONY and CLEOPATRA: Denarius, 32/31 BC
  (a) Obverse: Cleopatra's head with diadem and draped bust on
  prow of ship.
  Legend: CLEOPATRAE REGINAE REGVM FILIORVM
  REGVM.
  (Queen of Kings and her sons who are Kings).
  (b) Reverse: Antony's head, Armenian tiara behind.
  Legend: ANTONI ARMENIA DEVICTA
  This coin refers to the Alexandrian Donations and Antony's
  conquest of Armenia in 34.
  B.M.C. East 179.
  Seaby, Cleopatra and Antony, 1.

AGRIPPA and AUGUSTUS: Denarius, 13 BC
    (a) Obverse: head of Agrippa with mural and rostral crown.
    Legend: M. AGRIPPA COS. TER. COSSVS LENTVLVS.
    Cossus Lentulus was the moneyer responsible.
    (b) Reverse: head of Augustus with oak wreath.
    Legend: AVGVSTVS COS. XI.
    This coin, struck some eighteen years later, is one of the few
    denarii with a portrait of Agrippa.
    B.M.C. 4671 Imp.
    Seaby, Agrippa and Augustus, 1.

ANTONY: Denarius, 41 BC (Dustjacket)
    Obverse: Antony's head
    Legend: M.ANT. IMP. AVG. III. VIR. R.P.C. M.NERVA
    PROQ. P.
    M. Nerva was Antony's proquaestor or financial officer in the
    East. This coin was struck when Antony's brother was consul in
    41, and the reverse bears Lucius's balding head.
    B.M.C. East 107.
    Seaby, Lucius and Marcus Antonius, 2.

ANTONY: Denarius, 33 BC (Frontispiece)
    Obverse: Antony's head
    Legend: ANTON. AVG. IMP. III. COS. DES. III. III. V.R.P.C.
    Reverse: ANTONIVS AVG. IMP. III.
    B.M.C. East 177.
    Seaby, Antony, 2.

As well as the coins illustrated in this book the following are of interest:

i.   ANTONY: Legionary Denarii, 32/31 BC
On the obverse all these coins bear the legends ANT. AVG. III. VIR. R.P.C. and a galley; on the reverse LEG and the individual legion's number with the legionary eagle between two standards (the authenticity of coins of Legions XXIV to XXX, Seaby 61-65, is doubtful).
B.M.C. and B.M.C. East.
Seaby, Antony, 26 – 60.

ii.   OCTAVIA and ANTONY: Cistophoric tetradrachm, 39 BC
These coins, probably struck at Pergamum and Ephesus, celebrate the marriage of Antony and Octavia. One shows Antony's head bound with ivy, and on the reverse Octavia's on a cista mystica, a chest used in secret religious rites, between two serpents. The other has their conjoined heads, with Bacchus on the reverse standing on the cista mystica.
B.M.C. East 133 & 135.

iii.   ANTONY: Denarius, 39 BC
Obverse: Antony's head and legend: M. ANT, IMP. III. V.R.P.C.
Reverse: shows Jupiter or a soldier holding sceptre and olive branch with legend: P. VENTIDI to the right.
This coin celebrates Ventidius' victories over the Parthians.
B.M.C. Gaul 73.
Seaby, Antony, 75.

iv.   FULVIA: Quinarius, 43/42 BC
This coin struck at Lugdunum in Gaul probably bears Fulvia's head personifying Victory on the obverse. The reverse has a lion between A and XLI (Antony's age).
B.M.C. Gaul 48.
Seaby, Fulvia, 3.

v.   LABIENUS: Denarius, 40/39 BC
Obverse: head of Quintus Labienus and the legend: Q. LABIENVS PARTHICVS IMP., celebrating Labienus' conquest of Asia Minor for the Parthians early in 40.
B.M.C. East 132.
Seaby, Labienus, 2.

vi.	POMPEY: Denarius, 46/45 BC

vi.   POMPEY: Denarius, 46/45 BC
      Obverse head of Pompey and the legend: CN. MAGNVS
      IMP. It was struck in Spain after Pompey's death and before
      Munda.
      B.M.C. 79.
      Seaby, Pompey, 5.

vii. LEPIDUS: Denarius, 42 BC
      Obverse: Lepidus' head and the legend: LEPIDVS PONT.
      MAX. III. V.R.P.C.
      The reverse has the head of Augustus and the legend
      CAESAR IMP. III. VIR. R.P.C.
      B.M.C. Africa 29.
      Seaby, Lepidus and Augustus, 2.

viii. SEXTUS: Aureus, 42/40 BC
      Obverse: head of Sextus and the legend: MAG. PIVS. IMP.
      ITER.
      (In loyalty to Pompey the Great, Imperator again)
      Struck in Sicily
      Crawford 511.

Coin Portraits of Antony from Roman Denarii

Photographs by kind permission of the British Museum

c. 44 BC

c. 42 BC

41/40 BC

40/39 BC

36 BC

31 BC

Coin Portraits from Roman Denarii

Photographs by kind permission of the British Museum

Caesar c. 44 BC

Brutus c. 43/42 BC

Antony 32/31 BC

Cleopatra 32/31 BC

Augustus 13 BC

Agrippa 13 BC

Chapter Notes

(abbreviations at the end)

CHAPTER I

THE YOUNG ANTONY

8	Plut.,	*T. Grac.*, 9.
10	App.,	*Bell. Civ.*, I, viii, 72.
11	Orosius,	*Hist. Rome*, V.
14/5	Plut.,	*Ant.*, 1.
15	Plut.,	*Ant.*, 2.
22	Plut.,	*Pomp.*, 45.
25	Plut.,	*Ant.*, 2.

CHAPTER II

SYRIA, JUDAEA AND EGYPT

26/7	Jos.,	*Antiq. Jud.*, XIV, v, 2.
27	Jos.,	*Bell. Jud.*, I, viii, 4.
27	Jos.,	*Antiq. Jud.*, XIV, v, 3.
27/8	Jos.,	*Bell. Jud.*, XIV, v, 3.
28	Plut.,	*Ant.*, 2.
31	Plut.,	*Ant.*, 3.
31/2	Plut.,	*Ant.*, 3.

CHAPTER III

CAESAR'S LIEUTENANT

38   Cic., *2nd Phil.*, 2, 4.
38/9   Plut., *Ant.*, 4.

CHAPTER IV

MASTER OF HORSE

49   Cic., *Ad Att.*, VII, VIII – IX.
49/50   Cic., *Ad Att.*, VII, 15a.
49/50   Cic., *Ad Att.*, IX, 6a, 7a, 7b, 13a, 15.
51   Plut., *Ant.*, 5, 9.
51   Cic., *Ad Att.*, X, 86, Caesar to Cicero.
51   Cic., *Ad Fam.*, VIII, 16, Caelius to Cicero.
51   Cic., *Ad Att.*, X, 9a, Caelius to Cicero.
51/2   Cic., *Ad Att.*, X, 8a, Antony to Cicero.
52   Cic., *Ad Att.*, X, 8,
            enclosing *Ad Att.*, 8a, Antony to Cicero,
            and *Ad Att.*, 8b, Caesar to Cicero.
52   Cic., *Ad Att.*, X, 9,
            enclosing *Ad Att.*, X, 9a, Caelius to Cicero,
            and *Ad Fam.*, VIII, 16, Caelius to Cicero.
52/3   Cic., *Ad Att.*, X, 10, quoting Antony's
            second letter.
53   Cic., *Ad Att.*, X, 8 to *Ad Att.*, X, 18.
56   Consulars: see *Roman Revolution*, Syme, V. 61.
59   Incredibili fortuna: Caes., *Bell. Civ.*, III, 26.
63   Caes., *Bell. Civ.*, III, 88.
63   Plut., *Pomp.*, 64.
63   Caes., *Bell. Civ.*, III, 83.
63/4   Plut., *Pomp.*, 67.
64   Plut., *Pomp.*, 69.
65   Plut., *Caes.*, 46.
66   Achillas may have been captain of palace guard.
68   Etesian winds: Vegetius, Epit, Rei Milit.

CHAPTER V

CAESAR: DICTATOR AND TRIUMPHATOR

CHAPTER VI

CONSUL IN ROME

CHAPTER VII

MUTINA

CHAPTER VIII

THE CAESARIANS UNITE

* The authenticity of these has been questioned on the grounds that the querulous tone and ill expressed content are unlike Brutus' normal style. However these two letters existed in Plutarch's time and were then believed to be geniune: see Plut. Brut. 22.

CHAPTER IX

THE TRIUMVIRS

CHAPTER X

PHILIPPI

CHAPTER XI

CLEOPATRA AT TARSUS

CHAPTER XII

PERUSIA

CHAPTER XIII

BRUNDISIUM AND MISENUM

CHAPTER XIV

ANTONY AND OCTAVIA IN ATHENS

CHAPTER XV

TARENTUM AND SICILY

CHAPTER XVI

ANTONY AND CLEOPATRA IN ANTIOCH

CHAPTER XVII

THE PARTHIAN ADVENTURE

294	C.A.H. X, III, v, p.90/91.
294/5	Suet., *Aug.,* 70: Feast of Divine Twelve.
295	O.G.I.S. 195 and 453/5.
295	Fraser, J.R.S., 1957, p.71: basalt statue base from Alexandria with double date '19 which is 4', indicating Cleopatra's regnant years (19) and Cleopatra and Antony's joint regnant years (4), and equivalent to end December 34 BC.
295/6	Plut., *Ant.,* 68.
297	Vell., *Hist.,* II, 83.
298	Dio, *Hist.,* L, 3.
299	Dio, *Hist.,* L, 10.
300	Vell., *Hist.,* II, 86.

CHAPTER XXI

THE WAR IN GREECE

301	Plut., *Ant.,* 56, 61, 63, 68.
304	Plut., *Ant.,* 68.
304/5	Horace, *IXth Epode.*
305	Virgil, *Aeneid,* VIII, 678-81, 685-88.
305	Vell., *Hist.,* II, 83-86.
305	Nic., *Aug.*
305	Suet., *Aug.,* 17.
306	Orosius, *Hist.,* VI.
306	Florus, II.
305/6	Plut., *Ant.,* 65-68.
305/6	Dio, *Hist.,* L, 1-35.
307	Plut., *Ant.,* 62.
310	Dio, *Hist.,* L, 13.
313	Plut., *Ant.,* 68.
313	Dio, *Hist.,* L, 13.
315	Tarn, J.R.S., 1931, p.175. C.Q., 1932, p.75.
315	Horace, *IXth Epode.*

CHAPTER XXII

THE BATTLE OF ACTIUM

318	Dio, *Hist.,* L, 13, 8.
318	Vell., *Hist.,* II, 84, 2.
318	Dio, *Hist.,* L, 11-30.
318	Plut., *Ant.,* 65-68.
319/20	Tarn, *Actium,* J.R.S., XXI, 1931, p.173.
320	Orosius, *Hist.,* VI, 19.
320	Florus, II, 21.
320	1 nautical mile = 1850m.
	1000m = .54 nautical mile.
320	Plut., *Ant.,* 64.
322	Plut., *Ant.,* 64.
323	Plut., *Ant.,* 65.
324	Plut., *Ant.,* 65.
327	Plut., *Ant.,* 66/67.
327	Dio, *Hist.,* L, 31-35.

CHAPTER XXIII

THE BITTER AFTERMATH

329	Plut., *Ant.,* 68.
331	Plut., *Ant.,* 69.
332	Plut., *Ant.,* 69.
334	Dio, *Hist.,* LI, 2, 4.
334	Dio, *Hist.,* LI, 2, 5, 6.
334	Suet., *Aug.,* 13, 2.
334	Vell., *Hist.,* 86.
336	Dio, *Hist.,* LI, 3, 2, 3.

CHAPTER XXIV

OCTAVIAN: MASTER OF THE WORLD

342	Plut., *Ant.,* 69.
342	Dio, *Hist.,* LI, 9, 10.

CHAPTER XXV

THE LAST OF THE PTOLEMIES

For Cleopatra's death also see Grant, *Cleopatra,*
Chap.13, p.334/5 and notes.

Abbreviations:-

App.: Appian,	*Civil Wars: Bell. Civ.*
Aug.: Augustus,	
Caes.: Caesar,	*Civil War: Bell. Civ.*
Cic.: Cicero,	*Letters to Atticus: Ad Att.*
	to Brutus: Ad Brut.
	to his friends: Ad fam.
	Philippic(s): Phil.
Dio: Dio Cassius,	*Roman History: Hist.*
Jos.: Josephus,	*Jewish Antiquities: Antiq. Jud.*
	Jewish Wars: Bell. Jud.
Nic.: Nicolaus,	*Life of Augustus: Aug.*

Plut.:	Plutarch,	*Lives, Antony: Ant.*
		Brutus: Brut.
		Cicero: Cic.
		T. Gracchus: T. Gracc.
		Pompey: Pomp.
Suet.:	Suetonius,	*Life of Augustus: Aug.*
Tac.:	Tacitus,	*Annals: Ann.*
Vell.:	Velleius Paterculus,	*Roman History: Hist.*

C.A.H.   Cambridge Ancient History
C.Q.   Classical Quarterly
J.R.S.   Journal of Roman Studies
O.G.I.S.   Orientis Graeci Inscriptions Selectae

Ancient Literary Sources

These can be divided into the extant primary or contemporary sources and the extant secondary sources. The latter drew much of their material, either at first or second hand, from annals and records and lost primary sources such as Pollio's history and Augustus's autobiography, and also from Livy's history for this period a primary source lost except in epitomes or summaries.

The two decades from 62 BC to Caesar's death in 44 and Cicero's in 43 are perhaps the most fully documented from contemporary sources in all Roman history. After 43 the primary sources are meagre.

Apart from Appian's account of Octavian's Illyrian campaigns in 35 and 34 his extant history of the period ends with the death of Sextus in 35 in Book V of his Civil Wars; from here on the secondary narrative accounts rely largely on Dio Cassius's History and Plutarch's Life of Antony.

PRIMARY SOURCES

1. CAESAR, Gaius Julius Caesar, 100 – 44 BC

His Commentaries on the Gallic War, Books I to VII, are based on reports from his legates and on his own despatches to the Senate, and give a factual account of his campaigns in Gaul. Book VI was probably written by his legate, Aulus Hirtius. His Civil War, Books I to III, are his own account of the civil war. The Alexandrian War may have been written by Hirtius: if so he was not there himself but had access to the accounts of officers who took part. The African War was written by one of Caesar's officers who took part in it. The Spanish War was also written by someone who took part, but in this case his literary capacity was slight.

2. CICERO, Marcus Tullius Cicero, 106 – 43 BC

As well as other major literary works fifty eight speeches, among them the fifteen Philippics, and some eight hundred letters have survived; the latter include sixteen books of letters to his friend Atticus and sixteen books of other letters; with these some one hundred letters, written to Cicero by Caesar, Pompey, Antony and others, have survived.

While the Philippics were written for public delivery in the Senate and Forum, or for publication, or for both, most of the letters were private. These letters provide both a unique picture of the political scene and an insight into Cicero's character and his hopes and fears for the Republic; as with any letters not intended for publication they inevitably convey the mood of the moment rather than considered judgements.

3. SALLUST, Gaius Sallustius, 86 – 35 BC

Caesarian legate and governor of Africa, his History covering 78 - 67 BC is lost, but his Jurgurthine War and Conspiracy of Catiline survive: they were used by Plutarch, Dio, Appian and Suetonius, and influenced Nicolaus, Livy and Velleius Paterculus.

4. AUGUSTUS, Gaius Octavius, 63 BC – AD 14

Although his biography is lost his Res Gestae, a brief account of his own achievements first drafted in 8 BC, survives.

5. NICOLAUS, Nicolaus of Damascus, c 64 BC – AD 5

A Greek from Damascus who was tutor to the children of Antony and Cleopatra, and later secretary to Herod. His Universal History is lost, but his biography of Augustus using his memoirs survives.

6. There are other important references in the contemporary works of Virgil, Horace and Propertius.

7. The most important of the lost primary sources are:

(a) LIVY, Titus Livius, c 60 BC – AD 15

Perhaps the greatest of Roman historians he wrote his History of Rome in 142 Books; the thirty five which survive cover the earlier years. His account of the period 49/30 BC, written from his own first hand knowledge and experience, only survives in the Periochae or Epitomes: one by Florus written in the 2nd century AD, and one by Orosius in the 5th century AD. Writing in the early Principate he naturally took the orthodox Augustan line hostile to Antony.

(b) POLLIO, Gaius Asinius Pollio, 76 BC – AD 4

He wrote the history of his own times, history which he himself helped to make. One-time legate of Caesar and friend of Antony, he remained neutral in the Actium campaign. He was a soldier and a man of letters, of independent mind and spirit, patron of Virgil and the arts.

SECONDARY SOURCES

1. STRABO, 63 BC – AD 21

A Greek from Amaseia. His History is lost, but his Geography in seventeen books survives.

2. VELLEIUS Paterculus, c 19 BC – AD 30

A Roman army officer whose History of Rome survives: he draws on Livy and on Augustus's memoirs, and largely follows the Augustan line.

3. JOSEPHUS, Flavius, AD 37 – c 100

A pro-Roman Jewish priest who became a Roman citizen. He wrote a history of the Jews, Jewish Antiquities, in twenty books which survive, as do seven books of his Jewish War in a Greek translation of the original Aramaic.

4. PLUTARCH, Mestrius Plutarchus, c AD 50 – c 120

Born at Chaeronea in Boetia, Plutarch was a moral philosopher and a biographer. In his parallel Lives he links Greek with Roman, Antony with Demetrius as cautionary examples of what may befall great men. He is more concerned with dramatic effect and drawing a moral than with strict historical accuracy, though in some ways this enhances his work. He is more hostile to Antony than to his other subjects, perhaps as a result of the suffering of his great-grandfather as a press-ganged porter in the Actium campaign. Yet in its high drama, its portrayal of Cleopatra and its vivid anecdotes his Life of Antony is perhaps the most brilliant of all his Lives. It is also, as far as is known, the only account available to Shakespeare despite the widely different interpretation he puts on it.

5. SUETONIUS, Gaius Tranquillus, b AD 69

He wrote the Lives of Twelve Caesars from Julius Caesar to Domitian; as secretary to Hadrian he had access to imperial records, and generally quotes his sources accurately.

6. APPIAN, Appianos, c AD 90 – 160

An Alexandrian who became a Roman citizen and civil servant under the Antonines. He wrote a Roman History in twenty four books of which eleven survive. His Book V of Civil Wars ends with the death of Sextus in 35. He draws on Sallust and Pollio and is particularly interested in Rome's wars.

7. DIO CASSIUS, Cassius Dio Cocceianus, c AD 155 – 235

From Nicaea in Bithynia, son of the governor of Cilicia, Dio Cassius was praetor in AD 194, consul in 205 and for the second time in 229. He wrote a Roman History to 229 of which Books 36-54 covering 68 – 10 BC survive. He appears to draw on Livy for much of his material.

The Appendices Literary Authorities for Roman History to Volume IX of the Cambridge Ancient History, 133 – 44 BC, pp 882-890, and Volume X, 44 BC – AD 70, pp 886-876, contain a valuable appraisal of all the ancient sources.

The Oxford Classical Dictionary provides a biographical note on the writers and a summary of their works.

TRANSLATIONS

APPIAN
Roman History, Vols II, III & IV, Loeb Classical Library, 1913, parallel texts, trans. Horace White.

AUGUSTUS

Res Gestae Divi Augusti, (i) Loeb Classical Library, 1924, parallel texts, trans. F.W.Shipley, (ii) Oxford University Press, 1967, parallel texts, edited P.A.Brunt and J.M.Moore.

CAESAR

Conquest of Gaul, Penguin, 1931, trans. S.A.Handford, The Battle of Gaul, Chatto and Windus, 1980, trans. Anne and Peter Wiseman, Civil War, Penguin, 1967, also Alexandrian, African and Spanish Wars, (not by Caesar), trans. J.F.Mitchell.

CICERO

Philippics, Loeb Classical Library, 1926, parallel texts, trans. W.C.A.Ker, Ad Familiares, Loeb Classical Library, 1929, parallel texts, trans. W.Glynn Williams, Cicero's Letters to his Friends, Penguin, 1978, trans. D.R.Shackleton Bailey, Ad Atticus, Loeb Classical Library, 1918, parallel texts, trans. E.O.Winstedt, Cicero's Letters to Atticus, Penguin 1978, Cambridge University Press 1965/68, trans. D.R.Shackleton Bailey.

DIO CASSIUS

Roman History, Vols III, IV, V and VI, Loeb Classical Library 1917, parallel texts, trans. E.Cary.

HORACE

Odes and Epodes, Loeb Classical Library, trans. Odes Lord Dunsany, Epodes Michael Oakley.

JOSEPHUS

The Jewish War, Penguin 1959, trans. G.A.Williamson, The Works of Flavius Josephus, 3 vols, including The Jewish War and Antiquities of the Jews, Oxford 1839, trans. William Whiston.

PLUTARCH

Makers of Rome, Penguin 1965, trans. Ian Scott-Kilvert, Fall of the Roman Republic, Penguin 1958, trans. Rex Warner.

SALLUST

The Jugurthine War and the Conspiracy of Cataline, Penguin 1963, trans. S.A.Handford.

SUETONIUS
Twelve Caesars, Penguin 1957, trans. Robert Graves.

VELLEIUS PATERCULUS
History of Rome, Loeb Classical Library, 1924, parallel texts trans. F.E.Shipley.

VIRGIL
The Eclogues, Georgics and Aeneid, Oxford University Press, 1966, trans. C.Day Lewis.

Modern Bibliography

ANDERSON, R.C.   *Oared Fighting Ships*, Marshall, 1962.

BABCOCK, C.L.   *The Early Career of Fulvia*, A.J.Ph., 1965, 1-32.

BALSDON, J.P.V.D.   *Roman Women*, Bodley Head, 1974.
Rome: The Story of an Empire, Weidenfeld and Nicholson, 1970.
Life and Leisure in Ancient Rome, Bodley Head, 1969.
The Ides of March, Historia, 1958.

BENGSTON, H.   *Marcus Antonius*, Oscar Beck, Munchen, 1977.

BICKERMAN, E.J.   *Chronology of the Ancient World*, Thomas and Hudson, 1968.

BRADFORD, E.D.S.   *Cleopatra*, Hodder and Stoughton, 1971.

BRUNT, P.A.   *Italian Manpower*, Oxford, 1970.
The Army and Land in the Roman Revolution, J.R.S. 1962, 69-84.

CADOUX, T.J.   *Surrender of the Army*, J.R.S., 1956.

CARTER, J.M.   *The Battle of Actium*, Hamish Hamilton, 1970.

CASSON, Lionel   *The Ancient Mariners*, 1959.
Ships and Seamanship in the Ancient World, 1971.

CHARLESWORTH, M.P.   *Cambridge Ancient History*, Cambridge University Press.
Vol X, I, With W W Tarn II, III and IV.
Some fragments of the propaganda of Mark Antony,

C.Q. 1933, 172-77.
The Fear of the Orient in the Roman Empire, Cambridge Historical Journal II, 1926.

COOK, S.A., ADCOCK, F.E. & CHARLESWORTH, M.P. (Editors)
Cambridge Ancient History, Vol IX, Cambridge University Press.

CRAVEN, L.
Antony's Oriental Policy, University of Missouri Studies, III 2, 1920.

CRAWFORD, Michael
Roman Republican Coinage, Oxford University Press, 1974.
The Roman Republic, Collins, 1978.
Money and Exchange in the Roman World, J.R.S., 1970.

CROOK, John
A legal point about Mark Antony's will, J.R.S., 1957, 36-8.

DILKE, O.A.W.
The Roman Land Surveyors, David and Charles, 1971.

DUDLEY, Donald
Roman Society, Hutchinson, 1970, Pelican, 1975.
Urbs Roma, Phaidon, 1967.

FINLEY, M.I.
The Ancient Economy, Chatto and Windus, 1973.

FORSTER, E.M.
Alexandria: A History and a Guide, 1922, Archer Books, 1961.

FRASER, P.M.
Mark Antony in Alexandria, J.R.S.,1957, 71-73.
O.G.I.S. 195, Statue base.
Ptolemaic Alexandria, London, 1960.

GELZER, Matthias
The Roman Nobility, trans. Robin Seager, Basil Blackwell, 1975.

GRANT, Michael
The World of Rome, London, 1960.

	From Imperium to Auctoritas, Cambridge University Press, 1971.
	The Ancient Historians, Scribner, New York, 1970.
	Roman History from Coins, Cambridge University Press, 1968.
	Julius Caesar, Weidenfeld and Nicholson, 1969.
	Herod the Great, Weidenfeld and Nicholson, 1971.
	The Roman Forum, Weidenfeld and Nicholson, 1970.
	Cleopatra, Weidenfeld and Nicholson, 1972, Panther Books, 1974.
GRUEN, Erich (Editor)	*Imperialism in the Roman Republic,* Holt, Reinhart and Winston, 1970.
HAMMOND, N.G.L. & SCULLARD, H.H. (Editors)	*Oxford Classical Dictionary,* Oxford University Press.
HOLMES, T.R.E.	*The Architect of the Roman Empire,* Oxford, 1928.
	The Roman Republic, London, 1923.
HUZAR, E.G.	*Mark Antony,* University of Minnesota, 1978.
HYDROGRAPHIC DEPT. THE ADMIRALTY	*Mediterranean Pilot, Vol. III,* Admiralty, 1970.
JONES, A.H.M.	*The Cities of the Eastern Roman Provinces,* Oxford University Press, 1971.
	The Roman Economy, Oxford University Press, 1974.
KENYON, F.G.	*Rescripts of Mark Antony,* C.R. Vol. 17.
KROMAYER, J.	*Actium,* Hermes, 1898, 13-70; 1899, 1-54; 1933, 361-383.
	Antike Schlachtfelder IV, 1931, 662-71.

LANDELS, J.G.	*Engineering in the Ancient World,* Chatto and Windus/Book Club, 1978.
LEACH, John	*Pompey the Great,* Croom Helm/ Book Club, 1978.
LEWIS, N. & REINHOLD, M.	*Roman Civilisation,* Source-book I: The Republic. *Roman Civilisation,* Source-book II: The Empire, Columbia University Press, 1955, Harper Torchbooks, New York, 1966.
LINDSAY, J.	*Cleopatra,* Constable, London, 1971. *Mark Antony and his Contemporaries,* London, 1936.
LORD, Louis	*The date of Julius Caesar's departure from Alexandria,* J.R.S. 1938, 19-40.
MARLOWE, J.	*The Golden Age of Alexandria,* Gollancz, London, 1971.
MASSON, Georgina	*A Concise History of Republican Rome,* Thames and Hudson, 1973.
MEIKLEJOHN, K.W.	*Alexander Helios and Caesarion,* J.R.S., 1934, 191-95.
MORRISON, John	*The Ship, Vol 2, Long Ships and Round Ships,* National Maritime Museum, HMSO, 1980.
MORRISON, J.S. & COATES, J.F.	*The Athenian Trireme,* Cambridge University Press, 1986.
O'SULLIVAN, Firmin	*The Egnatian Way,* David and Charles, 1982.
PAGET, J.	*The Ancient Ports of Cumae,* J.R.S., 1968, 152-69.

PARKER, H.M.D.   *The Roman Legions,* London,
                                1928.

PAULY-WISSOWA   *RE Kleine Pauly,* Deutscher
                                Taschenbuch Verlag, 1979.

PEROWNE, Stewart   *Death of the Roman Republic.*
                                Hodder and Stoughton, 1969.

RICHARDSON, G.W.   *Actium,* J.R.S., 1937, 153-164.

SABBEN-CLARE, James   *Caesar and Roman Politics*
                                60-50 BC, Oxford University
                                Press, 1971, (Source material
                                in translation).

SCOTT, K.   *Octavian's propaganda and*
                                Antony's 'de sua ebrietate', C.R.,
                                1929, 133-141.

SCULLARD, H.H.   *From the Gracchi to Nero,*
                                Methuen, London, 1959.

SEABY, H.A.   *Roman Silver Coins,* Vol. I.
                                The Republic to Augustus,
                                Seaby, 1978.

SKEAT, T.C.   *The Last Days of Cleopatra,*
                                J.R.S., 1953, 98-100.
                                Surrender of the Army,
                                J.R.S., Vol. 56.
                                Notes on Ptolemaic Chronology,
                                J.E.A., 1960, 91-94.

SYME, Sir Ronald   *The Roman Revolution,* Oxford
                                University Press, 1960.
                                The Augustan Aristocracy,
                                Oxford University Press, 1986.
                                Who was Decidius Saxa?
                                J.R.S., 1937, 127-137.
                                Pollio Salonius and Salonae,
                                C.Q., 1937, 39-48.
                                Defection of Labienus,
                                J.R.S., 1938.
                                Illyrian Campaigns, J.R.S., 1933.
                                Imperator Caesar, Historia, 1958,
                                p.172.

TARN, W.W.   *The Battle of Actium,* J.R.S.,
                                1931, 173-199.

	Antony's Legions, C.Q., 1932, 75-89.
	Actium, a Note, J.R.S., 1938, 165-168.
	Alexander Helios and the Golden Age, J.R.S., 1932, 135-60.
	Cambridge Ancient History, Vol. X, with M.P.Charlesworth, chapters II, III and IV.
TARN, W.W. & CHARLESWORTH, M.P.	*Octavia, Antony and Cleopatra,* Cambridge University Press, 1965.
TAYLOR, L.R.	*Party Politics in Age of Caesar,* University of California, 1949.
TENNEY, Frank	*Caesar at the Rubicon,* C.Q., 1957.
TOYNBEE, J.M.C.	*Roman Historical Portraits,* Thames and Hudson, 1978.
VOLKMANN, H.	*Cleopatra,* trans. T.J.Cadoux, Munchen, 1953.
WATSON, G.R.	*The Roman Soldier,* Thames and Hudson, 1969.
WEBSTER, Graham	*The Roman Imperial Army,* A. & C.Black, 1969.
WEIGALL, A.	*The Life and Times of Cleopatra,* Thornton Butterworth, 1914. *Mark Antony, His Life and Times,* London, 1931.

Abbreviations used above:

A.J.Ph	American Journal of Philology
C.I.L.	Corpus Inscriptonum Latinarum
C.P.	· Classical Philology
C.Q.	Classical Quarterly
C.R.	Classical Review
J.E.A.	Journal of Egyptian Archaeology
J.R.S.	Journal of Roman Studies
O.G.I.S.	Orientis Graeci Inscriptiones Selectae

Table of Dates

All BC

83 or 82	14th January	Mark Antony born.
72		Death of Antony's father.
70		Crassus and Pompey consuls.
70 or 69		Birth of Cleopatra.
66/62		Pompey in the East.
63	23rd September	Octavian born.
60		First Triumvirate: – Pompey, Caesar and Crassus.
58/56		Caesar conquers Gaul.
55/54		Caesar's two expeditions to Britain.
57/54		Antony commands Gabinius' cavalry in Syria, Judaea and Egypt.
54/53		Antony joins Caesar in Gaul.
53/50		Antony Caesar's lieutenant in Gaul.
53	May/June	Crassus defeated and killed at Carrhae.
53/52	Winter	Antony in Rome, elected quaestor; marries first cousin Antonia.
50	10th December	Antony takes over as tribune.
49	January/March August	Caesar drives Pompey from Italy. Caesar defeats Pompeians at Ilerda in Spain.
	late Autumn	Caesar appointed Dictator.
48	January	Caesar crosses to Greece; Antony his legate.
	9th August	Caesar defeats Pompey at Pharsalus.

1

48/47	Winter	Caesar in Alexandria with Cleopatra. Antony in charge of Italy as Master of Horse.
47	Spring	Caesar restores Cleopatra to throne of Egypt. Antony divorces Antonia.
	2nd August	Caesar defeats Pharnaces at Zela.
	25th December	Caesar leaves for Africa.
	Autumn	Caesarion born.
47/46	Winter	Antony marries Fulvia.
46	6th April	Caesar defeats Pompeians at Thapsus.
	September	Caesar celebrates four triumphs.
	November	Caesar leaves for Spain.
45	17th March	Caesar defeats Pompeians at Munda.
44	1st January	Caesar consul for fifth time with Antony his colleague.
	15th March	Assassination of Caesar; Antony takes control as consul.
	Summer	Brutus and Cassius leave Italy; Octavian returns.
	September/December	Cicero's 1st, 2nd and 3rd Phillippics.
	28th November	Antony allotted the two Gauls as his proconsular provinces; leaves Rome and besieges Decimus Brutus in Mutina.
43	April	Antony withdraws to Provence.
	May	Joined by Caesarian legates Lepidus, Pollio and Plancus.
	August	Octavian proclaimed consul and in control of Rome.
	October/November	Second Triumvirate: – Antony, Octavian and Lepidus.
	November/December	Proscriptions; death of Cicero.
42	Autumn	Philippi campaign.
	23rd October	First battle; death of Crassus.

42	3rd November	Second battle; death of Brutus. Antony takes the East, Octavian the West.
42/41	Winter	Antony in Athens.
41		Antony summons Cleopatra to Tarsus.
41/40	Winter	Antony in Alexandria with Cleopatra.
	Winter	Lucius Antonius besieged by Octavian in Perusia.
40	Spring	Parthians overrun Roman East.
	February	Perusia falls.
	Summer	Antony returns to Brundisium and is reconciled with Octavian.
	October	Pact of Brundisium.
	October/November	Antony marries Octavia in Rome.
	Autumn	Birth of Cleopatra Selene and Alexander Helios in Alexandria.
Late 40/ early 39		Antony and Octavian make pact with Sextus at Misenum.
39		Ventidius recovers Asia Minor.
39/38		Antony and Octavia winter in Athens.
38	January	Octavian divorces Scribonia and marries Livia.
	June	Ventidius again defeats Parthians at Gindarus.
		Samosata surrenders to Antony; he prepares to attack Parthia in 37.
		Octavian defeated at sea by Sextus and appeals to Antony for help.
37	Spring	Antony meets Octavian at Tarentum; pact of Tarentum.
	Mid-summer	Renewal of Triumvirate.
		Agrippa builds new fleet and base at Portus Julius.
	Autumn	Antony 'marries' Cleopatra at Antioch.

36	Summer	Antony invades Media.
	Autumn	Retreat from Phraapa.
		Agrippa defeats Sextus at Mylae and Naulochus; Octavian recovers Sicily; downfall of Lepidus.
35/33		Octavian campaigns in Illyria and Dalmatia.
35		Death of Sextus in Asia Minor.
34		Antony recovers Armenia and makes it a Roman province.
	Autumn	Antony stages triumphal procession and the Donations in Alexandria.
33	Early summer	Antony on Araxes with Media as an ally; withdraws to Syria.
33/32		Antony and Octavian prepare for war.
	Winter	Antony and Cleopatra at Ephesus.
32		Antony divorces Octavia. Octavian declares war on Cleopatra.
31		The campaign in Greece; Agrippa seizes Methone; Antony trapped at Actium.
	2nd September	Battle of Actium.
30	August	Death of Antony; Death of Cleopatra.

MARK ANTONY, OCTAVIAN
AND THE JULIO CLAUDIANS

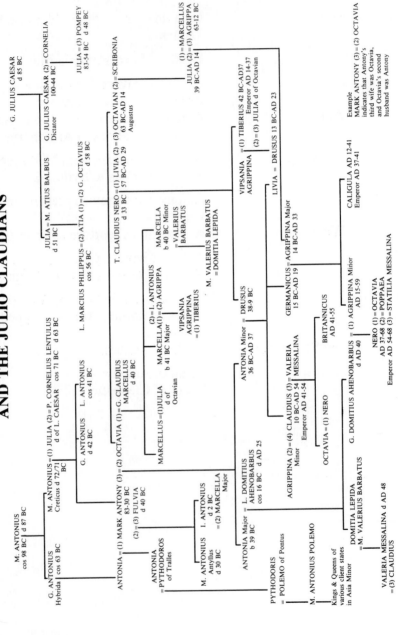

THE LATER PTOLEMIES

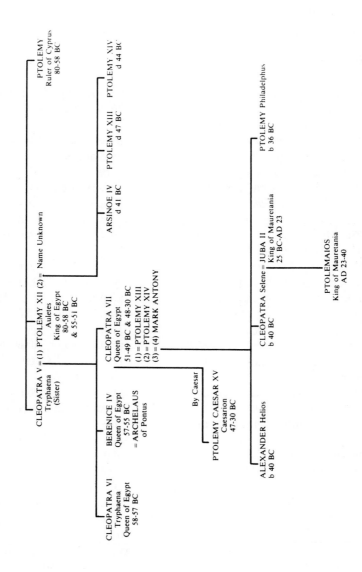

CLEOPATRA VI
Tryphaena
Queen of Egypt
58-57 BC

CLEOPATRA V = (1) PTOLEMY XII (2) = Name Unknown
Tryphaena
(Sister)
Auletes
King of Egypt
80-58 BC
& 55-51 BC

PTOLEMY
Ruler of Cyprus
80-58 BC

BERENICE IV
Queen of Egypt
57-55 BC
= ARCHELAUS
of Pontus

CLEOPATRA VII
Queen of Egypt
51-49 BC & 48-30 BC
(1) = PTOLEMY XIII
(2) = PTOLEMY XIV
(3) = (4) MARK ANTONY

ARSINOE IV
d 41 BC

PTOLEMY XIII
d 47 BC

PTOLEMY XIV
d 44 BC

By Caesar

PTOLEMY CAESAR XV
Caesarion
47-30 BC

ALEXANDER Helios
b 40 BC

CLEOPATRA Selene = JUBA II
b 40 BC
King of Mauretania
25 BC-AD 23

PTOLEMY Philadelphus
b 36 BC

PTOLEMAIOS
King of Mauretania
AD 23-40

General Index

younger son of Antony and Fulvia, 196, 218, 234, 297, 299, 359.

Antonius, Lucius, (*cos. 41*), youngest brother of Antony, 15, tribune 89, 110, 113, 116; at Mutina 135; commands cavalry 141/2; 154, 173, 175, 186, consul 188; dispute with Octavian 189/92; Perusine War 193/5; to Spain 197; 205, 207, 209/10, 212, 295.

Antonius, Marcus, (*cos. 99*), grandfather of Antony, 4, 9/10, 294, 359.

Antonius, Marcus, Antyllus, older son of Antony and Fulvia, 102, 128, 196, 218, 232, 234, 294, 297, 299, 344, 347, death 353.

Antonius, Marcus, Creticus, father of Antony, 10/1, 14/5, 17.

Antonius, Marcus, Mark Antony, (*cos. 44, 34*), 3/4, 11, 15/7, 25, in Syria 26/8, 30/1; in Gaul and Rome 34/5, 37/8; dress, character, coin portraits 38; 42, tribune 43/4; 45/6, Caesar's lieutenant 49/53; Pharsalus campaign 58/62, 65; Caesar's deputy 67, 72/4, 83, 87/9, 91/2; consul 97/121; after Caesar's death 97/103; funeral speech 104/5; coinage 109; relations with Octavian 111, 114; with Cicero 106, 113; leaves Rome 121/3; 124, Mutina campaign 125/38; withdraws to Provence 139/42; joined by Lepidus 143/4, 162; 146, 149/52, Second Triumvirate 152/5; role in proscriptions 155/61; 162, Philippi campaign 163/75; in Athens 179; in Asia Minor 179/82; meets Cleopatra at Tarsus 182/5; in Alexandria 185/6; 188/97, loss of the East 205/7; dispute with Octavian 208/11; Brundisium pact 210/2; marries Octavia 211/4; Misenum pact 215/8; 220/3, reorganises Asia Minor 223/4; 225/9, Tarentum pact 232; relations with Octavian 233/5; 240, to Athens 243; to Antioch 244; form of marriage with Cleopatra 244/5, 248; reorganises Levant 245/7; prepares to attack Parthia 245, 248/51; invades Media 251/3; besieges Phraapa 254/5; retreat from Media 255/60; assessment of campaign 260/1; at Leuke Come 261/4; rebuffs Octavia 263/4; in Alexandria 264/8; 270/1, in Armenia 272/3; triumphal procession in Alexandria 274/5; the Donations 275/8; 279, on the Araxes 279/81; 282, concentrates army at Ephesus 285/90; to Samos 290; in Athens 290/1, 296/7; coins in Italy 292; the war of words 292/6; divorces Octavia 297; his will 298/9; 300, to Greece 301; army dispositions 301/7; to Actium 307/8; the campaign 309/10; trapped at Actium 311/3; attempts to break out 313/5; the battle of Actium 307/28; the aftermath 329/37; return to Egypt 341/5; attempts to negotiate 346/8; the last battle 348/9; death 350/1; 352/61.

Aphrodisias, special relationship with Rome 224.

Apollo, 107, 293/5, 308, 335.

Aquillius Florus, 334.

Archelaus of Comana, given Cappadocia by Antony 245; 247, 285, 358/9.

Areius, 353, 357.

Aretas of Nabataea, 20.

Ariarathes IX of Cappadocia, 182, 245.

Ariobarzanes III of Cappadocia, 71.

Aristobulus II of Judaea, 19/20, 23,

lvii

cos. *63*, 34.

Cimber, Lucius Tillius, tyrannicide, 89, 91, 93, 102, 165.

Cinna, Gaius Helvius, 105.

Cinna, Gnaeus Cornelius, nephew of Sextus Pompeius, 288, 334.

Cinna, Lucius Cornelius, (*cos. 87/84*), 9, 11, 14.

Cinna, Lucius Cornelius, conspirator, 98, 102, 105.

Cinna, Lucius Cornelius, grandson of *cos. 87*, 288.

Claudia, daughter of Clodius and Fulvia, 155, 188, 192.

Claudius, Emperor AD 41-54, 290, 360.

Claudius Nero, see Nero.

Claudius Marcellus, see Marcellus.

Claudius, Pulcher Appius, (*cos. 54*), brother of Clodius, 33, 36.

Cleon of Olympos, 224.

Cleopatra VII, Queen of Egypt, the later Ptolemies 28; heir apparent 31; 35, co-ruler 66, 68; meets Caesar 68; his mistress 68; 70/1, 81, in Rome with Caesarion 86; 89/90, returns to Egypt 107; 162, sails to aid triumvirs 163; summoned to Tarsus 182/3; character, ambition 183/5; with Antony in Alexandria 185/6, 190; 193, 205, 210, twins born 218; 221, 223, 243/4, form of marriage with Antony 244/8; 251/2, to Leuke Come 260/4; returns to Alexandria 264; 267, 272, relations with Herod 264, 273; procession in Alexandria 274/5; the Donations 275/8; 278/80, with army at Ephesus 285/7, 289/90; at Samos 290; 291, coinage 292; 293, 295, at Athens 290, 296/9; vilified by Octavian 292/3; the war in Greece 301, 305, 307/8, 312; the battle of Actium 316/8, 320, 322, 324, 326/8; 329, return to Egypt

329/31; 333, 341/9, death of Antony 350/1; last days 352/6; death 357; 358/61.

Cleopatra VI, sister of Cleopatra, 29.

Cleopatra Selene, daughter of Antony and Cleopatra, 245, 275, 358.

Clodius, (Claudius), Pulcher Publius, 7, 15, prosecutes Catiline 15/16; 18, at Bona Dea festival 21; people's tribune 24; leader of urban mob 25; 26, 33, 35/6, death 40; 42/3, 83, 116, 155, 234.

Cocceii, 191, 288, see also Nerva.

Coinage, 38/9, 91, 109, 188, 223, 229, 248/9, 268, 292, 301.

Considius, Gaius Longus, Pompeian, 76.

Constantine, Emperor AD 307-337, 360.

Coponius, Lucius, 299.

Cornelia, wife of Caesar, 14.

Cornelia, wife of Pompey, 37, 66/7.

Cornelius Cinna, see Cinna.

Cornelius Gallus, see Gallus.

Cornelius Sulla, see Sulla.

Cornificius, Lucius, (*cos. 35*), Octavian's admiral and legate, 230, 238, 271.

Cornificius, Quintus, Caesarian, 65, in Africa 154, 161.

Cotison of Dacia, 294, 310, 313.

Crassus, Marcus Licinius, (*cos. 70, 55*), triumvir, escapes to Spain 10; consul 13; backs Sulla 13; 16, 21, 23, joins Caesar and Pompey in First Triumvirate 23/4; 24/5, 30/1, at Luca 32; death at Carrhae 33; 85, 90, 132, 182, 227, 250, 252/3.

Crassus, Marcus Licinius, older son of triumvir, 50.

Crassus, Marcus Licinius, (*cos. 30*), grandson of triumvir,

escapes from Castra Cornelia 55; governs Further Spain 89, 108; character 123/4; 128, 140, 144/5, joins Antony 150, 152; governs Cisalpina 154; 154, role in proscriptions 156/7; 175, 186, 189, 191, in Perusine War 192/6; in Venetia 195/6; negotiates with Ahenobarbus 207/8; supports Antony at Brundisium 209/11; 212, consul 213; 214, Antony's legate in Macedonia 220, 224; triumphs 224; 272, as historian 295; remains neutral 300.

Pollio, Salonius Asinius, son of *cos. 40*, 214. Also see Gallus Asinius.

Pompeia, granddaugher of Sulla, marries Caesar 14, divorced 21/2.

Pompeia, daughter of Pompey, 37.

Pompeius Bithynicus, in Sicily 159.

Pompeius Strabo, Gnaeus, (*cos. 89*), father of Pompey, 9, 228.

Pompeius Magnus, Gnaeus, Pompey the Great, (*cos. 77, 55, 52*), joins Sulla 11; in Spain 13; 13/4, defeats pirates 17/8; in the East 17/22; triumphs 22/3; First Triumvirate 24; 24/6, 29/31, triumvirate renewed 32; 33, 35/7, in Rome 40/5; defeated in Italy by Caesar 46/8; withdraws to Greece 48; 49/56, the campaign in Greece 57/66; Pharsalus 62/5; 66, death 67; 68, 74/6, 79, 81, 85/7, 90, 92/3, 98, 100, 109, 114, 134, 155, 173, 180, 182, 184, 214/7, 246, 249, 264, 266, 270, 278, 286, 302, 334, 341, 352.

Pompeius, Gnaeus, older son of Pompey, 57, 61, 66, 76, in Spain 79; 82, defeated at Munda 82; death 82.

Pompeius, Sextus, (*cos. 35*), younger son of Pompey, 66, sees father murdered 67; in Africa 76;

to Spain 79; 82, escapes from Munda 82/3; raises army in Spain 107; 112, negotiates with Lepidus 114, 127, 134; 139, 144, 149, in Sicily 154, 159/60; rescues proscribed 161; repulses Salvidienus 161; 163/4, 173/5, 182, 186, 188, 191, gives sanctuary to Livia and Julia 195/6; 207/8, supports Antony 208/10; 214/5, Misenum pact 215/8; 230, defeats Octavian 230/1; 232/4, defeated by Octavian 235/9; flees to East 239; 243, 260/1, in Asia Minor 264/6; death 266; 268, 270, 277, 291, 303, 306, 316/7, 323, 332, 334, 347.

Pontifex Maximus, 16, 21/2, 63, 84, 105, 239, 333.

Poplicola, Lucius Gellius, (*cos. 36*), Antonian admiral, 288, 313, at Actium, 316, 320, 323/7.

Poppaedius Silo, Quintus, commands Ventidius's cavalry 220/2, 228.

Populares, 7/9, 12, 15, 41, 46, 56/7.

Porcia, daughter of Cato, wife of Brutus, 90.

Postumius, Quintus, 315.

Pothinus, 66/9, 81.

Proculeius, friend of Octavian, 238, in Alexandria 348, 351/3.

Propaganda, 192, 194, 244, 273/4, 278/9, 293/4.

Propertius, 356.

Proscriptions, 11, 155/60.

Provinces, 24, 34, 40, 88/9, 102, 108, 113, 153/4, 211.

Ptolemaeus of Chalcis, 185, 206.

Ptolemaios, son of Juba II and Cleopatra Selene, 359.

Ptolemies, 5, 28, 245, 248, 273, 275, 335, 344, 347, 355/6, 357.

Ptolemy XII, Auletes, 25, 28/32, 66, 68, 182.

Index of Place Names

Place Names

Arpinum	III	Castra Cornelia	III
Arretium	III	Caucasus Mts.	II, V
Artaxata	V	Cephallenia	IV, VI
Asculum	III	Cetina, River	III
Asia (Province)	II, V	Cevennes Mts.	I
Asparagium	IV	Chalcide Peninsula	IV
Assyria	V	Chalcis (Syria)	V(a)
Aternum	III	Cilicia	II, V
Athens	IV	Cisalpine Gaul	II
Avenio	I	Claterna	III
Avernus, Lake	III	Clupea	I
Azov, Sea of	II	Coele Syria	II, V
		Cologne (Colonia Agrippina)	I
Babylon	V	Commagene	II
Bactria	V	Coracesium	II
Bagradas, River	I, II	Corcyra Nigra	III
Baiae	III	Corduba	I
Balearics	I	Corfinium	III
Beneventum	III	Corfu (Corcyra)	IV, VI
Berytus	V(a)	Corinth	IV
Bitter Lake	V(a)	Corsica	I, III
Black Sea	IV	Cos	IV
Bon, Cape	II	Crete	II, V
Bononia	III	Crimea	II, V
Bosphorus	IV	Croatia	I
Britain	I	Cularo	I
Brundisium	III, IV	Cumae	III
Bruttium	III	Curicta	III
Buthrotum	VI	Cydonia	II
Byblos	V(a)	Cyprus	II, V
Byzantium	IV	Cyrenaica	II, V
		Cyrrhestice	V
Calabria	III	Cyrus, River	II, V(a)
Campania	III	Cyzicus	IV
Cannae	III		
Canusium	III	Dacia	II, IV
Cappadocia	II, V	Dalmatia	I, III
Capua	III	Damascus	V(a)
Carana (Erzerum)	V	Danube, River	I, II
Caria	II	Dead Sea	V(a)
Carrhae	II, V	Decapolis	II
Carteia	I	Dertona	III
Carthage	I, II	Domitia, Via	III
Casilinum	III	Dordogne, River	I
Caspian Sea (Hyrcanian)	V	Drave, River	II
Cassia, Via	III	Drin, River	IV

Picenum	III	Sicyon	IV
Piraeus	IV	Sidon	V(a)
Pisaurum	III	Sinai	V(a)
Pisidia	II	Sinope	II
Placentia	II, III	Sipontum	III
Po, River	II	Siscia	III
Pola	III	Skilla, Cape	VI(a)
Pollentia	III	Smyrna	IV
Pontus, Kingdom of	II	Somme, River	I
Postumia, Via	III	Spain	I
Praeneste	III	Spain, province of Further	I
Preveza	VI	Spain, province of Nearer	I
Priene	IV	Sparta	IV
Provence	I	Spoletium	III
Psamathos	IV	Stratonicaea	IV
Puteoli	III	Strymon, River	II
		Styllis	III
Ravenna	III	Sulmo	III
Rhegium Lepidum	III	Susa	V
Rhine, River	I	Sutrium	III
Rhodes	IV	Syracuse	III
Rhone, River	I	Syria	II
Rome	III	Syrian Gates	V(a)
Rubicon, River	III		
Ruspina	I	Tabriz	V
		Taenarum, Cape	IV
Saguntum	I	Talkheh, River	V
Sahand Mt.	V	Tarentum	III
Salonae	I, III	Tarsus	II
Samaria	II	Tauromenium	III
Samos,	IV	Taurus, Cape	III
Samosata	II, V(a)	Taurus Mts.	II
Santa Andrea, Island	III	Teanum	III
Sardis	IV	Tenos	IV
Sardinia	I, III	Tergeste	III
Save, River	III	Thames, River	I
Scodra	I, II, IV	Thapsus	I
Scolacium	III	Thasos	IV
Scylla, Cape	III	Thessalonica	IV
Segre, River	I, II, III	Thessaly	IV
Seine, River	I	Thrace	II
Seleucia (Cilicia)	II	Thurii	III
Seleucia (Syria)	V(a)	Thysdrus	I
Sentinum	III	Tiber, River	III
Sicilian Straits	III	Tibur	III
Sicily	III	Toryne	VI